W9-BEM-176

THE COMPLETE GUIDE TO

Choosing a Cruising Sailboat

ROGER MARSHALL

INTERNATIONAL MARINE/McGRAW-HILL
Camden, Maine • New York • San Francisco • Washington, D.C. • Auckland • Bogotá • Caracas • Lisbon • London • Madrid • Mexico City • Milan • Montreal • New Delhi • San Juan • Singapore • Sydney • Tokyo • Toronto

International Marine
A Division of The McGraw-Hill Companies

10 9 8 7 6 5 4 3 2 1

Library of Congress Cataloging-in-Publication Data
Marshall, Roger.
The complete guide to choosing a cruising sailboat / Roger Marshall.
p. cm.
Includes index.
ISBN 0-07-041998-1 (alk. paper)
1. Yachts—Design and construction. 2. Sailboats—Design and construction. I. Title.
VM331.M368 1999
623.8'22—dc21 98-52773
CIP

Questions regarding the content of this book should be addressed to
International Marine
P.O. Box 220
Camden, ME 04843
www.internationalmarine.com

Questions regarding the ordering of this book should be addressed to
The McGraw-Hill Companies
Customer Service Department
P.O. Box 547
Blacklick, OH 43004
Retail customers: 1-800-262-4729
Bookstores: 1-800-722-4726

This book is printed on 70-pound Citation, an acid-free paper

Printed by R. R. Donnelley, Crawfordsville, IN
Design and page layout by Faith Hague
Project management by Janet Robbins
Production assistance by Shannon Thomas
Edited by Jonathan Eaton, Jane Crosen, Scott Kirkman, and D. A. Oliver
All illustrations by the author except for the following: illustrations on pages 43, 46, 59, 72, 86, 94, 102, and 133 by Marcus Schone
Photos courtesy the author unless otherwise noted

Contact the author's design firm at
Roger Marshall, Inc., 44 Fort Wetherill Rd., Jamestown, RI 02835

For David and Michael, Optimist sailors, taking their first step along the road to a life of sailing

Other books by Roger Marshall

Designed to Win
Race to Win
Designed to Cruise
Yacht Design Details
A Sailor's Guide to Production Sailboats
Marshall's Marine Sourcebook
Better Sailing
Peace of Mind in Heavy Weather

Contents

Drawings

Use this list to locate all the drawings for each of the five concept designs.

The Weekender

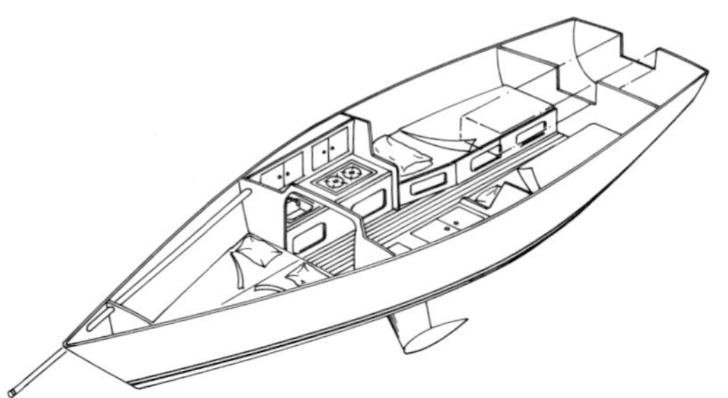

The Cruiser

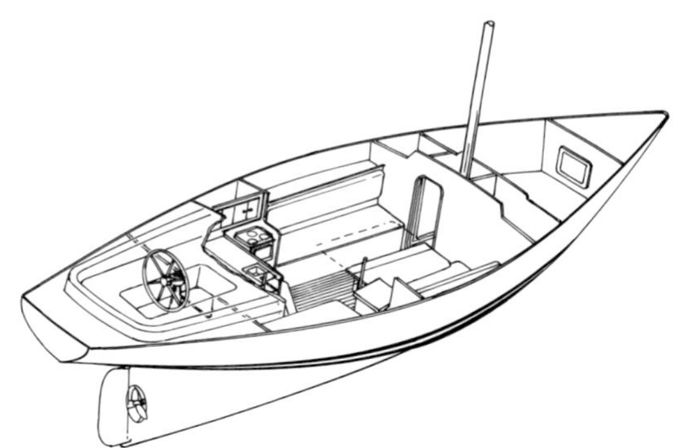

Acknowledgments

It's the writer's name that is on the cover when the book hits the bookstores, but even though the writer puts the actual words to paper, many other people are involved in the ideas expressed—some in a direct way, others in an indirect fashion. This book has many indirect contributors. Over the years I have been fortunate to have worked alongside some of the finest designers in the world, for five years at Sparkman & Stephens where Olin and Rod Stephens were free with their comments and help. Since those days I have exchanged ideas with most of the world's designers—the late Gary Mull, Laurie Davidson of New Zealand, in-house designers at many of the major boatbuilders. Each of these people added to my knowledge and the information in this book.

I have also been fortunate in writing for some great editors. Charles Mason, executive editor of *SAIL* magazine, Bill Sisson of *Soundings*, and Dean Clarke of World Publications in Florida are three of the very best. Each of them in some small way added to my skills as a writer, and indirectly improved this book. Another editor with whom I worked for the first time recently is Jon Eaton of International Marine, publisher of this book. Jon's touch added yet another layer of comments, suggestions, and improvements to the manuscript.

This February my skills as a writer were also recognized by my peers. Boating Writers International, the leading association of professional writers in the marine industry, gave me two first-place awards and one second-place award for my technical writing in *Soundings* magazine, where I am technical editor. In addition, one of my designs has been nominated for inclusion in *Ocean Navigator*'s American Yacht Review of the finest boats built in America in 1998 and 1999.

Not only have editors and designers given freely of their ideas, but boatbuilders have, too. Howdy Bailey in Virginia and Steve White and his late father Joel White of Brooklin Boat Yard in Maine have built my designs and added their own touches to them. In Rhode Island, John Merrifield and Kim Roberts of Merrifield-Roberts, Barry Carroll of Carroll Marine, and others have helped make concepts into reality. I've spent hours over a beer or three talking with Rich Worstell, president of Valiant Yachts, and many of his clients about what they want in their ideal cruiser. Plus, I have been fortunate enough to review hundreds of cruising and racing boats for various marine magazines.

In the marine industry others have given freely of their time. Dick Rath of Lewmar Marine, Jeff Rice of J. C. Rice International, Bill Larson of Exmar, Jim Archibald of the Jamestown Boatyard, and Brodie McGregor of Concordia are but a few. Yacht broker Scott Heckard and his fellow broker Walter Ackerman of Annapolis Sailyard, Inc. were extremely helpful in providing information for this book.

Finally, my wife Mary has not only read and commented on the manuscript but also bore the brunt of my complaints as the project progressed. Without her help this book would not have the fluency, style, and authority that it has. Thanks to all of you and to all the other sailors who have added to my knowledge and skills.

Roger Marshall
Jamestown, Rhode Island

Introduction

What do you look for when you set out to find your ideal boat? Do you look for a boat at the right price? For a boat that will carry you to far-off lands? For a boat that can carry you and your family safely? A boat is probably one of the most expensive purchases you will ever make, next to your home. Getting the boat that best suits your purposes is difficult; it takes knowledge and a lot of work. This book is intended as a guide to the best features to look for in a new or used boat. As yacht broker Jeff Rice of J. C. Rice International in Saunderstown, Rhode Island, says, "There's a boat out there for everybody, but you have to do some work to find it. You need to be honest with yourself about what you want the boat for. Don't buy a boat to sail to Bermuda or transatlantic if you will only sail around Narragansett Bay."

Finding the right boat means you must do your homework and pick the boat for the area in which you are going to sail. It means understanding why a particular boat is or is not suited to your style of sailing. For example, a few years ago I sailed on a ruggedly built 50-footer designed to be sailed around the world. The owner had fitted the boat out with a full inventory of cruising sails, including storm sails. It had radar, VHF, GPS, a life raft, and an inflatable dinghy with a 7-horsepower outboard. Below decks it had a huge freezer, a four-burner stove, twin showers, harness strongpoints, and leecloths. The boat was fitted out for long-distance voyaging. It was, however, sailed on a man-made lake that was about 5 miles long and 3 miles wide. When asked, the owner said that he wanted to go around the world, but he wanted to get some practice first. About three years later I passed through the same area. The boat was still there, and my inquiries about it revealed that it was rarely sailed. It had become too much trouble to get ready to sail around the lake. How sad.

Jeff Rice summed it up in my conversation with him, "Don't buy a boat to sail around the world five years from now. Buy a boat to suit your sailing needs today, and in five years' time buy a boat to sail around the world. Most people buy too much boat when they first get into sailing. It becomes a drain on their pocket, a lot of work to keep up, and is often at the limit of the owner's ability to handle."

Giving you the right tools to buy the most suitable boat for you is the purpose of this book. To do this, we have worked up five concept designs, representing five basic categories of use, pointing out what you should look for in each type of boat: a Weekender, a Cruiser, a Voyager, a Single-Hander, and a Cruiser/Racer.

The Weekender is definitely a fun inshore boat (in fact, I have an identical design sitting in my backyard), intended for evening sailing and club-level racing. It is very basic; staying aboard is like camping out. But the fun of this boat is that it is inexpensive and simple to have built or to build yourself.

The Cruiser can be sailed farther offshore out to islands and secluded coves, although it is intended to stay within reach of rescue services. This is not a sporty boat like so many cruisers are these days, but is intended to be comfortable: a boat where you can leave the helm with the pedestal brake on for a few minutes to put the kettle on; a boat that you can enjoy and have a lot of fun with. It can easily be made larger or smaller, depending on your needs.

The Voyager has the capability to cross

oceans. In my early days I would have made the helmsman stand out in the open, but as I grow older I better appreciate the satisfaction of getting out of the elements, so this boat has a doghouse. It also has a watermaker and a generator. I make no apology for adding complex mechanical items; today they are reasonably reliable and work well if maintained properly.

I have raced and cruised extensively all over the world, and one of the most comfortable trips was from Padanaram (South Dartmouth), Massachusetts, to Bermuda aboard a boat with a watermaker. A hot shower once a day is a boon to morale and well-being. Being able to run a computer via a generator or inverter makes modern communication easy and reasonably trouble free. (You can e-mail Mom and put her anxieties to rest, or even tell the office that you are hard at work!) Although some cruisers prefer to sail with minimal equipment, I, and many of my clients, want some semblance of modernity when we sail. Yes, this gear takes some maintenance, but what else are you going to do with your time on a cruise, watch TV via satellite?

The Single-Hander is moderately leading edge. There are other, more extreme ideas I would add if it were to be built for racing (see the carbon fiber mast of the concept design on page 210). The Single-Hander was included to show that water ballast can be fitted to a performance boat. However, in my opinion, water ballast is not needed for cruising performance. It takes up space, adds plumbing complications, lowers resale value, and requires a very beamy boat to make it most effective.

The Cruiser/Racer reflects the current thinking among designers that the hull and rig must be as fast as possible, and the "cruising" part is simply the interior arrangement. While this boat is not designed to a specific rule, it reflects some of the current design thinking for cruiser/racer-style boats. Unfortunately, this style of high-performance "cruiser" is becoming very common, but for comfortable cruising it is not the best option. A cruising boat, whether for offshore or inshore sailing, needs to be flexible. It needs some performance. (A slow boat spends longer at sea and is more liable to be hit by bad weather.) It *will* be loaded down with gear. It *will* go aground as the crew explore a cove or creek. It should not fatigue the crew unduly. And it *should not* leave the owner wondering if a part is going to break or bend if it is slightly overstrained.

In addition to these five concept designs, I have included other designs as examples to show how, given the parameters, a boat can be designed to suit any particular purpose. For example, page 24 shows the lines of a steel 35-foot chined hull using conic sections. This boat was requested by a client who intended building it himself and wanted the construction to be as simple as possible. Page 44 shows a boat designed for an older client who could no longer climb up and over the side deck. The transom door and open cockpit (from sportfishing boat design) were our solution to his boarding problem. The radar arch holding the mainsheet can be seen on many Hunter boats (Hunter Marine, Alachua, Florida). The sail-handling system makes use of the latest in winch and capstan technology. This boat gave my client what he wanted and suited his type of sailing. You probably won't find a design like this from a production boatbuilder.

One other point that I should mention is that all of these designs are from my design office. Few production builders are willing to give me, a writer/designer and a potential competitor, enough information to show the entire design process as displayed here. While these plans come from my office the ideas they represent can be applied to almost any production boat.

Hopefully, this book will provide you with a lot of ideas to help you make an informed decision when you buy a new or used boat. But remember, as Jeff Rice says, be honest about what you want to do with the boat.

One

What Do You Want in a Cruising Boat?

How do you tell the difference between a boat meant to be sailed across lakes and bays and a boat intended for crossing oceans? What makes one boat faster, another drier, another easier to handle, and yet another easier in its motion? The short answer to all such questions is that they were designed that way.

Cruising boats don't just happen; they are designed for particular purposes and conditions. One boat might be designed to cruise with a family of four in shallow waters in winds that are light in the morning but turn strong by late afternoon, as in the Chesapeake Bay or coastal New England. This type of sailing requires a boat that can sail well in light winds or a short chop. If you have direct access to the open ocean, on the other hand, your sailing might be a little different. In this case, the boat may have to weather long combers as it leaves the harbor with light and variable winds; such conditions are found off San Diego. A different kind of boat is required for sailing in the English Channel, where strong westerlies can be upon a sailor almost before the weather forecast mentions them.

It would be wonderful, of course, if one sailboat design could answer to all uses and conditions, but that is impossible. Every design is a compromise, and the designer's art rests in realizing the primary objectives as fully as possible while sacrificing as little as possible in other attributes. You should learn to recognize the style of boat that best suits the conditions in your cruising area. It may be a shallow-draft boat with a powerful rig to drive it through the Chesapeake chop, or a tall-rigged sloop to make headway against Pacific swells in light air, or a well-built cutter to pound into a strong breeze in the English Channel. The choice of boat ultimately rests with you, so it behooves you to understand why one boat works better for your needs than another.

When you're shopping for a boat, several avenues are open to you. You can purchase a used boat. You can buy an off-the-shelf production boat. (We'll explore both of these options further in chapter 7.) If you are reasonably intrepid, you can buy a "bare" hull and deck, and finish the boat out yourself. Or, if you have made a lot of money in the stock market or come into an inheritance, you can have a custom boat built. Each of these avenues has its advantages, but whichever you choose, you are still going to have to learn to evaluate a boat.

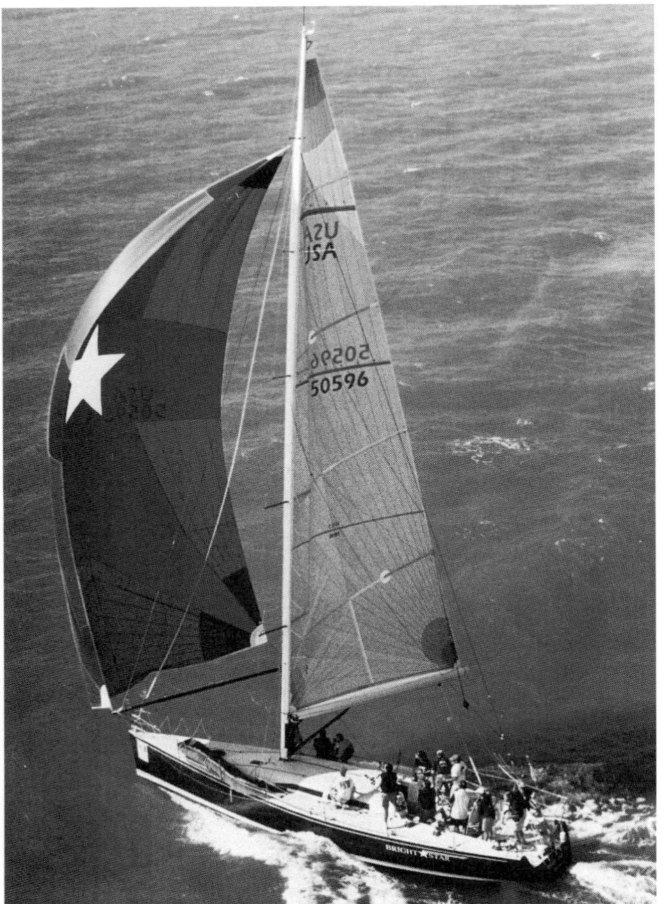

This Carroll Marine 46 CR makes a high-performance cruiser for speedy trips. *(Photo courtesy of Carroll Marine)*

Evaluation begins with an understanding of a boat's lines, as shown in the design drawing, or *lines plan*. (We will take a closer look at lines and hull shapes in chapter 2.) The lines tell you many things. Why does one hull go to windward like a banshee, while another sails 5 degrees lower and a knot slower? Why on one boat is the hull perfectly matched to the rig, the deck, and the interior, while on another the parts seem to have been assembled at random? An informed scrutiny of the lines will give you some of the answers, though not all. In evaluating a boat, you'll learn why certain features are essential on some boats and a nuisance on others. For example, a watertight door might be considered essential on a transoceanic vessel, but nothing more than a nuisance on a boat that never leaves sight of land.

Choosing Your Ideal Boat

Should the boat you buy have long overhangs? Should it be a heavy-displacement (heavyweight) vessel, a lightweight flyer, or somewhere in between? Should it have a large sloop rig or a moderate ketch rig? The answers to these and many other questions all depend on what you want to do with the boat.

Suppose you like to sail into secluded coves where you can anchor off and let the kids take the dinghy to explore the area. This alone tells you several things about what to look for. First, the boat should probably have a bow roller, substantial ground tackle, a windlass and a chain locker, plus a space to store the dinghy. These features in turn might dictate that the hull have more buoyancy forward to support the additional weight of ground tackle there.

By asking yourself more questions, you can narrow down your choices even further. For example, you may sail in Maine during the summer, then travel down the Intracoastal Waterway to

Florida and from there to the Caribbean. This means that your boat will be anchored both near rocks and near coral, so your anchor rode should be chain rather than rope. Travel down the Intracoastal will be under power, which brings into focus engine size and range, and in turn fuel capacity. Unless you plan to unstep it, the mast should not be more than 66 feet from the waterline to the top (63 feet may be a more practical limit), because this is the height to the underside of several fixed bridges along the route. Of course, traveling down the Intracoastal and later through the Bahamas raises the question of draft, too. Must it be restricted? If so, by how much?

When you have asked yourself all the pertinent questions and have a list of features for the boat of your dreams, check over production sailboats to see which ones best match your list and your pocket. You may have to make a few compromises based on what is realistic. For example, you may want the draft restricted to about 6 feet in order to get into certain harbors in the Bahamas. On a 40-footer, that is not a problem, but on a larger boat, say a 60-footer, the reduction in draft may give the boat less stability. So on a 60-footer, you may have to accept slightly more draft, say 6 feet, 9 inches, and avoid certain shallow harbors. Or you may have to accept less stability and make the boat a little more of a motorsailer by relying on a larger engine. Another option is to take the shallower draft and use a lightweight carbon fiber spar to gain additional stability. This option brings cost into play as well, since a carbon fiber spar is two to three times more expensive than an aluminum one. Whatever you decide, your list of questions and answers will ultimately ensure that the choices you make will be the best for you.

If you are not sure what questions to start with, try taking the quiz that follows. It will help you decide which of five basic types of boats is best suited to you—a Weekender, a larger Cruiser, a long-distance Voyager, a Single-Hander for single- or short-handed sailing, or a Cruiser/Racer. Then, at the end of this chapter, we'll lay out some ideas for what a boat of each of these types might look like.

The Island Packet 320 is very similar to our inshore Cruiser with its long keel and comfortable interior.
(Photo courtesy of Island Packet Yachts)

Question Time

The following questions are aimed at helping you find the right style boat for your needs, based on your existing sailing patterns. The quiz is divided into three parts: your cruising style, boat and gear specifics, and safety. For each section, your score will indicate the style(s) of boat appropriate for your present level of experience.

Your Cruising Style

1. How often do you sail?
   a. One to five times per season
   b. Six to fifteen times per season
   c. Every weekend
   d. Every weekend and most evenings
   e. Every weekend, most evenings, and vacations

2. How concerned are you with racing and sailing performance?
   a. Never race
   b. Race occasionally
   c. Race at yacht club level once or twice a week
   d. Race every weekend
   e. Race every weekend and evenings

3. When you sail, you:
   a. Plot a course and sail as long as it takes to get to your destination, even overnight
   b. Sail just for the sake of sailing; your destination is not too important
   c. Choose destinations that allow you to sail for three or four hours at a time
   d. Sail from one marina to another
   e. Sail for an afternoon and always go back to your home marina

4. How far from land do you sail?
   a. I stay inside a bay or harbor
   b. I go up to 5 miles from land
   c. I sail up to 15 miles from land
   d. Most of my sailing is done over 15 miles from land
   e. I regularly sail out of sight of land

5. When you moor in a strange marina, what do you do first?
   a. Check out the local restaurant listing
   b. Head for the marina shower
   c. Get power and water hooked up
   d. Make sure the boat is secure
   e. Check the local weather forecast

6. How often do you sail overnight?
   a. Never
   b. One to three times per year
   c. Four to eight times per year
   d. Eight to fifteen times per year
   e. Fifteen times or more per year

7. You could single-hand (or handle with your spouse or partner) a boat of the following length:
   a. 20 to 25 feet
   b. 26 to 30 feet
   c. 31 to 35 feet
   d. 36 to 40 feet
   e. 41 to 46 feet
   f. Over 47 feet

8. Your sailing experience is:
   a. Less than one year
   b. One to three years
   c. Three to six years
   d. Six to ten years
   e. More than ten years

9. How often do you buy new sails for your boat?
   a. Never; I buy a new boat every three years and go with the sails onboard
   b. One sail every two to three years
   c. One sail every year
   d. Two or more sails each year
   e. A full set of sails about every two years or so

10. How often have you sailed in heavy weather (winds over 35 knots)?
    a. Never
    b. Occasionally
    c. Once a season
    d. Regularly
    e. Very often

Scoring

1. a. 1 point, b. 2 points, c. 3 points, d. 4 points, e. 5 points
2. a. 1 point, b. 2 points, c. 3 points, d. 4 points, e. 5 points
3. a. 5 points, b. 4 points, c. 3 points, d. 2 points, e. 1 point
4. a. 1 point, b. 2 points, c. 3 points, d. 4 points, e. 5 points
5. a. 1 point, b. 2 points, c. 3 points, d. 4 points, e. 5 points
6. a. 1 point, b. 2 points, c. 3 points, d. 4 points, e. 5 points
7. a. 1 point, b. 2 points, c. 3 points, d. 4 points, e. 5 points, f. 6 points
8. a. 1 point, b. 2 points, c. 3 points, d. 4 points, e. 5 points
9. a. 1 point, b. 2 points, c. 3 points, d. 4 points, e. 5 points
10. a. 1 point, b. 2 points, c. 3 points, d. 4 points, e. 5 points

Over 45 points. If you scored over 45 points on this section, you are probably an experienced sailor and know what you want in a boat. You could sail any of the boats in the design series.
Over 35 points (but less than 44). You might be more interested in the Cruiser or Voyager.
Over 25 points (but less than 35). The type of boat you might prefer is the Weekender, the Cruiser, or possibly the Cruiser/Racer. You should ask someone with experience to help you decide what is the best boat for your needs.
Under 20 points. You should gain more experience sailing the Weekender or Cruiser/Racer. You should also have someone help you select the right boat.

Boat and Gear Specifics

What gear do you want on your boat, and how much? Some cruisers prefer as little power-consuming gear as possible, and if you are one of them you will probably have a low score for this section; but how much gear to carry is up to you. When most cruisers think of heading offshore, they want enough gear to give them independence from land-based resources. With the array of equipment available on today's cruising boats, your technological proficiency is one measure of your readiness to head offshore. There's no sense carrying a full suite of electronics, though, if you're not going to use them. The following questions attempt to gauge your comfort level with a fully equipped modern cruising boat.

1. You have used the following items on your boat or on somebody else's boat (include all that apply):
   a. Roller-furling gear
   b. Generator
   c. Reverse-osmosis watermaker
   d. Inverter
   e. Microwave
   f. Electric winches
   g. In-mast furling gear

2. Your ideal boat should sleep:
   a. One person
   b. Two people
   c. Two to four people
   d. Four to seven people
   e. Eight or more

3. Your boat should have (include all that apply):
   a. No anchor
   b. A plow anchor on a bow roller
   c. A Danforth-style anchor on a bow roller
   d. A fisherman-style anchor on a bow roller
   e. A windlass or capstan capable of handling heavy ground tackle
   f. A low-profile windlass
   g. A chain anchor rode
   h. A nylon anchor rode with a short length (2 fathoms) of chain

4. Your boat should carry a dinghy, yes or no? If yes, what type and how should it be powered? (pick any combination of dinghy and outboard):
   a. A fiberglass dinghy
   b. An inflatable
   c. A rigid-bottom inflatable
   d. An outboard of up to 9 horsepower
   e. An outboard of 10 horsepower or more

5. In the galley you would like (include all that apply):
   a. An icebox
   b. A freezer
   c. A refrigerator
   d. A two-burner stove
   e. A three- or four-burner stove with oven
   f. 110-volt outlets

6. The stove is to be fueled with (select only one):
   a. LPG (liquefied petroleum gas), or propane
   b. CNG (compressed natural gas)
   c. Diesel
   d. Electricity
   e. Wood
   f. Alcohol

7. Your boat should have the following rig (select any combination—for example, a and f):
   a. A masthead rig
   b. A fractional rig
   c. Sloop with 150-percent headsail
   d. Sloop with double head (headsail) rig
   e. Cutter (double headsail) rig
   f. Ketch rig
   g. Yawl rig
   h. Schooner rig
   i. Cat rig

8. The boat should have the following keel configuration (select one):
   a. A conventional long keel with rudder attached
   b. A cutaway keel with a separate skeg-hung rudder
   c. A fin keel with a skeg-hung rudder
   d. A fin keel with a balanced rudder
   e. A long-span bulbed keel with a balanced rudder
   f. A winged keel
   g. A keel/centerboard
   h. A centerboard in the hull
   i. A daggerboard

9. Which of the following do you do from your boat? (include all that apply):
   a. Fish
   b. Swim
   c. Snorkel
   d. Sailboard
   e. Barbecue
   f. Use a dinghy, either to board the boat or to sail for fun

10. Your boat should have the following (select any two):
    a. A hard dodger
    b. A soft (canvas) dodger
    c. A Bimini top
    d. A sheltered area for the crew
    e. A pilothouse
    f. A windshield

Scoring

1. Award yourself 2 points for each item.
2. a. 2 points (are you really that unsociable?—the Single-Hander is for you), b. 3 points, c. 4 points, d. 5 points, e. 3 points
3. a. 0 points, b. 3 points, c. 4 points, d. 2 points, e. 5 points, f. 3 points, g. 2 points, h. 3 points
4. If you answered no, give yourself 0 points. If yes, you earn: a. 3 points, b. 3 points, c. 1 point, d. 3 points, e. 2 points. (Whether you have a hard dinghy or an inflatable is a

matter of personal choice, so the same number of points apply.)

5. a. 2 points, b. 4 points, c. 3 points, d. 3 points, e. 4 points, f. 1 point. (An offshore cook would prefer a large freezer and a three- or four-burner stove with an oven.)
6. a. 3 points (LPG has a higher heat value than LNG, diesel, wood, or alcohol), b. 3 points (where CNG is available), c. 2 points (electric stoves do not gimbal), d. 2 points, e. 1 point, f. 2 points.
7. a. 4 points, b. 3 points, c. 3 points, d. 4 points, e. 4 points, f. 4 points, g. 3 points, h. 3 points, i. 2 points. (A masthead sloop rig, described in chapter 6, is the simplest to use. While the schooner rig is romantic, it is complex for the average sailor. A cat rig can be used offshore in the hands of a skilled sailor, but it is not a long-distance offshore rig. See chapter 6 for further discussion of the various rigs.)
8. a. 4 points, b. 4 points, c. 4 points, d. 4 points, e. 3 points, f. 3 points, g. 3 points, h. 2 points, i. 1 point.
9. a. 2 points, b. 2 points, c. 2 points, d. 2 points, e. 2 points, f. 2 points.
10. a. 3 points, b. 3 points, c. 3 points, d. 2 points, e. 2 points, f. 1 point.

If you scored over 65 on this section, you'll be happy with all the gear a 50-foot Voyager could throw at you. If you scored 55 or over, you could probably adapt to any of the designs. If you scored 31 to 54 points, you should probably stay with the simpler Cruiser or Cruiser/Racer. Below 30 points, you might prefer the Weekender or possibly the Cruiser/Racer.

Safety

1. Which of the following should your boat carry?
   a. An engine-driven pump only
   b. An engine-driven pump and a battery-powered pump only
   c. In addition to either of the above, a single hand pump
   d. In addition to a. or b., two hand-operated pumps—one below deck and the other accessible from the deck
   e. Only hand-operated pumps—one below deck and the other operated from on deck

2. Your boat should carry (include all that apply):
   a. Life jackets for all the crew
   b. Harnesses for all the crew
   c. A life raft capable of holding the entire crew
   d. Horseshoe life rings
   e. A first-aid kit with seasickness pills

3. Your boat should have (include all that apply):
   a. Strongpoints (such as padeyes) for hooking safety harnesses into
   b. Jacklines on deck
   c. Personal strobes
   d. Inflatable life jackets
   e. Personal flares

4. Your boat should have the following available (include all that apply):
   a. VHF radio
   b. SSB radio
   c. Internet access
   d. Method of connecting to the outside world without using VHF or SSB radio
   e. GPS
   f. Loran
   g. EPIRB
   h. GPS-linked EPIRB or GPIRB

5. What would you put in your grab bag? (select all that apply):
   a. I don't know what a grab bag is
   b. Fishing hooks and line

c. Sunscreen
d. Water
e. GPS
f. VHF radio
g. Weather radio
h. Can opener
i. Freeze-dried foods
j. Canned foods
k. Long-sleeved shirts or sweaters
l. Compass
m. GPS
n. EPIRB

6. What charts do you carry aboard your boat? (select all that apply):
   a. An electronic chart plotter
   b. A chart for the harbor that you normally sail out of
   c. A chart for the local area
   d. A set of charts for your region, plus local charts
   e. Separate charts for the area in which you are sailing plus local harbor charts as needed

Scoring

1. a. 1 point, b. 1 point, c. 2 points, d. 4 points, e. 3 points. Engine-driven or electrically driven pumps can be put out of action if the engine or battery is flooded. So it is better to have at least one hand-operated pump and ideally two, one below deck and the other operable from the cockpit.
2. a. 5 points, b. 5 points, c. 5 points, d. 4 points, e. 3 points
3. a. 3, b. 2, c. 2, d. 4, e. 2. Strongpoints can be added later, if desired. As long as the fittings are available jacklines can be added for offshore sailing.
4. a. 3 points, b. 4 points, c. 1 point, d. 1 point, e. 3 points, f. 1 point, g. 4 points, h. 5 points (GPS-linked EPIRBs or GPIRBs can lead rescue services directly to you without a search.)
5. a. 0 points, b. 2 points, c. 2 points, d. 2 points, e. 2 points, f. 2 points, g. 2 points, h. 2 points, i. 1 point, j. 2 points, k. 2 points, l. 2 points, m. 2 points, n. 6 points for a 406 MHz EPIRB (2 points for a 121.5 MHz EPIRB). Freeze-dried foods take water to reconstitute, and you may not have enough water in a liferaft.
6. a. 1 point, b. 2 points, c. 3 points, d. 4 points, e. 5 points

A score of 55-plus indicates that you are safety conscious and can sail anywhere; any of the designs would suit your style of sailing. If you scored between 45 and 50, you could make do in any of the designs. If you scored between 30 and 45, you shouldn't go too far from shore; the Cruiser or Cruiser/Racer would be more suitable to your style of sailing. If you scored between 20 and 30, you should probably sail the Weekender or the Cruiser/Racer in sheltered waters.

Our Designs

The results of the quiz suggest what kind of sailing you favor and therefore what type of boat might best suit you. This provides only a general guide, however—not hard and fast rules. We sail for pleasure, after all; if your heart is set on voyaging but the quiz pegs you as a coastal cruiser, don't be deterred. There are successful voyagers out there in small, spartan boats, and others who set sail with little experience. Perhaps you will be one of them.

The five designs we turn to next—a Weekender, a Cruiser, a Voyager, a Single-Hander, and a Cruiser/Racer—were selected because they are so different from one another. They are not intended to be defining examples of a type, but merely typical. They also allow you to see that many features can be incorporated into another boat; for example, the Single-Hander or the Cruiser could have a pilothouse as is shown on the Voyager.

Throughout this book we will follow the development of these five designs. Each one is characterized by different goals and equipment, with the overall goal being to fulfill the design criteria in the most efficient way. The boats will take shape through the chapters that follow. Here we introduce the starting concepts. If you're anxious for a peek at what results, you can view the final designs in chapter 9.

The Weekender

A weekender is a small boat meant for inshore sailing in coastal waters where rescue is quick and a safe haven is nearby. The boat's length is typically 20 to 26 feet. Being fairly small, the Weekender is relatively light and simple, with few amenities. In fact, living aboard is more like camping out than living in luxury.

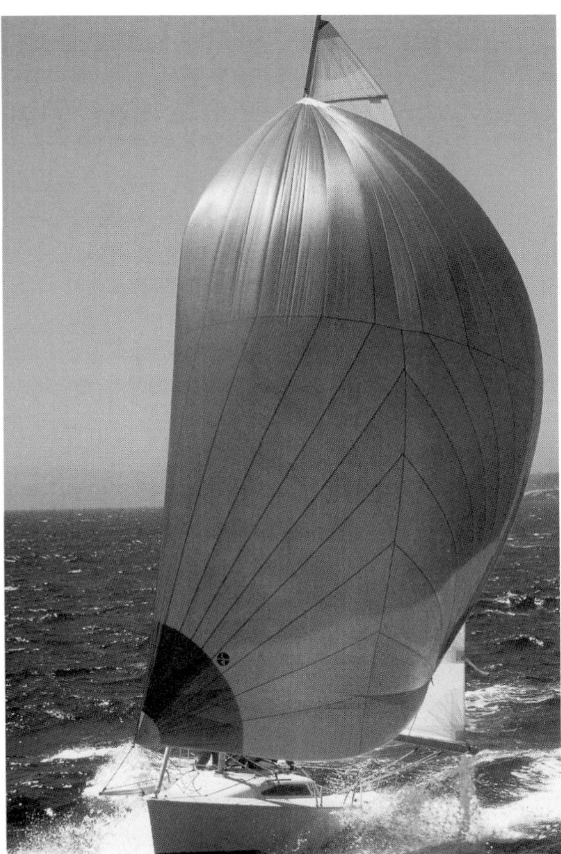

The Ultimate 20 one-design shows a fine turn of speed under spinnaker and is a good example of a weekender. *(Photo by Patrick Short courtesy of Ultimate 20 Sailboats)*

The typical weekender will have up to four bunks, a large cockpit, a small galley, a large built-in icebox (possibly accessible from the cockpit), an open head compartment closed off with a curtain, a small anchor for anchoring overnight (although most weekend sailors keep their boat in a marina or on a mooring), and a main battery with battery-powered navigation lights. The battery may be charged by an inboard or outboard engine. Because of the boat's light weight, it may be raced. Performance may be supplemented with a traditional spinnaker or with a pole-mounted multipurpose spinnaker (MPS) or genniker (genoa-spinnaker hybrid).

The Cruiser

The Cruiser is a larger boat with an overall length in the 34-to-36-foot range. It is aimed at the couple who would like a reasonably sized

The Beneteau 42 is a comfortable production cruiser for most conditions. *(Photo courtesy of Beneteau)*

boat that is easy to handle under all conditions. Speed is not important, but handling and seaworthiness are. This boat is intended to be cruised not more than 30 miles offshore, and will most often be used for weekend or weeklong cruises along coastlines and out to coastal islands.

The typical cruiser has four to six bunks that may be settee/berths or dedicated berths. It usually has a full galley, with a three- or four-burner stove and an oven. For instant meals, there may be a microwave driven either by a small generator or by an inverter. Such a boat will have an enclosed head and shower, a comfortable dining area, and a cockpit dining area as well. The cockpit may not be large, but it is comfortable. In the cockpit there may be a table with a barbecue on the rail. Other commonly seen features are roller-furling gear, a small windlass for anchor handling, and a fully battened mainsail with lazyjacks.

The Voyager or Long-Distance Cruiser

The Voyager or long-distance cruiser is larger than the first two types, as befits a boat that will cross oceans or explore fairly remote coasts. Its overall length is around 45 to 47 feet, and the construction is strong enough to withstand a severe storm.

For sailing in a comfortable long-keeled cruiser, the Island Packet 45 is one of the best boats on the water. *(Photo courtesy of Island Packet Yachts)*

There are two schools of thought about gear on offshore voyagers. One says that systems should be kept to a minimum lest something go wrong and you end up having to tote around a large lump of metal that doesn't work. The other says that you should carry whatever gear you need to enjoy the trip and enough spares to make repairs. We will design a boat that subscribes to the second school of thought.

In keeping with offshore performance capability, the cockpit on a long distance cruiser is typically small but comfortable. Safety lines are provided on deck with strongpoints in the cockpit. The hull will have a fin keel with a skeg-hung rudder to reduce wetted surface and to enable the boat to make fairly fast passages. While some sailors equate voyaging with long-keeled boats, more modern shapes make for a faster, more comfortable trip. The hull shape should be compatible with the goals of offshore voyaging, seakeeping, and crew comfort. Below deck, the bunks should be near the fore-and-aft centerline of the boat for easy motion when the crew is off watch, although that might not be possible when the dining area, galley, and engine compartment also need to be in the middle of the hull.

To allow for pleasant extended passages, the boat should have a large battery bank, which leads to the requirement for a strong, multifaceted charging system. In our particular Voyager we'll incorporate solar chargers, but as solar cells are unlikely to generate enough power, we may have a wind generator, plus a diesel genset. We will also incorporate an inverter into the engine compartment to give the boat 110 volts AC from the battery bank when the generator is not running. If possible, over the battery bank and generator we'll install a workbench so that repairs can be made. This means a walk-in engine compartment large enough to hold all the gear. Rather than have a wet locker, we'll make the engine compartment do double duty and install drying racks there.

While some cruisers prefer to keep things simple and postpone clean clothes and a shower until the end of a passage, this boat will also have a reverse-osmosis watermaker to make enough water to keep the tanks topped up when exploring remote areas. The watermaker should be sized to provide enough water for a clothes washer/dryer. The galley will be capable of supporting a crew of four to six people on an extended cruise, which means that it will have a freezer, refrigerator, and a four-burner stove with an oven. There will also be a microwave and various 110-volt appliances for use when the generator is running.

On deck the boat will carry substantial ground tackle, possibly two bow rollers with anchors, a nylon anchor line on a reel as well as a chain rode stored in a chain locker, and a fairly heavy-duty windlass. For getting ashore, a hard dinghy would be too large to carry on deck, so an inflatable will be used. With transom davits, or chocks over the main cabin, a hard-bottomed inflatable can be carried, but it is more likely that the inflatable will be a Zodiac Roll-up type. Of course, this means an outboard engine, which will be mounted on the stern rail when not in use.

The Zodiac Roll-up inflatable makes an ideal tender for a voyager or an inshore cruiser. *(Photo courtesy of Zodiac USA)*

The Single-Hander

In contrast to a voyager, a single-hander has a minimum of equipment. Our boat will have a length of 45 to 50 feet to make it fast when traversing large bodies of water and easy for one person to sail without feeling too cramped.

Most cruisers who single-hand adapt an existing design to their needs. Purpose-built single-handers are constructed for races such as the single-handed round-the-world (now called Around-Alone) race or the single-handed transatlantic race. We will assume that our purpose-built boat is intended for the latter.

The central concerns of this design are that all the gear is within reach of the helmsman, and that the boat has adequate safety features to keep him or her aboard under all conditions. Our boat will have a pilothouse-style cabin that extends aft to give some shelter when the crew is on deck. The cabin will have plenty of ports to enable the crew to watch sail trim while staying under shelter. It will also have a large navigation area, with a comfortable chair for the navigator/crew who may sleep in the seat from time to time. This navigation table/seat unit may be gimbaled to keep it level underway.

To gain stability and directional control the boat may have water ballast, a very deep keel with a bulbed bottom, and a deep rudder. A deep rudder is essential to give the autopilot control in what could be a fairly beamy boat. The rudder may be designed to have a canting blade or there may be twin rudders, depending on the beam at the transom. To drive the autopilot, there will be a large battery bank, a small generator on the main engine, and a wind generator or solar cells.

The Cruiser/Racer

A more popular boat than the Single-Hander is the Cruiser/Racer. This boat is basically a cruising interior fitted in a racing hull. Its length is between 32 and 36 feet, with a beam of around 10 to 12 feet. The hull should have a relatively small wetted surface and a relatively deep keel with a bulb to maximize stability. If the boat is to sail under the International Measurement System (IMS) or Performance Handicap Rating Factor (PHRF) rating rules, it will not be allowed to use water ballast, but under the racing rules for the single-handed transatlantic or round-the-world race it can. Most likely, the boat will not have water ballast, although the possibility should not be ruled out. (Designing to the rating rules is covered in more detail in chapter 2.)

The cockpit in a cruiser/racer is laid out for efficiency during sail changes and to position the crew in the best location from a weight standpoint. This probably means that the cockpit is fairly large, limiting headroom and space below deck.

This boat will not sail far from shore, so the structural strength and the seakeeping ability are not primary concerns. The rig can be either a fractional or masthead rig (see "Sloop" in chapter 6), depending upon the skill levels of the sailors racing the boat. The crew will not usually spend a long time aboard the boat except during a cruise. Accommodations should be carefully thought out to minimize weight and to locate watch crew weight to best advantage.

Production Boats

It will be informative to follow the development of the five designs in this book, but when it comes time to buy a boat, most people buy a design in production from one of the major builders. For example, a weekender-style boat is available from companies such as Melges Boatworks in Zenda, Wisconsin; Hunter Marine Corporation of Alachua, Florida; and J/Boats of Newport, Rhode Island. You might also consider a multihull from a builder such as Corsair Marine of Chula Vista, California, builders of F-yachts.

For a cruiser-style boat you might go to Island Packet Yachts of Largo, Florida; Catalina Yachts of Woodland Hills, California; Pacific Seacraft Corporation of Fullerton, California; Jeanneau USA and Beneteau Yachts, both French built and imported; or Tartan Yachts of Grand River, Ohio. Hunter Marine Corporation and Freedom Yachts of Portsmouth, Rhode Island, might also fit into this category.

In the voyager category, you will need a boat with the ability to cross oceans safely. At the top of this category (read most expensive) are boats from the Hinckley Company of Southwest Harbor, Maine; Baltic Yachts and Oy Nautor of Finland; and Oyster Marine from Great Britain. One of the top ocean cruising yachts, with a huge number of round-the-world voyages to its credit, is the Valiant 40, now made as the Valiant 42 and Valiant 50, available from Valiant Yachts in Gordonville, Texas. You might also look at some of the larger boats from Waquiez of France, and Hallberg-Rassey of Sweden. These imports are well built and have transoceanic capability. Some of the boats from our cruiser category have been pressed into service as voyagers and proven themselves well, usually after some refitting for offshore work.

Few single-hander yachts are built for production, but many production boats in the voyager category can be adapted. As of this writing I know of no production boats that use water ballast in the manner described in the following pages, although many custom boats have been built with water ballast.

Cruiser/racers abound. You only have to look at the results of any major race week or yacht club regatta to find boats from Carroll Marine in Bristol, Rhode Island; Dehler Yachts from Germany; and others. Don't forget that many one-design boats fit into this category. For example, some Tartan Yachts and J/Boats fit the bill as one-design cruiser/racers.

Two

Hull Shapes

Designers don't look at boats the way sailors do. When sailors look at a boat they might see a hull with an attractive sheerline, plenty of beam, a bow that conforms to the latest in design thinking, and a transom that has steps to help them get aboard. They spend time looking at the keel and ask about its draft and its ability to get them to windward. They might look at the rudder, but usually only to make sure it is large enough to steer the boat properly.

In contrast, designers looking at the same boat perceive details and nuances. They mentally impose a set of lines over the hull, and then analyze the hull shape. For example, a designer might look at the bow area and wonder why the bow shape is fuller than normal; a fuller bow is not quite as efficient to windward as a fine bow. Windward performance for a cat or a schooner is not as good as for a sloop, so a fuller bow would be perfectly acceptable on a cat or schooner. Likewise, windward performance is not as good for shallow-draft boats, so the bow of a shallow-draft boat can be slightly fuller.

Designers don't look at the hull without looking at the entire boat. A different rig or keel shape, a nontypical deck layout, heavy anchors forward, or a large aft cabin can lead to changes in the hull shape. These changes are often a critical part of the boat's overall success or failure.

The hull shape is critical to the performance of a boat, but many other factors can influence how a designer modifies the hull to suit the boat's in-

The Lines Plan

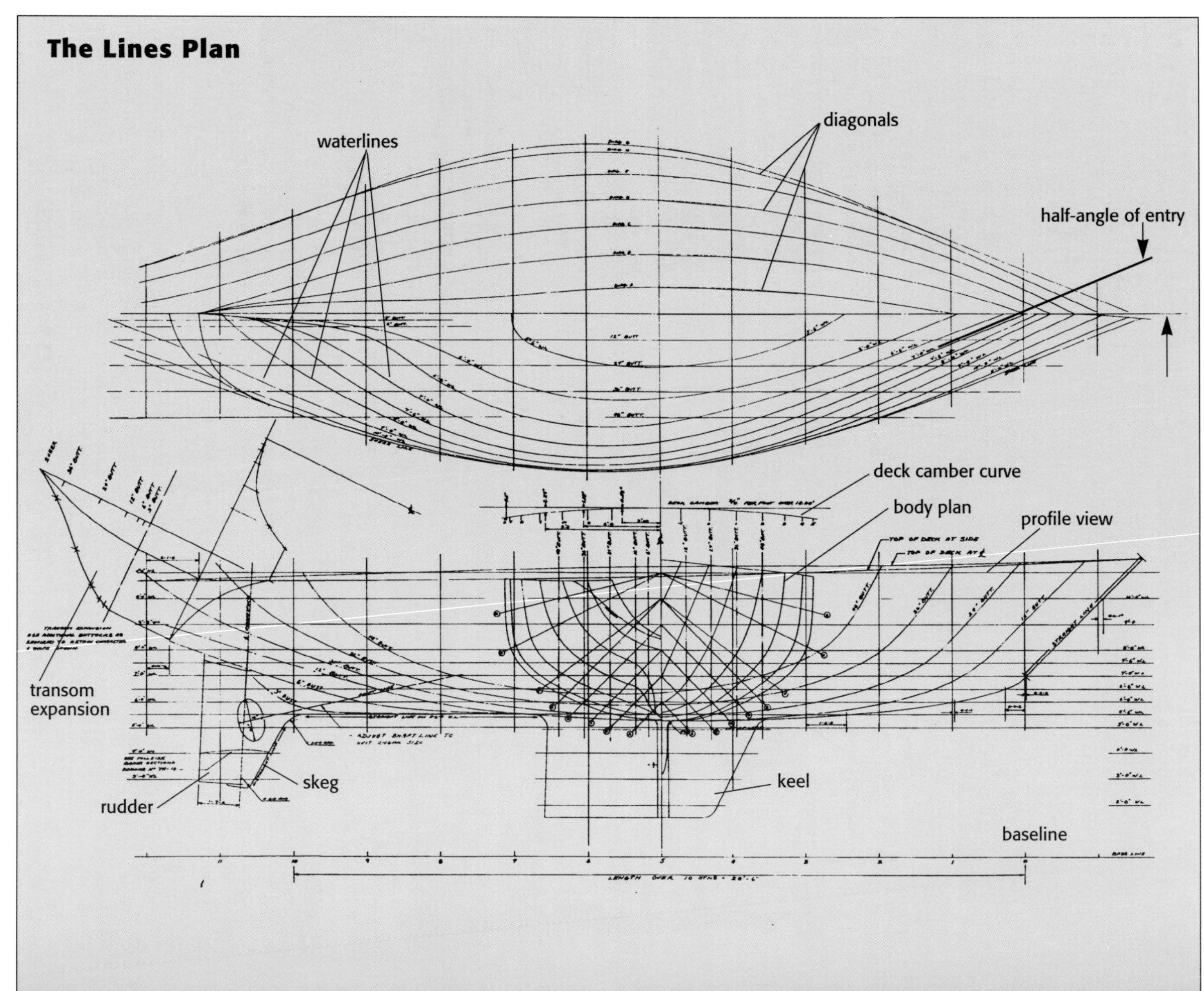

The lines of a boat are rarely drawn completely today. Most lines are developed on a computer. This set of lines from an older boat shows the standard views. At the bottom of the grid is the *baseline*, which is usually divided into 10 stations spanning the waterline length of the boat.

Immediately above the baseline is the *profile drawing* showing the *buttock lines*. This boat uses a number of buttocks, starting with a 12-inch buttock and going out to 48 inches. Additional 3- and 6-inch buttocks are added aft to show the shape of the skeg. On this hull the 10 stations are taken to the *fairbody* line of the hull (the centerline of the hull if the skeg were not shown). Often the lines are taken to the centerline of the rudder, but this rudder has been pushed farther aft, almost to station 11, thus lengthening the waterline. The large skeg on this boat houses the propeller, affording it complete protection. A three-bladed prop would work best in this type of skeg to avoid a lot of vibration.

The *sections* are shown in the *body plan* superimposed on the profile. Note that the sections amidships are reasonably flat-bottomed to allow for a shallow-draft keel. Notice how the sections have no tumblehome and carry some fullness into the bow area to provide reserve buoyancy in a seaway. Above the sections is the *deck camber curve*, which shows the builder precisely how much camber, or crown, to use on the deck. A curve of ¾ to 1 inch would make the lee-side deck very steep to walk on, while a curve of less than ¼ to 1 inch tends to look very flat.

Above the profile view are the *waterlines* and *diagonals*. The waterlines are shown at 6-inch intervals where hull curvature is pronounced and 12-inch intervals (above the 8-foot waterline) where the hull is relatively flat. The diagonals (also marked on the body plan as [A] through [H]) show nice, smooth curves with no distortions. They give the designer an idea of the curve of the hull when heeled, and serve as additional fairing points when the hull is lofted. With computer-aided design, diagonals are no longer shown.

Notice the half-angle of entry of the bow, shown on the waterline view. This is a fairly normal half-angle of 22 degrees. Under sail the boat tends to throw spray clear of the hull without a lot of water coming aboard, although the relatively flat panels in the bow area do tend to pound in a seaway.

On the profile view, at the stern, is shown a *transom expansion*. This shows the shape of the transom when it is "unwrapped," and tells the builder how much material is required.

Larger-scale drawings of the rudder and keel would be provided with this boat, to avoid cramming all the information on one page where it might be too small and confusing.

tended purpose. For example, rating rules often lead designers to distort racing hulls in pursuit of a good rating. International Offshore Rating (IOR) boats of the late 1970s and early 1980s sometimes had grossly distorted hulls, to gain a rating edge. Consequently, it is important to understand how the lines of a boat are developed, the factors that go into developing the lines, and how they influence the shape of the hull.

We will begin with the basics. Unlike a house, where the walls are usually straight both vertically and horizontally, and sharp corners define turns, a boat hull is curved in both directions. To define the curvature the hull is sliced into sections, buttock lines, and waterplanes. A drawing showing the sections, buttocks, waterlines, and diagonals is known as the *lines plan* or more simply, the *lines*.

Sections (usually 10) are made by cutting the hull at 90 degrees to the fore-and-aft centerline. (In the early days of hull design, builders made a wooden half-model of the hull, which was then sliced into sections; measurements taken from these sections were then scaled up and laid out full size on the lofting floor.) If the edges of each section were painted black and viewed from ahead, you would have a sectional view (or *body plan*) of the hull.

Buttock lines are vertical slices along the hull parallel to the centerline of the boat. Buttock lines appear in the *profile view* (or side view) of the boat. As we'll see later, buttocks give a designer a good idea of the shape of the stern wave as it leaves the hull.

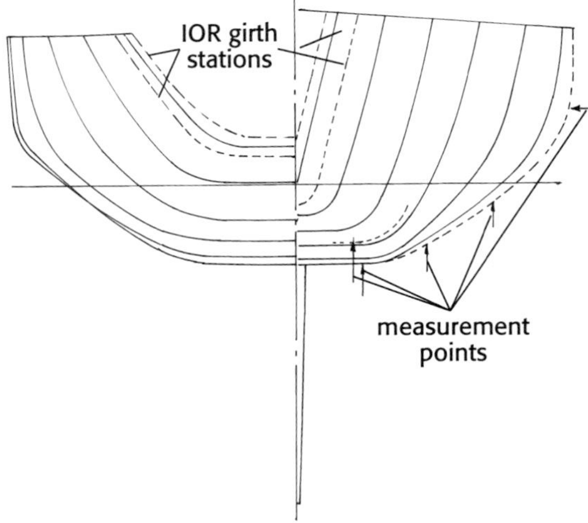

The sections of an IOR racer from the late 1970s. Note how the sections are distorted at rating points to minimize the overall rating. Rating points are indicated with arrows, while the girth stations are shown dashed.

The girth stations were distances measured as fractions of the overall beam of the boat. In order to measure the slope of the stern and bow various corrections were calculated to arrive at a derived sailing length known as L. The rated displacement of the boat was calculated from measurement points at various distances along L and the combination of sailing length, displacement, sail area, and stability were all figured into the rating calculation. In the early days of computers this information was often scaled out on a drawing and calculated using hand-held calculators.

Because measurement distances, girth lengths, and certain other factors were based on B or the rule beam of the boat, designers made B as large as possible, leading to excessively beamy designs with acute hull distortions.

Waterplanes or *waterlines* are horizontal slices along the length of the hull, and are viewed from above or below the hull. Waterplanes affect such aspects of the hull as stability, waterline beam, and interior roominess.

Diagonals are lines cut through the boat from forward to aft at an angle to the waterplane. The diagonals were traditionally inserted to give fairing points in areas of sharp curvature where waterplanes or buttocks did not define the hull well enough. Computer-generated offsets have superseded this use for diagonals, but many designers consider them useful for defining the shape of the hull when the boat is heeled. Diagonals are usually labeled with letters to set them apart from the waterplanes or buttocks.

A designer looks at the lines to get a feel for a hull's overall characteristics. The shape of the sections at the bow, for example, gives an idea of the wetness of the boat in a seaway. The shape of the sections aft can often tell how well the boat will steer.

By studying this chapter and making a habit of observing hull shapes, you will begin to develop an eye for a boat's probable performance. After you have examined a hull and drawn your conclusions, sail that boat. This firsthand experience will probably confirm your impressions, but it may also change them. Only by sailing a large number of boats and looking at a lot of hulls will you develop the ability to make an accurate assessment of a boat just by looking at its hull.

Sections

As mentioned, there are usually 10 sections which show the shape of the boat at designated *stations* when viewed from ahead or astern. The stations start at the bow, with station 0 at the intersection of the waterline and the bow, and continue to station 10 at either the rudderstock or the intersection of the hull centerline and waterline. Stations forward of station 0 are usu-

Computers and the Lines Plan

In days of old, construction of a boat started with the building of a half-model, and the half-model was cut up and scaled up to provide full-sized *offsets* (offsets are dimensioned, scaled off the drawing, and used to lay out the full-sized hull on the lofting floor). But during the nineteenth century, boat designers starting drawing the lines of boats on paper, and providing the builder with a *table of offsets*. The table of offsets enabled the boatbuilder to scale the paper lines up to full-size lines.

Today most designers use specially developed computer programs to draw the lines of a boat and use CAD (computer-aided design) programs to draw interior, sail, deck, and other plans. You are unlikely to see a drawing of true sections, buttocks, or diagonals. You may see representative lines, but what you see will depend on the way the designer works and the program used to develop the lines plan. Familiarity with the computer program is essential to comparing several sets of computer-generated lines.

Most of the work of fairing the lines on a computer is done using polylines (see drawing on page 19) and a b-spline surface (a mathematical term) and other equations that allow the designer to fair the hull without having to draw lines as we know them. This means that you may not see true section, diagonal, or buttock lines, only polylines. For the sake of this discussion we will continue to interpret the lines as if the boat were drawn by hand. This will enable you to get a better understanding of hull shape.

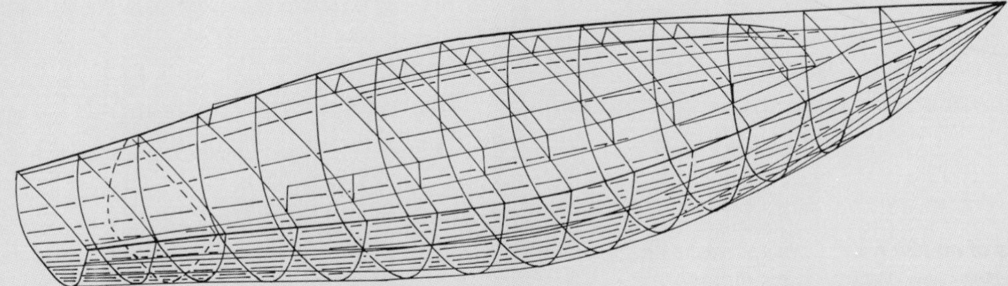

Here is a set of lines as drawn by a computer using the Nautilus program from New Wave Systems, in Jamestown, Rhode Island. The longitudinal lines are not diagonals or waterlines, but polylines, a collection of straight line segments that are short enough to look like a curve when displayed on the screen. In the program, however, the actual lines are displayed as a b-spline surface.

ally written as negative values, for example, −1 or −2. When the lines continue aft of station 10, the number is simply increased.

Typically, the front half of a boat is shown on the right side of the section or body plan drawing and the back half of a boat on the left side of the drawing; this is done to avoid drawing the middle sections on top of each other where they may be confusing to read. The sectional shape of the boat is determined by the characteristics the designer wants. For example, the sections of a 12-Meter are deeply veed due to the influence of the rating rule. Deeply veed sections are said to have *slack garboards*, which makes the keel relatively ineffective. (In traditional plank-on-frame construction, the garboard plank was the one next to the keel, into which it was rabbeted. Slack garboards made the plank easier to install because it followed the natural curve of the hull.) The sections of a lightweight high-performance boat, on the other hand, are usually dinghy-like and very flat at the bottom. This is intended to make the boat sail fast when upright and to enhance keel efficiency.

The depth of the sections gives a good idea of the boat's *displacement*, the volume or weight of the vessel when afloat. Deep sections, like those of a 12-Meter, indicate a very heavy boat. Typically a 65-foot 12-Meter weighs in at around 55,000 pounds. In contrast, a lightweight racing boat of similar length, with fairly flat sections, might weigh about 20,000 pounds.

12-Meter sections

A 12-Meter is designed to a rating rule, but the hull shape is typical of some older cruising boats. The sections show a fairly narrow hull with a deeply veed shape. This immediately suggests that the boat has a heavy displacement and that the keel is not very efficient. It also suggests that the boat has high wetted surface (about 620 square feet, compared to a similar-sized flat-bottomed boat at about 490 square feet) and will not be a sparkling performer in light winds. However, in heavy winds the combination of a deeply veed hull and heavy displacement will give the boat a relatively smooth ride with little slamming. A smooth ride leads to much less crew fatigue. The deeply veed hull will also make the boat tend to track in a straight line rather than meander, making it easier for an autopilot to steer.

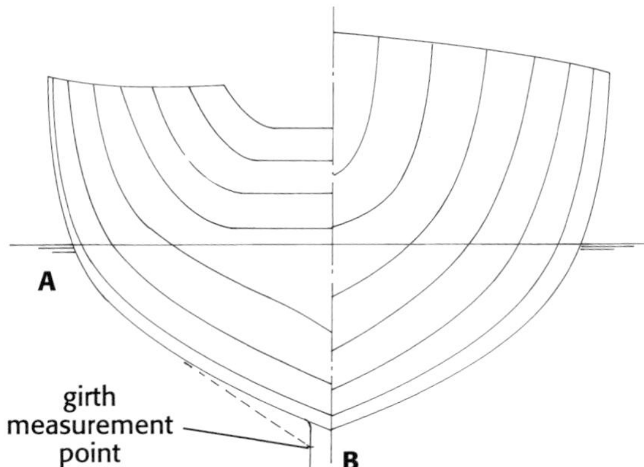

Typical sections for a 12-Meter hull. These hulls are heavy (about 55,000 pounds on a 45-foot waterline). The rating rule also incorporates a girth difference between a point on the hull at the waterline (A) and a point on the keel (B), which is actually measured between the skin girth and a straight line (shown dashed). To keep the difference small, designers pull the hull down amidships, making it even deeper.

There is easily enough headroom inside the hull, so the freeboard is usually quite low. Because of the large amount of ballast, a boat of this style typically heels readily up to about 20 degrees, and then becomes very hard to heel further. This too says that freeboard need not be high, except in the bow area. Because of the high displacement and relatively low freeboard, however, sailing this boat in a seaway would be a wet experience as waves break over the bow.

Because the boat is narrow, it requires a large amount of ballast that will usually fit easily into the deep bilges and keel. Although the keel is inefficient, the narrow beam raises the hull's windward efficiency.

Dinghy sections

Dinghy sections are the opposite of 12-Meter sections. Because dinghies use their crew for stability, they do not need space for ballast, which enables them to sail faster than 1.5 x $\sqrt{LWL}$

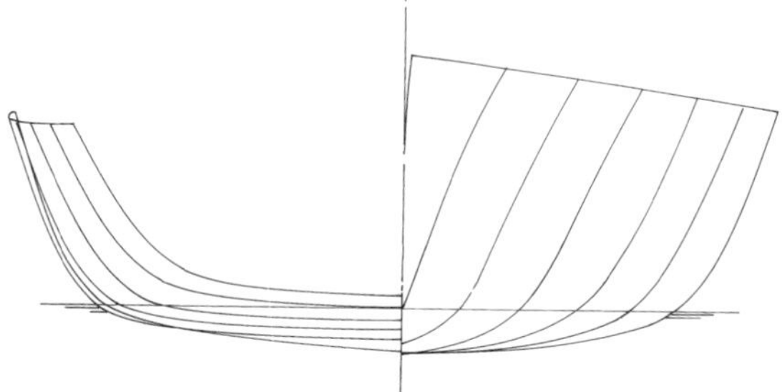

These dinghy sections support the weight of the crew, but no ballast. Consequently, they are very shallow, leading to shallow buttock lines and much higher speed potential.

(see the sidebar "Waves and Boat Speed" on page 23). The midship section is very flat, and the flatness is carried aft. This flatness can lead to pounding in the chop or short steep waves that might be kicked up in a sheltered bay.

To get the crew out as far as possible and increase stability, the sections are flared outboard. While this increases the effect of crew weight, it also helps the lee side scoop water into the boat when it is heeled more than usual. Self-draining ports must be fitted, since the crew on the rail will not be able to get inboard to bail the boat.

The lack of ballast, flared sections, planing ability, and crew stability gives this hull a very high speed potential, making it fun to sail in sheltered waters. But it is liable to capsize or fill with water, which are not good features for a cruising sailboat. High acceleration, high speed, and light weight all tend to lead to early crew fatigue in strong winds. Overall, this hull is not one that could be labeled seaworthy or seakindly.

Cruising boat sections

The sections of a modern cruising boat will often show a fairly flat underbody to enable the boat to carry plenty of displacement and still have a shallow but efficient keel. In a boat intended for offshore sailing, we would want the sections slightly deeper to confine water to the bilge when heeled and to give the boat better directional stability under autopilot. But deeper sections increase overall draft, so the depth of the sections, or in designer talk, the *canoe body* depth or draft, should suit the area in which the boat is going to sail. Deeper sections develop slightly more hull lift than do shallow sections, but the keel loses efficiency because it has less span from top to bottom. Overall, a shallow hull with a deep keel is slightly more efficient than a deep (12-Meter-style) hull with a relatively short keel span. For inshore sailing, where draft is often critical, the hull shape shown in the drawing represents the best compromise between hull depth and keel draft.

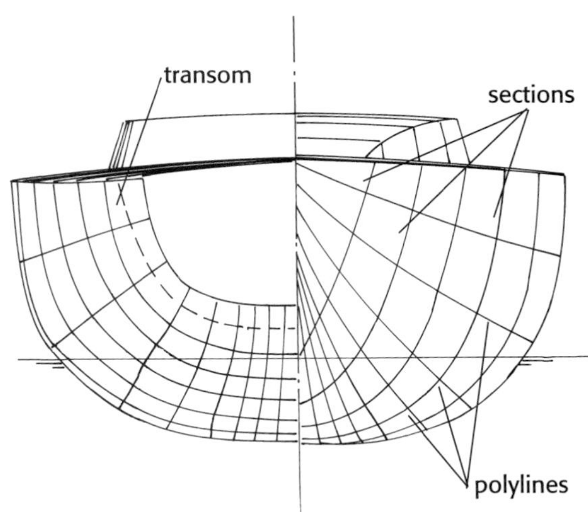

The sections of a cruising boat as drawn on a computer. The longitudinal lines are polylines, and often they don't look fair. This hull is relatively flat bottomed because a shallow draft is required. The bow sections have a slight curvature to reduce pounding. Notice also that there is a section aft of the transom (shown dashed). The hull lines are faired beyond the ends of the hull to make sure the hull stays fair to the transom. The deck camber and cabintop are often made as a separate "layer" in a computer program and added later.

Cruising boat sections also want good beam and a relatively high freeboard (we'll examine freeboard's effect on seaworthiness in chapter 3). Stability is a function of beam and weight of ballast, so increasing the beam helps to increase the boat's stability without incurring the need for additional ballast. Increasing the beam also gives greater volume inside the hull to make the boat more spacious without increasing its displacement. This makes the boat roomier for its price.

High freeboard is needed to get headroom inside a shallow hull. Very few sailors will buy a boat without adequate headroom. In general, at least 6 feet, 2 inches of headroom is required over the cabin sole. Fortunately, the cabin sole tends to be in the middle part of the boat where the hull is deepest. When we are designing the interior, we need to keep in mind the shallowness of the hull and make sure that we do not put a walkway in an area where headroom is restricted.

Finally, notice how the shape of the midship section is carried through to the aft end of the hull. When the smaller stern sections carry a shape similar to that of the midship section, water moving along the hull flows smoothly aft, which, in theory at least, will make the boat faster.

Buttock Lines

The buttock lines run from bow to stern and show how the shape of the hull changes as it goes from forward to aft. The critical parts of the buttocks are the bowlines (the buttocks are sometimes called the bowlines in the forward part of the boat), and the run aft. In a heavy-displacement boat, the buttocks are fairly steep both forward and aft. Steep buttocks aft limit boat speed rather severely by effectively trapping the boat in its own stern wave.

Rounded stern

A cruising boat with a rounded stern has buttock lines that follow the contour of the stern. When the boat is sailing upright (for example, sailing downwind), the stern wave tends to follow the buttock lines until gravity stops it from growing any higher; the wave then breaks and will not get any longer. When the distance from the end of the designed waterline to the crest of the stern wave is small, the hull is effectively locked into a maximum speed. The only time that speed might be exceeded is when surging down the back of a wave.

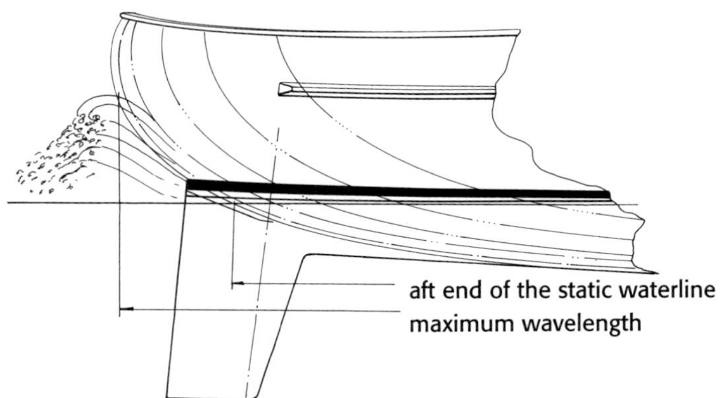

A rounded stern has steeply upswept buttocks. This tends to pull the stern wave upward at the stern, keeping it very short. In other words, the boat is "locked" into a certain wave length, no matter how hard the wind pushes it. Additional power builds the wave higher but adds little in the way of boat speed.

Canoe stern

Unlike a rounded stern, a well-designed canoe stern can have fairly flat buttocks that allow water to flow easily past the stern and smoothly across the rudder, making the boat easier to steer. Canoe sterns also tend to have an easier motion through the water because of the easier buttock lines. Because a canoe-sterned boat is often symmetrical forward and aft, however, it may pitch in a seaway.

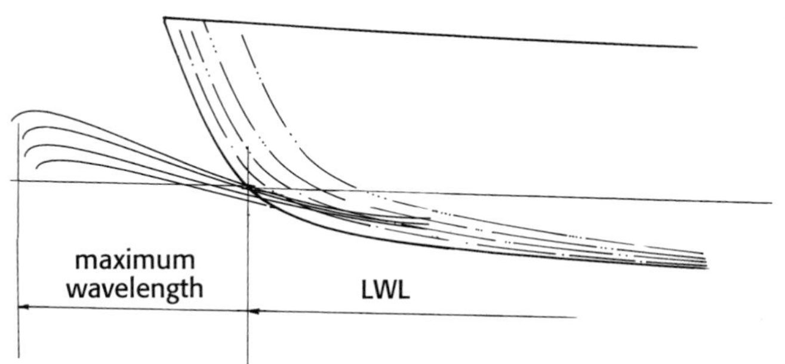

A canoe stern has flatter buttocks than a rounded stern, and is not locked quite so tightly into a wave length. Because the hull shape forward of the waterline is fairly flat, a canoe-sterned hull can be quite fast.

Typical transom stern

In this shape the buttocks describe a shallow angle and the stern wave can move well aft before it crests. Consequently, this stern shape tends to give the boat a slightly longer stern wave, which translates to a higher speed potential. Further, the wave crest tends not to be as high as with a rounded stern, and thus is unlikely to break until higher speeds are reached.

Dinghy stern

The buttocks on a dinghy tend to be much flatter. Because the dinghy is light and does not carry ballast, it has the potential to plane. In the planing mode the boat is no longer bound by Froude's law (see sidebar "Waves and Boat Speed" on page 23), and a 15-foot hull may reach speeds of 12 to 15 knots. Notice how the stern wave crest has moved a long way aft. Because it is fairly flat, it is unlikely to break until the boat is moving at a very high speed.

Waterlines

The shape of the waterplane area is best viewed from above, and the lines that show its area are usually called the *waterlines* or *waterplanes*. *Waterplane areas* give the designer an idea of the stability of the boat and its sea-keeping ability. For example, a boat with a diamond-shaped waterplane, as many IOR-style boats had a few years ago, derives relatively low stability from its waterplane area. The ends of its hull are pinched to get a rating reduction, while the middle of the boat is fat to increase beam and further contribute to a lower rating. As a result, the boat is liable to pitch and is often difficult to control at higher speeds.

Today most boats have a gently rounded waterplane with fuller ends and a conse-

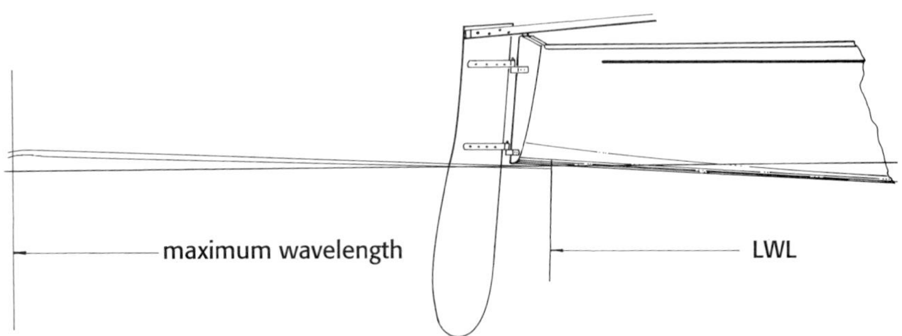

When a flat dinghy-like stern is combined with a lightweight hull, the potential for planing is always present. Under normal conditions the stern wave of this dinghy hull is much farther aft, creating greater speed potential.

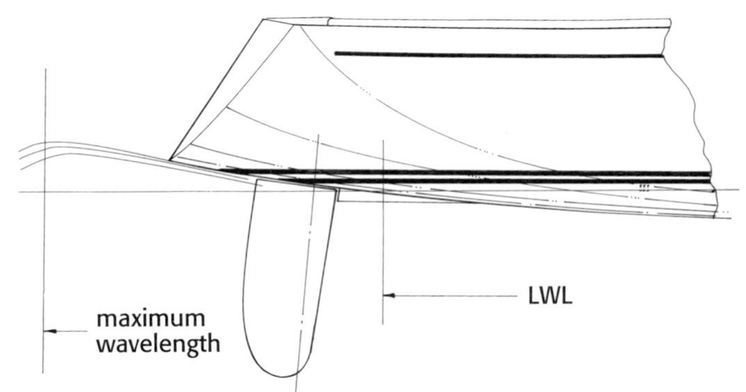

A conventional transom stern has flat buttock lines and a long stern wave. In extreme conditions this type of hull may surf or surge down the backs of waves, exceeding its hull speed by a considerable amount. Under normal conditions the stern shape allows the stern wave to move much farther aft than a rounded stern shape.

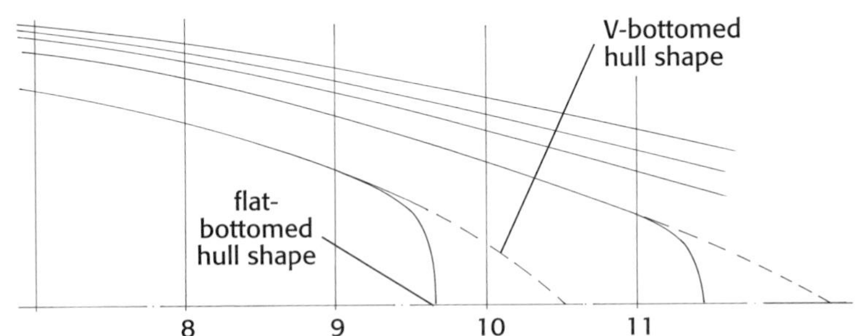

The angle at which the stern waterlines approach the centerline indicates whether the boat is flat- or V-bottomed. This hull is fairly flat, but if the waterlines were developed as shown by the dashed lines, it would be veed.

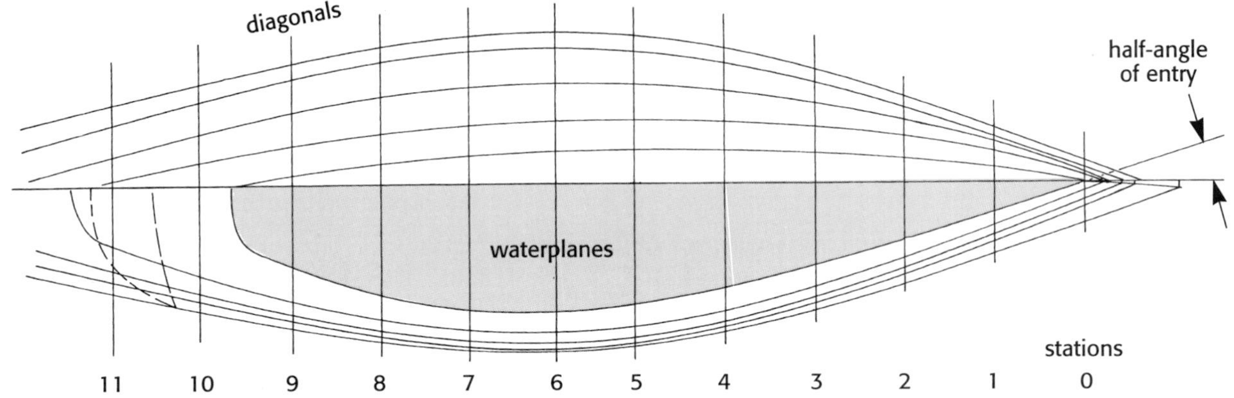

The half-angle of entry on this hull, shown at the waterline at station 0, is 20 degrees. On the upper half of the drawing are the diagonals, and on this hull they describe a smooth curve. This tells the designer that water is likely to flow easily (fast) along the hull.

quent increase in stability. An important part of the waterplane is the bow area, where designers tend to be concerned with the *angle of entry*. The bow's angle of entry affects the boat's ability to sail to windward. For example, in days of yore when sailing frigates plied the oceans, the half-angle of entry might be as high as 40 degrees to create a stable gun platform. Today the half-angle of a fat-bowed boat might be 25 degrees. This style of boat will probably not sail to windward well in a seaway. However, a fine entry (with a half-angle of 15 to 18 degrees) often produces a boat that sails bow-down or is wet forward. A half-angle of 20 to 22 degrees is a good compromise.

A look at the aft shape of the waterplane can quickly tell a designer whether the boat is flat-bottomed or veed. If the waterplanes cut in sharply and approach the centerline at 90 degrees, the boat is flat-bottomed. In general, the more acute the angle at which the waterlines approach the centerline, the more veed the bottom of the boat.

Lines for Different Designs

Small changes in a boat's lines can have a large influence on performance. Here we'll take a macro look at the five design concepts introduced in chapter 1 and see what hull forms are best suited to each. In the five boats that take shape throughout this book, the differences have been emphasized to better illustrate the trade-offs and decisions that go into a design.

The Weekender

Our Weekender will be a fun family boat of about 22 feet overall. Our main requirement is that it accommodate a family of two adults and two small children on weeknights and weekends. The family may sleep aboard for one night, but that is about all. They will usually moor in a marina and use the marina showers and restaurant, so onboard cooking is minimal. The boat should also have a good performance potential, because owners of weekenders often want to compete in the local yacht club's evening race series in spring and fall; these races usually last about one to two hours. In keeping with many of the more performance-oriented boats, this hull will be of the style that is known as a sport boat, as built by companies such as Carroll Marine in Bristol, Rhode Island, or Melges Boatworks in Zenda, Wisconsin.

Waves and Boat Speed

Back in the 1890s, William Froude determined that a displacement hull obeys a certain physical law. This law, known to designers as *Froude's law*, says that the speed at which a boat can sail depends upon the wave length created by that boat. The wave length, in turn, is a function of the waterline length (LWL) of the boat.

Froude determined that the maximum speed a boat could attain was $1.37 \times \sqrt{LWL}$. In other words, a boat with a 25-foot waterline could sail at $1.37 \times \sqrt{25}$ or 6.85 knots. This is true if the boat is blunt-ended with a 25-foot waterline. But most boats have some overhangs that increase the sailing waterline length when heeled. Consequently, a better rule of thumb is to assume that the maximum speed of a displacement boat is about $1.5 \times \sqrt{LWL}$, or in this case, $1.5 \times \sqrt{25} = 7.5$ knots. If the boat is moving slowly and has three or four wave crests alongside the hull, its speed can also be calculated. When the boat has three crests and two waves along the hull, its speed is $(1.37 \times \sqrt{25})/2 = 3.425$ knots. When the boat has three waves along the hull, the speed is $(1.37 \times \sqrt{25})/3 = 2.28$ knots.

The shape of the buttocks affects the wave length in that flat buttocks tend to lengthen the stern wave, while steep buttocks tend to shorten it. On very light hulls with flat buttocks, as speed builds up, the hull of the boat is supported by *dynamic lift* (just as an airplane wing generates lift). This lift causes the boat to rise out of the water slightly and enables it to *plane*. Because a planing hull is no longer in the displacement mode, the crest of the stern wave moves a long way aft of the hull. The boat may now move at $\sqrt{LWL} \times 2$ or more.

Bow

A weekender will not go far from the shoreline. This means that the boat is not likely to encounter large ocean swells, although the waves it does encounter will be relatively large for its size. As a result, for windward performance, the bow should be fairly fine. Because the crew is unlikely to spend much time on the foredeck and the boat will not carry a heavy anchor or anchor chain, a fine entry (see "Waterlines," on page 21) is perfectly acceptable. A fine entry will make the bow sections fairly U shaped. But a fine bow will have to have enough room to house the spinnaker sprit, which will run out beside the headstay. Consequently, as we get further into the design, we may have to widen the bow sections at the deck slightly to accommodate the sprit housing.

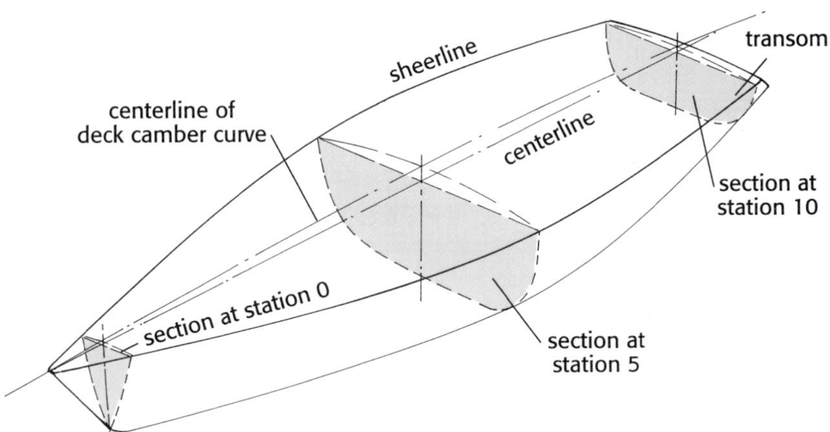

From the bow, midship, and stern sections, the shape of the hull begins to emerge.

Lines for a Steel Multichine Hull

The lines for this multichine steel-hulled boat, 35 feet length overall (LOA), have no conventional buttocks, diagonals, or waterlines because the chines would distort them, making fairing difficult.

These lines were developed using conical

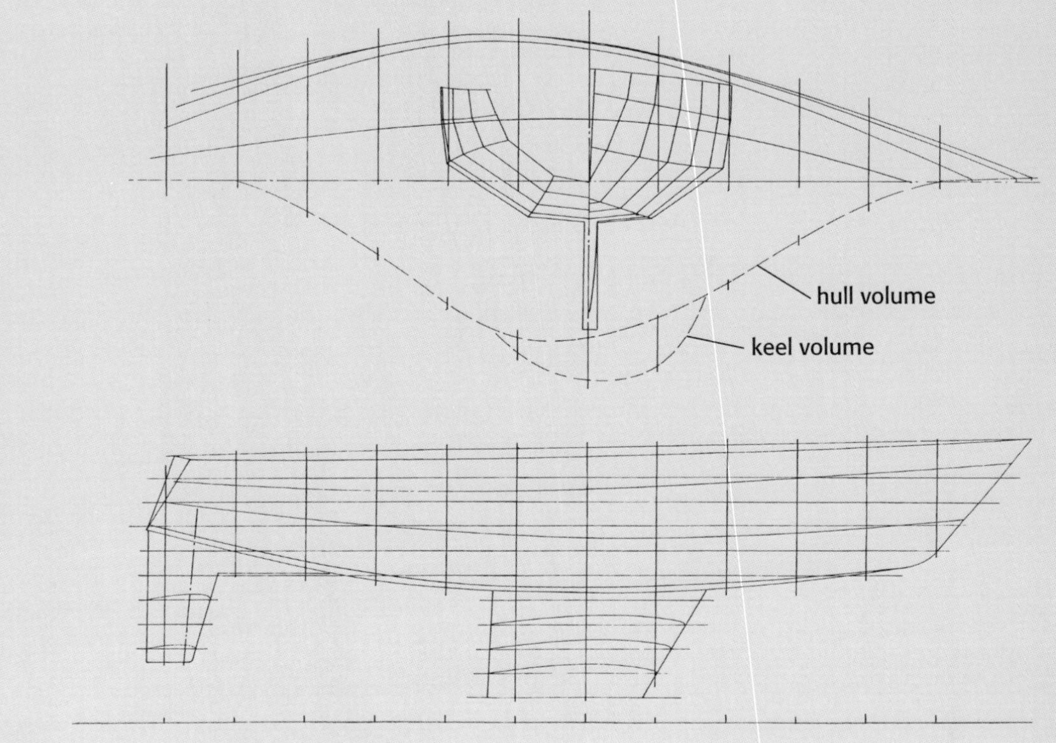

Stern

The Weekender's stern will carry most of the weight of the crew as they sit in the cockpit. It will also have an outboard motor on an outboard bracket or in a well below the cockpit. This means the stern sections have to support a large portion of the weight of the boat. By making the stern sections fairly wide, we will be able to keep the buttocks relatively flat, but still give enough buoyancy aft. This will also increase the cockpit volume and make additional room inside the hull for two quarter berths. In general, a smaller boat with greater crew weight will need fatter stern sections to support that weight.

Maximum beam

Because a weekender is small enough to carry on a trailer, its beam should not be so large as to pose a trailering problem. In most states the maximum beam for trailering is 8 feet, 4 inches, so we'll increase beam to 8 feet, 4 inches to take it to the maximum. The midship sections will have some flare to make more room for interior accommodations and to get the crew weight outboard if the crew want to sit on the rail during club races, but it will not have much depth because the hull is very light.

The beam will be carried well aft to suit the

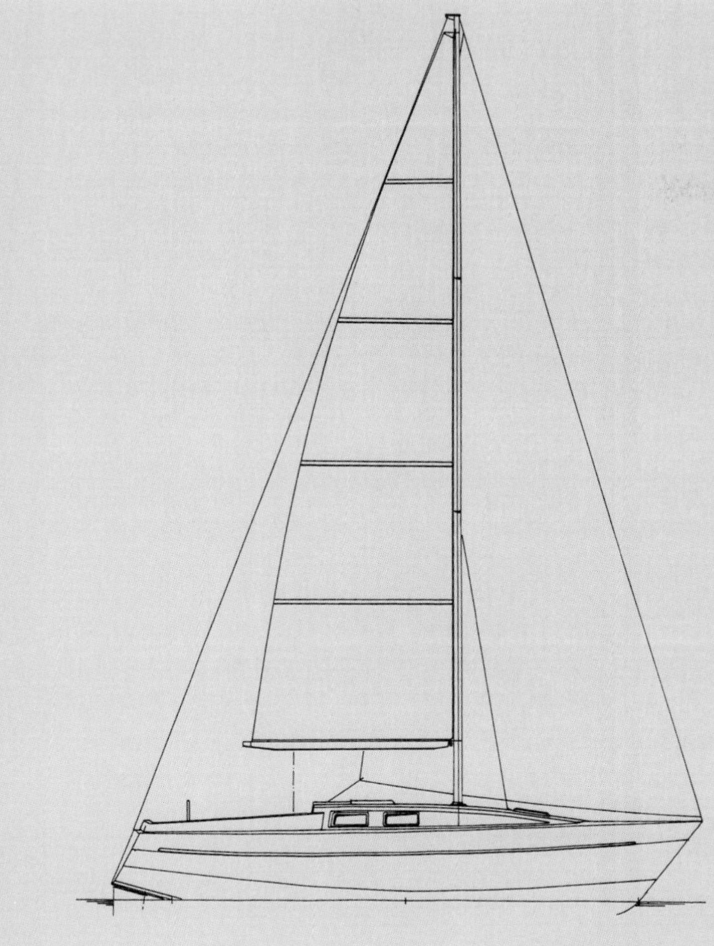

sections (conic sections assume that each panel of the hull between the chines is part of a cone). Today, the same lines would be drawn with a computer, which could also show the plate development (how the steel plates must be cut before they are rolled around the curved hull). The use of conical sections ensured that the ⅛-inch steel hull plating is bent in only one direction and therefore easy for an amateur to bend. The major curvature on this hull is in the keel sections to make them reasonably airfoil shaped. Frankly, a 35-foot hull in steel is very heavy, but with chine construction this hull can be built by any amateur who can weld thin (⅛-inch) plates.

The sail plan shows a boat that looks fairly conventional despite its multichine construction. To save weight and increase stability, we would recommend a plywood deck bolted to welded steel deck beams. An ambitious builder could easily lay teak strips over the plywood to make the deck very attractive.

weight of the crew in the cockpit, plus it will allow the cockpit to be wider, giving more legroom for the adults.

The Midbody

The midship sections should suit the style of boat. In this case they will be flat-bottomed to make the keel most efficient and to help keep the displacement light. This will also help the anticipated high level of performance for such a relatively light boat. The *prismatic coefficient*—that is, the ratio of the midship section area multiplied by the waterline length to the volume of the hull (see chapter 5)—will be fairly high, probably in the 0.56-to-0.57 range.

The midship sections are also flat to enable the boat to be trailered easily. In fact, it would be reasonable to design this boat with a weighted daggerboard instead of a fixed keel, making trailering even easier. With the board and rudder fully raised, the boat would then have a draft of just 8 inches. For overall performance and ease of use, however, let's stick with a fixed deep keel. The boat will be slightly harder to trailer, but with an overall weight under 2,000 pounds it can still be towed behind a medium-sized vehicle.

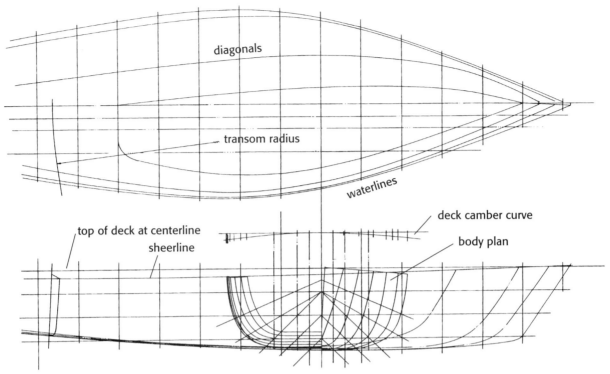

A simple set of lines for the Weekender, showing easy buttock lines and flat-bottomed sections with a little flare. The waterplanes carry a slightly finer entry than usual to cope with bay chop. The diagonals are smooth, with no distortions. All in all, this is a very simple, easy-to-sail boat design.

Freeboard

We don't intend to have a full 6 feet of headroom on this boat, as it would make the boat look ungainly. We'll settle for 5 feet, 6 inches, which means that we'll have to carefully adjust the height of the freeboard and the cabintop so that neither looks too high. This is the trickiest part of the midship section trade-off. Too much headroom, and the boat will look ungainly; too little, and it will be hard to sit or stand inside.

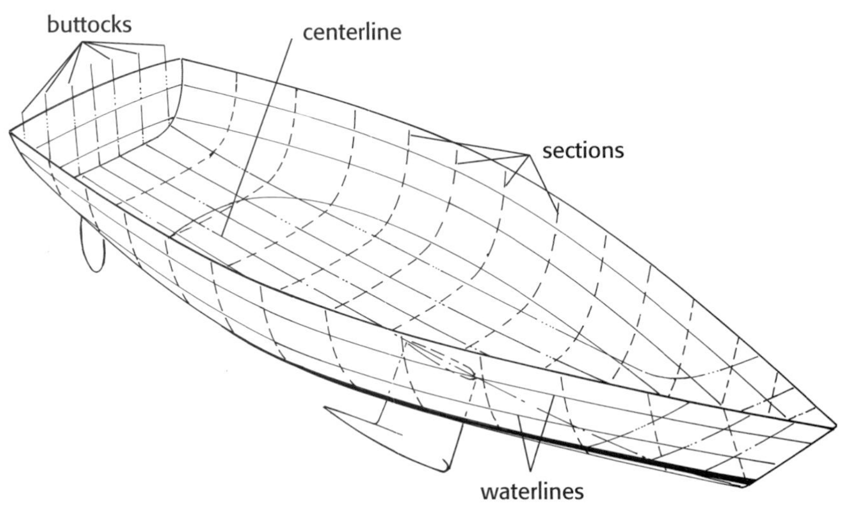

The same set of lines seen in three dimensions highlights how lines drawn by a designer define a curved hull shape.

By keeping the freeboard lower, we trade off headroom for aesthetics, but if we wanted to go higher we could. In this case, rather than make the boat look ungainly, we can add horizontal stripes to make the boat appear longer and disguise the high freeboard.

Integrating the pieces

The next step is to put the bow, midship, and stern sections together and integrate them into a one-piece hull as shown at left. By carefully fairing the sections together we get a hull that is reasonably flat bottomed, with its beam carried aft, and a veed bow section. The three sections can then be developed into a full set of sections. Years ago this took a skilled draftsman several days, but today a computer will fair the lines in a few minutes, leaving time for the designer to tweak them until they are virtually perfect. The lines are also shown here in three dimensions to help illustrate how, together, they define the shape of a hull.

The Cruiser

What do we look for in an inshore cruiser? Typically, an inshore cruiser will be kept at a marina all week and used only on weekends. Most sailors use their boat as a recreational center. It gets them out on the water, and they can swim or fish from it, sunbathe on it, cook a meal in the galley or go ashore to eat. Many of the features that affect hull shape are not hydrodynamically selected for optimum performance, but are trade-offs made when designing the rest of the boat. For example, a builder might decide that the boat is less expensive to build using a one-piece mold. This means that the hull will have a slight flare in the topsides to make it easy to pop out of the tooling. If a boat has tumblehome—that is, if the topsides near deck level turn inward toward the centerline, as in a Valiant 42—a two-piece mold is required, which increases the cost of building the hull.

Let's assume our inshore Cruiser will not be used for racing. This means we can incorporate a traditional long keel. This hurts our sailing performance a bit but confers other advantages, as we'll see. The resultant hull sections will more closely resemble an Island Packet cruiser than an inshore sport cruiser. We'll make up the bow, midship, and stern sections in a manner similar to our Weekender, but the trade-offs will be different. We'll assume an overall length of 34 feet for our Cruiser.

Midbody

The drawing of the midship section should show headroom requirements as well as the hull shape. Most sailors require full standing headroom, which translates into a minimum of 6 feet, possibly 1 or 2 inches more. A boat with a long keel is likely to have a fairly high displacement, allowing the hull to be relatively deep. Furthermore, we can get more headroom in a veed hull because the hull depth is slightly greater near the centerline. As full headroom is only required in the areas where people walk, we will keep the bunks to the sides of the boat when we work on the interior and leave space down the middle. By increasing deck camber we can also add another inch or two of headroom.

Given these parameters, we get a midbody that is relatively beamy and deep, with plenty of headroom and a little flare in the topsides. However, we do not want too much beam. According to the capsize study undertaken by USYRU (United States Yacht Racing Union, now the U.S. Sailing Association) and SNAME (the Society of Naval Architects and Marine Engineers), excessive beam encourages a boat to stay inverted should it capsize. *

*(The United States Yacht Racing Union and the Society of Naval Architects and Marine Engineers joint committee on Safety from Capsizing. Interim report April 1983, 2d interim report of the directors June 1984, Final report of the directors June 1985.)

Stern

For most cruising boats, the stern shape is secondary to obtaining the best space inside the hull. Because we intend to install a quarter berth in this Cruiser, the beam and headroom should be carried aft. But the boat has a long keel and a spoon-shaped bow, so a conventional counter stern matches the bow shape and makes the hull lines more aesthetically pleasing than a relatively beamy cruising boat stern like that of the Island Packet. This also shortens the waterline

The Island Packet 320 typifies the style of our Cruiser.

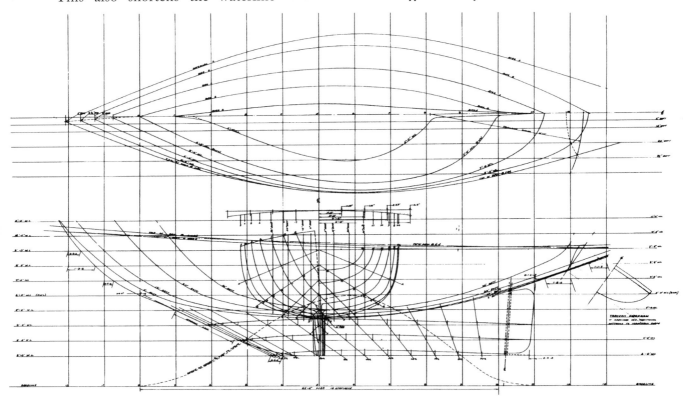

The lines of our Cruiser. On this 34-foot boat the hull and keel are integrated. The hull bottom is quite shallow, but not totally flat. The long keel increases wetted surface but also gives the boat tremendous directional stability if an autopilot is to be used. Above the sections is the deck camber curve. It is fairly flat (3/8 to 1 inch), making the deck easy to walk on at all angles of heel. The buttocks show easy curves that indicate the boat will sail quite nicely before the wind. From the waterplanes and diagonals, which show no distortions, we reach the more general conclusion that this boat should sail well under all conditions. A simple counter stern completes the lines. Note how all the lines are faired to station 13, even though the transom crosses station 12.

slightly, but as the boat is only going to be used for coastal cruising we can live with that.

We also need to be able to board the boat from a dinghy or from a dock. Typically, boarding from a dinghy requires a boarding ladder on the hull side or steps in the transom. Given that the stern is conventional, we will use a boarding ladder on the hull side. Because we have increased the beam aft, we will need to decide how far aft we can push the cockpit and how large it should be. The cockpit can then be integrated into the overall layout without hurting the interior accommodation.

The bow

Most cruising sailors like to drop the hook while they have a picnic or sleep overnight, so we'll need an anchor, bow roller, and small capstan. One of the relatively light, low-profile windlasses will do just fine. This means that the bow can be flared slightly, but reserve buoyancy is not as large a factor as it might be in a boat going around the world. Because the hull shape is reasonably conventional, we'll stick with a spoon bow. Aesthetics are important too!

With a few small changes we could easily incorporate a clipper bow, which would fit well with a slightly different stern and the long keel. This hull shape would be especially appropriate if the boat were to have a schooner rig. But not many schooners are built as production boats, so we'll stay with our original plan.

Freeboard

As the boat will not be going far offshore (a maximum of 20 miles is about the limit for most cruisers), freeboard can be as low as is consistent with adequate headroom inside the boat. There are two ways of doing this. One is to set the freeboard and fit a cabinhouse to it at whatever height is required. Often this can place a high cabinhouse on an attractive hull. The other option is to raise the freeboard a few inches, which has the effect of lowering the height of the cabinhouse. By juggling these two features we can arrive at a cabin and hull that look attractive.

The Voyager

The Voyager is designed to travel across oceans, to be self-sufficient for long periods of time, and to carry a family of two adults and two children on those journeys. It will have to carry a large amount of stores, which means a relatively heavy displacement. Let's assume that it will also carry a hard dinghy, a life raft, a sailboard, an outboard motor, and an inflatable.

Displacement

Our first task when determining displacement is to decide how far we might sail in a single voyage and how long it will take us. Assuming the boat is 48 feet overall with a waterline of 40 feet, the vessel's best speed is close to 9 knots, but a more likely average is 6 knots. If we intend to cross the Atlantic (about 3,000 miles), it will take a boat of this size about three weeks. Consequently, we will need to carry food for four people for a minimum of three weeks, with emergency rations (freeze-dried foods) for another two weeks. This means an additional 600 to 1,000 pounds of weight, plus the extra clothes and gear that might be carried for a long trip.

Two factors must therefore enter early into the design equation. First, the boat must have good performance both lightly loaded and fully loaded. And second, the hull must be roomy enough to accommodate a substantial amount of food and gear.

Bow

On this boat there will be a pair of heavy anchors, mounted on bow rollers for instant use when sailing into a strange port. Although most long-distance sailors leave their anchors on the bow rollers when under passage, strictly speaking they should be removed and stowed below where they can add to the vessel's stability.

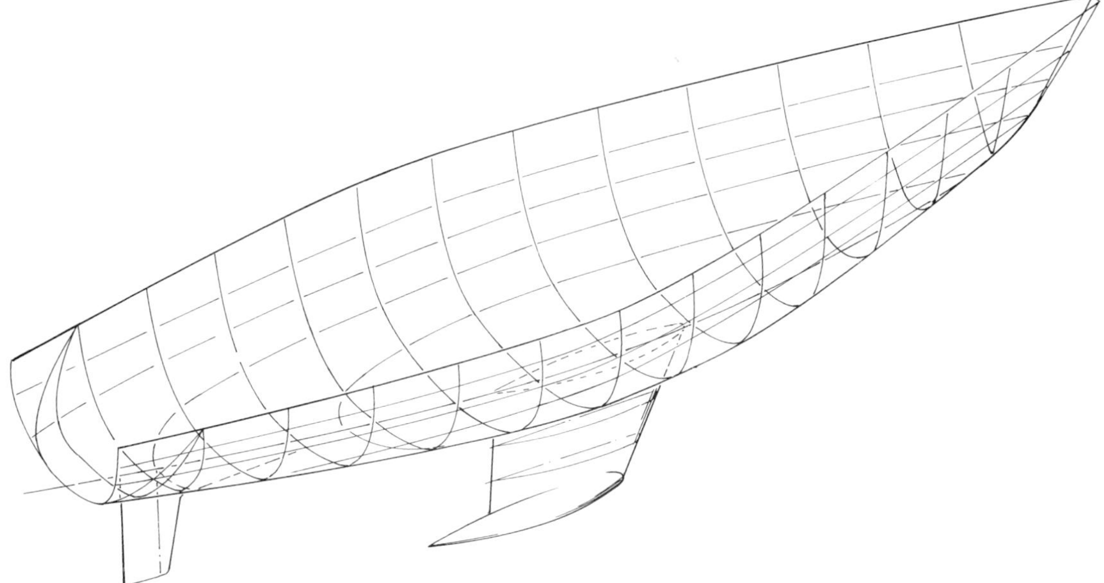

The Voyager's lines were developed on the computer and are simplified here, with the keel and rudder added. Overall length is 48 feet. The bow has an entry angle of 19 degrees, putting it right around the norm. The beam is carried well aft to accommodate a large aft cabin, a crew cockpit, and a dinghy carried on transom davits. There is a transom scoop (running almost to the end of the lines) aft of the watertight transom. The rudder has a small skeg to protect against weeds and lobster pot warps.

There will also be an anchor windlass, 200 feet of chain, and anchor line stowed in the bow area. The headstay will have roller-furling gear, and we'll need anchor-handling space on the foredeck. There will be a head compartment and a V-berth forward of the mast. All these features add up to a lot of weight forward. This dictates a fairly full bow section with plenty of reserve buoyancy, and a high sheerline to reduce the amount of water that comes aboard.

Midbody

The Weekender is flat-bottomed, and even the full-keeled Cruiser is relatively so. But while that improves the efficiency of the keel, it also allows even a small amount of bilgewater to roll around the inside of the boat and get everything wet. A seagoing boat wants deeper midship sections to help keep the bilgewater where it belongs. Typically, a boat might heel to 25 degrees, so the bilges would need to have an angle greater than that. As that is not usually feasible, we will incorporate a bilge sump to contain any water that flows into the bilges.

Freeboard will be high to give the boat full headroom (a minimum of 6 feet, 3 inches) and to keep the height of the cabin down slightly, thus presenting less surface for storm seas to hammer. As with the inshore Cruiser, a slight flare in the topsides will enable the boatbuilder to use a one-piece mold.

Stern

Because this boat will be at anchor most of the time and the crew will use the dinghy to get to shore, we will install transom steps and a scoop stern. (With careful design we'll be able to build in lockers for LPG tanks in the transom steps.) We'll also add dinghy davits and a radar arch. All these features require space. As the dinghy will be 9 feet long, the transom should be fairly wide. It need not be 9 feet across, but if we assume that the radar arch/davit structure is 7 feet across, the stern should be slightly wider at the deck. We also need to check that the wheel can be bypassed easily and that the rudder quadrant can be fitted under the cockpit.

It has been said that a scoop stern can cause problems by holding a lot of water when sailing downwind in heavy seas or when hove-to. I have installed this type of stern on two designs now, and neither boat has had any problems shipping excess water over the stern when hove-to in a Force 9 gale. Certainly, however, the step should be modest.

Keel

This boat will spend most of its time cruising, but it will also need to get into some fairly shallow harbors. To get into many of the harbors in the Bahamas, the draft should be about 6 feet, but that is fairly shallow given that the boat will spend a few weeks transiting the Bahamas each year. In this case, we'll make the draft about 6 feet, 6 inches and use a bulbed keel to gain stability.

I believe that the bulbed keel gives the best compromise among stability, speed, and safety. A long-keeled boat is slowed by the additional wetted surface of its keel, and this could add two or three more days to a transatlantic crossing or prevent the boat from dodging a severe gale. A long-keeled boat will hove-to more comfortably and may track more easily, but my clients report no problems with the bulbed keel when hove-to or when the autopilot is driving the boat.

Rudder

The boat will also cruise along the coast of Maine where there are many lobster pots. This means that the rudder should be well protected against snagging pot warps. A balanced rudder will do the job of steering quite well, but often, even with a pin in front of the rudder, a weed or rope will catch between the rudder and the hull. For that reason, we will use a rudder with a small skeg in front of it, as shown in the figure on page 32, to provide more protection against snagging a pot warp.

The Single-Hander

Our Single-Hander will be a Cruiser/Racer in that we will apply lessons learned from the long-distance single-handed races, but the boat will also incorporate a comfortable interior, an inside steering station, and other cruising amenities. The idea is to create a boat that is capable of racing in the transatlantic single-handed race, but can also be cruised easily.

Single-handed racing boats usually use a deep keel to keep the boat light and maximize stability. Unlike cruiser/racers, they lack crew to increase stability underway, and for this reason many can scoop up water ballast and pump it to the high side to increase stability. Most offshore races that allow water ballast limit the resultant stability increase to 10 percent, but for a pure cruising boat there is no limit. Our boat will use water ballast, but only to the 10-percent limit, as if the boat will be entering a single-handed race. That means we'll optimize every parameter that makes it fast for racing, but you should note that this boat is not taken to the extremes of some solo racers. Many of the features shown for this boat, such as watertight compartments, a small cockpit, and redundant steering systems can be used on any cruiser.

There are two schools of thought concerning the beam of a single-hander. The first says to make the boat very narrow; this will enable it to sail fast upwind, but offwind performance will be moderate. Water ballast will not be very effective on a narrow hull, however, because its distance from the hull centerline, and therefore its righting moment, is small. A second school of thought recommends a beamy hull, which will sail well off the wind but only moderately upwind. Another drawback to beamy hulls, again,

Rudder Shapes

Rudder shapes have been debated for as long as ships have sailed the seas. Today the major discussion is between skeg-hung rudders (A) and balanced rudders (B). A balanced rudder is more sensitive than a skeg-hung rudder, and requires slightly more work to keep the boat on course. This would make an autopilot work harder, which is one reason to choose a skeg-hung rudder for a cruising boat. A skeg also supports the bottom of the rudder, making a slightly smaller-diameter rudderstock possible. The disadvantage of a skeg-hung rudder is that the stock runs from the top to the bottom of the rudder, and a heavy pintle shoe must be fitted. On a balanced rudder the stock can end halfway down the rudder, making it much lighter and enabling the blade to be tapered. This advantage must be weighed against the possibility of the bottom half of the blade breaking off.

The best of both worlds in terms of efficiency is the hybrid rudder (C). This rudder has a skeg in the top portion and is balanced over the bottom portion. For larger vessels this is the best compromise, but it has a major drawback in that lines can easily be trapped between the rudder and the skeg.

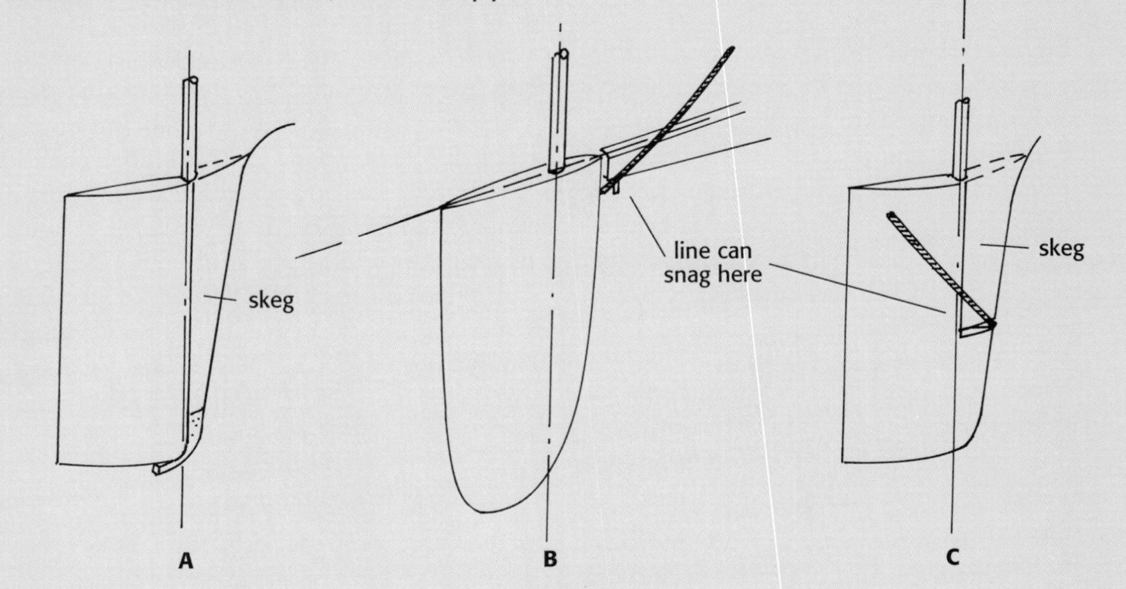

is that they tend to stay inverted if they capsize.

When a boat is designed for a particular race, it will be optimized for the expected wind conditions and the competition. If an entire racing fleet consists of beamy boats, an incremental increase in upwind speed will win the race. But in a mixed fleet the winner will most likely be determined by the length of time spent offwind versus the length of time spent sailing upwind. Most single-handed races have a significant portion of offwind sailing, often at high speeds. So the shape of this boat will be fairly beamy—not as extreme as some of the beamiest boats, but wider than the average hull. We will take special precautions to ensure that the boat is self-righting in the event of a capsize.

Bow

With no additional weight forward except for a spinnaker pole, the bow can be relatively plumb. If the boat were designed for any of the single-handed races where length is limited, speed would be maximized by having the waterline the same length as the overall length, making the boat plumb ended. This is what we'll do for our boat. We'll also keep the angle of entry of the bow fairly fine to enable the boat to sail to windward as well as possible. If the race has a significant upwind portion, we would hope that the boat would stay with the fleet upwind and sail away from it offwind.

Midbody

As mentioned, the boat should be beamy to maximize the potential of the water ballast. In the last BOC race (now known as the Around-Alone race), one or two 60-footers had a beam of 20 feet, or a 3 to 1 ratio. Our boat will have a 2.8 to 1 ratio, which gives it a beam of 17.8 feet on a 50-foot hull length.

To minimize the wetted surface for such a large beam, we'll use rounded sections and carry the roundedness well aft. Because the boat will be built as lightly as possible, the buttock lines will be fairly flat. This makes the hull look rather dinghy-like, but helps speed as soon as the sheets are eased.

Stern

Because of the large beam relative to most cruising boats, the stern of this hull will be designed to minimize wetted surface. This will make it fairly round, but we'll modify that rounding by making the transom a little squarer to keep the buttocks fairly flat when the boat is heeled.

The large beam is carried well aft, and as the boat heels a centerline rudder may come out of the water. For this reason, we'll look at using two rudders. (Another option is to make a deep, canting single rudder.) We'll design the twin rudders to minimize their drag, making one come almost out of the water when the boat heels.

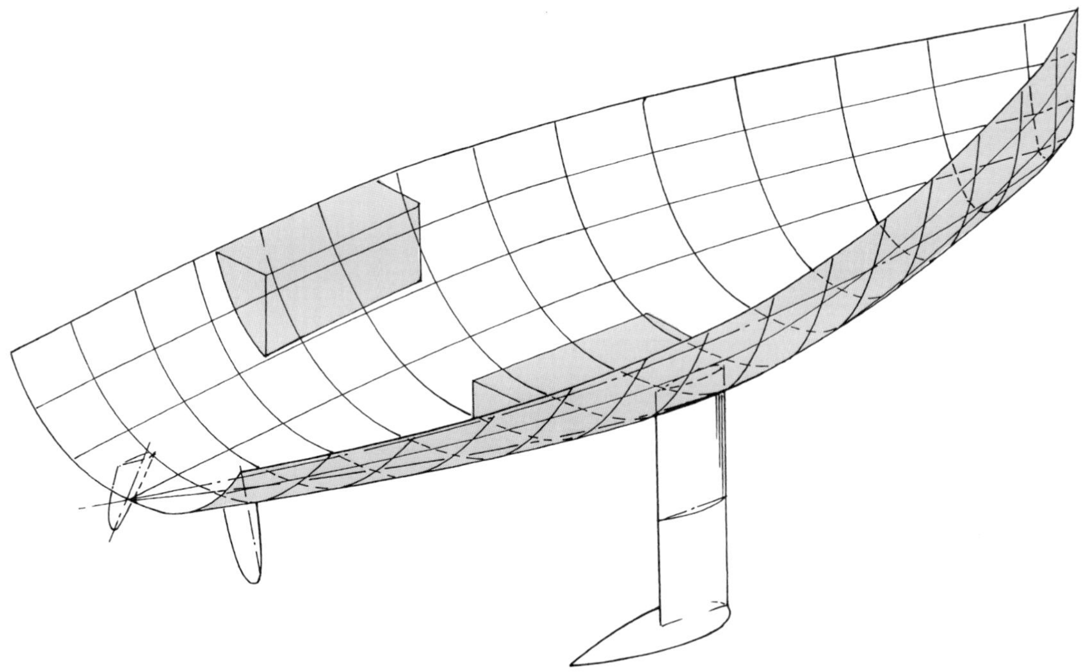

The Single-Hander's lines show twin rudders and a deep keel with a bulb. This boat is wide and shallow, with water ballast tanks high on the outboard side of the hull. The overall length and waterline length are both 50 feet, indicating that bow and stern are plumb.

Water ballast

When designing the lines, we need to look at the position of the water ballast under all sailing conditions. It needs to be located so that the longitudinal center of gravity (LCG) of the boat is optimized at any angle of heel and with any amount of ballast. Because the longitudinal center of buoyancy (LCB) of the boat changes when the boat heels, a designer has to perform extensive center of gravity (CG) calculations to determine the best angle of trim for a given sailing condition.

Heading upwind in light air, for example, the boat may sail better with the bow trimmed down slightly, but as the wind increases a better performance is achieved with more weight aft. This implies that the water ballast tanks should be empty in light air (giving the boat slight bow-down trim), and as the wind increases the tanks should be filled to trim the boat slightly by the stern.

The Cruiser/Racer

The lines of our Cruiser/Racer demand yet another approach. It is out on the racecourse to win, so every aspect of the hull and rig should be scrutinized with a view to maximizing performance. However, a cruiser/racer must also be comfortable for cruising, so it must have more than the bare necessities below deck. The interior, in fact, can be luxurious as long as it doesn't add too much weight.

The first step in this design is to determine which rating rule the boat will conform to. In the U.S. it might be designed to the International Measurement System (IMS), but only about 5,000 boats worldwide use this system. It might also race under the Performance Handicap Rating Factor (PHRF). This rule is much more arbitrary, rating boats based on how fast a panel thinks it will go. In Europe, the Channel Handicap System (CHS) is in wide use, with over 6,000 boats rated to it. Boats can be designed to sail well under this system, although the rule is based on boat performance rather than design features.

Once the rating rule under which the boat will race has been determined, the hull shape can be worked up. Unfortunately, rating rules are designed to tax the speed-increasing factors in any design. Consequently, race boats minimize these factors to get a low rating. One outcome of this is that production boats designed to look like rule beaters are often slow. As we are developing a production boat, we'll acknowledge rating rules where applicable, but our main emphasis will be on speed and safety.

Displacement

Our Cruiser/Racer should be moderately light, but interior joinerwork can be both expensive and heavy. One builder's solution to this problem (Carroll Marine of Bristol, Rhode Island, builder of a number of raceboats) is to fabricate a lightweight interior liner using sophisticated laminating techniques (see the discussion of SCRIMP in chapter 3), and trim the boat out with lightweight wood or small amounts of heavier wood. Another technique is to make the interior joinery of lightweight sandwich materials such as Nomex honeycomb core. Such materials tend to be pricey, however. In this design we'll use a combination of these and other techniques to keep the boat light without breaking the bank.

Bow

Because the IMS Rule penalizes the overall length of a hull, bow overhangs on recent cruiser/racer designs have become much shorter. As we are acknowledging the IMS Rule in the design of this boat, we will make the bow overhang minimal. This leads to U-shaped sections forward, which limit the amount of weight that we can locate forward; this in turn dictates a small anchor stowed below deck and a nylon anchor rode on a reel, but no chain or windlass.

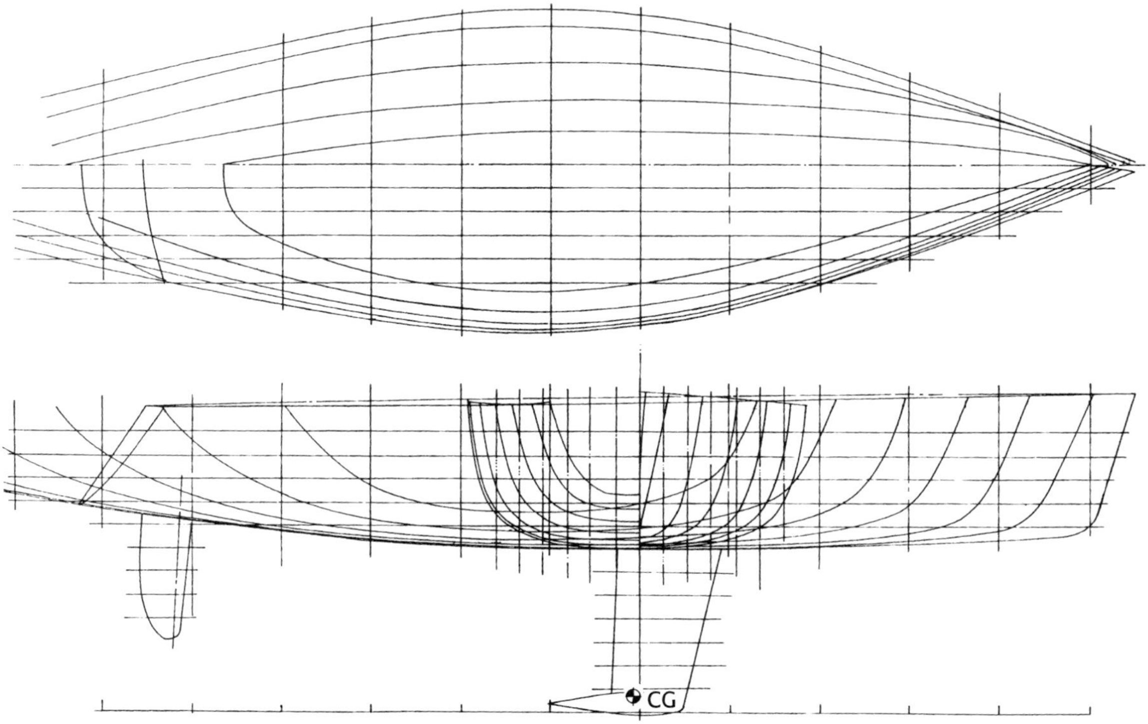

The lines of the Cruiser/Racer. The bow on this hull is close to plumb, and hull beam is carried well aft. The keel is deep and has a triangular bulb to keep the center of gravity (CG) of the ballast low and to reduce wetted surface. The overall length is 37 feet with a 33-foot waterline.

Stern

Influenced partly by the rule and partly by the need for high offwind speed, we'll make the stern fairly wide. This will help support crew weight aft, make the buttock lines fairly flat, and help the boat surf offwind. A relatively wide stern may also give us enough interior volume to accommodate a double berth aft. A wide, fairly flat stern will also help the boat surf on waves, momentarily increasing speed.

Midbody

In keeping with the wide stern, we'll make the midbody beamy and flat bottomed, which will increase the efficiency of the keel. A slight roundness to the bottom will keep wetted surface down, which should increase speed in light air.

We want to minimize the waterline beam yet keep a fairly wide beam on deck to get crew weight outboard. This means that the hull sides will have some flare, plus we'll make sure that headroom is a minimum of 6 feet to the underside of the cabintop. The side decks should be wide enough to allow crew to sit and lean outboard through the lifelines.

The Cruiser/Racer's hull lines differ somewhat from those of the other designs because they are intended for a different purpose. Without carefully considering a boat's purpose, where it will sail, and who will be sailing it, a design can become a mongrel. If every facet is considered at the design stage, it is possible to produce a fast, well-styled boat that does everything required of it under most or all conditions.

Three

Seaworthiness

When considering seaworthiness, the first step is to determine under what conditions the boat is likely to be sailed. A boat that is intended to sail around the world has a much different set of seaworthiness standards than a boat that will primarily be sailed in a sheltered harbor. The round-the-world boat will have features such as a strong hull, a small cockpit with large drains, substantial lifelines, small windows, and possibly watertight compartments. The bay sailor has no need for all these features, and if they were fitted on the boat they would probably make it overly heavy, slow to tack or jibe, and would, in fact, detract from its seaworthiness. Seaworthiness, in this context, means the way the boat is designed and fitted out for the conditions in which it will be used. A boat that accommodates these conditions well is a seaworthy boat.

Because of the high costs of building boats fit to encounter serious storms, only production builders such as the Hinckley Company, Nautor (who build the Swan line of boats), Valiant Yachts, Oyster Marine, and a few others build boats intended to survive truly bad conditions. This is because they know their clients are likely to sail their boats in heavy weather.

Other builders assume that the boat will be in harbor or, better yet, hauled out before a severe storm hits. A designer should design for a major storm only if the boat is likely to encounter one. If the boat is only sailed in fair weather, storm design features can be minimized. Such a boat will still be seaworthy for its intended purpose.

Design Factors That Affect Seaworthiness

It is interesting that the most seaworthy boats are built by people who sail regularly. Once boatbuilders have rapped their shins on a poorly placed locker, or reached for a handhold and found that there wasn't one, they quickly think in terms of locating those features. (We'll take a closer look at handholds and other specific items later in this chapter.) If you step aboard a boat built by Lyman-Morse in Thomaston, Maine, for example, you'll find that everything is properly placed and handholds are numerous. Cabot Lyman, who runs the company, has sailed around the world and makes sure that the seaworthiness of Lyman-Morse boats is never in question.

Among the many factors that affect seaworthiness, some are intrinsic to the hull itself, such as a hull of the right shape and construction. Others are part of the deck cabin and cockpit structure and layout. Large windows, for example, are great in harbors or near a coast, but at sea they can easily be stove in. Still other factors in the seaworthiness equation can be found inside the boat. Nobody wants a battery to fly out of its box and come crashing across the cabin, but it has happened. Gear below deck should be strongly secured. Solid, well-placed handholds, nonskid floor surfaces, and ergonomic cabin furniture design are essential to prevent falls and injuries. In the sections that follow we'll look at seaworthiness as it relates to the hull, the cockpit, the deck, the interior, and the boat's mechanical components.

Seaworthy Hull

What makes a hull seaworthy? Is it the shape of the hull, the curve of the sheer? Or is it the depth of the keel, the structure of the bow sections? Seaworthiness is all of these and more. A seaworthy hull has a strong structure throughout and a smooth motion in a seaway to reduce crew fatigue. It also has many other intangible features that usually only become apparent as the weather worsens.

A seaworthy production cruising hull is usually not lightweight. Light hulls tend to have a faster, jerkier motion than heavier hulls. A displacement/length ratio of under 80 represents a lightweight hull. It is widely accepted that most production cruisers have a displacement/length ratio between 150 and 270. This is not to say that light hulls cannot be seaworthy; they can be, as well as fast enough to get you to port before bad weather hits. However, seaworthy light hulls are usually slightly more costly to build (about 5 to 10 percent more), and ultralight hulls can be very expensive (up to 50 percent more).

Which brings up the question of structure. Structural weight should not be confused with engineering. Many heavy boats have been built that were not engineered properly. A well-engineered boat, no matter what the material used in its construction, can be seaworthy whether it is light or heavy. If weight were the only criterion for a seaworthy boat, all boats would be made of lead!

Hull beam

The hull of a seaworthy boat must be of the right shape. A long, narrow hull sails better to windward than a beamy hull, but a narrow hull requires more keel weight to achieve the same stability as a wider hull. A narrow hull also has less room for accommodations. So, hull beam often becomes a trade-off between accommodations and seaworthiness: If the hull is too narrow it can be highly cramped below deck, but if the hull is too beamy it can impair the boat's sailing performance. However, we must look at that statement in light of the current crop of Around-Alone boats. Some of these boats have a beam of 20 feet on a 60-foot LOA. This is very beamy relative to the boat's length, but the beam is carried well aft, making the buttocks flat, water ballast highly effective, and giving the boat high speed potential. If a boat were to be beamy and have pinched ends, it would tend to pitch and would be unseaworthy.

Bow

Another factor in seaworthiness is the shape of the bow, the part of the boat that is most likely to slam into waves. Large, flat panels with little or no furniture behind them will bang and resonate, making a lot of noise. Eventually the flexing of these panels may lead to failure. Rounded panels that use some of the hull curvature to absorb wave loads can be better.

Sheerline

The sheerline of a boat is another factor that counts toward seaworthiness. A high sheer forward will reduce the amount of green water that comes aboard, although it will never eliminate it. A sheerline should have a nice, sweet curve to it—high at the front, and lower aft. Ideally, the low point of the sheerline should be around station 8, which is where most water drains off the boat. On many modern boats an aluminum rail runs along the sheerline. This can make it easy to clip on items such as blocks and tackles, in a sense making the boat more seaworthy. I have to admit, however, that there is nothing quite so pretty as a varnished wooden toerail.

Freeboard

According to the USYRU/SNAME capsize study referred to in the previous chapter, freeboard has a mixed effect on the stability of a boat. On the one hand, high freeboard can be good because it keeps the sheer out of the water longer and reduces the chances that the deck might dig in and become a pivot point for a capsize. On the other hand, high freeboard exposes more of the hull side to a wave strike. It also increases windage when sailing to windward.

From a designer's and a builder's point of view, freeboard gives headroom, and most people want full headroom in their boat. High freeboard can be disguised with longitudinal stripes or false sheerlines, but in general it is not good to have too much freeboard. The biggest problem with high freeboard is that it makes it difficult to do a man-overboard recovery or board the boat from the water or from a dinghy. (To make it easier to board, the transom can be designed with steps or a boarding ladder fitted to the side deck.)

Weights

The distribution of weights throughout the hull affects seaworthiness. If all the weight is in the ends (for example, the anchors, chain, and windlass forward; stores, a dinghy, and heavy tools in the lazarette), the boat is likely to pitch more, making it more fatiguing for the crew. This is also shown in the figures on page 132.

Vertical weight distribution should also be concentrated around the middle of the boat. Extra weight aloft—for example, a heavy mast or radar at the masthead—can detract from stability and increase pitching.

Keel

A boat that has a deep keel with a very short chord may be fast in light winds, but it may not be able to heave-to in a storm. It will need to be sailed through bad weather (as did many of the boats in the 1998 Sydney-Hobart Race), which could lead to crew fatigue. A keel with enough lateral area to prevent a large leeway angle in heavy weather works better than a keel that is superefficient upwind in medium and light winds, and a longer-keeled boat with a compact sail plan is easier to heave-to in inclement conditions. However, a keel with too

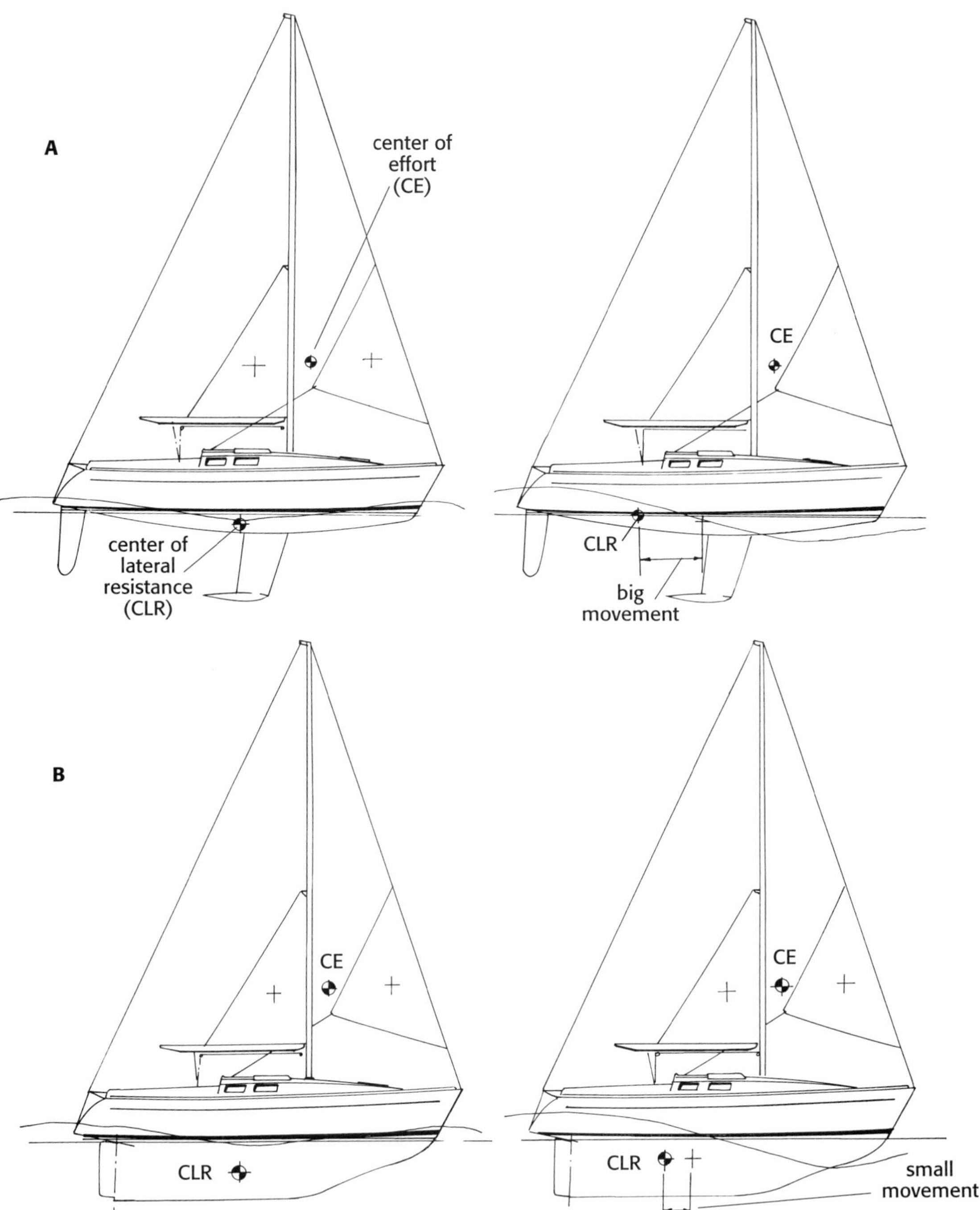

The CLR (center of lateral resistance) moves around less in large seas on a boat with a long keel. When that factor is coupled with the resistance to yawing of a long-keeled boat, it becomes apparent that a long-keeled boat is better for heavy weather. The trade-off is that it has more wetted surface and sails slower in lighter winds. (A) shows the movement of the CLR on a short-keeled boat, and (B) shows it on a long-keeled boat. The waves and sail plan are the same in both cases.

much lateral area will have an extraordinarily high area of wetted surface.

The lateral area of the keel is found by multiplying the chord and span. The location of the keel affects the location of the center of lateral resistance (CLR) of the underwater area. The CLR is the center of the hull, such that, if a piece of string were to be attached, the hull would move sideways without yawing. As attaching a string is impossible at the design stage, it is found by locating the center of the lateral profile of the entire area below the waterline. This is an assumed location and does not account for the curvature of the hull. For the sake of easy calculations all the hull forces are assumed to act through the CLR.

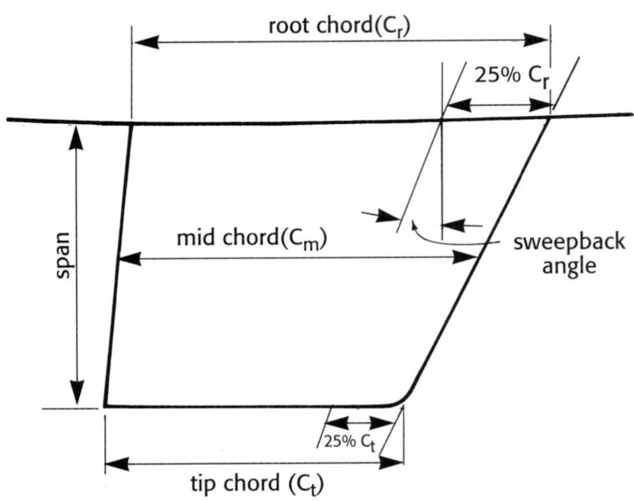

Keel shape is defined by the span, chord lengths, and sweepback angle. The sweepback angle is measured at 25 percent of the chord length aft of the leading edge. A keel such as that on* Australia II *where the leading edge slopes forward instead of aft is said to have reverse sweepback.

The vertical distribution of the keel ballast also enters the seaworthiness equation. A properly shaped keel with plenty of stability enables a boat to sail well to windward or offwind. A keel that does not give the boat adequate stability forces the skipper to reef earlier, sail more conservatively, and be more aware of how the sail area is affecting the boat.

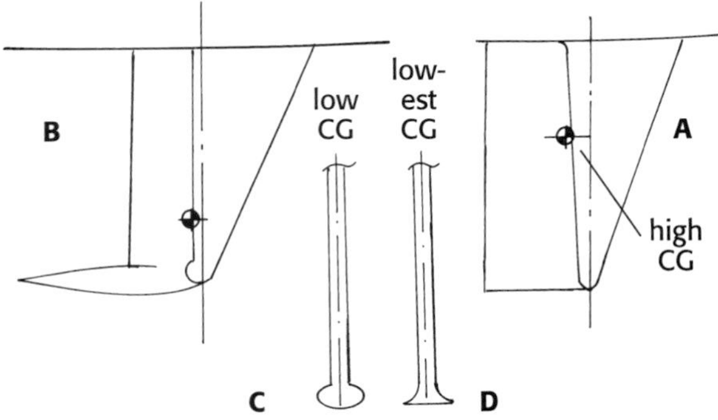

The center of gravity (CG) of a keel has a very large effect on the stability of a boat. (A) shows a conventional keel with a CG near the middle of the keel. If a circular bulb is used (B), the CG drops to the lower third of the keel, depending on the size of the bulb. Designers make the bulb oval shaped (C) to lower the CG another inch or two, or triangular shaped (D) to lower it even more.

Ballast weight

The weight of ballast in a boat no longer plays as important a part in the seaworthiness of a hull as it once did. In the days of long-keeled boats, the amount of ballast was critical because all hull shapes were similar. As we saw in chapter 2, a bulbed keel can have a much lower center of gravity than a fin keel—which, in turn, means that we can use less ballast to get the same amount of righting moment (a *moment* is the product of a lever arm length times a weight) than we could with a fin-keeled boat. It is the *distribution* of the ballast that is important today.

Rudder

The rudder can be a factor in seaworthiness. A balanced rudder makes the boat much more

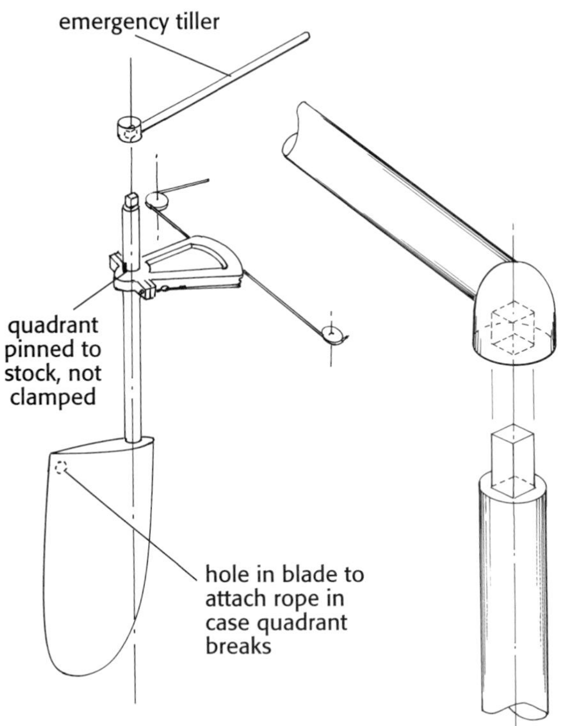

Typical steering gear layout. The quadrant is keyed to the rudder shaft and wire cables lead to the steering pedestal (left). An emergency tiller is fitted to the top of the rudderstock as shown at right.

sensitive, gives greater control, and usually makes the boat faster. But unless the rudder is carefully built, it can fail. In 10 trips to Bermuda and upward of 50 crossings of the English Channel, the boats I have sailed have lost their rudder three times. On each occasion we were able to jury-rig a solution and limp home; access to the steering gear was critical in every case.

The rudder should also be "forgiving"—that is, it should not be so sensitive that the boat is on the edge of control as soon as the breeze comes up. Typically, sensitive rudders have thin blades. Most designers make the thickness 10 percent of the chord length of the rudder. The thickness can be as low as 8 percent in high-performance rudders, but when it gets down to 6 percent the rudder tends to stall easily and becomes overly sensitive, making the boat hard to steer.

A skeg-hung rudder, as we have seen in the previous chapter (page 32), gives better protection than a balanced rudder, but rudder design also enters into the equation. A balanced rudder has so much in its favor (better boat speed, more responsiveness, less wetted surface) that it has the edge for most conditions. Only if you

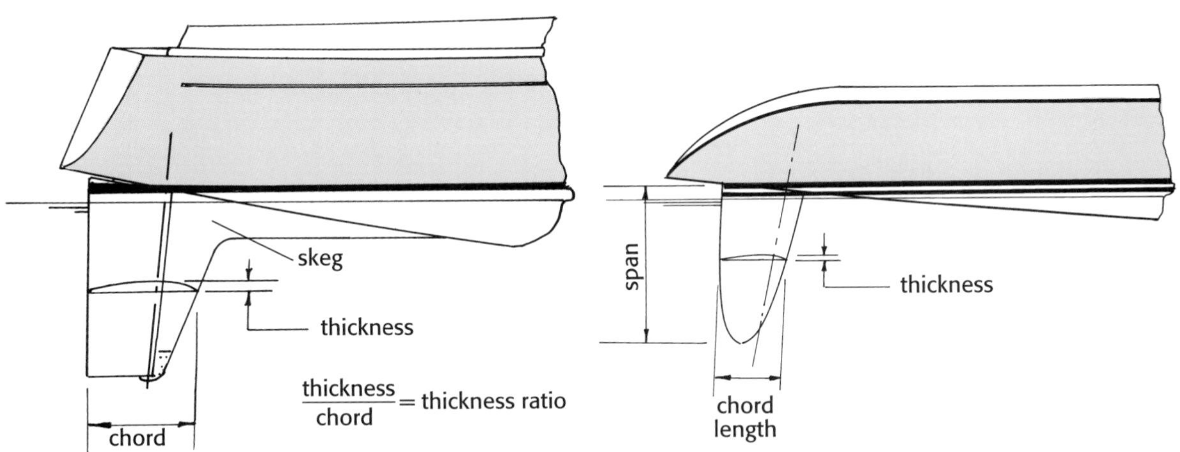

Rudders should be "forgiving"—that is, if you make a mistake, the boat should not immediately broach or wander off course. In general, rudders with a thickness ratio (the ratio of blade thickness to chord length, multiplied by 100) of less than 6 percent are not forgiving. For a cruising boat the thickness ratio should be 8 to 10 percent. As mentioned in chapter 2, a skeg-hung rudder (left) is less sensitive than a balanced rudder, but is also less likely to foul lobster pot lines and weed.

are likely to sail in areas where there is a lot of debris or gear in the water will a skeg-hung rudder be more useful. (Along the coast of Maine, for example, there are so many lobster pot warps that you can hardly avoid them.) Lying hove-to in a storm puts a different complexion on things. When hove-to, a boat will probably be moving backward or slowly forereaching. In this situation, a skeg-hung rudder will generally hold up better.

Going aground appears to pose little danger to the rudder, considering that it is usually about 60 to 75 percent of the draft of the keel. Most of the time the boat goes aground from ahead. In the few times I have seen a boat that has gone aground from astern, neither type of rudder has fared well—the skeg broke off one boat, causing it to fill with water.

Hull shape and crew fatigue

Hull shape plays a part on seaworthiness through its effect on the motion of a boat in a seaway, which in turn affects the crew, in that a tired crew may make errors that jeopardize the safety of their boat. A boat with a fine bow, a narrow stern, and poor weight distribution will pitch and lead to crew fatigue. On the other hand, a boat with a narrow bow and a fat stern tends not to pitch so much, because the fat stern dampens pitching. Light boats tend to have a faster, jerkier motion than heavier boats, again leading to crew fatigue. A well-balanced boat also requires less effort to steer.

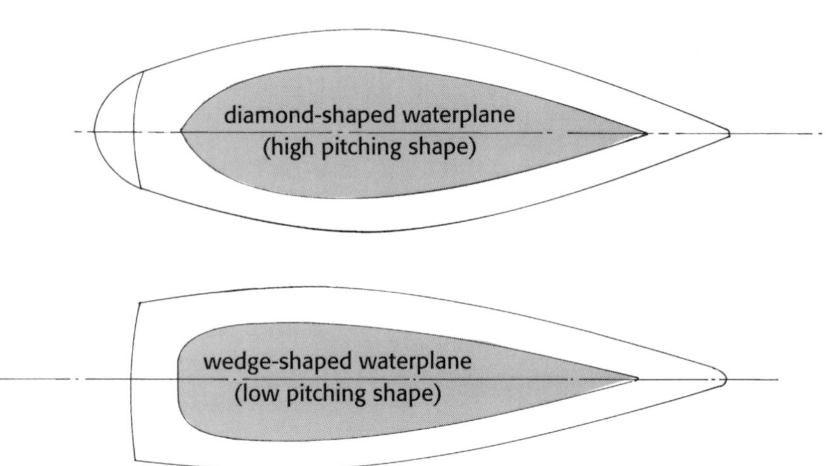

A diamond-shaped waterplane (top) encourages pitching. A boat with a wedge-shaped waterplane (bottom) is less likely to pitch, and the crew are less likely to get fatigued on a long trip.

In the Cockpit

Another major area of the boat that must be considered in the seaworthiness equation is the cockpit. On some boats, steering from the cockpit is a problem in that the helmsman cannot see forward over the cabintop or under the headsails. Steering might also be a problem if the helm seat is not properly positioned or at the optimum height. On other boats, sitting in the cockpit becomes difficult because there is nowhere to brace yourself as the boat heels. The consequences of such design shortcomings might be as trivial as snagging an unseen lobster pot buoy, or as serious as a collision. Every sailor should keep a sharp lookout; it is part of good seamanship. But a boatbuilder or designer should make it easy to maintain that vigilance.

Visibility

If you're planning to take out an unfamiliar boat, stand behind the wheel for a moment and look forward. Make sure you can see the bow and any person on the bow (who might be handling the anchor). Check to see how much of the ocean in front of the boat is visible. On boats with a high cabin you may find it easier to look through the windows rather than over them.

Look at the side decks to check whether you can see the dock and fenders as you come alongside. Make sure the helm moves easily and freely. Perform the same tests while sitting at the wheel. While these tests may seem minor at the dock, they become of great importance when the boat is at sea. Check to see how far in front of the boat you can see a buoy. Spotting another boat in time to avoid a collision is a primary requirement for good seamanship.

Check also to see how far you can see under the headsail. If you can see only a few feet, you may have to post a watch to leeward to make sure you can see opposite-tack boats on a collision course.

Harness strongpoints

In heavy weather your crew should be tethered to the boat. Stand in the cockpit and look

(continued on page 46)

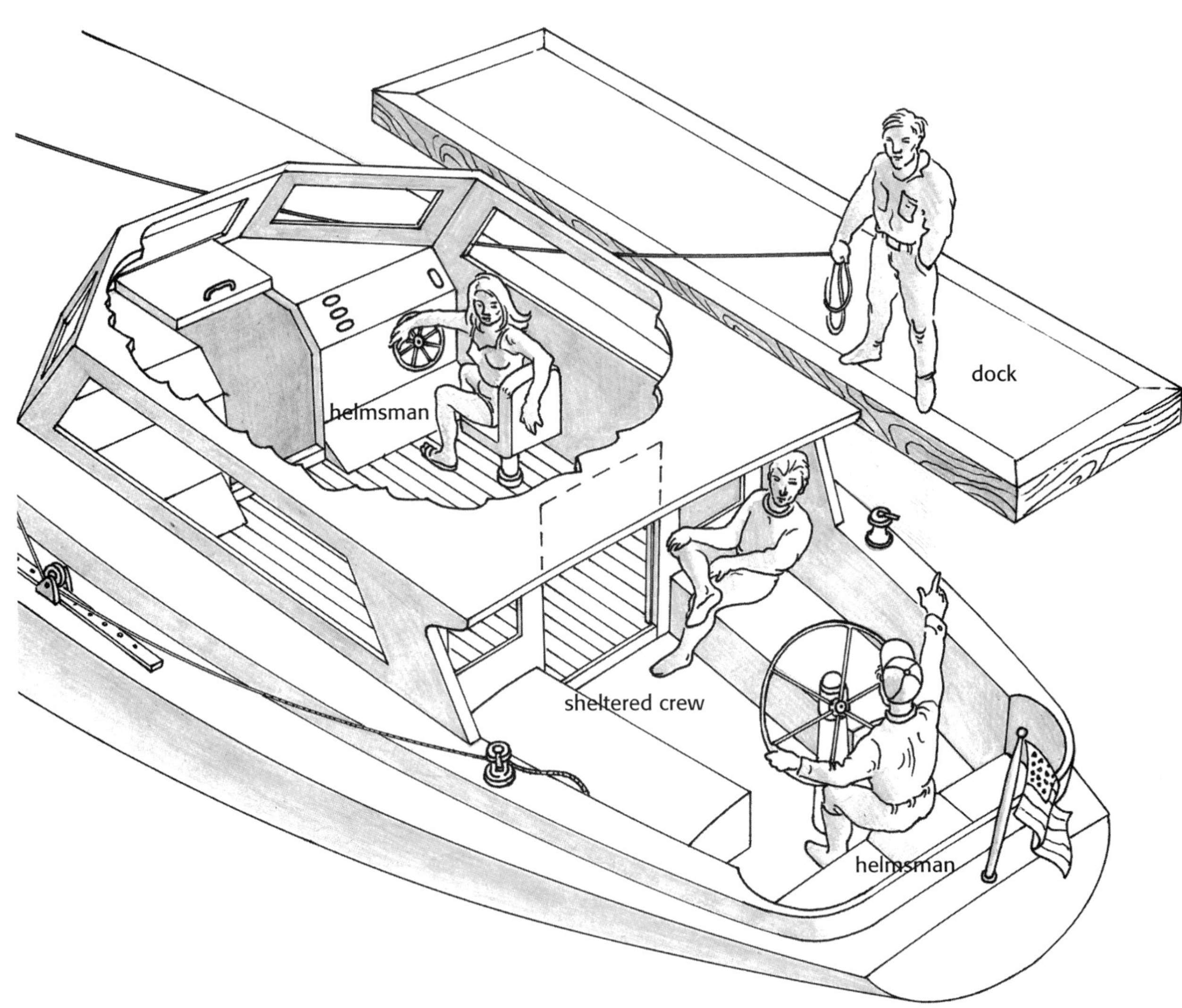

Docking the boat using the inside steering station can be difficult due to restricted visibility. The inside steering station is best used when motoring.

A Boat for Older Sailors

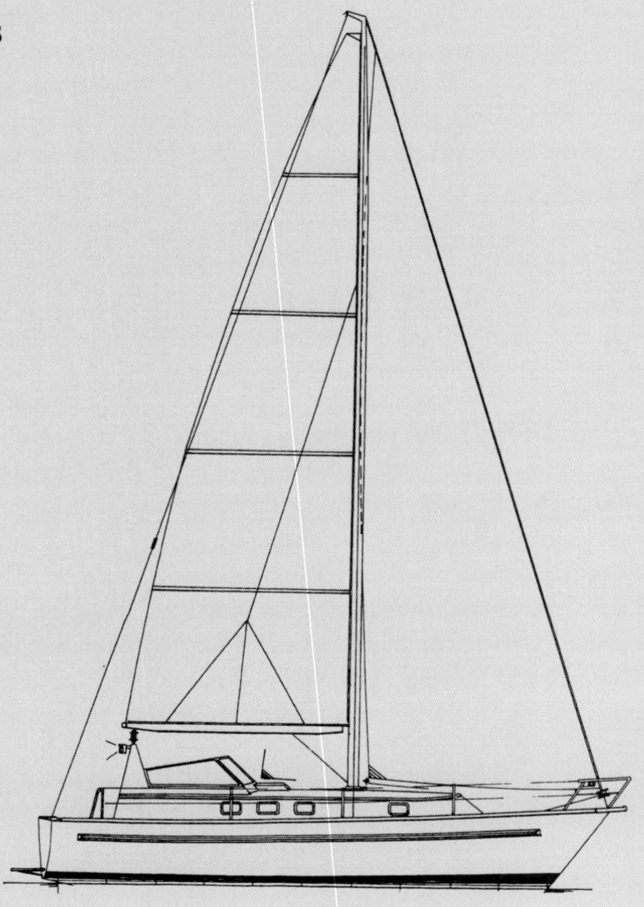

Many sailors are older and less spry than they were 10 or 20 years ago. They no longer want to climb over coamings and go forward to set a spinnaker or play with heavy anchors while balancing on the bow. Neither do they want to have to take crew with them to do all these chores.

A retired neighbor of mine sold his 54-foot yawl to buy a Nonsuch 36. He said the Nonsuch was a boat in which he could comfortably cruise without having to find crew every time he went sailing. That was his solution, but his pet peeve was that he still had to climb over lifelines and coamings just to get aboard.

I once had a client a year or two from retiring with the same problem. He wanted to be able to step aboard the boat and sail it from the helm position. He did not want to have to wind winches; "I'm too old for that," he told me at our first meeting. He needed to be able to contact his business on his days off until he retired permanently. He also wanted to be able to take his grandchildren fishing, or sail with his children and their families to their favorite cove and anchor as needed. Another requirement was to be able to carry an inflatable dinghy.

The design we came up with allows the owner to step from the dock onto the transom platform and go through the stern gate into the cockpit. He can also use the cockpit for fishing with his grandchildren. The helm seat is to starboard, with a single electric winch aft of it. (We originally showed a helm seat back aft in the conventional location, but the client vetoed that. "I want to be able to fish with the grandchildren and walk aboard easily," he repeated.) All the lines on the starboard side lead to the main winch through sheet-stoppers, with a similar arrangement for the other side of the boat. There are only two electric winches onboard to do all the work.

The cockpit is completely open, with lockers on each side for collapsible chairs. The chairs and coffee table are used when the boat is at anchor. With an open cockpit, the boat can easily carry a cooler for drinks if a large number of people are aboard.

All the controls are concentrated at the helm

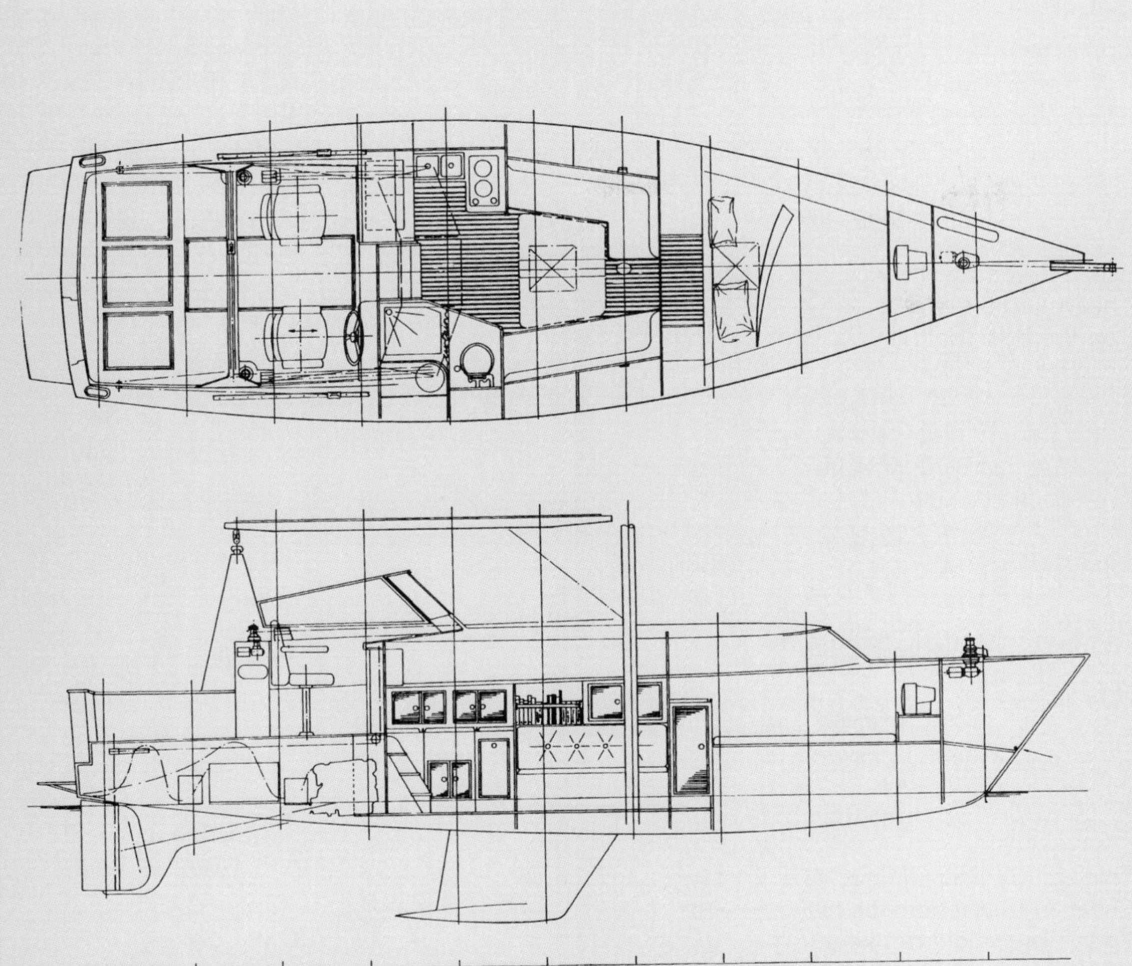

position. Engine controls are on the dash in front of the helm, as is the anchor control. An autopilot gives the skipper time to make coffee or just enjoy effortless sailing. The anchor is a Lewmar Concept system operated entirely by joystick from the helm. This means that nobody has to go forward at any time, except to undo the mainsail ties and put them back on at the beginning and end of each trip. The fully battened mainsail falls into lazyjacks and is totally contained. It is sheeted on the radar arch to keep it out of the cockpit. The arch also serves as a Bimini foundation.

Inside the hull, the boat is fairly conventional, except for the TV located on the forward bunk. The entire boat is wired for stereo and TV, plus it has a cell phone (which can be used up to 20 miles offshore in most areas), a computer for e-mail, and Internet access. All this in a 36-footer!

This boat fitted the bill for that particular client. It was aimed squarely at an older client who wanted to be able to sail, but also wanted to be able to enjoy taking his family out. This boat was a custom design, and a custom boat is one way of getting something tailored specifically to your needs. But once you understand the concepts that go into a design, you can adapt a production boat to suit your pocketbook and your sailing style.

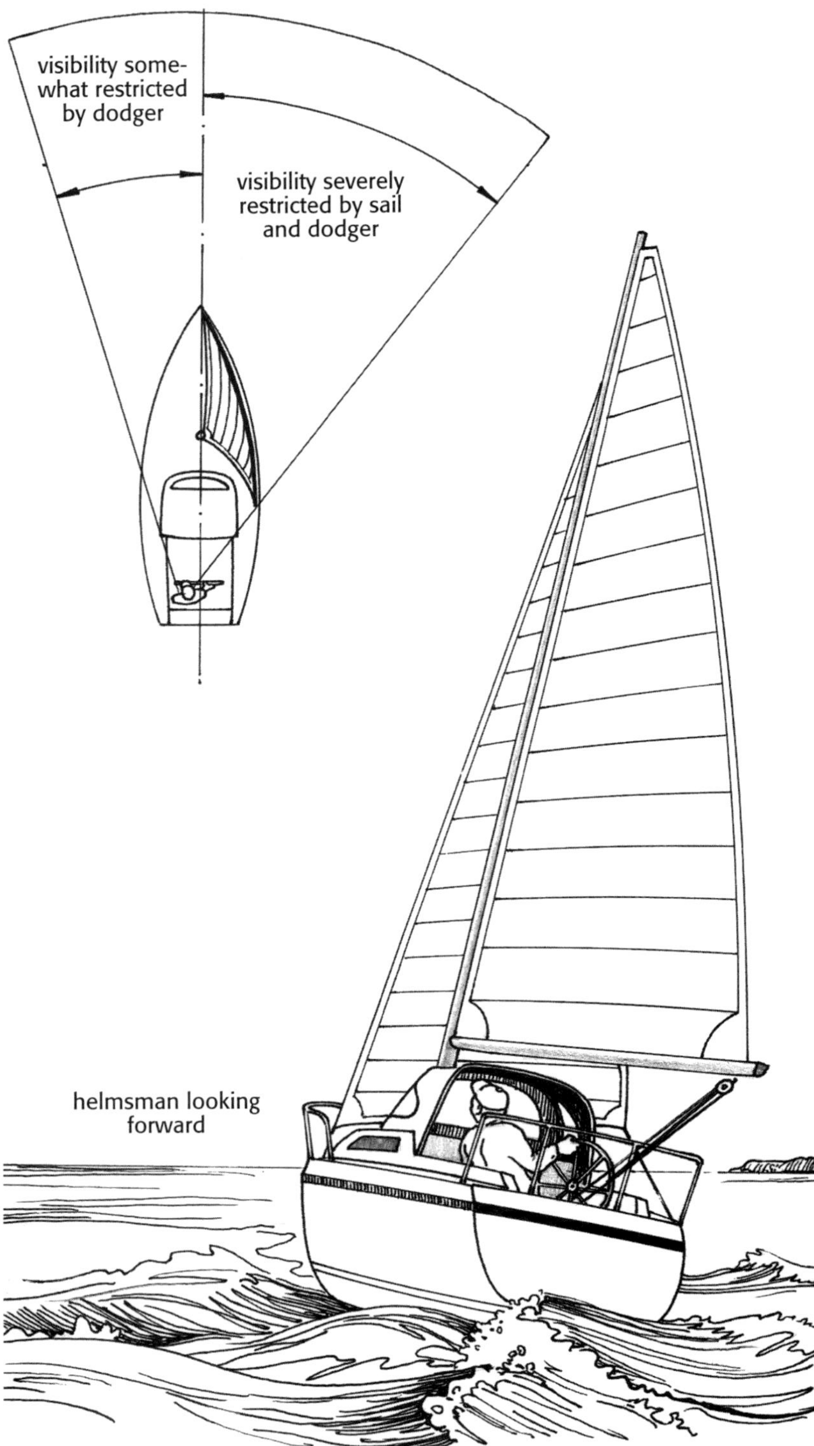

Stand behind the wheel of a boat and check the visibility forward. If you cannot see other boats, you can get into serious trouble under sail.

around you. Is there a strongpoint (for example, a padeye or jackline) to hook a lifeline? Can you hook on before you come out of the cabin? Can you fit jacklines or hook onto a strongpoint before you leave the cockpit? On the boat shown you will need to unclip from the cockpit jackline to get to the jackline running down the side deck. But note that a large number of handholds are provided.

Sitting in the cockpit

Can you sit comfortably and brace yourself when the boat is heeled? If not, you may become fatigued, and fatigue plays a large part in poor decisions at sea. If the cockpit well is no more than 24 inches across, it is relatively easy to brace yourself.

Cockpit drains

Check the cockpit drains to make sure they work efficiently. If in doubt, fill the cockpit to the level of the seats, or as high as possible, and let it drain. According to the late Rod Stephens, the cockpit should take less than three minutes to drain; if it takes longer, the drains are not large enough. The Offshore Racing Council (ORC) regulations call for drain areas to total at least 4¾ inches for boats over 28 feet. Even if your drains

Staying Aboard

Jacklines: Make sure that your boat has strongpoints forward and aft to attach a jackline in heavy weather. The jacklines should be within easy reach of the cockpit to enable a crew to clip on before leaving shelter. Jacklines are not shown on this boat, but there might be one inside the cockpit well, and another running along each side deck from just forward of the sheet turning blocks (outside the shrouds but inside the lifelines) to a strong padeye on the foredeck.

Seating: When sitting in the cockpit the crew need to brace themselves against the boat's heel. In general, a 24-inch-wide cockpit sole is ideal. If the sole is 30 inches wide, crew have difficulty bracing themselves and may slide or sit to leeward. To shelter the crew in bad weather, a dodger should be fitted.

Handholds: These should fall to hand when you walk forward. On this boat a crew going forward to the bow will hold the cabintop handrail, the shrouds, and the lifelines. Note the safety netting strung between the lifelines to prevent sails, sailbags, and crew from slipping over the side. Around the mast are bars to hold the crew in place when operating halyards. To sailors these are known as "granny bars."

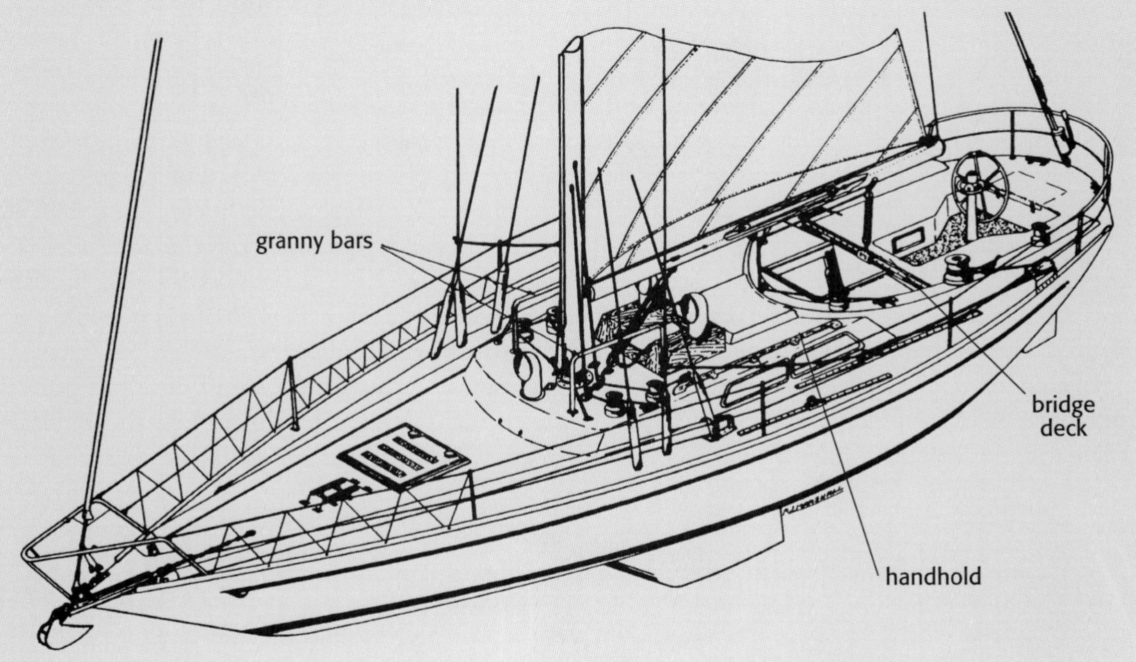

measure up, check to see if they have a non-return valve; this can restrict some of the flow, making the drains slow to empty the cockpit.

In many late-model boats the cockpit runs all the way to the transom, and drain slots or *scuppers* are cut in the transom; this is the fastest way to drain the cockpit. Also check the drains when the boat is heeled. Quite often water backfills the cockpit as soon as the boat heels because the heeled cockpit corner goes below the level of the seawater. When this happens, the helmsman ends up standing in a puddle of water while the remainder of the cockpit stays relatively dry.

Free-Surface Effect

If you have ever stepped into a partially flooded dinghy you have probably found that the dinghy is extremely easy to capsize. This is because of the water in the dinghy. If the water is allowed to slosh around as the dinghy is tipped (in other words, the water has a free surface), its center of gravity moves toward the low side and helps to tip the boat over. This effect can happen to a boat that has a lot of water in the cockpit or in the cabin. Free surface can also occur in large half-filled tanks without internal baffles, which is why it is better to keep them fully filled or entirely empty.

You should also be aware of the cockpit size. A large cockpit introduces *free-surface effect* and drains slowly unless it has an open transom. Free-surface effect can make the boat more liable to capsize. For this reason, in a boat that is to sail offshore, the cockpit should be kept to a reasonable size.

Bridge deck

Can water go below deck from the cockpit? A bridge deck may make the companionway ladder one or two steps longer, but it stops water from going below should the cockpit fill. It also helps the overall rigidity of the boat and adds extra interior locker space.

Coamings

On a cruising boat, coamings should be high enough to keep green water that lands on deck from flowing into the cockpit. Typically, coamings are used as sites for winches, but often little thought is given to the efficiency of the person using the winch. By making the coamings slightly higher in the design stage, by locating the winch on the cabintop, or sometimes by changing the slope of the coaming sides or top, the winch can be made easier to use.

Moving around the Deck

If the cockpit is seaworthy, it is time to move forward and check the deck layout. First step out of the cockpit; hopefully you will be stepping up over the coaming and onto a side deck that is at the same height as or higher than the cockpit seat. On some boats the side deck is lower than the cockpit seat and if you are not expecting it, you can be tipped outboard toward the rail.

Side decks

Walk along the side deck and check that you aren't going to stub your toes on badly placed deck gear. Make sure there are also strongpoints

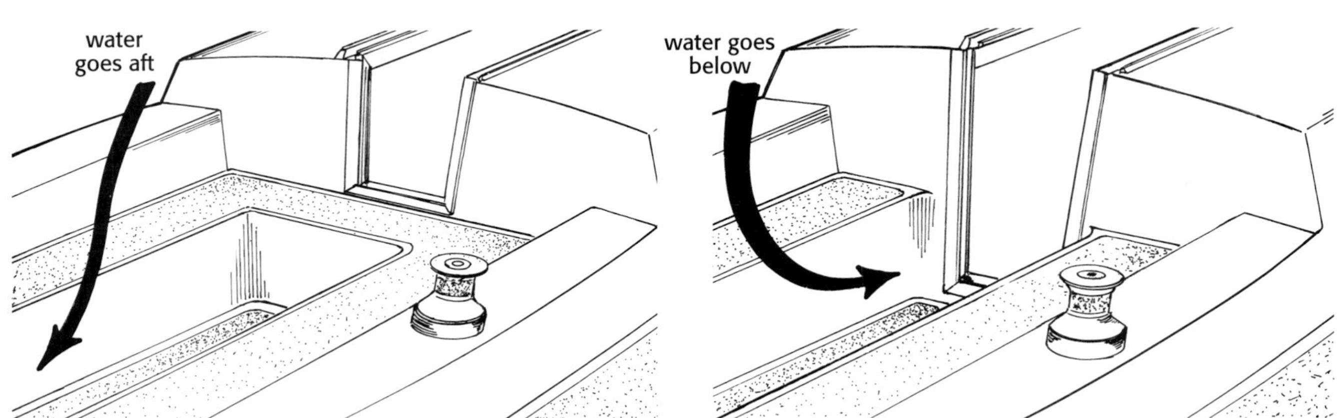

A bridge deck helps to prevent water going below, and should be incorporated into any boat heading offshore.

for jacklines if you intend to sail offshore. Check the toerails. They should be strongly fastened and relatively high on a cruising boat. Quite often, if you walk down the lee side of a boat that is heeled, you end up walking on the toerail, and if there are no toerails you may slip through the lifelines into the water. Next check the placement of the shroud chainplates. Are they positioned to one side of the walkway? If they are like those on the Whitby 42, an out-of-production cruiser designed by Ted Brewer, they will be in the middle of the walkway and you will not be able to walk inboard of them because of the lower shroud. Going around them on the outboard side is also difficult because the lifeline is so close. Getting forward on this boat is difficult. You want to have easy access forward, because you may have to go up there on a dark night in an emergency situation.

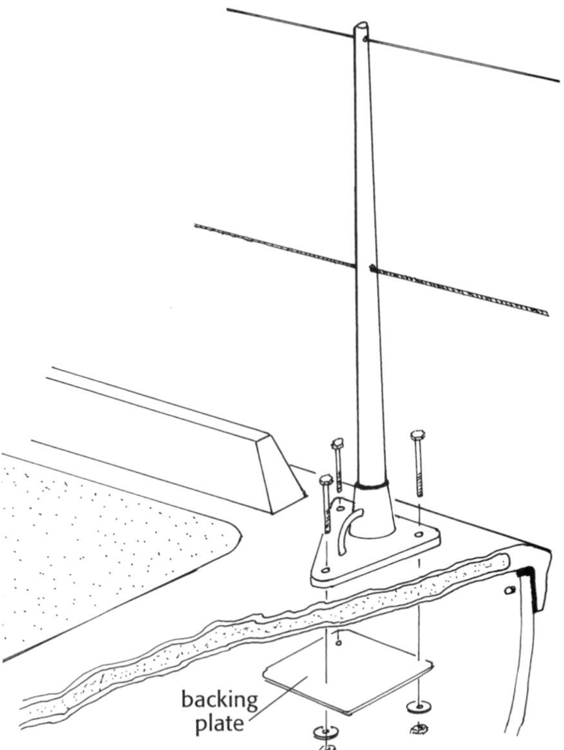

Lifelines should be strongly through-bolted and should have a backing plate below deck. Spacers are inserted through a sandwich-cored deck, like the one shown here, so that the deck is not crushed if a crewmember falls against the stanchion.

Lifelines and stanchions

Lifeline stanchions should be strongly through-bolted, and most are. But sometimes backing plates are not used. If you can see behind the headliner inside the cabin, check the backing plates. A stanchion mounted without backing plates could tear out of the deck if fallen on heavily.

Look at the lifelines. Are they plastic coated? The plastic-coated lines can get nicked, and when that happens water can get into the core and corrode it. I know of two people who have gone overboard because a lifeline parted. The better lifelines are stainless steel wire with a turnbuckle on each end. If the lifelines have a gate, make sure that it can be closed easily and that the clips are taped when you go sailing. That way they won't come open unexpectedly.

Deck strongpoints

Make sure that every operation can be performed while crewmembers are tethered to the boat. There should be strongpoints for harness tethers around the mast, near winches, on the side decks (for jacklines), and near the helm station. If in doubt, put on your harness and try each operation. Try grinding on all the winches on deck without removing your lifeline. It is no use to find out when the boat is hove-to in a gale that you can't reach a winch when you are harnessed.

Handholds

On deck, check for handholds as you walk forward. Take the boat for a sail, and check again for handholds; they should fall easily to hand. Handholds should be placed on the cabintop, near the mast, near any foredeck hatches and the companionway, and near the steering wheel. A handhold or two on the mast and on the forward end of the boom is also not a bad idea.

Hatches

The companionway hatch is a likely source of leaks and should be well made. The best hatches slide on metal or plastic tracks to ensure that they are watertight when closed. A dodger groove around the hatch allows a small dodger to be fitted, which also helps keep rain from going below.

The hatch washboards should not be hinged, but should be in two or three parts. If they are hinged, they will bang together as the boat pitches and keep the off-watch awake. Washboards should also incorporate vents so that in severe weather the hatch can be closed tightly, yet still admit air into the boat. The boards should fit together with a lip or sloped edge to stop water from going below.

Below Deck

There are a number of seaworthy features to look for below, ranging from handholds, to galley stove safety bars, to the ease of walking through the cabin, to whether you can stay in your bunk on either tack in bad weather. Wide open spaces below deck are dangerous. I sailed a large boat last year in which the dining saloon extended clear across the hull. Any crewmember trying to traverse it had no handholds, and had to sprint across while trying not to be thrown off balance. Eventually one crewmember was hurt while trying to cross the saloon.

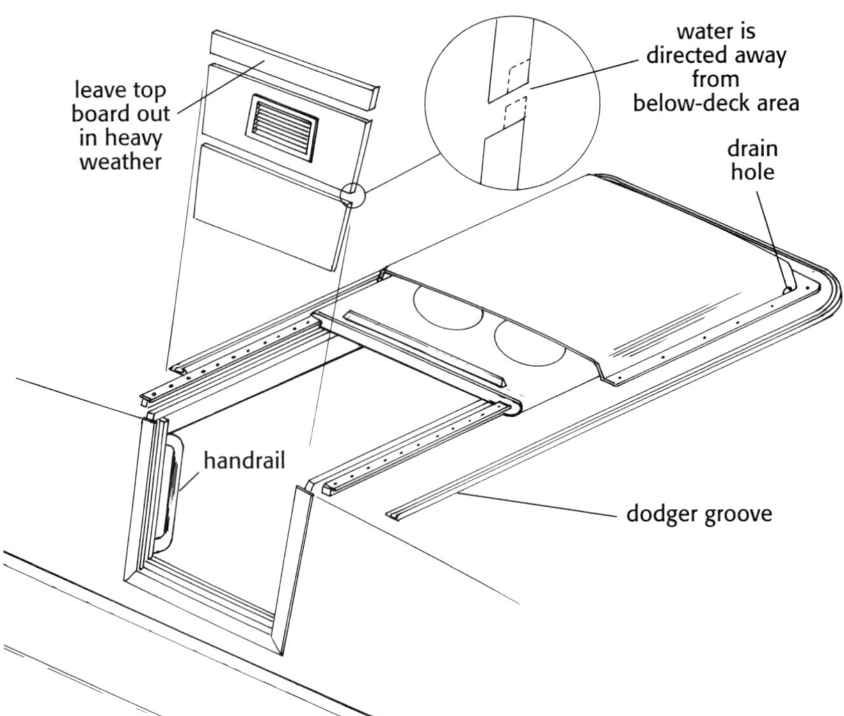

This main companionway hatch includes a number of clever features that might not be apparent at first glance. The hatch wraps around the slides to help prevent water ingress. The hatch cover has drain holes to facilitate draining. A dodger groove goes around the hatch, so that a dodger can be fitted to keep rain and spray from going below. Note the handhold inside the hatchway. The washboards are made in three separate parts, which allows crew to insert one or two parts as the weather worsens. The narrow top washboard is almost never inserted underway; it lets air into the boat even under storm conditions. The joints of the washboards all slope outward to shed water.

Cabin sole

Some boats feature a split-level cabin sole. You will learn where the step is after you have fallen once or twice. The best option is to have one level throughout the boat, even if it slopes slightly at either end. The worst option is a step that is only one or two inches high; you will inevitably forget it is there and trip over it fairly often. Steps that are 6 to 8 inches high rarely get tripped over. The worst place for a step is going into or out of the galley—sooner or later the cook, arms loaded with food, will trip over it.

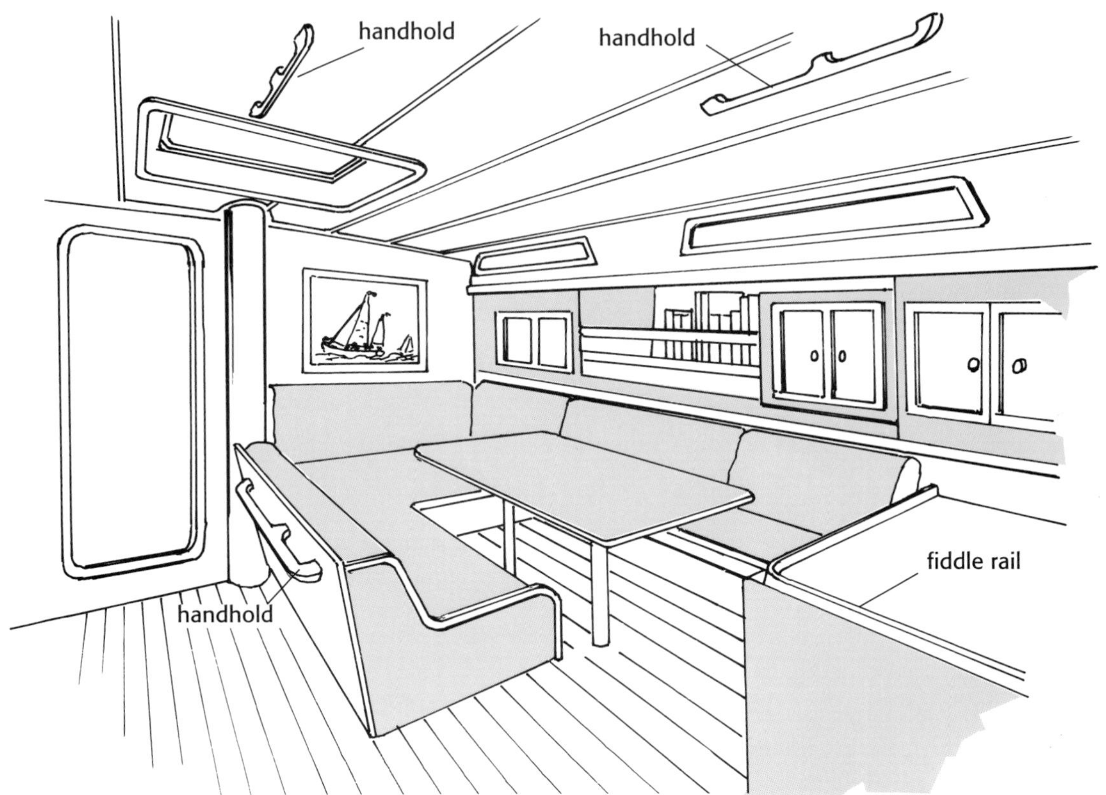

Handholds are important below deck, too. Here, several handholds are shown on the seatbacks and on the overhead. A crew could also grab the fiddle rail in an emergency.

Cabin soles should also be non-slip. Yes, many sailors want a nicely varnished sole, but have you ever walked on a varnished sole when it is covered with a film of water? Experienced offshore sailors have an oiled or bare cabin sole if it is wood, or a nonskid surface on fiberglass.

Handholds

Below deck look for easy-to-reach handholds when the boat is upright *and* when it is heeled. Walk through the boat in harbor and feel for handholds; they should fall naturally under your hand. Check again when the boat is heeled. Quite often you'll find that you need handholds in different places to help you get through a heeled cabin. Below-deck stanchions are good handholds, available for people of any height. But too many stanchions can make the below-deck area look like a forest of chrome trees.

Drawers

Check that drawers cannot slide out as the boat heels. I prefer the lift-and-pull type of drawer, but some manufacturers use mechanical latches. Even the best boatbuilders forget the details sometimes in the rush to get a boat ready. I once boarded a Hinckley and found that not one drawer had been properly fitted. The reason given was that the catches had not arrived by the time I looked over the boat. To check whether a drawer is of the lift-and-pull type, first lift and pull it out of the drawer slot, then turn it over. It should have a pair of notches on

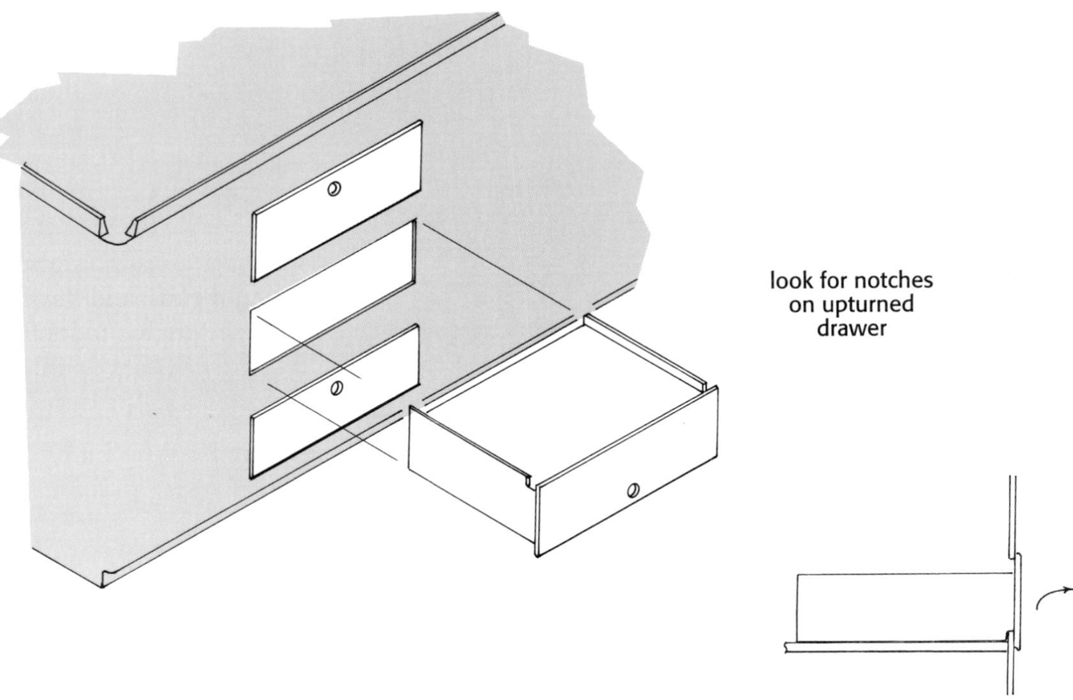

Drawers should be of the lift-and-pull type, to ensure that they cannot open when the boat sails off a wave. To check, remove the drawer, turn it over, and look for the notches at the front.

each side that stop the drawer from sliding out when it is closed.

Cabin table

Check that the table will not collapse if a person falls against it. Tables should be strongly bolted to the cabin sole, and the sole should be bolted to the cabin foundations or floors. On one boat I sailed, the table was bolted to the sole but the sole boards could be lifted out! The table is probably the piece of saloon furniture most often used as a support when the boat is heeled, so it should be strongly bolted down.

Head compartment

Look at the head compartment. If the head is at an angle to the boat's centerline, and you need to use it in a seaway, it is usually very difficult to stay in place unless you can brace yourself properly. This usually means that the head should face either fore-and-aft, or transversely. The best heads to use in a seaway have some furniture around them so that you can hold yourself in.

The head unit should also have plenty of handholds to make it easy to hold on while dressing. Another feature to look for is a separate shower with a curtain or door that is not adjacent to the head; if a curtain is inboard of the head, you will have nothing to lean against when the boat is heeled. Even the shower should have handholds in case the boat lurches while you are getting wet.

Movable gear

There is always a fair amount of gear that can move around below deck. The stove moves in its gimbals. Batteries can be lifted out of the boat, as can extra ballast, and in some boats the tanks can be removed. Imagine what would happen if the boat were knocked on its beam ends. What would come crashing across the boat? The stove should be gimbaled in such a way that it cannot fly out of the gimbals even if the boat were to be totally inverted. Likewise with the batteries and any tanks. You should also check cabin sole boards, especially if you store heavy items such as canned foods and spare water canisters beneath them.

Fire Extinguishers

Under the heading of seaworthiness we should include fire extinguishers. The Coast Guard recommends that every boat have at least two onboard, in a suitable location. I recommend that you have one extinguisher in the galley and another near the engine compartment. A third, smaller extinguisher can be stowed forward, near the forward head on a larger boat. You never know when you'll need it.

Fireboy-Zintex fire extinguishers. *(Photo courtesy Fireboy-Zintex)*

Mechanical Items

Also below deck are a large number of mechanical items, ranging from the main engine, to the batteries, to pumps and compressors for the refrigerator or freezer. You might also have bilge pumps, water pumps, and a water heater. These items should be strongly fastened down. Do not, however, fasten fuel lines too tightly. The engine vibrates when it runs, and flexible lines are used to connect the engine to its fuel and water supplies. Should these lines be tightly fastened, they might wear and break at fastener points.

Engine

A seaworthy boat will have an adequately sized engine. I once sailed on a 40-foot boat with a 25-horsepower engine. The engine gave the boat plenty of power when the wind was light, and the vessel could cruise at around 7 knots. But as soon as the wind came up to 15 to 20 knots from ahead, speed over the ground dropped to 2 knots. As the wind increased beyond 20 knots, boat speed almost ceased. This was not a seaworthy boat. A seaworthy boat has an engine powerful enough to get you off a lee shore in a gale. On this 40-footer that meant refitting a 40-horsepower engine.

The new-boat data chart in chapter 5 (see page 112) shows the ratio of displacement to engine size. The lower the number, the more power there is available to push the boat through the water. Remember that compressors, alternators, and pumps attached to the engine each drain a few horsepower, making the available power output lower than the listed number.

Propellers

Your choices are two- or three- (or four- or five-) bladed propellers; fixed, folding, or feathering props; or a saildrive. Which one is best for your boat? The best propeller depends on the situation in which it is likely to be used. For example, on a long-distance voyager the best

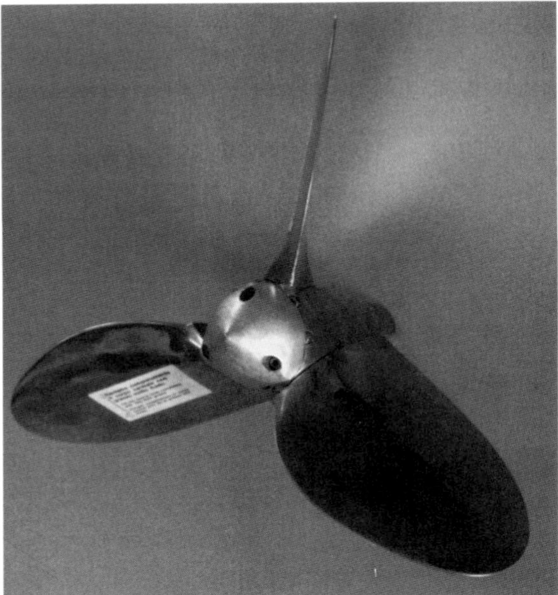

A three-bladed feathering prop shown with the blades open (top) and feathered (bottom).

prop is one that feathers to provide least resistance when the boat is under sail.

The number of blades your propeller has directly affects its efficiency. More blades give more blade area, and more blade area makes the propeller more efficient. In practical terms, three blades are about all that can be used on folding or feathering props. Fixed-bladed propellers can use up to five blades, although the extra blades do cause extra drag, which slows the boat under sail. In general, if your propeller is revolving in open water, two or three blades are all you need. If your propeller is in an aperture (as the Cruiser prop is), it should have three blades so that only one is masked by the deadwood at any time. Vibrations are a concern with two-bladed props: vibrations are caused by the prop being in open water when it is horizontal and masked behind the deadwood when the blades are vertical.

Feathering props align the blades so that each blade is parallel to the water flow past the hull. When the prop shaft turns, the blades automatically kick out to the best pitch. They are usually almost as efficient going astern as they are going forward. Feathering props can be purchased with either two or three blades. The drawback to a feathering prop is that sometimes it won't open when the shaft is turned unless the boat is completely stopped. To get it to open you may have to stop the boat completely and then spin the prop by putting the engine in gear.

Folding props have blades that fold down toward the center of the prop to minimize contact with the water. Folding props are remarkably efficient when the boat is moving ahead, but often they are very inefficient when going astern. They also sometimes fail to open unless the boat is completely stopped. Under sail, folding props sometimes let one blade drop which can cause additional drag, although this can be remedied by having a crew dive down and put an elastic band over the prop. Of course, you would only do this if you were going on a long trip under sail or racing.

Fixed-bladed props produce the most drag of all and in my opinion should only be used on motorsailers or on boats heavily oriented toward using the engine. However, many cruisers like the security of having a prop that is ready immediately despite the drag.

Saildrives are rather like an inboard/outboard unit on a powerboat in that the entire engine, transmission, and propeller come as one unit that is simply dropped into the boat. There is no doubt that saildrives, when combined with feathering or folding props, are efficient. They are also relatively trouble free and are being installed by more and more manufacturers.

Through-hulls

Another feature to check inside the boat is access to through-hulls and intakes. Should a hose clamp or intake let go, you want to be able to reach the through-hull and hammer a bung into place to stop the water from flowing into the boat. If the boat has a liner or built-in furniture over the through-hull and it cannot be reached, the fitting will not get maintained and eventually something *will* fail.

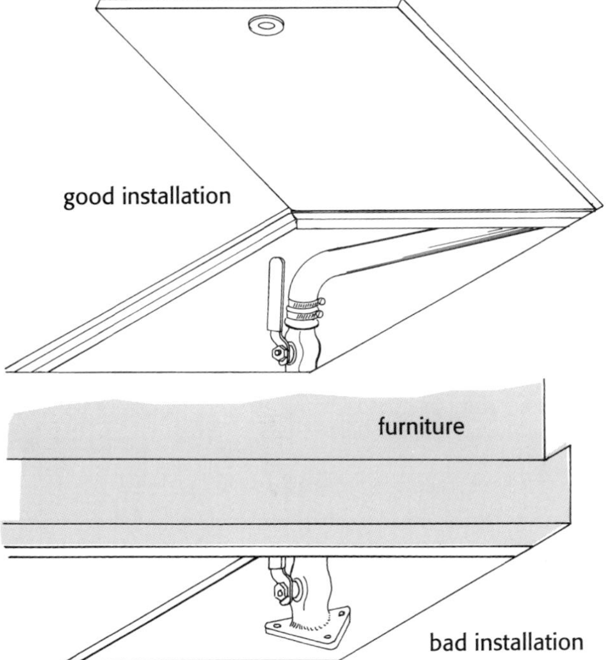

A through-hull partly hidden by furniture is unlikely to be maintained properly.

Pumps

You need access to all pumps in case a belt goes or the pump jams while the boat is underway. Make sure that you can reach everything you might need access to; then take another look when the boat is underway.

Joints

When production cruisers are built, the deck is usually assembled with all its fittings and then bolted to the hull. Similarly, the keel is often bolted to the hull (some keels have the lead encapsulated in the hull/keel mold). These joints are a vital part of the seaworthiness of the boat. After all, it is difficult for a boat to sail if the keel falls off or the deck peels off the hull (it has happened!). The deck also keeps the water out and contributes to the overall strength of the boat.

Hull/deck joint

If you want to know how much a deck contributes to the strength of the hull, you can make a simple test. Remove the lid from an empty shoe box, and push the ends of the box inward. They bend easily. Now put the lid back on and tape it to the box. Squeeze the ends and notice how much harder it has become to make the box bend. The same thing is happening on your boat, when the mast and keel exert loads that tend to deform the hull. The deck (or shoebox lid) helps to stiffen the structure.

Hull/deck joints can take many forms. One of the strongest is the coffee-can joint, where a flange on the edge of the deck fits over the hull. The flange is then screwed and glued to the hull to become a solid unit. Typically a toerail is bolted over the hull/deck joint to hide it. Another deck joint places the flange on the hull with the deck laid on top. A toerail is bolted through both the deck and the hull to make a strong, stiff joint.

Hull/keel joint

Another critical joint is the hull/keel joint. On

Various Hull/Deck Joints

A hull/deck joint typically used in one-off construction is shown in A. The deck is made slightly larger than the hull, which has an outward-turning flange. Bolts are installed through the flange and deck, then the inside is glassed in place. The flange is cut off and the exterior glassed and faired. This makes a strong, rigid joint. B is known as a coffee-can joint because the deck is made with a downward-turning flange and the hull has a slight recess. The deck is lowered over the hull and through-bolted at the rubrail. It may or may not be glassed over inside the hull. B1 shows the hull without a recess and the joint hidden by the rail. C shows the deck with an inward-turning, recessed flange. The deck is trimmed to fit the flanged area. Because this type of joint requires great precision, the joint shown in C1 is usually used. The joint shown in D is not a very good one, but is often used on less-expensive boats and powercraft. Both the deck and the hull have outward-turning flanges, which are bolted and glassed together. The joint is hidden with a rail. D1 shows another variation on the same joint. If a boat has bulwarks, the joint is usually made as shown in E. This is a very strong joint and rarely leaks.

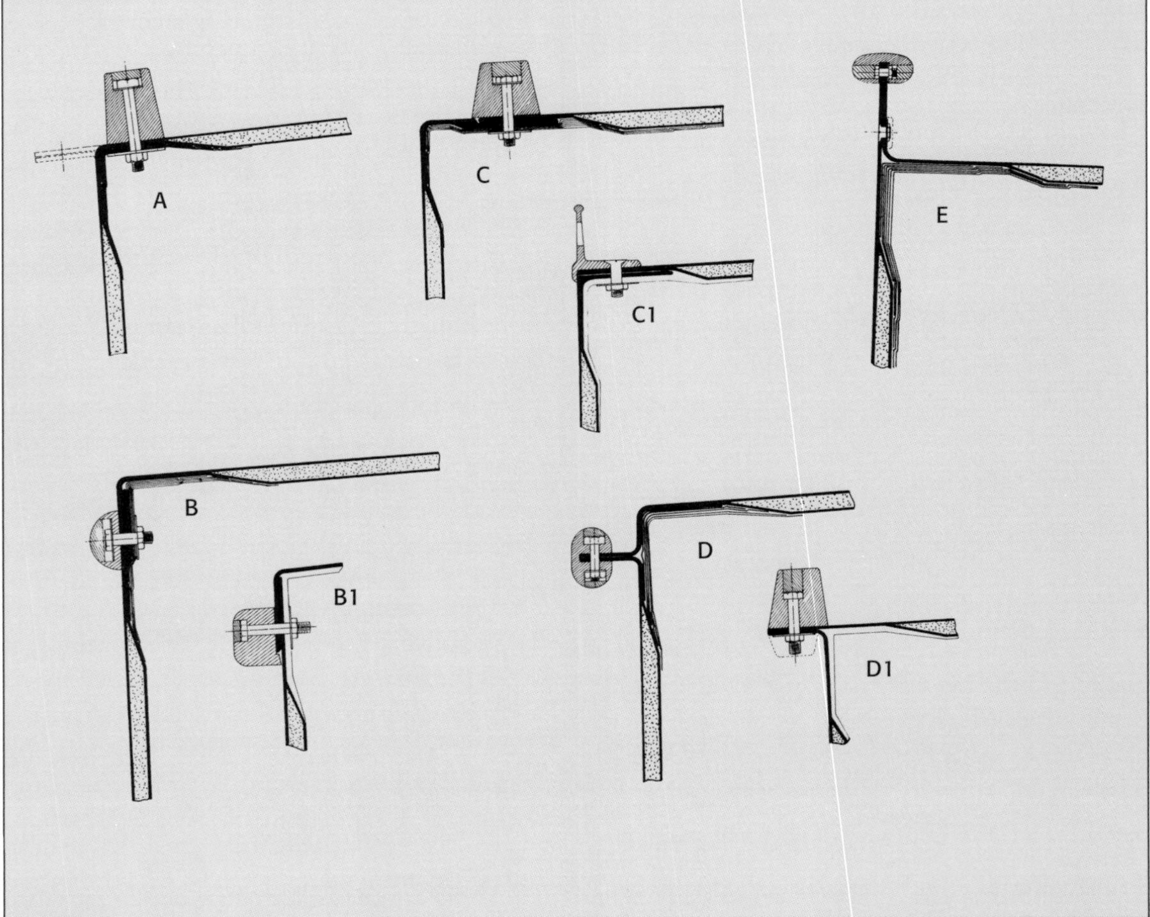

older boats, this joint was an easy one to make, since the keel was wider at the top than at the bottom. Today, however, the hull/keel joint can be complex (see chapter 8, page 199). Some of the latest keel blades are very thin at the top and difficult to bolt to the hull. These keels often have large bulbs attached to the bottom that create a large bending moment that has, in some cases, caused the keel to break off.

Our Designs

On the boats we are developing in this book, we'll look at seaworthy features that can be incorporated while the boats are being built. We'll try to make the boats more seaworthy even if it means sacrificing an iota of speed. We want the boats to be safe and able to sail in their intended venues without problems.

The Weekender

The Weekender is probably the least seaworthy of our boats, but it is intended to sail close to shore, it is fast, and it will usually be sailed in the company of other boats. Because it is small, its compartments can be made completely watertight, or they can be filled with foam to render the boat unsinkable.

Also because the boat is small, the bunks are in the ends. This spreads the weight out and makes the boat more liable to pitch, which reduces crew comfort and increases fatigue. But as the crew will only spend weekends aboard, fatigue is not a huge problem.

Construction

As this boat is unlikely to sail in the deep ocean, the structure can be very light. One of these designs has been built using WEST System cold-molded construction (a ¼-inch wood laminate), another using a cored S-glass laminate. The hull/deck joints were made using a triangular piece of foam glassed in place, with the deck fitted to it. Both were then glassed together from the inside. Neither structure is intended for high impacts, but

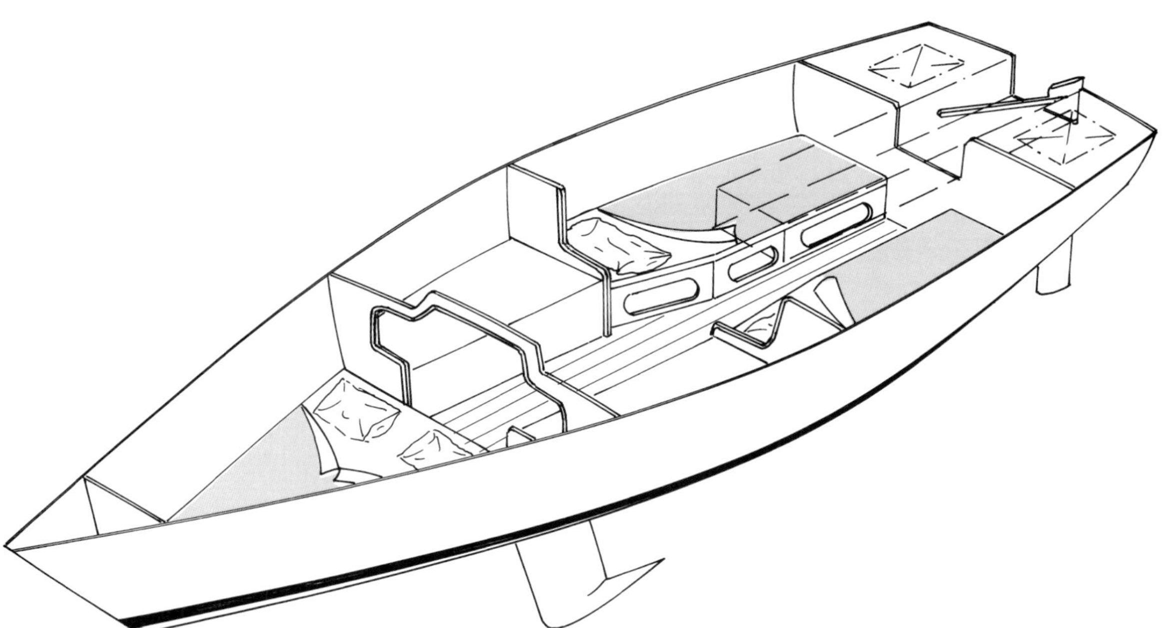

The bunks on the Weekender are in the ends of the boat, but because the crew are aboard for such a short time they are unlikely to be fatigued by pitching.

both do the job. A hull designed to withstand high stresses would require another layer of hull material, which would add unacceptable weight to this hull. Neither boat has an interior hull liner, so bolts, backing plates, and other structural details are easy to inspect and service.

Cockpit

The cockpit drains over the stern and is sloped so that water will naturally drain aft, but that will not prevent water from going below. All this boat has for keeping water from going below is a 3-inch sill at the bottom of the companionway. This is not ideal, but it makes the companionway easier to use, and is consistent with an inshore boat that is unlikely to take a wave over the transom.

Engine

The engine is an 8-horsepower outboard mounted on a transom bracket, which requires a reinforcing block bonded inside the transom. This arrangement is not particularly seaworthy, because the operator has to hang over the transom to get the engine started. Under sail the engine can theoretically be lifted inboard and stowed on the cabin sole, where its weight would help stability. In practice, however, with a family of four packed aboard for the weekend, that won't happen, especially since even an 8-horsepower engine is a heavy, unwieldy beast. Rather, it will be tilted out of the water but remain on the bracket. Fortunately, its tendency to make the stern squat (both in use and not in use) is counteracted by the Weekender's wide beam aft. An engine this small is likely to make heavy work of it if called upon to power upwind in a blow.

Winches

The halyard winches are mounted on the aft end of the cabin, which is the most usable position. The primary winches are located on the deck where the crew can reach them easily. This is not the best position for winding the primaries, but it is a good position for using them while sitting to windward. To do so, the headsail sheet leads will need to be taken from the turning block across the cockpit. This introduces slightly more friction, but the gain in stability (by having another warm body on the weather rail) is well worth the compromise. On a boat this small, winch locations must be a compromise among ergonomic considerations, stability, and fair sheet and halyard leads.

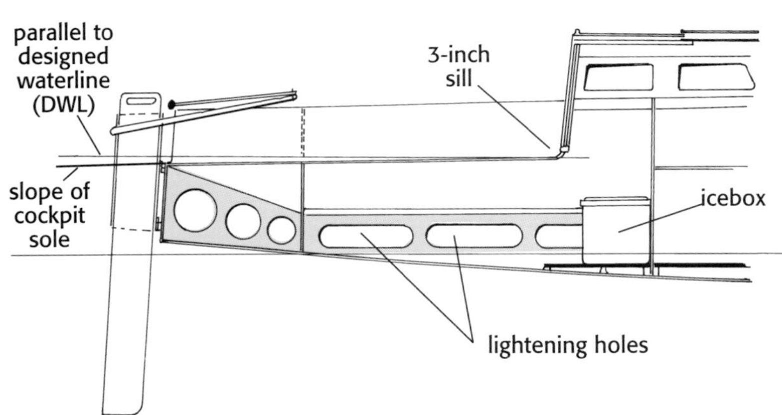

The cockpit has a slight downward slope to help water drain over the transom. The lightening holes in the furniture below deck are clearly shown in this view, as is the icebox step.

Helm position

The helmsman is located aft of the mainsheet, where he or she can sit outboard, operate the mainsheet, and sail the boat. If the helmsman trims the mainsail as well as steers, the boat's balance will be better and the boat is less likely to encounter an unexpected situation. When racing, the other crewmembers can concentrate on headsail trim and tactics. If the Weekender

On a boat this small, crew weight plays an important part in stability, so the deck layout must be worked out to enable crew to sit to windward and to operate the boat properly. The helmsman sits abaft the mainsheet and steers. In heavy conditions he/she can also operate the mainsheet to keep the boat sailing without being overpowered.

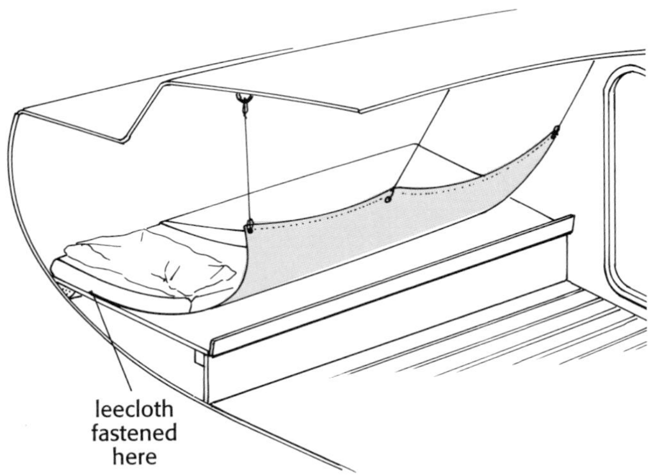

When fitting a leecloth, make it wide enough to be screwed to the bunk flat about one-third of the way from the outboard side of the bunk. This enables a crewmember to raise the cushion slightly and sleep more comfortably.

is to be cruised, not much adjustment needs to be made to the mainsheet or jibsheet, and the helmsman can steer and easily reach all the sail controls.

Handholds and leecloths

Below deck, seaworthiness is reduced to the bare essentials. Handholds should be placed in every possible position. Leecloths should be installed on all the bunks if the boat is to be sailed overnight, and everything should be fastened down tightly.

Sail plan

Like the rest of the boat, the sail plan is not particularly seaworthy, but in keeping with the boat's inshore personality, it does not need to be. The sail plan is large, for good light-air speed rather than storm sailing. The headsail may be roller reefed, again for cruising performance rather than seaworthiness. The mainsail is fully battened and reefed using reef lines inside the boom.

Fractional rig

The fractional rig (described in chapter 6 under "Sloop") is good for performance, but not so good when it comes to seaworthiness. Typically, fractional rigs require running backstays or swept-back spreaders to maintain tension on the headstay. This boat has swept-back spreaders, which keep the afterdeck clear but make it difficult to adjust the headstay tension while underway. Consequently, permanent backstay tension will be required to keep load on the headstay, or the headstay can be allowed to slack off and the boat to sail below its windward potential.

In its favor, the fractional rig can easily be depowered with vang tension when a gust hits, and this mainsail can be reefed quickly using the jiffy reefing system installed on the boom. With the small foretriangle, sail can be carried at all times to make the boat manageable in all but the worst conditions.

The Cruiser

I recently read a study that said that more than 90 percent of today's sailors venture no farther offshore than 40 nautical miles. For the average cruiser, that is six to eight hours of sailing. Seeing that we now get satellite reconnaissance pictures of the weather 24 to 48 hours in advance, most sailors should have plenty of time to get to shore when a major storm is approaching and to tether their boats safely. Consequently, there is little incentive to build boats that can survive severe storms.

Most boats in America today are designed and built to survive moderate storms or inshore sailing; they are not overbuilt to survive the rigors of offshore storms. This is fine as long as the boats are in port before bad weather hits, where the crew can be ashore enjoying the storm from the local restaurant or bar. But even a boat sailed mainly inshore needs some seaworthy features.

Construction

As weight is not a critical factor in the performance of this boat, it is designed to be built using a single-skin fiberglass laminate. The laminate was designed to be fairly straightforward, allowing the boat to be built over a wooden mold. If this were a production boat, the keel could easily be designed to encapsulate the lead. In this method the keel is laminated as part of the hull, eliminating a hull/keel joint, and a mixture of lead shot and resin is poured into the keel cavity. If the boat were to go aground and tear a hole in the keel laminate, the lead shot would be contained within the epoxy resin. While this method does not give maximum stability, it offers a good compromise with the cost of casting a keel and bolting it in place.

Cockpit

Note how the coamings around the cockpit are deep and the seatbacks are high. These are good features from the perspective of comfort, but they are not so seaworthy. Should the cockpit fill with water, there will be a lot more of it to get rid of. On the other hand, a small cockpit doesn't allow many people to sit around and enjoy the sail. The designer's dilemma is to make the cockpit large enough for a group to enjoy, but not so large that it endangers the boat. The cockpit also needs efficient drains (discussed

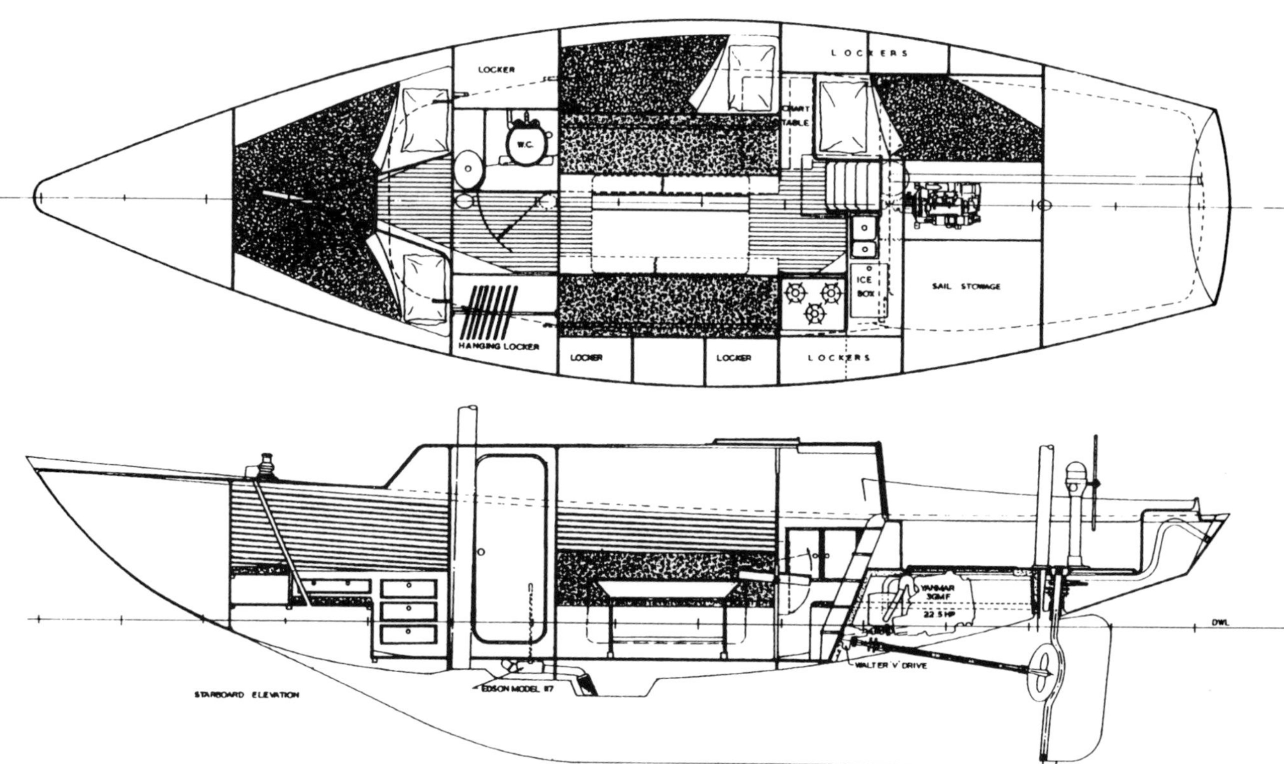

The arrangement plan of the 34-foot Cruiser shows a small, comfortable boat easily handled by two people. The engine is under the cockpit and is removed via a cockpit hatch. Because it is so far aft, a V-drive is fitted. Below deck the galley is to port with a large dining area ready for those long evening games when you have guests aboard. Small children can be ushered forward at bedtime to sleep in the V-berths while your evening continues. Note the heavy-duty pump with its strum box in a sump. On the Cruiser the chart table is unlikely to see a lot of use (most navigation will be done by pilotage), and it is made to fold away.

earlier in this chapter) to quickly get rid of any water that comes aboard.

Hatches

In addition to small opening ports around the main cabin, this boat has two large hatches on deck. If the boat were to make an offshore passage, it would need plywood panels to cover the hatches in storm conditions, as well as some ready method of fastening the panels.

Hatches are typically installed for ease of access, which means their hinges are located at the back. This is not a seaworthy arrangement, however, because if green water comes on deck it will get sluiced below through an open hatch. Better to face the hatches aft so they will be slammed shut by a boarding wave. On this boat there are tracks around the hatches to carry protective dodgers.

Vents

While it may not seem important, the vents on this boat have a low profile to minimize snagging of sheets as the boat tacks. But this means that they may be submerged if green water comes aboard. From the strict standpoint of seaworthiness, the vents should be higher off the deck. They are also designed as part of a halyard tail

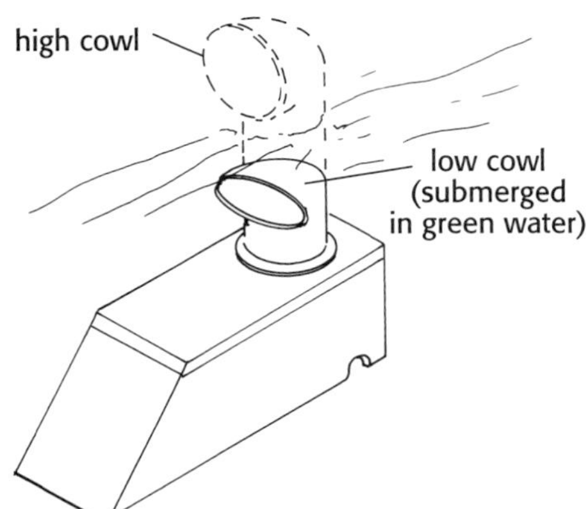

Dorade vents have low-profile cowls to reduce snagging by lines. If the boat were to go farther out to sea, higher cowls should be fitted to prevent green water going down the vents.

locker just abaft the mast to stop lines from falling overside. (See also the deck plan in chapter 6.)

Anchor chain stowage

Our Cruiser has a bow roller forward with an anchor stowed on it and a chain locker below deck. This makes it easy to drop the hook and to keep the deck clear when the anchor is not in use. But the arrangement puts a lot of weight forward, plus the anchor well and chain locker can fill with water in a sea (despite being tightly sealed). In this boat the chain locker has been pushed aft as far as possible, and the hawsepipe doubles as steps for the forehatch. In this sloping pipe, the anchor chain lies against one side and is less prone to bang and rattle.

Head compartment

When a storm lasts a long time, a well-laid-out head compartment makes the entire crew more comfortable. In this boat the head is fitted transversely, which enables the crew to wedge themselves in place. If the head were fitted fore-and-aft, using it at large angles of heel might require foot braces higher on the compartment sides than you might expect. Since the easiest way for men to use the head in a seaway is to kneel down, a kneeling pad is provided on either side of the toilet. The head should also have a sink for hand washing and, if possible, a shower, more for personal hygiene than seaworthiness. But as the crew are likely to be aboard only for short periods of time, a shower is not essential.

Sail plan

For a comfortable, seaworthy sail plan that is easy to handle, the roller-furled sloop rig is one of the simplest, but to break up the sail plan into even smaller increments for an older couple to handle, we'll show a ketch rig (see the Cruiser's sail plan in chapter 6). With a roller-furling headsail and a roller-furling mainsail, all the sails can be set and secured by one person and trimmed from the cockpit. On this boat an

MPS (multipurpose spinnaker) will be set without a spinnaker pole. This will keep the offwind sails to a minimum and make sail handling relatively simple, thus enhancing seaworthiness.

Dinghy

Because this boat will be kept at a mooring, a dinghy is essential. The dinghy can be left behind on the mooring, towed astern, or carried inverted on deck. None of these locations is particularly seaworthy, but davits on the transom would add weight aft and detract from the looks of the boat. The best location for the dinghy is on the cabintop, and even though visibility from the helm is hampered, chocks have been provided.

The Voyager

The Voyager will travel long distances, and will be at sea in a storm, so it should incorporate features that make it as seaworthy as possible for this type of sailing. The boat will probably not have watertight doors, as most sailors prefer to have the interior open for good airflow throughout; plus there will usually be enough crew to handle an emergency. The seaworthy features of this boat are a skeg-protected rudder, an easily handled sail plan (possibly broken up into small areas), a minimum number of through-hull fittings, a small cockpit with which drains over the transom, a sheltered area at the forward end of the cockpit, and strongpoints at all locations where the crew will

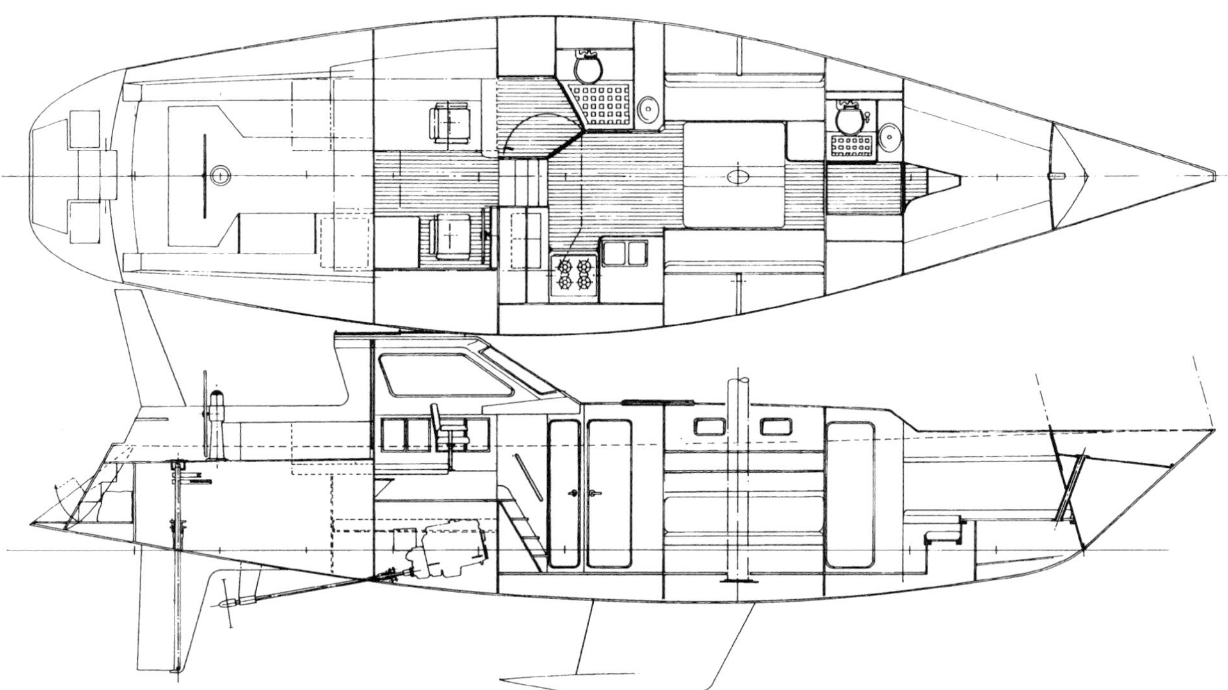

The arrangement plan of the Voyager shows a pilothouse over the engine compartment. To port of the pilothouse is the owner's stateroom with a double berth. A large galley is to starboard with an icebox, stove, and freezer. This location for the freezer means that its compressor is just abaft in the engine compartment, to increase its efficiency. Under the cockpit sole is plenty of space for stores, as well as easy access to the steering gear and engine compartment. Note the raised cockpit sole, which puts the helmsman's eye level over the pilothouse. The drawback of this arrangement is the lack of a bridge deck to stop cockpit water from going below. For this reason the pilothouse door to the cockpit has an insert for heavy weather.

work—that is, near winches, near the helm station, and near the companionway, where a person can hook on before leaving the shelter of the cabin.

Although this boat should have a bridge deck, this would make the steps into the pilothouse difficult to use. For this reason we have eliminated a bridge deck, but have provided the pilothouse door with washboards. In heavy weather the washboards would be locked in place to serve as a bridge deck. With the open transom, any water that gets into the cockpit should drain freely astern.

Pilothouse

On a long cruise it is nice to be able to shelter from the elements while the autopilot does the work of steering. The Voyager has a pilothouse to shelter the crew and expand the living area of the boat. It features opening windows and opening overhead hatches for viewing the sails. The forward windows will require reinforced construction and plywood emergency panels.

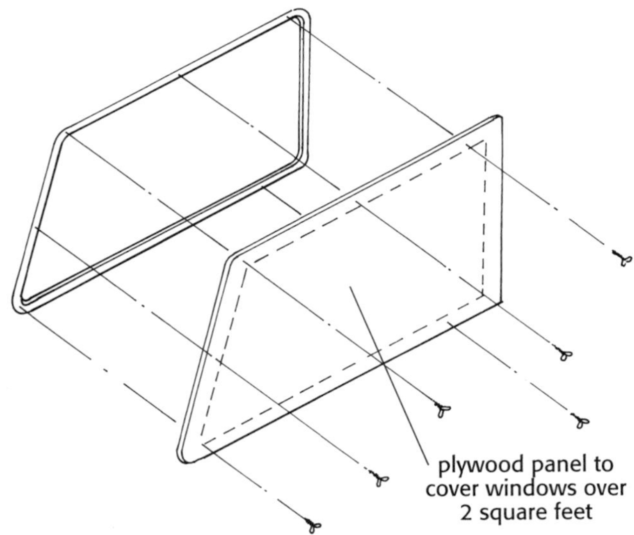

On the Voyager, the pilothouse windows are larger than 2 square feet; consequently, plywood storm panels should be made for emergency use. These panels can be held in place with wing nuts to make them easy to install and remove.

Inside steering

The inside steering station makes visibility forward difficult, but the aft steering station can be used in good weather. You wouldn't want to dock the boat from the interior helm station, as you couldn't see the fenders or the dock when the boat came alongside. Because the inside steering station is to starboard, visibility to windward will be almost impossible on port tack. Consequently, additional crew may have to be posted to look to windward when the inside steering station is in use.

Access

An offshore boat needs easy access to all critical components, such as the steering gear, the engine compartment, and all pumps and compressors. The hull should also be easy to check in case it is holed. Therefore the interior will be developed to ensure that every item of importance can be checked and maintained easily.

Construction

The Voyager's original design called for cold-molded wood-laminate construction using the WEST System, but there is no reason why the hull cannot be somewhat high-tech, with some unidirectional carbon fiber along areas of high stress, and a Kevlar laminate on the outside of the hull for impact resistance. As a production boat, the entire structure might be laminated using the SCRIMP method to eliminate secondary bonding of fiberglass components (see sidebar, "SCRIMP," page 65).

Ground tackle

Because this boat is designed to anchor on unfamiliar shores, the anchors and gear should be overweight, with a spare anchor carried in the bilge. The windlass, too, should be stronger than usual. One of the best windlasses I have come across is made by the Ideal Windlass Company, in East Greenwich, Rhode Island. Their windlasses are cast using the same molds

SCRIMP

If you have ever been in a fiberglass shop, you will have noticed the smell of styrene and other volatile organic compounds (VOCs, the feds call them). A few years ago laws were passed in California limiting VOCs, and laminating a fiberglass hull with a wet laminate exposed to air became a thing of the past in that state. Other states have imposed similar restrictions on VOC emissions, and the trend may soon be nationwide. To eliminate VOCs, other methods of laminating were sought and developed. At Tillotson-Pearson Inc. (TPI) in Warren, Rhode Island, as well as a number of other production builders, the SCRIMP system has taken hold. (SCRIMP is an acronym for Seemann Composites Resin Infusion Molding Process, after Seemann Composites in Mississippi, which developed the process.)

For the reader who is familiar with vacuum-bagging, another so-called "closed-molding" system, the process is similar, but for those who are not, here's a quick rundown. Unlike normal "open-molding" laminating methods, in which layers of fiberglass cloth are laid in a mold and wetted out before being rolled, boats built with the SCRIMP process are laid up dry. In a typical mold the gelcoat is sprayed on and the outer fiberglass layer, the core, and the inner fiberglass layer are lightly glued in the mold. (The method can be used for both cored and non-cored hulls.) The entire layup is covered with a layer of peel-ply and a special SCRIMP cloth. A vacuum bag is then placed on top of the SCRIMP cloth and the air is sucked out, putting the entire layup in a vacuum. Various hoses lead into the bag, and each hose is clamped until it is needed. The entire layup is still dry at this point.

When it is time to put the resin into the mold, the hoses are simply dropped into a bucket of resin and the clamp on each hose is opened as the resin is infused. The pre-accelerated resin flows through the hose and into the layup. The whole laminating process takes about half an hour, depending upon the size of the boat. The vacuum is held until the laminate is dry, and then the vacuum bag, SCRIMP cloth, and peel-ply are simply pulled off the molded shape. That's it—no voids, no drips, no mess, and no unproductive tool cleanup time. The job is much cleaner than the conventional wet-laminating approach. Using the SCRIMP method, stringers and floors are built into the layup dry and wetted out when the resin is infused. This saves time and eliminates secondary bonding—a major plus for boats with lots of floors and framing. Another plus is the elimination of lightweight fabrics, cloths, and mats. SCRIMP can use very thick fabrics, in some cases up to 120 ounces per square yard, although the more standard fabric is about 60 ounces.

Because the bagging and vacuum pressure is controlled during all phases of the process, the job can be repeated with an accuracy previously obtainable only with pre-pregs and vacuum-bagging. According to the SCRIMP brochure, the Navy has tested the method on laminates up to 6 inches thick and has found that voids cannot be detected using any of the current American Society for Testing and Materials (ASTM) testing methods. (Typically a hand laminate might have 8 to 10 percent voids, while a pre-preg might have 2 percent voids.)

In terms of tensile and compressive strengths, SCRIMP, vacuum-bagged, and autoclaved laminates are compared in the SCRIMP brochure using a 140-degree post-cure. Tensile and compressive strengths are similar for SCRIMP and autoclaved laminates, while strengths for vacuum-bagged laminates are slightly lower.

as windlasses built 40 years ago, but the working machinery has been continually updated.

The bow roller on this boat will be strong, with pins to hold the anchors in place. I once saw a 75-pound anchor leap out of the bow roller with enough force to bend the pulpit 2 feet above it. The anchor was supposed to be tied down, but the continual motion of beating into a seaway had worn through the lashing. Our Voyager's twin anchor rollers carry a Danforth lightweight anchor on one side, and a Simpson-Lawrence CQR or plow anchor on the other. Both rollers are aligned with the chain gypsy on the capstan. Note that the capstan is recessed into its own locker to keep the deck clear. The locker has a drain at the forward end to get rid of water that might get through the hatch seals.

Cockpit

As this boat will be sailing offshore, it has a small cockpit with protection from the elements for the crew. Both seats (berths) in the cockpit are a minimum of 6 feet, 4 inches to allow a crewmember to stretch out. The pilothouse berth runs under the cockpit seat to port, which limits seat hatches on that side. The cockpit drains directly over the transom. Note how the cockpit sole is sloped to drain aft.

Transom

Getting on and off the boat at anchor or in port may require the use of a dinghy. Consequently, the ideal transom should have steps to allow crew to board easily. These steps also facilitate getting a man overboard back on deck.

Stowage for a life raft is in a transom locker. In order to get the life raft into the water quickly, the transom has a lifting step. In theory, it is possible for the crew to cut or untie the life raft lashing, lift the step, and kick the life raft over the transom into the water. Because the life raft is stored in a dedicated locker, it will not need a fiberglass casing.

To the starboard side of the steps, CNG or LPG tanks will be stowed, with drains venting directly over the side. To port is stowage for scuba gear and air tanks. We should also see if a scuba compressor can fit in the locker or in the engine compartment. While we would like to add all these features to the transom, we will have to see if they fit when the design comes together.

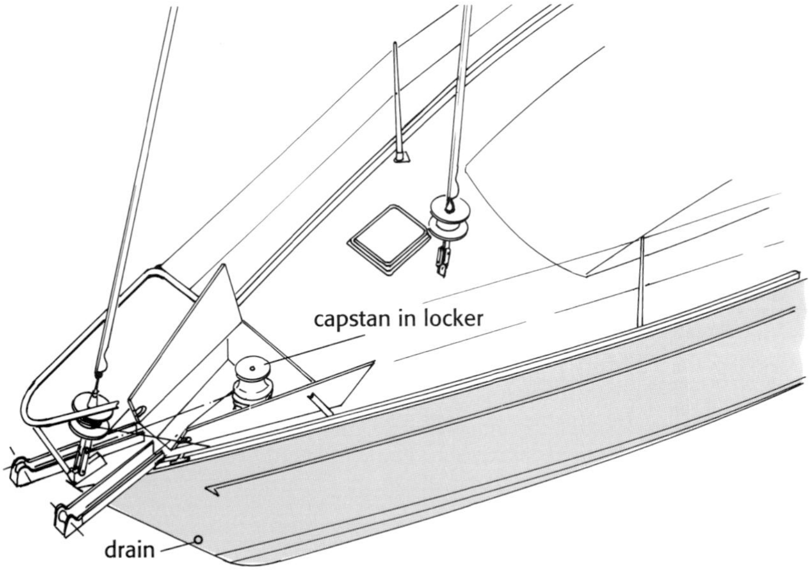

The capstan is installed in its own locker to keep the foredeck clear for sail handling. Bow rollers lead to the locker, which has a large drain hole in the forward end.

Radar arch

The radar arch is an important piece of gear on this boat. In addition to the radar, the arch will support solar cells (to help charge the batteries) and carry all of the vessel's antennas. (We may also include the Edson Company's tilting radar stand, which enables the radar to be used when the boat is heeled.) On the outside of the

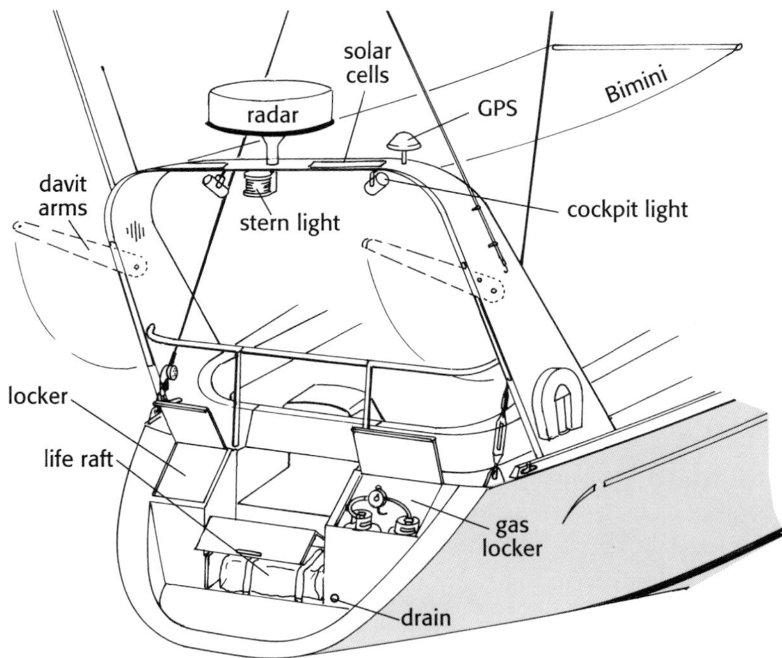

In place of a conventional transom, the Voyager carries a boarding ladder, life raft stowage (under the steps), gas bottle stowage, and even a freshwater shower. After removing the helm seat and the steering wheel in port, the steps can be used as the main boarding location. The radar arch also helps to position gear out of harm's way. SSB, VHF, GPS, and other antennas are located on the arch as well as the radar, solar cells, boarding and cockpit lights, and a high stern light. If desired, a roller-furled Bimini can be fitted on the forward side of the arch to shelter the cockpit in hot weather.

arch is a horseshoe life ring with a strobe, drogue, and dye marker. Inside the upper part of the arch are cockpit lights, lighting for the boarding platform, a hot and cold freshwater shower, stereo speakers, and the stern light. To accommodate the arch, the backstay will need to be split, but this allows a Bimini top to be fitted and led forward to the end of the main boom. At the back of the arch are foldaway davits that can be lowered to carry the dinghy for short trips.

Cabin sole

In this boat the teak and holly-splined cabin sole will not be varnished with high-gloss varnish. Instead it will be lightly oiled or varnished with a semigloss Cape Ann water-based varnish to protect it and provide a firm footing in heavy weather. In the galley we'll use a non-slip polyurethane floor covering made by TBS in France and imported by Wichard, Inc. of Simsbury, Connecticut. This flooring can be cut to form a mat or glued in place to become part of the floor.

Wet locker

Ideally the foulweather gear locker should be located near the companionway. This allows the crew to take off wet gear before they go below. It is surprising how a little water below deck can make life miserable.

A wet locker should be laid out to help wet gear dry. In this layout the locker has posts for boots or gloves at the bottom, and hooks for scarves on the sides. The bottom is a grating that drains to the bilge. A hanger rod lets foulweather gear dry easily on coat hangers, while above it there is a grating shelf for hats and other gear. The last detail is a vent from the engine compartment or a heater to bring hot air into the locker to dry clothes faster. If space permits we will add a locker with these features in the pilothouse.

Bunks

Bunks should be located near the middle of the boat for easy sleeping, but that space is often taken up with a dining area. Consequently, the dining-area settees on this boat are convertible to bunks for long trips. Each settee has a leecloth, as does every bunk.

On this boat the double bunk in the master stateroom to port (partly under the pilothouse) is fitted with a divider down the middle. A wide double bunk is difficult for one person to sleep in at sea. Should the boat tack, the sleeper rolls from one side to the other unless sailbags are put in the bunk or a divider is fitted.

Single bunks on this boat are all larger than the minimum to enhance comfort, but not so wide that the sleeper rolls around in a seaway. If the boat should get into a storm, the crew could use sailbags to fill out the bunks and make them smaller; this prevents the occupant from bouncing around as the boat sails off a wave. A bunk for the navigator is fitted in the pilothouse. If the boat is being sailed by a couple, one person could keep a lookout while the other person sleeps in the pilothouse bunk, ready for an emergency. (We'll take a closer look at the bunks in chapter 4.)

Galley

In the ideal galley there should be enough room for the cook to stand to one side of the stove. That way, if a pot is thrown off the stove, it will hopefully miss the cook. There should also be one or two strongpoints in the galley and overhead so that the cook can wear a harness and clip on in heavy weather. A bar in front of the stove stops anyone from falling into the stove. The stove should be gimbaled and have a gimbal brake as well as being fastened securely in place. The accompanying sketch shows what we hope to achieve, but it will depend on the space available in the galley.

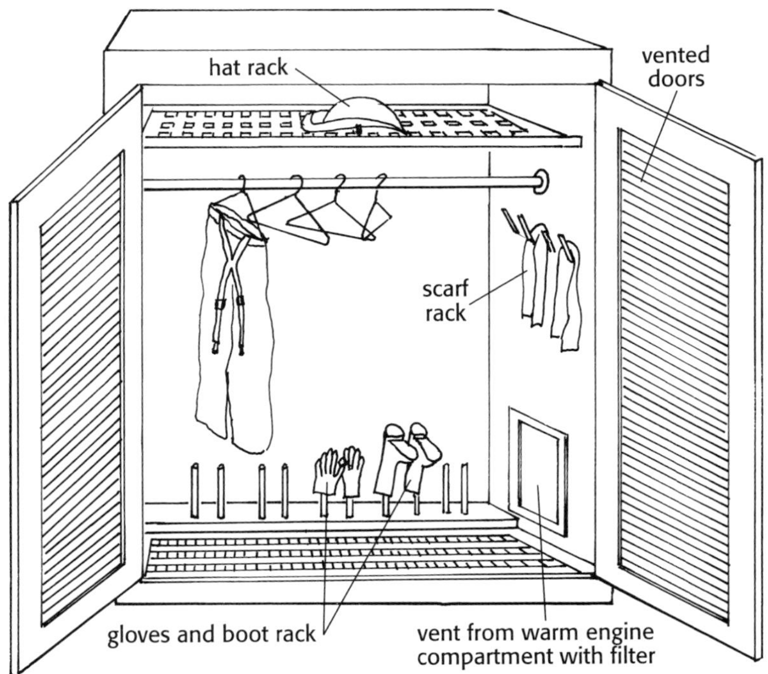

The ideal hanging locker is laid out as shown. A bottom grating lets water drain to the sump; pegs hold boots upside down for easy draining; on the sides are pegs for scarves and hats, while foulweather gear is hung on the rack. A shelf along the top of the locker holds hats or other small gear. The entire compartment can be warmed with engine heat, and louvered doors allow good circulation.

Engine compartment

The 76-hp engine is easily accessible through the pilothouse sole. Fuel and water filters will be located where they can be changed easily, and all plumbing will be fitted on vibration-proof mountings.

Both the engine and generator will be well insulated to minimize noise. On this boat we'll fit a Westerbeke generator, with a noise-dampening box. While it doesn't come directly under the heading of seaworthiness, the generator is used to charge the batteries, which power the autopilot, the nav lights, and the onboard electronics.

Batteries, their boxes, and all other heavy gear should be strongly fastened. In this case, an insulated bar is bolted across the top of the battery bank to

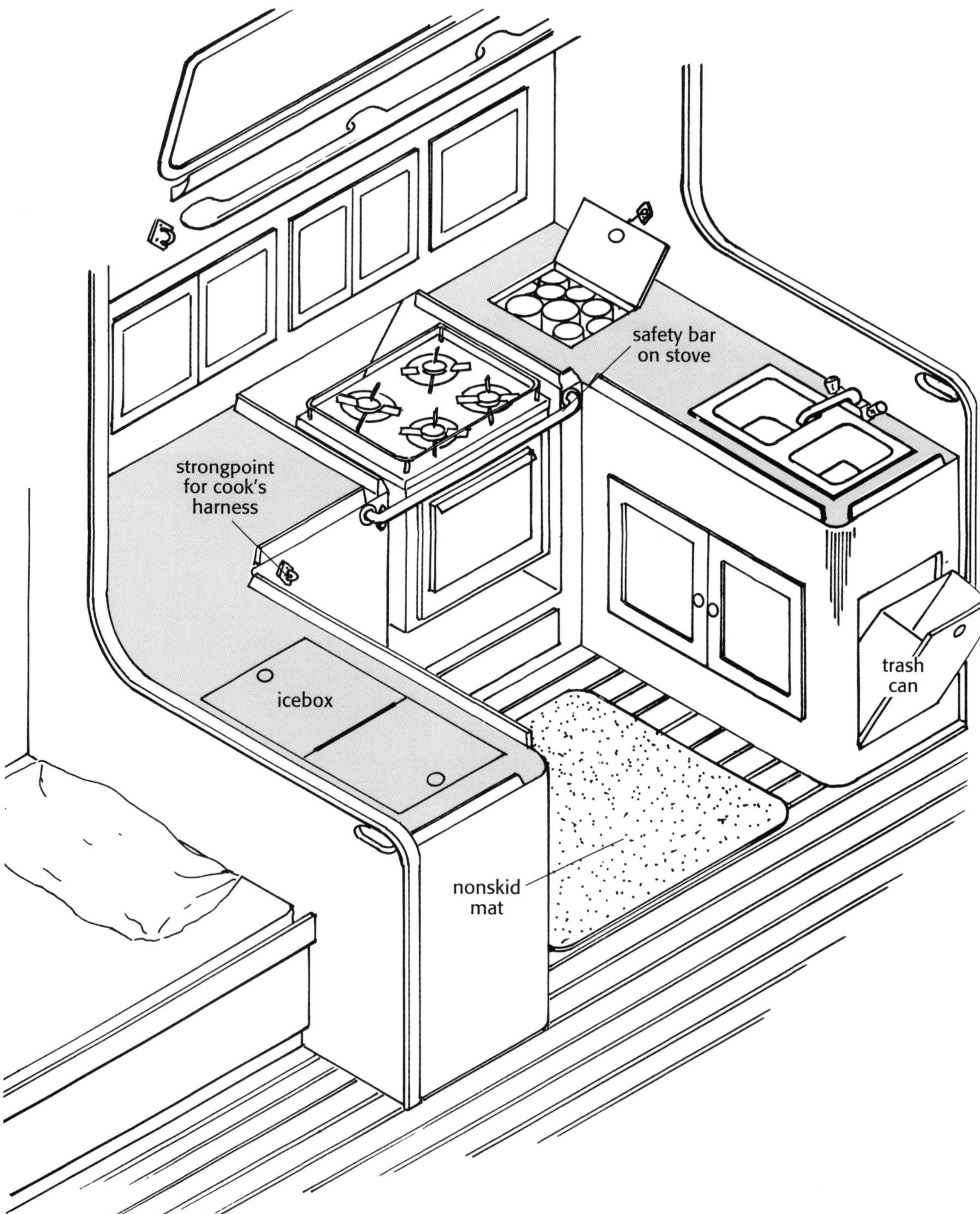

The ideal galley has space for the cook to stand to one side of the stove, a large freezer or icebox, a gimbaled stove with an oven, twin sinks as close to the centerline as possible, and a pull-out trash can. Note the handholds and strongpoints for the cook's harness.

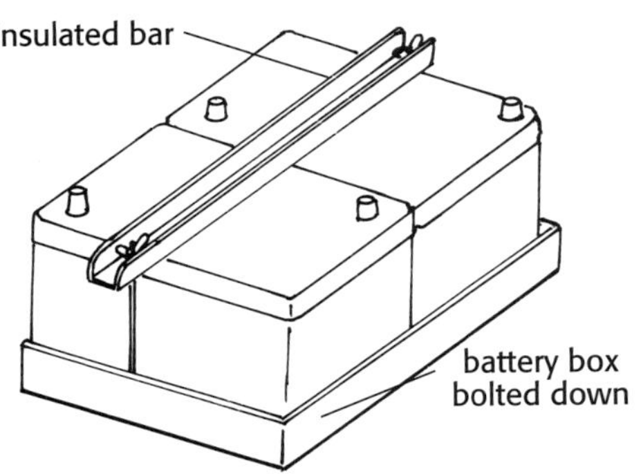

Batteries are strongly bolted to the battery tray, which is in turn bolted to its foundation.

hold the batteries down. The battery tray is bolted to its foundation.

A backup 110-volt alternator is also installed on the main engine. This unit comes from Balmar, which makes several sizes. Solar cells on the radar arch, and possibly on the dodger, also help to keep the batteries charged. This should give the boat ample electrical power.

The Single-Hander

People who sail alone cannot keep watch all the time, so a boat for single-handed sailing cannot be truly seaworthy. However, we can make it as seaworthy as possible and hope that the skipper takes a prudent approach to sailing in shipping lanes and other hazardous areas.

Because the Single-Hander is going to be out in all weather conditions, it needs to be strongly constructed. Should something fail for several days at sea, the skipper cannot stay awake long enough to nurse the boat into port. Typically, a single-handed boat has minimal accommodations and may even be empty, apart from a few light sails forward. This makes it easy to see the hull and identify any problems that might occur. It also means that there are

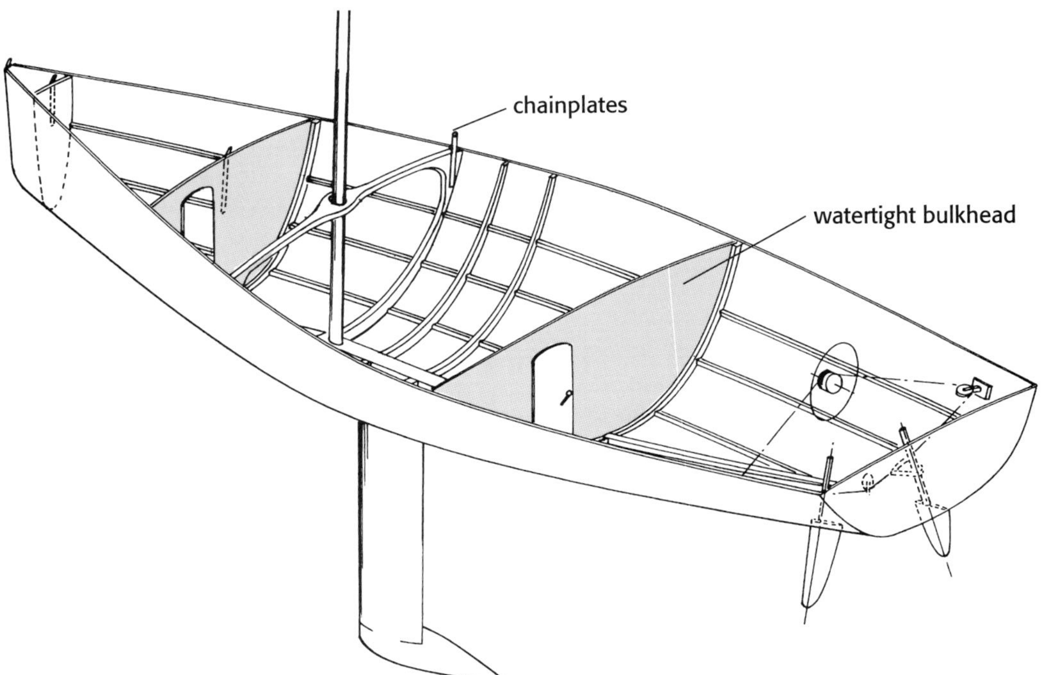

The Single-Hander has two watertight bulkheads at intervals along the hull. This divides the hull into three sections. If one compartment is flooded, the other compartments should be able to keep the boat afloat. Forward, a collision bulkhead goes from waterline to deck. Ring frames are shown where they support the mast and chainplates.

fewer bulkheads inside the hull to provide extra transverse strength and rigidity to the hull structure. The bulkheads fitted are often watertight. Our boat will have an interior, but much of the hull will still be visible. The single-handed race around the world requires that watertight bulkheads be fitted to divide the boat into approximate thirds, the idea being that if one compartment is flooded, the boat can still stay afloat. For safety's sake, we will use the same criterion.

With only one person onboard, the accommodations are usually concentrated around the middle of the boat, both in order to minimize crew fatigue and to reduce pitching to get more speed. Because of the physical demands of single-handed sailing (sailors often stay up 24 hours or longer), everything should be carefully thought out to permit the minimum expenditure of energy.

Construction

In order to make this boat strong but light, it will be made entirely of carbon fiber using the SCRIMP process (see sidebar, "SCRIMP," page 65). Both the deck and the hull will be SCRIMPed to eliminate secondary bonding and provide a rigid monocoque (one-piece) shell. The watertight bulkheads will be located about one-third of the way back from the bow and forward from the stern, with a small watertight collision bulkhead just abaft the bow waterline. The actual location of these bulkheads will be determined from a flooded stability curve developed from the hull lines. When making this calculation, we locate the bulkheads so that the boat will float with any one compartment flooded; this increases the boat's chances of getting home should one compartment be holed.

Hull/keel joint

This joint is going to be extremely tricky to engineer in that the root of the keel is very thin. For this reason we will build a box in the SCRIMPed hull and bolt the keel to the hull horizontally. Not only will this provide a watertight, rigid hull/keel joint but, according to Euler's theorem, it will also help to reduce the bending of the long keel blade with a heavy lead bulb at the bottom.

Cabin

On a single-handed boat the skipper spends a lot of time navigating, watching the sails, and keeping a lookout. The cabin should be designed to accommodate all these tasks. When viewed from the exterior, the cabin on our boat is streamlined and tapered to provide something of an end-plate effect to improve mainsail efficiency when the boat is sailing to windward. It has large curved windows of heavily reinforced plastic, giving good visibility in all directions (the curvature also increases the strength of the window panels), although visibility may be limited when the boat is heeled 25 degrees or so. The cabin is also high, for two reasons: The first is, again, to create the end-plate effect between the boom and the hull. The second is to provide a large, watertight pod, which serves as a pivot point to help the boat return to the upright position in the event of a capsize. At the back of the cabin is a watertight door to keep the elements out, which can be opened by the solo sailor at any time.

The end-plate effect happens when a blocking surface is placed on the end of a wing, sail, or keel to eliminate or reduce air or water flow in a span-wise direction. In other words, an end plate keeps the liquid flowing across the foil rather than down the length of the foil, increasing the foil's efficiency. For example, *Australia II*'s keel had large wings that also served as an end plate for the water flowing across the keel. An end plate also increases the efficiency of the keel, sail or wing by eliminating flow around the bottom. A well-designed end plate can increase efficiency by up to 2 times. By making the cabin-

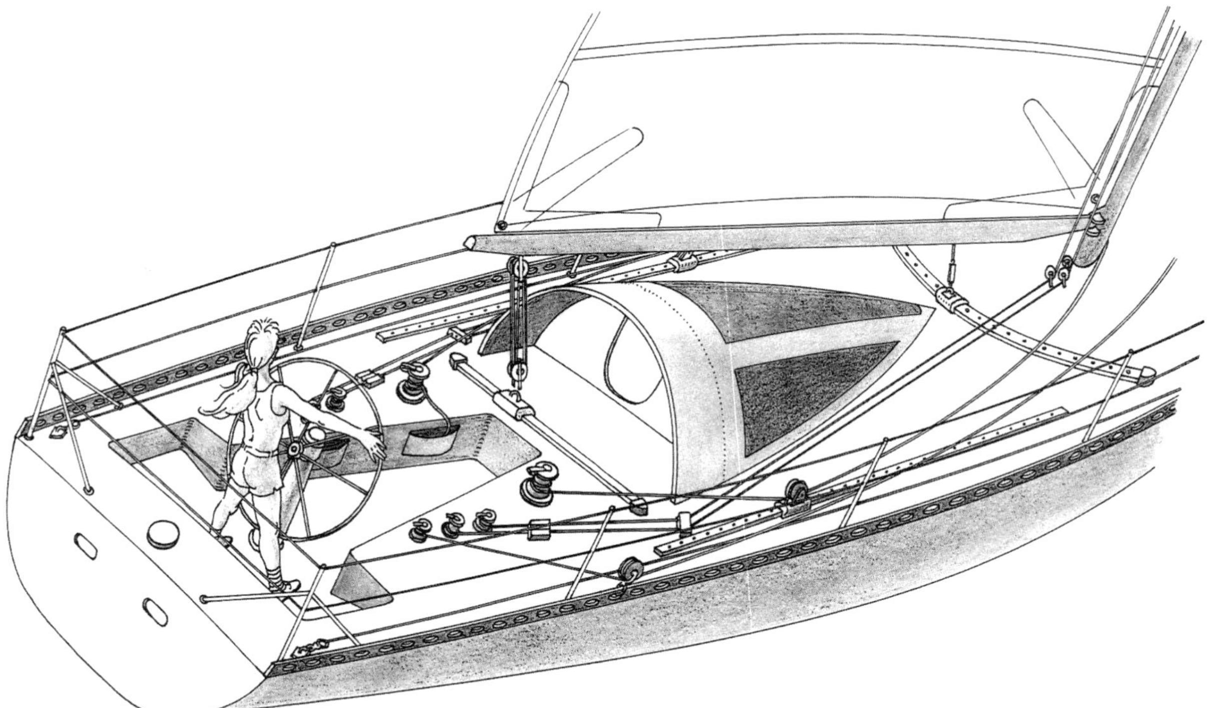

The wedge-shaped cabinhouse is intended to form a seal between the boom and the deck to help increase the end-plate effect and make the mainsail more efficient. A watertight door at the aft end of the cabinhouse helps keep water out of the boat in the event of a capsize. All deck gear leads back to the cockpit.

top the end plate for the sail plan it is hoped that the efficiency of the mainsail will be increased.

Inside the cabin is the navigation station, an inside steering station, the galley, and a large, comfortable chair. Few solo sailors have a lot of time to sleep. Most of their sleep time consists of napping in the navigator's chair. If this chair can be used as a steering seat, so much the better, although most single-handers have an electronic autopilot on board.

Navigation station

The nav area might not seem like a subject for a seaworthiness chapter, but most single-handed sailors spend a lot of time there. Ideally, the nav area should be located as close to the center of the boat as possible. On a single-handed boat, though, keeping a good lookout is also important, so the navigation area will be in the cabin near the inside steering station and the galley. The skipper's bunk can be near the center of the hull, as can stores, the engine, and other heavy items.

Galley

On a single-hander the galley is often very basic. Most single-handers have little time to make a good meal and rely instead on freeze-dried, frozen, or canned foods. This galley has a three-burner stove with an oven, twin sinks, a microwave, and storage for food pouches. (The boat will have a reverse-osmosis watermaker in the engine compartment to make enough water to use freeze-dried foods.) In the middle of the boat is a small freezer/refrigerator and storage for bulk foods, which can be taken up to the cabin galley in smaller quantities.

Because of weight considerations the galley

will be kept low, just forward of the nav area. On some boats designed for single-handing, the entire nav station and galley are mounted on gimbals to adjust for the heel angle. While this is certainly feasible, we will not do so here to keep weight to a minimum.

Cockpit

With only one person aboard, the cockpit does not need to be large. In fact, the smaller the cockpit, the less likely it is to be flooded. It can also be designed to drain through the transom to eliminate through-hulls. Note the jacklines running just outboard of the cockpit well: the solo sailor can clip on before leaving the cockpit and go aft to the wheel without unclipping.

Steering systems

At the aft end of the cockpit, there is a large-diameter steering wheel for entering and leaving harbor and for emergency use. Inside the cabin there is an additional steering system for use in the cruising mode. Both systems are cable-operated, with clutches to enable the helmsman to get some rudder feedback and to remove the drag of one or both wheels while the autopilot is in use. Another method is to run the cables from the below-deck station to a separate quadrant. All these systems not only give redundancy to the system, but allow the solo sailor to decide where to steer from. An emergency tiller can be fitted to the head of either rudderstock for a third level of emergency use.

Furling gear

All headsails on our Single-Hander have roller furling for ease of use, with the furler lines led back to the cockpit. Because roller-furling sails do not hold their shape well in heavy weather,

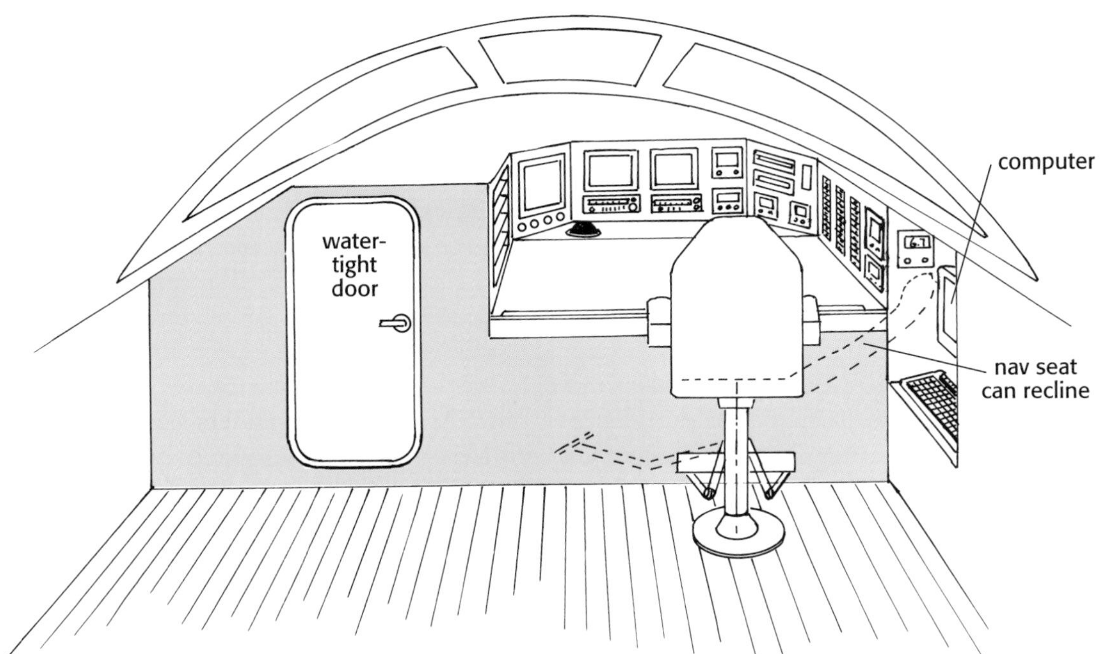

A second watertight door from the pilothouse to the hull helps to ensure the watertight integrity of the hull should the boat be holed. The solo sailor will spend a lot of time in the nav area, so comfort is essential to good seamanship. The navigator's chair can recline to any angle of heel to allow the navigator to take catnaps while fully dressed. Note that screens that need to be read are directly in front of the navigator, while switches and nonessential dials are to one side.

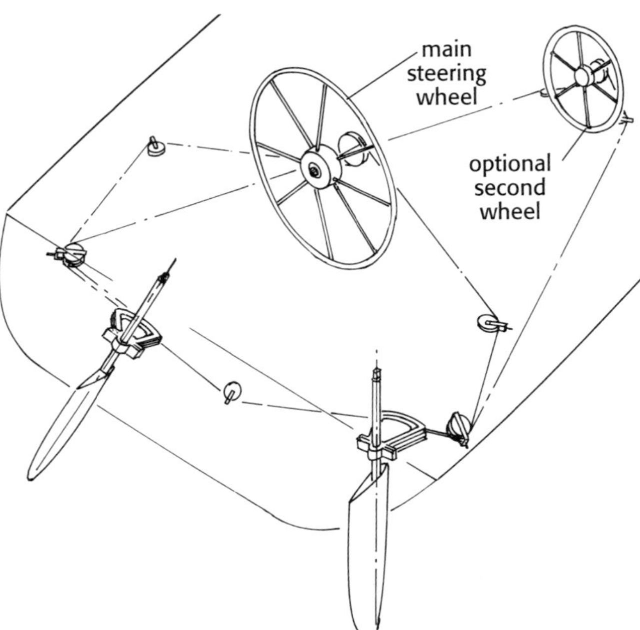

The cable steering is reasonably simple. Two cables lead forward from a double quadrant (or two single quadrants)—one set goes to the aft steering wheel, the other to the below-deck steering station.

there is a second removable stay in front of the staysail furling gear. This stay has a hanked-on storm jib for heavy-weather sailing. When not in use, it rests alongside the mast where it can be tied back and kept under tension.

Spinnaker

As this boat is a racing boat, it will usually carry a spinnaker. Spinnakers are an unseamanlike sail but must be used offwind to get the best from the sloop rig. Setting a spinnaker on a large, heavy pole can be very demanding for one person, keeping him or her on the foredeck a long time; this can lead to fatigue. Running under a spinnaker can also lead to loss of control, which may be very difficult for one crew. For this reason, we will use a multipurpose spinnaker (MPS) or genniker attached to a centerline sprit. By using the boat's polar diagrams, the skipper should be able to optimize the course to avoid going directly downwind and to keep the boat going as fast as possible.

Polar plots or diagrams show the boat's speed at any wind angle. They are developed for true and apparent wind angles. Most of today's racing boats use polar plots developed from the boat's IMS rating and installed on the boat's computer system. Using a polar plot, the navigator can pick off a wind angle to find the boat's best speed for that wind angle.

Mast and rig

In order to minimize windage and increase stability, the boat will have a triple-spreader carbon fiber mast. With this mast precise bend can be developed to optimize the efficiency of the sails for maximal boat speed. The rig is a definite compromise between speed and seaworthiness. A double-spreader rig could easily be fitted and would be slightly more seaworthy but slightly less efficient. Provided it is tended regularly, a triple-spreader rig offers weight and performance gains that other styles do not.

Radar reflector

Any boat that is heeled over may not show up very well on the radar of an approaching vessel because the boat is heeled and the signal will bounce off the hull and spar, and not go back to the transmitter. To ensure that the boat is visible to radar, we will install a Lensref radar reflector near the masthead. This reflector is lighter than our second choice reflector, the Cyclops, and concentrates the incoming signal onto a reflective surface at the back of the reflector. Its Luneberg lenses look like an onion with multiple layers, and each layer bends the incoming signal to the reflective point at the back of the reflector. A 12-inch-diameter reflector weighs 14.4 pounds.

The Cruiser/Racer

Cruiser/racer-style boats are designed to go fast yet still have accommodations for reasonably comfortable cruising. This is, for example, the basic premise behind the IMS (International Measurement System) Rule. But designers, because their future income is predicated upon their boats winning as many races as possible, tend to make a cruiser/racer as race-oriented as possible, and minimize the interior layout.

Boats go fastest when they are kept relatively light, so production cruiser/racers are often made with a hull liner or pan that fits inside the boat. The liner includes molded bunk flats, galley lockers, the shower pan and locker, V-berths, and engine beds. In fact, quite often the engine, icebox, bulkheads, wooden trim, and electrical wiring are all installed on the pan before it is fitted into the hull. While this keeps the boat relatively light and makes it speedy to build, it can be a nightmare for an owner. Unless the builder takes special care, wiring and plumbing may not be accessible, through-hulls may be hidden by the pan, and bulkheads may not fit properly. Not all builders make these errors, but a buyer looking at a production boat with a pan liner should carefully consider access to all parts of the hull.

Deck layout

Typically, on a boat that will be raced, the deck layout is set up for maximum efficiency. That often means a large cockpit, a large steering wheel, a lot of space for crew to trim sails, jibe, or tack the boat, and wide side decks for crew to sit outboard. These factors make the boat sea-

Production cruiser/racers are built on an assembly line. A shows decks with all the deck gear fitted, ready to be installed on hulls. B is an interior pan liner ready to be fitted into a hull. In C the pan has been dropped into the hull and is being glassed in place.

worthy for racing in reasonably sheltered waters, and seaworthy for deep-water racing in reasonable weather. Because the crewmembers are usually fairly experienced, a lack of seaworthiness on the part of the boat can usually be compensated by the crew, although the margin for error can become thin.

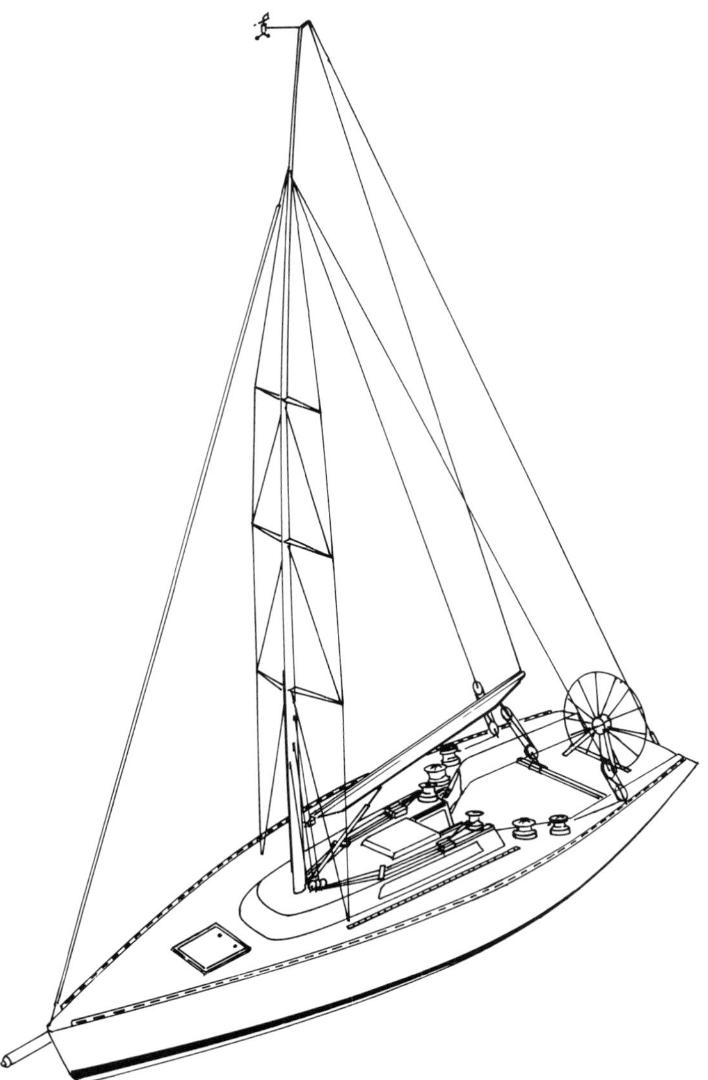

The Cruiser/Racer features a triple-spreader fractional rig, a large wheel aft, a sprit forward, and few winches. All lines are led through line organizers and sheet-stoppers before being taken to winches.

Sail plan

Cruiser/racers may have a masthead rig or a fractional rig (see chapter 6). Both are equally viable, but the fractional rig takes more skill to control; this is because mast bend plays a larger part in the mainsail shape of a fractional-rigged boat than it does on a masthead rig. As a result, the fractional rig is slightly less seaworthy in the hands of an inexperienced crew.

On a cruiser/racer the mast is usually optimized to help the boat stay light and go fast. This means that the mast has a small section and many sets of spreaders. Our boat will have two or three sets of spreaders, depending on the mast inertias required. The mast inertias will be worked up when the mast is designed. Masts of this style tend to fall if they get out of column, so great care must be taken to set the mast up properly. Losing the mast does not a seaworthy boat make.

In all our designs the features used are tried and true rather than new technology. When considering seaworthiness, features that have worked and are known to be seaworthy are better ones to go with than those that seem to be good ideas but have yet to be tried under arduous conditions. Although our designs may seem a little conservative, they should sail long distances without gear or crew failures.

Four

Comfort and Ease of Handling

What is comfort? Sitting in a plush seat with a glass of wine in hand? Lying in a comfortable bunk? Having plenty of headroom? Humans adapt easily to some discomfort. But discomfort on a boat usually leads to fatigue, and that's when mistakes are made. For example, on one trip I made across the English Channel, the navigator's berth was on the windward side of the boat. There was no belt or harness to strap the navigator in, so he had to brace himself against the galley counter in order to work on the navigation table. During the night, he made an error that resulted in our missing the harbor entrance buoy by several miles. Fortunately, we were able to figure out where we were and sailed along the coast to reach our destination. But had we been sailing in thick fog, we may well have put the boat on the bricks.

Comfort means that every part of the boat is ergonomically designed, from minor details to overall placement. All corners on furniture should be rounded and provided with handholds so that people can grab on, or if they miss, they aren't hurt when they fall against a corner. And, of course, furniture should be located in the part of the boat with the best motion. For example, the ideal location for the galley, engine, and navigation area is in the middle of the boat, where there is the least pitching motion. This is also the best place for bunks, so that a sleeper suffers as little movement as possible; however, these often take the form of convertible settee berths, since bunks take up a lot of space and space is at a premium in the middle of the boat.

Comfort also requires giving the hull shape an easy motion through the water. On one boat I sailed, the bow slammed into each wave with a tremendous bang. The slamming sound could be heard throughout the entire boat and kept the off-watch crew awake most of the night. A slightly different hull shape would have eliminated slamming and let the crew sleep.

Heel angle also causes discomfort. A bunk that is perfectly adequate when the boat is upright may be totally unacceptable when the boat is heeled. A typical case in point is a transverse bunk or a double bunk. In a transverse bunk the occupant may have to sleep head-up, until the boat tacks and then sleep head-down. Worst of all are bunks set on a diagonal; these cannot be used when the boat is heeled in any direction.

Comfort, then, is a combination of many things. It requires space to move around in, but space that can be restricted when the boat's motion increases. It means designing a hull shape that will not become too lively as the weather deteriorates. It means standing and sitting positions designed for human dimensions. And it means retaining these features whether the boat is heeled or upright.

Of course, comfort is also related to the size of a boat. A weekender, for example, will not have the comfort level of a larger boat. But as the Weekender will only be used for relatively short periods of time, some discomfort can be accepted. This is not true of a boat intended for single-handed sailing, where a high level of comfort is needed to prevent fatigue and mistakes.

The relative amount of open space a boat has for its size is an important ingredient in comfort. To compare available elbowroom in different boats, I developed a simple Comfort Factor. It divides the boat's displacement in pounds by 64 to get cubic feet. From that number is subtracted the ballast volume, which is found by dividing the weight of lead ballast by 700 (700 pounds of lead per cubic foot). Water ballast is divided by 64 (64 pounds per cubic foot). The resulting volume is then divided by 2, because the boat's furniture and mechanical gear use half the interior. Finally, the halved volume is divided by the number of permanent bunks to get an idea of the volume per person on board. Larger boats offer more volume per person than smaller boats, which immediately suggests dividing by the waterline length to make the result less dependent on length. But sailors aboard smaller boats, such as the Weekender, know they have less space and are unlikely to compare their accommodations with those of a 50-footer. Clearly, the Comfort Factor is best used to compare boats of similar size.

For example, the Comfort Factor for a Valiant 42 is

$$(24{,}500/64 = 382.81 \text{ cubic feet}) - (9{,}500/700 = 9.29) = 373.52/2 = 186.76$$

$$186.76/4 \text{ bunks} = 46.69 \text{ cubic feet/person}$$

If we divided that number by the waterline length, we would get a figure of 46.69/34.5 = 1.353. Using this number we could compare many boats of various sizes, but we would still find the Comfort Factor to be weighted in favor of larger boats.

When thinking more broadly about comfort in a boat, it helps to consider each part of the boat separately. In this chapter we look at comfort as it relates to the hull, the interior accommodations, and the deck, before turning to comfort features included in each of our five boats.

A Comfortable Hull

What factors make for a comfortable hull? A hull that slips through the waves easily and quickly will be comfortable. Generally, that is a very slim hull, as in the style of a 12-Meter. The drawback is that a long, slim hull has accommodations that feel like the interior of a railway car. Increasing the beam increases the available accommodation volume and makes the boat seem more spacious. The beam of a boat is not the only factor that affects a boat's comfort, of course. The shape of the bow, midship sections, and stern affect comfort, too.

Bow

A bow with some convex curvature in its topside panels is less likely to slam than a bow with flat panels. Carrying a rubrail up into the bow of the boat invites noise forward, as water spreading up from the forefoot hits the underside of the rail with a tremendous bang in a serious seaway.

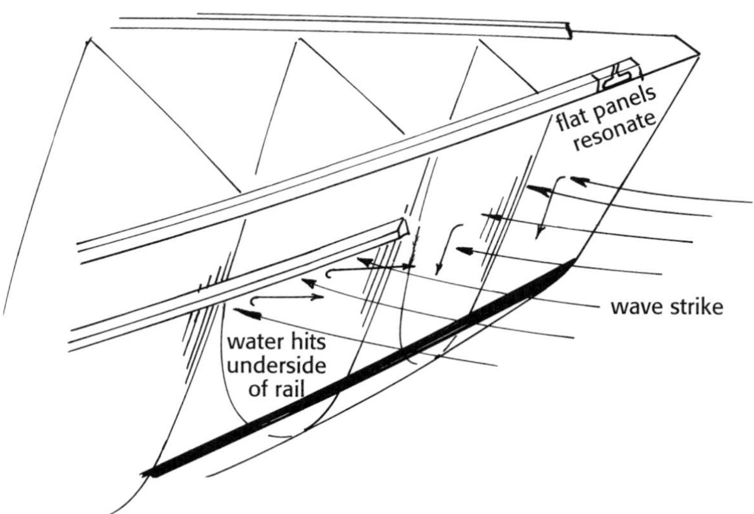

When waves slam against a bow with flat panels, the panels resonate and the banging can be heard throughout the hull. On one boat I sailed, the rubrail became a source of noise when waves struck the underside. The force of the waves caused the area to bang loudly in any kind of a seaway. If the rubrail had ended farther aft, the noise would not have been so pronounced.

Midbody

Reasonably veed midship sections, rather than a flat bottom, also cut down on hull noise and make the hull more seakindly. Veed midship

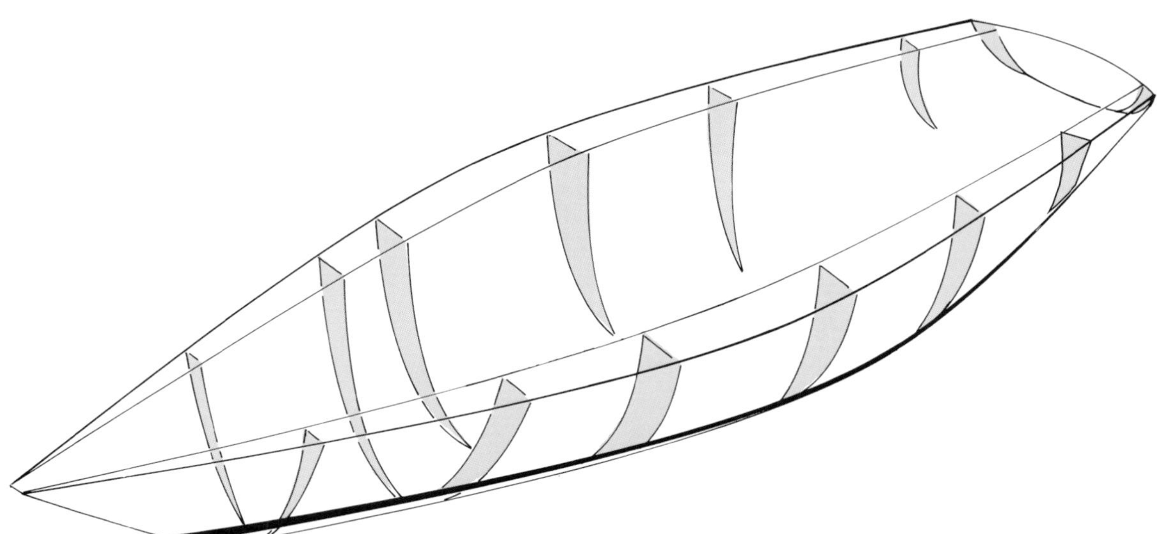

A beamier hull has more interior volume than a narrow one. With a slightly beamier stern, the designer can carry the extra volume through to the end of the boat.

Forty Feet of Comfort in Steel

Steel boats, because of their weight, can be very comfortable. The boat shown here has a steel hull and keel with scrap lead poured into the keel and covered with a welded steel plate. The hull on this boat is mostly flat with a radiused chine along the middle of the hull at about the level of the boottop. It was designed for advanced amateur construction.

Inside, the boat has a large galley and icebox with twin sinks on the centerline over the en-

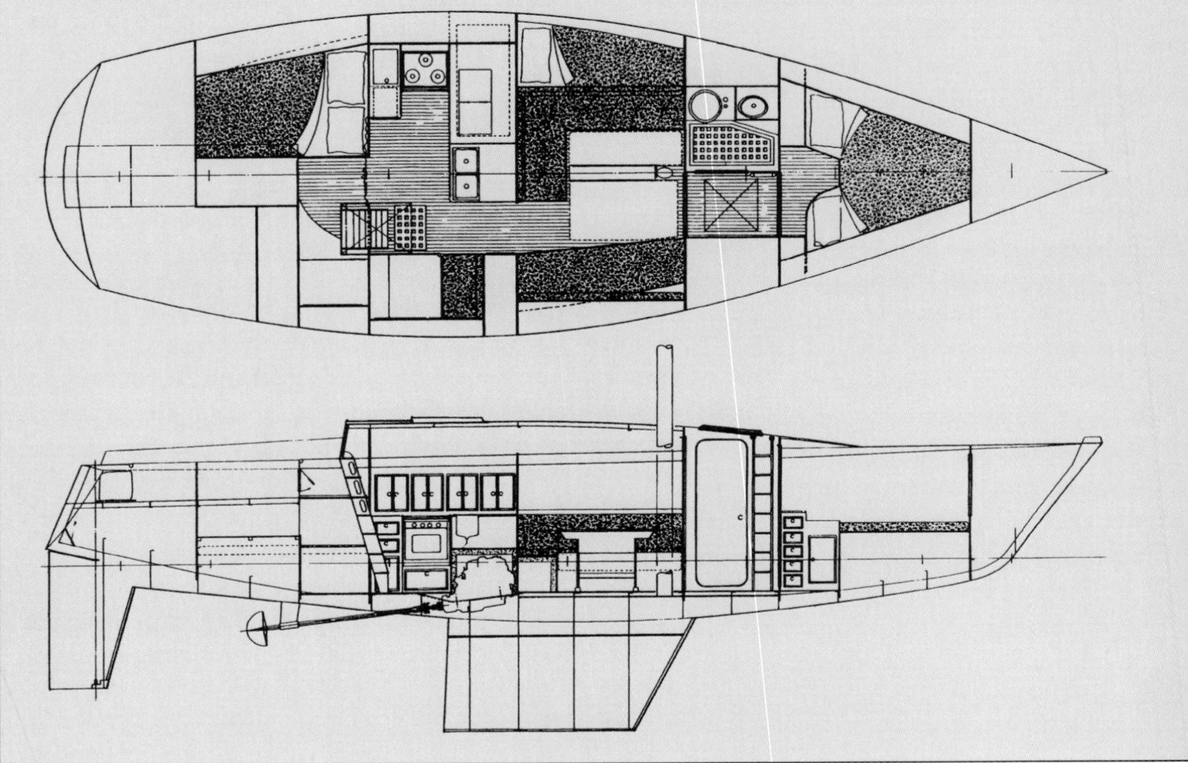

sections, while they are not in current vogue, help keep bilgewater down in the bilge where it belongs, rather than letting it slop all over the interior as happens in flat-bottomed boats. Veed sections also make slamming motions easier when a boat is pounding into a head sea.

Stern

A stern shape that is fairly beamy will dampen pitching, making a sailing trip more enjoyable, but a stern that is too beamy might have steering problems as the boat heels. The buttocks and waterlines around the stern should be shaped so that waves leave the hull cleanly without dragging a large wake. For example, the 12-Meter *Mariner* had a chopped-off stern (known as a destroyer stern in powerboat circles). The crew said that this stern shape dragged a turbulent wake behind the boat, making it quite slow.

Noise

The shape of a boat's hull can have a major effect on hull noise levels, as we've already gine box. With a crew of five, the Comfort Factor is 39.5, making it quite spacious for a boat of only 40 feet overall. If the boat were to be sailed by two crew, the Comfort Factor would rise to almost 100. Because weight is not a major factor on this boat, it would be easy to incorporate a lot of bookshelves, a heating stove, and other amenities to make it into a comfortable medium-distance Cruiser.

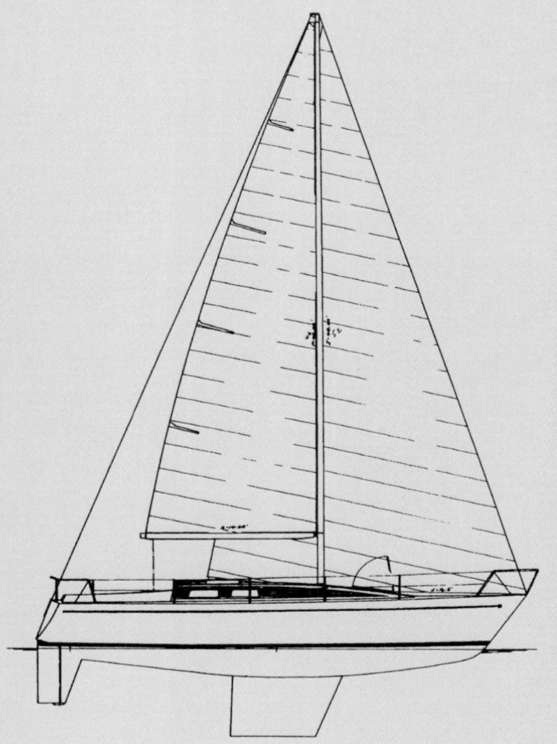

Opposite the galley is a good-sized nav area. If I were to do this boat again, I would push the cabintop a little farther aft and use the space opposite the owner's berth to install a washer/dryer or watermaker. With the nav area farther aft, the interior would feel even larger. I would also put the head to starboard to balance the transverse weights a little more evenly. Notice the offset companionway ladder and hatch, to allow easy access to the owner's cabin.

With its steel construction the boat has a high displacement/length ratio of 271 and a low sail area/displacement ratio of 14.5. (For a full discussion of performance ratios, see chapter 5.) These are typical numbers for a steel-hulled boat, with sail area restricted by the height of the mast. (If the mast were too high, the boat would get a little squirrelly with a tendency toward early broaching.) To increase sail area and performance, a sail handling/anchor platform could be fitted at the bow and a cutter rig installed. With a slightly longer boom to balance the increased headsail drive, this could be a steel-hulled boat with a solid performance.

mentioned. A properly shaped hull will transmit minimal wave noise into the interior. Having furniture and some insulation inside the hull further cuts down on noise. In contrast, an empty hull often resonates like an empty drum.

Another noisy item below deck is the engine. Quite often there is inadequate insulation around the engine, which gives rise to high noise levels. A decibel meter will quickly tell you if noise levels are too high. When the engine is running, check other sources of noise as well. Secondary vibrations are commonly transmitted to the hull and may increase the noise level while being masked by the engine's roar. To eliminate secondary vibrations you may have to put the engine on flexible mounts, install flexible lines between the engine and the hull, fasten piping and exhaust lines down firmly, and then gradually eliminate other rattles. There are companies, such as Soundown, Inc., in Boston, Massachusetts, that specialize in noise reduction.

Freeboard and headroom

Freeboard and headroom are two other hull factors that contribute to comfort. A boat with low freeboard and low headroom is uncomfortable unless you are sitting down. In the main cabin standing area, the headroom should be at least 6 feet, while sitting headroom should be at least 3 feet above the seat. Too little headroom makes a boat feel cramped and uncomfortable.

On boats under 28 feet, getting enough freeboard is difficult, especially with light displacement. In contrast, on boats over 30 feet LOA there is no excuse for inadequate headroom unless the boat is intended for racing. Larger boats have little problem with headroom, and 6 feet, 4 inches of headroom makes the interior light and airy. Be wary of having more than 6 feet, 6 inches of headroom, though, or handholds will be hard to reach for shorter people.

Accommodations

Making the interior comfortable is a job that has teased designers for hundreds of years. In eighteenth-century men-of-war, the remainder of the ship not used for stores or guns was a communal living area. Considering that ships like HMS *Victory* housed around 600 men in a ship that was less than 200 feet overall, space was at a premium, and each man was given only 18 inches of space to sling his hammock in.

Even today, space on a boat is at a premium, and designers and boatbuilders struggle to decide what amenities to give their clients. Different people want different things inside their boats. Some want a large galley, others a large navigation area. Some want eight bunks, while others are content with two. Designing the perfect interior is a challenging task and requires a thorough knowledge of the buyer's requirements, the buyer's sailing style, ergonomics, a boat's behavior in a seaway, as well as materials and fabrics and how they hold up on the water.

Comfort in the Dining Area

Sailors seem to spend a lot of time sitting around the dining table during and after a meal, so the dining area needs to be comfortable. Seats should be 16 to 18 inches from the cabin sole, and they need to be 16 to 18 inches deep. More comfortable seats have a seatback that slopes from 2 to 4 inches depending upon its height. (A minimum of 2 inches per foot is recommended, with more comfortable seats having lumbar support and a slope of about 4 inches per foot.) There should also be at least 3 feet of headroom above the seat (a minimum of 42 inches is better), and about 20 to 24 inches of width per person (30 inches is better).

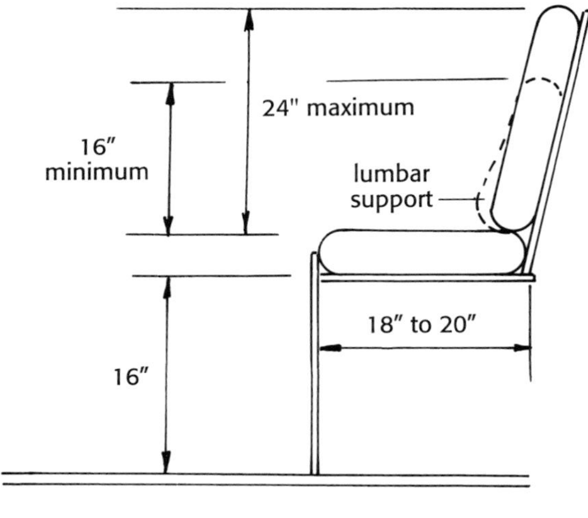

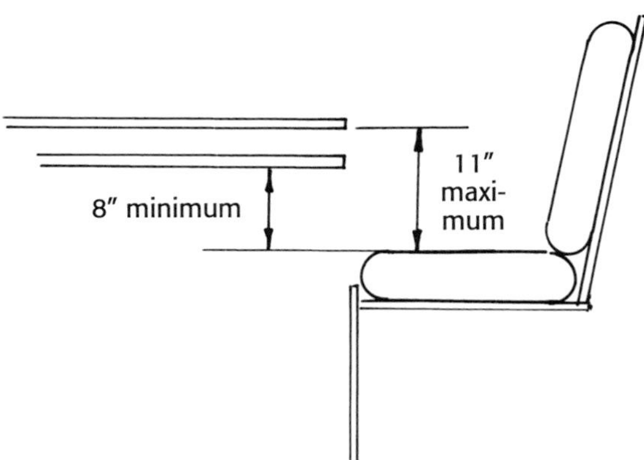

Seat dimensions need to be adjusted carefully to ensure comfort. The tabletop should not be less than 8 inches above the seat.

The dining table should also have about 20 to 24 inches of width per person, and should be located about 8 to 11 inches above the top of the seat. Its distance above the seat will vary according to the height of the seat. There should also be about 10 to 18 inches of space at either end of the table to allow crew to move around if they need to. (See page 89.)

The location of the dining area is also critical. If the dining area were in the forward part of the boat, it would be very difficult to eat there in a seaway because the greatest pitching moment is forward. Since the middle of the boat has the smoothest motion, as well as the greatest width, dining areas are generally placed there.

Comfort in the Navigation Area

The navigator's comfort is important. If the navigator gets tired, he could lose concentration and make mistakes. Navigators also have to control and operate many electronic devices aboard today's boats, so comfort, both upright and when heeled, is critical. Machines with dials, wind speed and direction and boat speed indicators, a compass, the loran or GPS receiver, and a computer or calculator, all need to be located so as to avoid glare or reflections which could make them hard to read. Machines that need to operated, such as computers or calculators, need to be close to hand and at the right height. There should also be room for a chart and navigation tools. Getting all this gear in a space where they can be properly and comfortably used is quite a feat.

Typically, the radar, chart plotter, wind instruments, loran, and GPS should be in front of the navigator. Switches and controls should be offset to the right (for right-handed people). A calculator can also be set off to the right. The compass should be in the middle of the panel in front of the navigator. The chart table itself should be large enough to accommodate a folded chart. Navigation tools can be stored on the left side of the front panel, as can items such as a handheld compass or GPS.

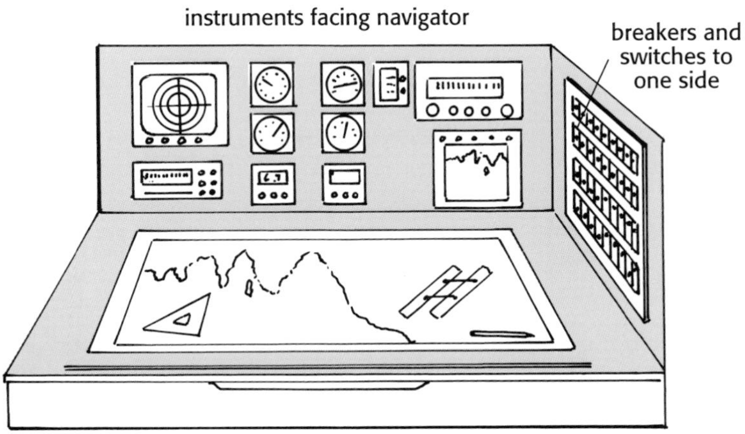

A comfortable nav station puts frequently viewed instruments directly in front of the navigator. Switches and nonessential instruments can be mounted to one side.

Comfortable bunks

The location of the bunks in a boat is critical to the comfort of the crew. V-berths in the forepeak are virtually uninhabitable in a seaway. The bow of the boat pitches as it plows into a sea, so a berth forward of the mast is subject to a lot of bouncing up and down. The noise of the bow slamming into the seas only makes it harder to sleep. At sea the most comfortable bunks (and the easiest to get out of in an emergency) are those in the middle of the boat where the pitching motion is least. If possible, I prefer to use these bunks when at sea.

Generally, however, bunks in the middle of the boat are converted settee berths, which can have their own disadvantages. For example, if one watch is eating while the other watch is trying to sleep, one of the watches has to leave the dining area. When the boat is in port, settee berths are one of the least desirable bunks on a boat, because diners occupy them, often until late, and people moving through the cabin disturb sleepers. Finally, it is often necessary to move bags and cushions to gain access to a settee berth.

Quarter berths, often located on either side of the cockpit, are the next most comfortable, but they too can have drawbacks. For example, most quarter berths are wide at the shoulders and narrow at the feet because they follow the contour of the hull. However, when the boat heels the bunk is tipped downwards, forcing the occupant to sleep head-down. I have seen many sailors sleep in a quarter berth with their head at the foot end, but often this end has poor air circulation and the sleeper wakes up with a headache. To keep a sleeper horizontal when the boat heels, furniture should be positioned outboard of the bunk. As they are removed from the traffic centers of the boat, quarter berths can be very comfortable in port, when the boat is stationary.

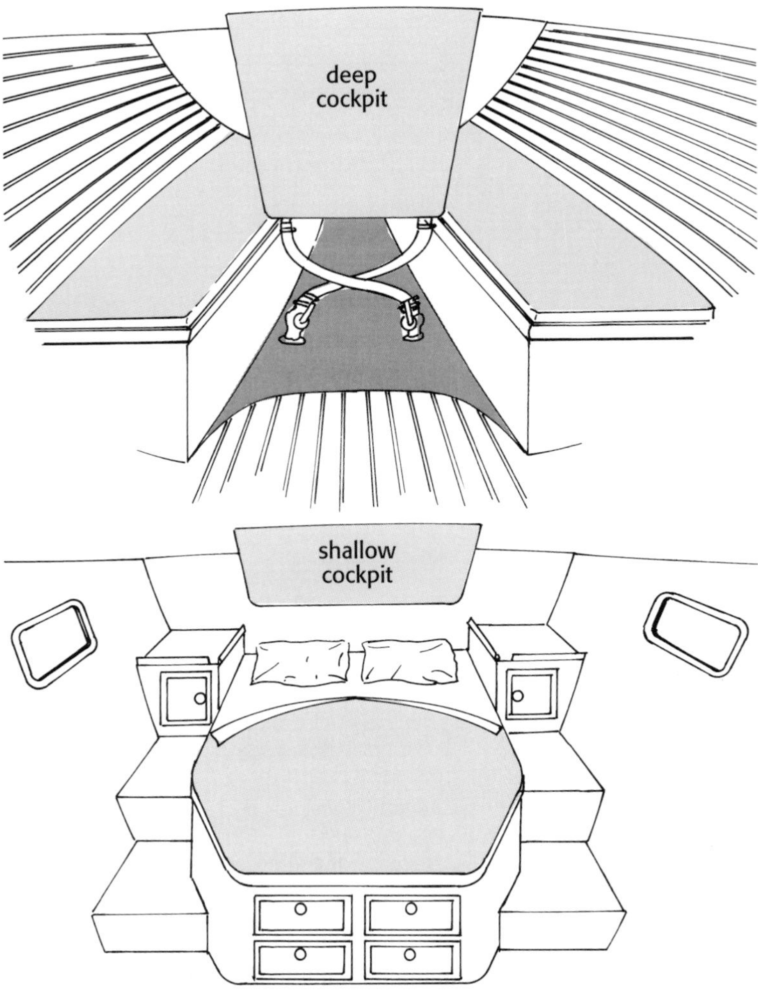

The old-style aft cabin (top) was dominated by the bottom of the cockpit and the cockpit drains. Newer cockpits are shallower and drain over the transom, allowing a larger double berth and a luxurious feel in the aft cabin (bottom).

The proximity of the underside of the cockpit can make the quarter berth area seem cramped and uncomfortable. Many designers get around this by making the cockpit quite shallow, at the same time improving the seaworthiness of the boat. There is a trend in the latest cruising boats to move the cockpit farther aft and the aft cabin slightly forward to make the aft cabin more habitable. This has led to many boats with a double berth partly under the cockpit.

Double berths are great for harbor use when the boat is upright. In this situation it doesn't matter if the berth is fore-and-aft or transverse. Because of the height of the berth, steering gear can be easily hidden under it. But at sea it is a different matter. Double berths can be slept in, but only as long as the boat is not tacking to windward. If a double berth is to be used at sea, it should have a leecloth divider down the middle to make it into twin single berths.

Double bunks should be a

minimum of 54 inches wide, but even that is too narrow when the occupants move around a lot during their sleep. If you are trying out a boat and want to feel how wide the double berth is, try putting a blanket the same width as the bunk on your bed at home and sleeping under it with your spouse or partner. You may be surprised at how cozy you become.

Despite their disadvantages at sea, V-berths do have some merit elsewhere. In harbor they offer plenty of space and sleeping options. They can be used as a double or two singles for both adults and children. For children, the forepeak area with a V-berth is ideal, because the children can go to bed early and leave parents and guests undisturbed in the dining area.

Galley Comfort and Safety

Like your kitchen at home, the galley is probably the most dangerous part of the boat. A lot of danger can be eliminated or reduced with good design, however.

To make the galley comfortable, we need to make sure it is ergonomically designed with plenty of handholds, rounded corners, a nonslip sole, and *all* the cook's tools stowed securely.

Small features make a galley more comfortable. Plates should be stowed where they cannot move around. The usual method is to use three or four vertical rods to hold the plates in place. Often cups are stowed on hooks, but in any seaway they rattle and bang together. It is better to stow them between three rods set vertically.

Galleys can be laid out in several styles. The most common are the U shape, the L shape, and the straight galley. In larger boats, other shapes are used. No matter what the shape, however, the basic work flow is the same: The food is taken out of a locker or refrigerator and placed on a countertop work area, where it is prepared, then taken to the stove (or arranged on a serving plate in the case of salads). Even meals prepared ahead of time will be taken from a locker or the icebox to the stove or serving plate. The food-filled serving plate is delivered to the table, and after the meal it is returned to the galley to be cleaned and stored. Cutlery and crockery must be delivered to the table, along with beverages and glasses. Thus the flow of utensils and food toward the table is a primary consideration for an efficient galley layout.

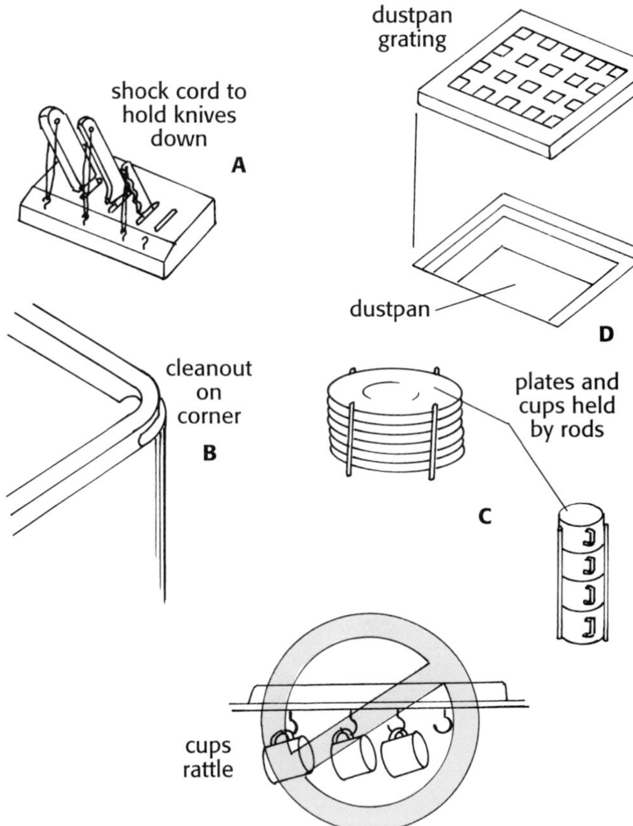

Galley gear can be dangerous in the event of a knockdown. If you have a knife rack, make sure the knives cannot fall out by threading shock cord through each of the handles and hooking it on the bottom of the rack (A). The corners of cabinets should have handholds and spaces for crumbs to be swept off the counter (B). Plates and cups should be held securely in doweled racks (C). Cups should not hang on hooks, as they will bang and clatter as the boat pitches. A lift-out pan in a grating in the cabin sole makes it easy to sweep up crumbs and other galley debris on the sole. When the pan is full, it is lifted out and the contents disposed of (D).

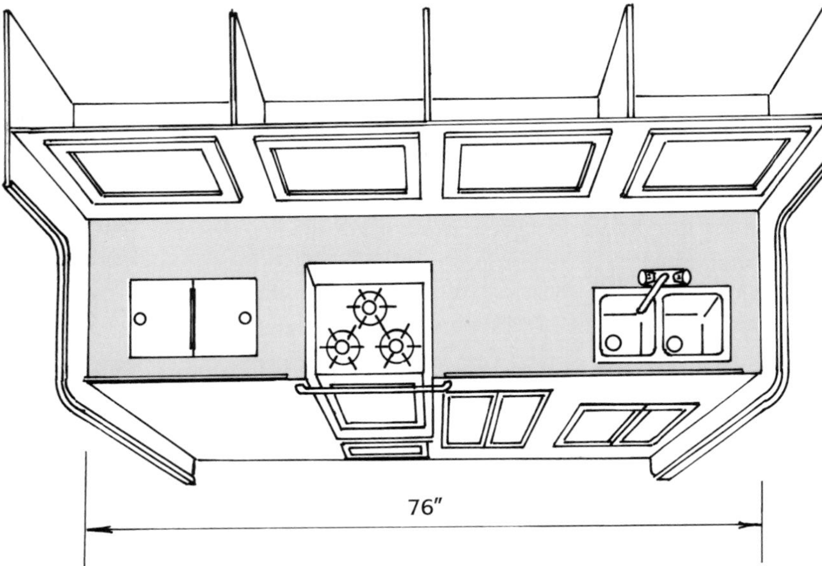

A straight galley seen from above. Note how food can be removed from the icebox, cooked, assembled on the worktop, and taken to the table on serving dishes. From the table the dishes return to the counter and go into the sink, where they are washed up and put back in their lockers at the back of the galley.

Galley stove

There should be a safety bar in front of the stove in case a person falls against it. The stove should have clamps to hold pots in place, and it should be strongly fastened on its gimbals. It should also have some form of locking mechanism for use in harbor and a clamp to slow down the gimbal action. Suppose you want to take a roast out of the oven while on a cruise. Typically, you open the oven door and the stove tips forward, making the roast slide forward. I once watched a cook catch a roast barehanded as it was headed for the floor. A clamp on the stove gimbal will enable the cook to slow the swinging down long enough to take food from the oven.

If the stove is fueled with LPG or CNG gas, it should have a turn-off valve at the stove and another at the tank. The boat should also have a gas-detecting device fitted to find any gas leaks before the stove is lit.

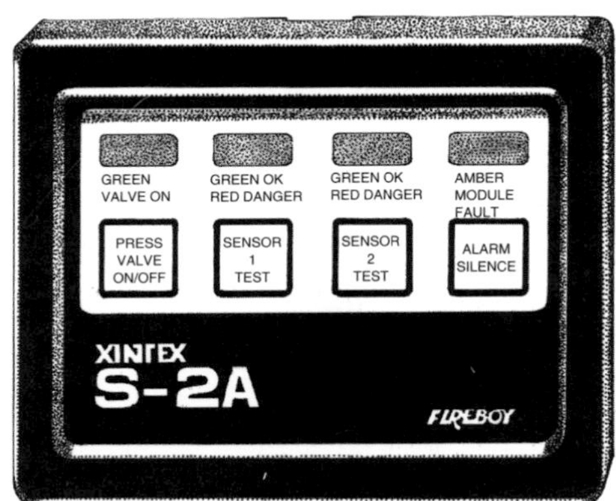

The Xintex propane sensor. A sensor such as this one should be aboard every boat with a propane stove.

Features found in every galley include a stove and possibly a microwave, either one or two sinks, an icebox, a refrigerator or freezer, storage for pots and pans, lockers for cutlery, crockery, and glassware, and a bin for waste disposal. Some galleys may even have a second bin for recycled items.

Cook's harness

A strongpoint and sling should be located to one side of the stove. This will ensure that the cook is out of the line of any pots that might topple off the stove in heavy weather.

Gear stowage in the galley

Knives should be stowed in their own slots in a drawer or fastened down in a knife rack. Heavy pots and pans are stowed low to keep weight down and prevent them from becoming eye-level projectiles. Pots are usually stored in the locker under the sink or stove. If you want pots to be secure in bad weather, you should probably make racks or put shock cord loops through the handles to stop them from flying out of their lockers.

Refrigerator/icebox

Top-opening refrigerators are the most common in boats because they lose little cold and none of their contents when opened, and are easier to build. A side-opening unit can be just as efficient, but its contents can fall out if the door is opened when the boat is heeled. Unfortunately, items in a top-opening refrigerator tend to pile up on top of each other. To make it easier to find things, wire frame baskets should be used to organize foods.

The refrigerator/icebox should have at least 3 inches of insulation around it to keep the contents cool. In my design office we normally specify 4 inches of insulating foam where the refrigerator/icebox is against the exterior hull. For a freezer we specify an extra inch of insulation all around the unit. Extra insulation is especially beneficial in the lid, which should fit tightly to prevent loss of cool air. Make the lid lockable to keep it from flying off in a knockdown.

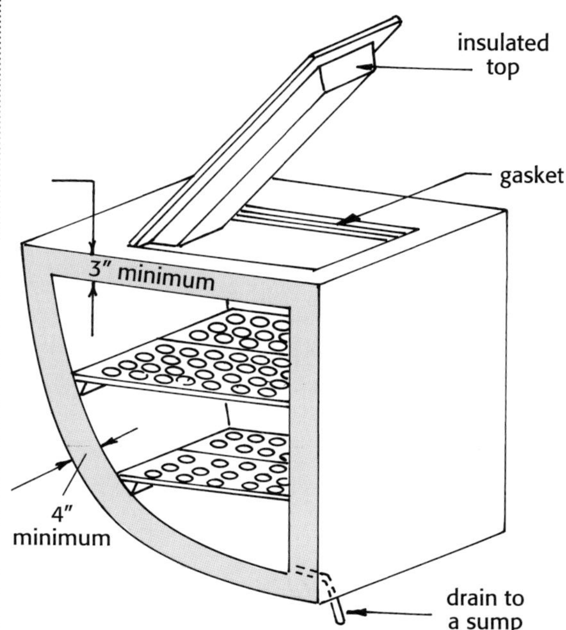

A top-opening icebox or freezer needs plenty of insulation—at least 3 inches on inboard surfaces and 4 inches against the hull for iceboxes, with an additional inch for freezers. Shelves are in two or three parts, to make it easy to reach the bottom. The icebox drains to a sump tank; do not drain your box into the bilge, as it can make the bilge smell.

Galley lockers

The galley should have plenty of locker space for stowing pots and pans, plates and mugs, cutlery, and all the equipment used in preparing a meal. Generally, lockers are located outboard of the stove or icebox and in any other available space.

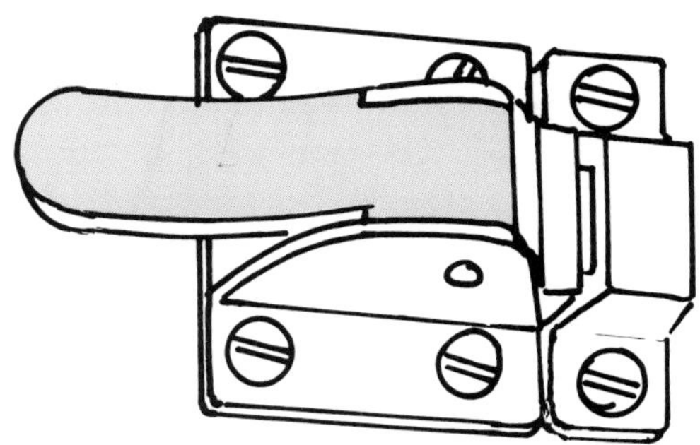

Use a finger catch on locker doors.

Each locker should have a strongly fastened door. Doors with magnetic catches can fly open if a can or other heavy item rolls against them as the boat tacks. Catches with carbon steel springs may eventually rust, making the catch useless. The best door locks are finger pulls with stainless steel springs.

Sinks

Ideally, deep twin sinks are best for a boat. With twin sinks dishes can be placed in one and washed in the other. If there is a draining rack fitted, washing up becomes easy. Sinks should be placed near the centerline of the boat so that they will not backfill as the boat heels, forcing you to close the seacock every time you set sail. If you are worried about someone filling the

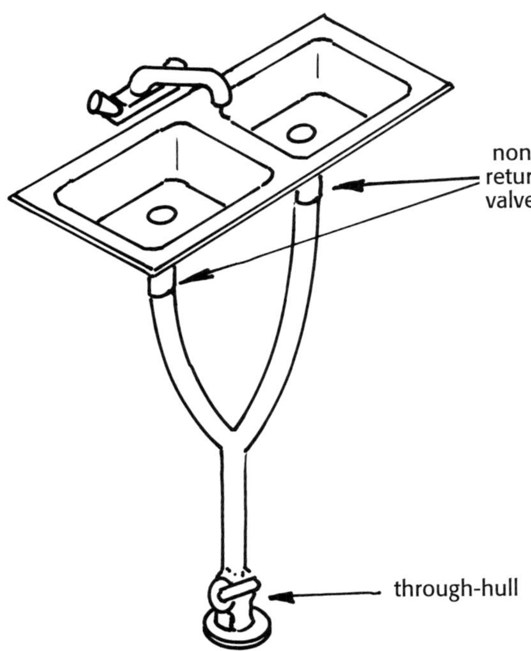

Deep twin sinks are best for most cruising boats. The sink drains should go to a through-hull or sump tank. If there is any possibility of backfilling, the sinks should be fitted with a non-return valve.

sink without opening the drain or leaving the drain open while you are underway, a one-way valve can be fitted that allows the sink to drain but prevents backfilling.

110-volt system

If the galley has enough space, it can be wired for 110-volt (220-volt in the U.K.) sockets. These enable home appliances such as microwaves, blenders, toasters, and can openers to be used onboard, making cooking much easier. Of course, you will also need a generator, a shore supply, and/or an inverter. If an inverter is used, however, you will have to watch battery drain carefully.

Freezer

As the chief cook, I find that a freezer makes meal preparation much easier. I can make up soups and stews at home, freeze them in square 1-quart Tupperware-style containers, and take them aboard the boat. The food is given a quick thawing in the microwave, a slice of French bread is added, and lunch is ready. You can also take frozen goods from the supermarket aboard and keep them ready for almost instant use.

Because freezers are not used continuously in the galley, they can be tucked away anywhere on the boat there is a large enough space. For example, on one boat the freezer was in the lazarette, while on another it was under the settee berth.

Overhead storage

Quite often little thought is given to storing gear up high, but with a little ingenuity it can be done. On one French boat I sailed, sausages hung from the overhead handrails and melons hung in onion bags from hooks in the galley. A spice rack was fitted on the aft bulkhead, and a mesh net held baguettes and fruit. If you lack storage in your galley, consider adding nets or fitting overhead racks.

Making a Layout Modular

When designing an interior layout, the dining area, the galley, the bunks, and the navigation area can be thought of as a series of modular units. Each unit takes up a certain minimum amount of space, and the locations can be juggled to get the best accommodations. Bunks, for example, should always be a minimum of 6 feet, 4 inches long, which gives us a minimum size for each module.

A dining area can be built around the modular concept, too. Consider a 33- to 38-foot cruiser, not unlike the 34-footer we're developing in this book. If each person requires a minimum of 20 by 10 inches of space at the table, and the children 16 inches, there should be 112 inches of usable table perimeter to accommodate six people. A 40-inch-long table that is at least 36 inches wide will be adequate for group dining. Because space is limited inside most boats, the table should be made to do double duty. It can be a dropleaf table that is only 8 to 12 inches wide when both leaves are collapsed, or it can have a fixed tabletop that drops to form part of the double berth. The fixed tabletop will take up substantial space, but the space can be reduced by making one side fold down.

By making the table 40 inches long and the settee bunk 76 inches long (6 feet, 4 inches), we make room for a seat at either end. (Seats are generally 16 to 18 inches front to back, thus 40 + 16 + 16 = 72 inches.) But that does not leave any room for people to get in around the table, so the smart decision is to put a seat at one end of the table (with a drop-in seat across the doorway), and use the other end for access. The drop-in seat can be used for a second child.

The typical seating depth of a settee is about 17 or 18 inches, but a bunk should not be less than 24 inches at the shoulder. This poses a quandary for the designer who must make a settee serve both seating and sleeping functions. One solution is to give the berth a transom; in

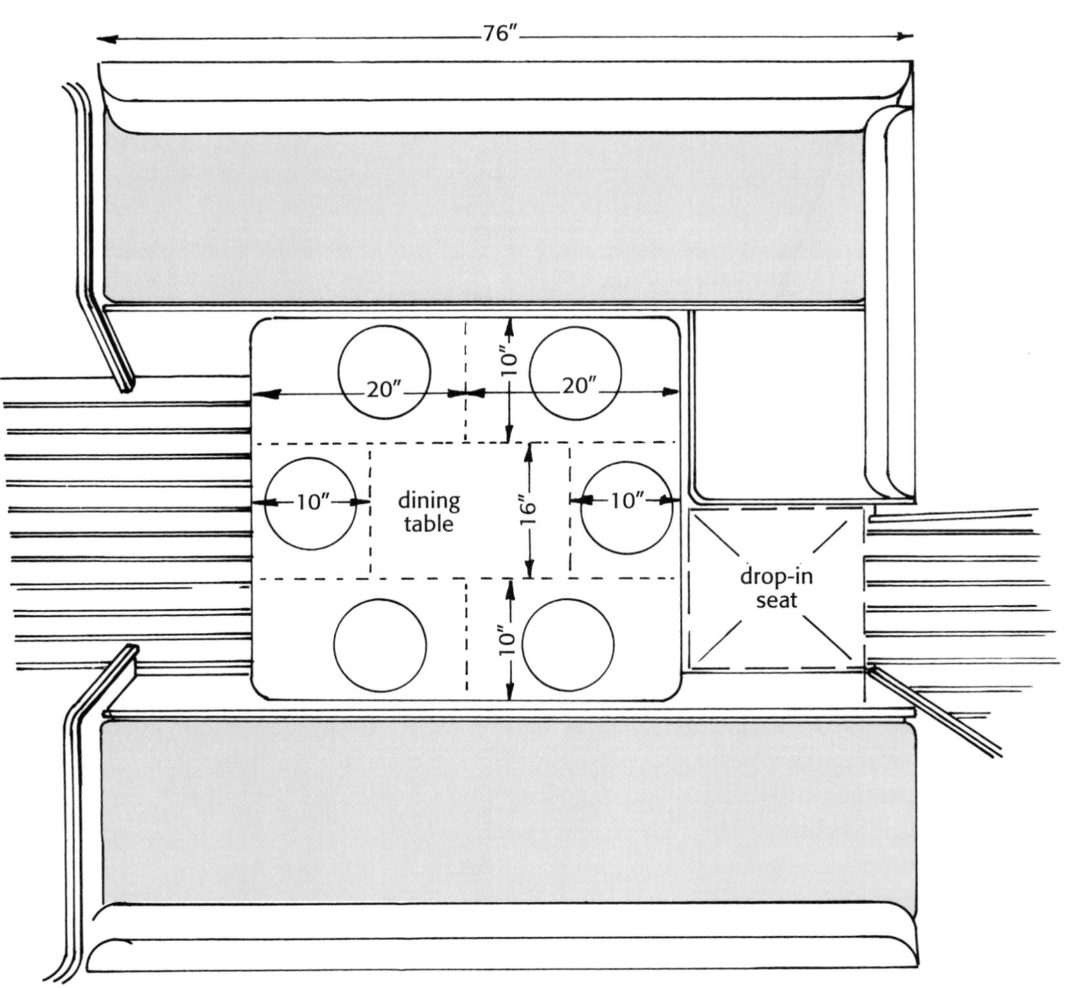

Because a fixed tabletop takes up substantial space, most builders use a dropleaf table. This view shows how much space is required to fit six people around a dining table. The seat in the passageway drops in to give additional space. The overall length of this module is 76 to 78 inches.

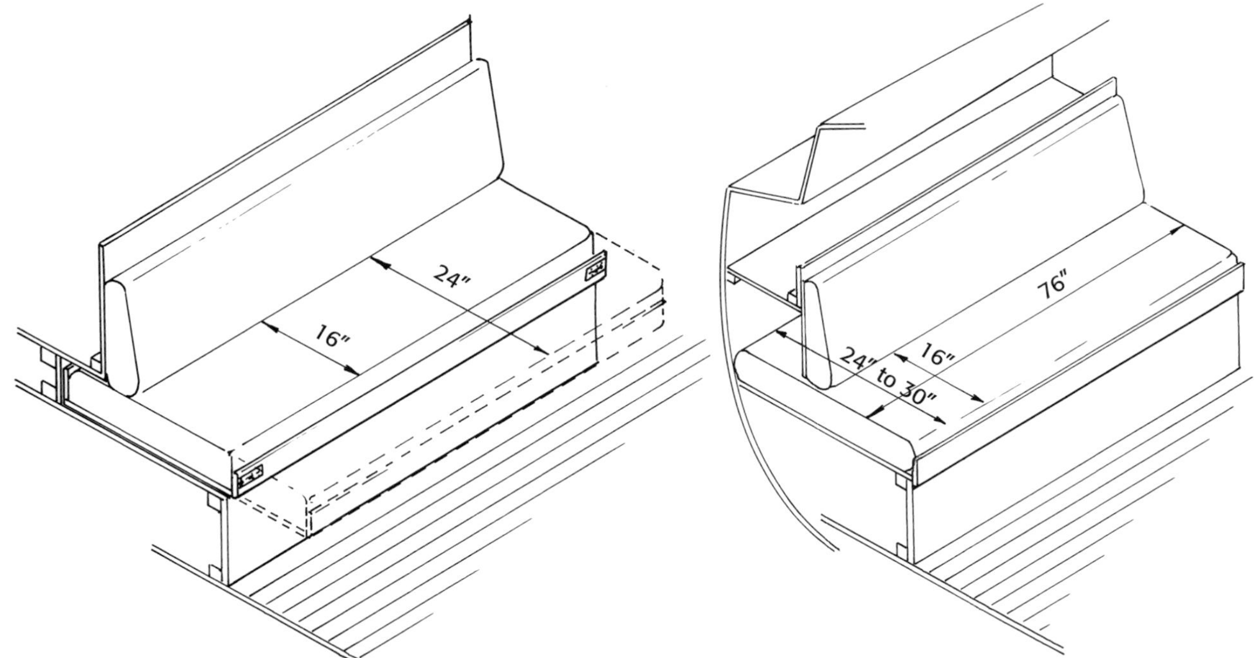

Seats are most comfortable when they are between 16 and 18 inches deep, but a bunk must be a minimum of 24 inches wide to be comfortable. To accommodate the difference, a slide-out transom can be used, as shown here. The cushion and its support are pulled out from under the seatback and held in place by barrel bolts.

Another method of expanding a settee berth is to make the seatback removable and utilize the space behind it.

a settee transom berth, the cushion and bunk flat slide out for sleeping and are held in place by a barrel bolt at each end. The alternative is a fixed settee with a hidden recess behind the seatback cushions (this space can often be used to stow bedding and pillows); removing the seatback reveals the full width of the bunk flat. If space were cramped behind the seatback, removable extra-wide cushions could be fitted and the space eliminated. When the table is designed to drop down into a double berth using an adjustable table sup-

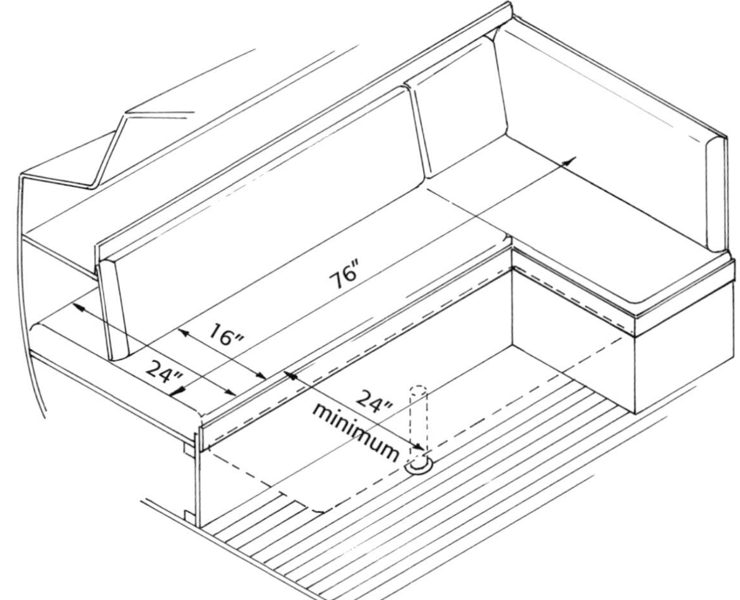

A dining table can be converted to a double bunk by lowering the tabletop. The seatbacks are used as the mattress.

port column, the seatbacks become the mattress for the double.

We can also estimate whether the galley will fit as a module. If we make the galley as small as possible, a straight galley will take up at least 76 inches (more for comfort) and will be about 30 inches wide. An L-shaped galley, at 76 inches, is more spacious, but at the price of an increase in width. If we make the galley U-shaped, the sinks can be nearer the centerline, making them less likely to backfill. The icebox will be larger, and we will have a small space on one side of the stove for drawers. Now the galley size is close to our modular size, about 6 feet, 4 inches long.

If we fit a nav table that is 24 inches deep and 30 inches wide with a seat 18 inches deep, we get an overall depth of 42 inches. By adjoining a hanging locker or bureau that is 34 inches wide, we can make a modular unit that is 76 inches long. This gives us another 6-foot-4-inch module that can be placed opposite the galley. By putting the galley and the nav area on opposite sides, their weights tend to cancel each other out.

We should probably fit the head on the same side as the nav area to balance out the galley weight completely. The minimum size for a head compartment is about 22 to 24 inches. Much less, and large people might not fit; much more, and you have difficulty bracing yourself in a seaway. Next to the head will be a hand basin, located in the countertop. Hand basins are usually around 12 inches in diameter, or they may be oval, so we can allow about 16 inches. A shower unit should be about 36 inches square for easy showering. You can make it as small as 28 inches, but you won't be able to work up a good lather.

The head unit, sink, and shower can be made to fit in a length of about 6 feet, 4 inches, which enables us to position it opposite a bunk or any other of our modules. The accompanying sketch shows the modules roughed out in a typical hull of, say, 38 feet. Starting at the helm seat, we must

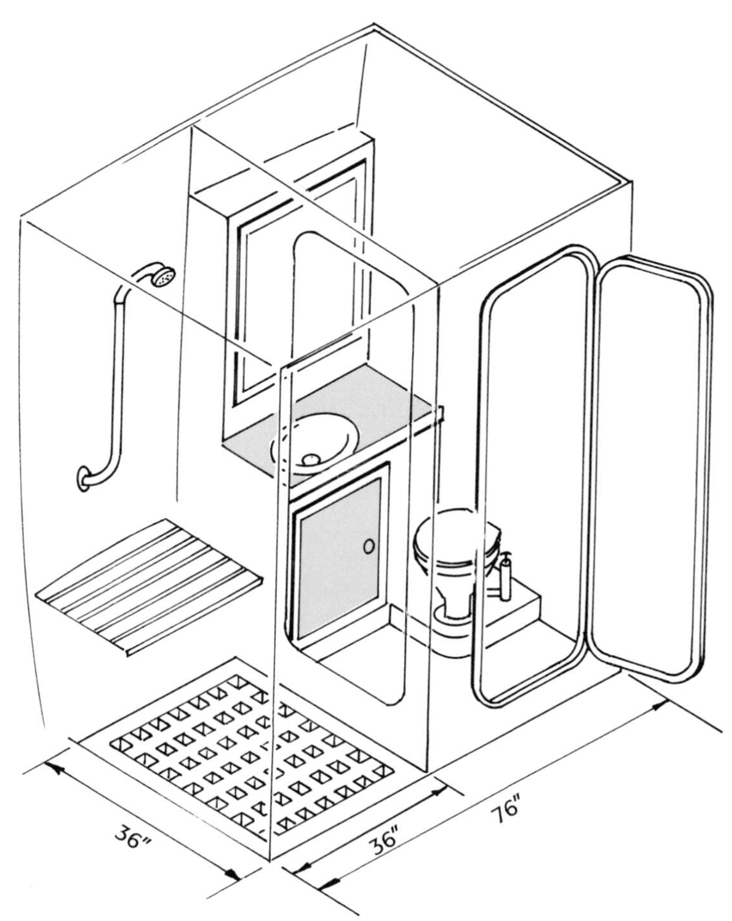

A head unit showing the dimensions of the layout to make it fit into our modular scheme. The shower is about 36 by 36 inches for easy use, and the head is 36 to 42 inches long by 36 inches wide. If interior space allows, the head can be larger, but space is often limited and a builder will juggle inches to make everything fit.

allow space to stand at the helm, which fixes the position of the steering wheel. Because the crew needs to move around the wheel, the cockpit seats are cut back next to the wheel. Below deck, we put a bulkhead just forward of the steering gear, and then measure 6 feet, 4 inches from the bulkhead forward; this module will probably be a quarter berth space. Now we go to the front of the boat and locate the V-berths. To get the dining area module in the middle of the boat, we locate two modules near the center of the hull. This leaves a small area between the V-berth and the main dining area. As it isn't quite 6 feet, we'll use it for a single head/shower unit.

Now we are ready to fill in the modules and make small adjustments. By juggling inches in this fashion we can develop the interior layout. Notice how bulkheads are placed opposite each other to make construction easier and the hull stronger. The next step is to integrate each feature with the next, making sure that access, ease of use, and ergonomics work for the benefit of the entire design.

Comfort on Deck

Sailors spend most of their time on deck, and this means paying careful attention to where people without much protective clothing might step or lie. For example, cleats and chocks can cause major damage to a barefoot sailor who inadvertently kicks one; and a nice spot to stretch out and read on the foredeck can be ruined by one misplaced cleat. When laying out the deck, performance and efficiency have their place on a racing boat, but compromise can be allowed on a cruising boat.

Cockpit

As the most used part of the boat, the cockpit should be as comfortable as possible, but, unfortunately, too few cockpits are. Seats should be long enough—at least 6 feet, 4 inches—to lie down on, and wide enough to sit comfortably, with a fairly narrow cockpit well so that you can brace yourself when the boat heels. Experience shows that 24 inches is about the maximum width of the well for most people. If a table is fitted, you'll need 12 to 17 inches between the seat and table in order to move around. The art of making a cockpit comfortable comprises many elements, among them seats, seatbacks, the helm seat, and shelter in the form of a dodger or Bimini top.

Cockpit seats

Most cockpit seats are uncomfortable without cushions. They are flat, unyielding, and the front faces drop vertically. Some of these problems stem from production engineering. For example, there are two reasons for the flat front face with no room to tuck your legs in under: One is that the mold tooling cannot be recessed without additional expense and complication. The other is that often the face of a cockpit seat forms the side of a passageway or locker below deck.

With a little more effort, cockpit seats can be designed to fit the average rear end. Lumbar support can be provided without creating contours unworkable in a production deck mold. Unfortunately, even a comfortable seat in the upright position can become uncomfortable when the boat heels or when someone decides to lie down. Because boats change heel angles and people move around, making a contoured cockpit seat to suit every situation is difficult. It is easier to adjust the cushions if someone wants to sit lengthwise. Of course, the cushions need to be fastened with studs or Velcro so they won't slip off the seat, but that's a simple matter.

Seatbacks

How often have you sat down in a cockpit seat and felt a stab of pain as the coaming hits you right about the belt line? A simple solution to a low coaming is to make a seat cushion with a raised back. Human beings are not square. We don't fit on a flat seat with a flat vertical surface

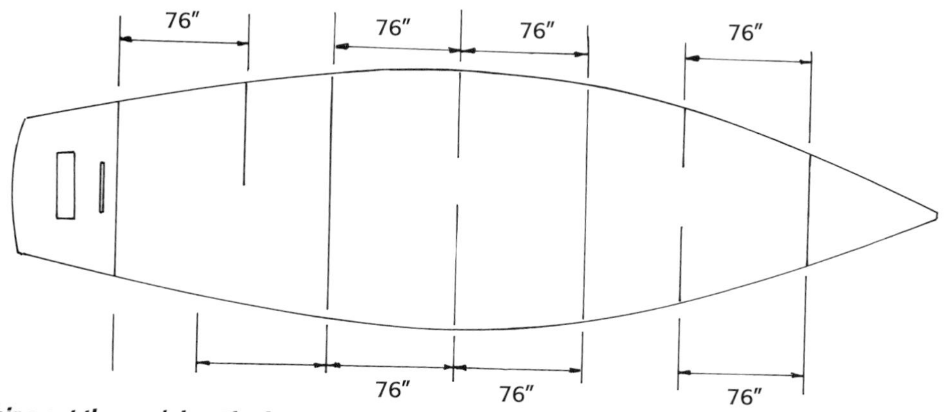

Roughing out the modules. The forwardmost module is for V-berths, with the middle areas for the dining area and galley. Aft is space for quarter berths. A forward head can be fitted between the V-berths and the dining area. As this space is too small for a module oriented fore-and-aft, the head unit will be fitted transversely.

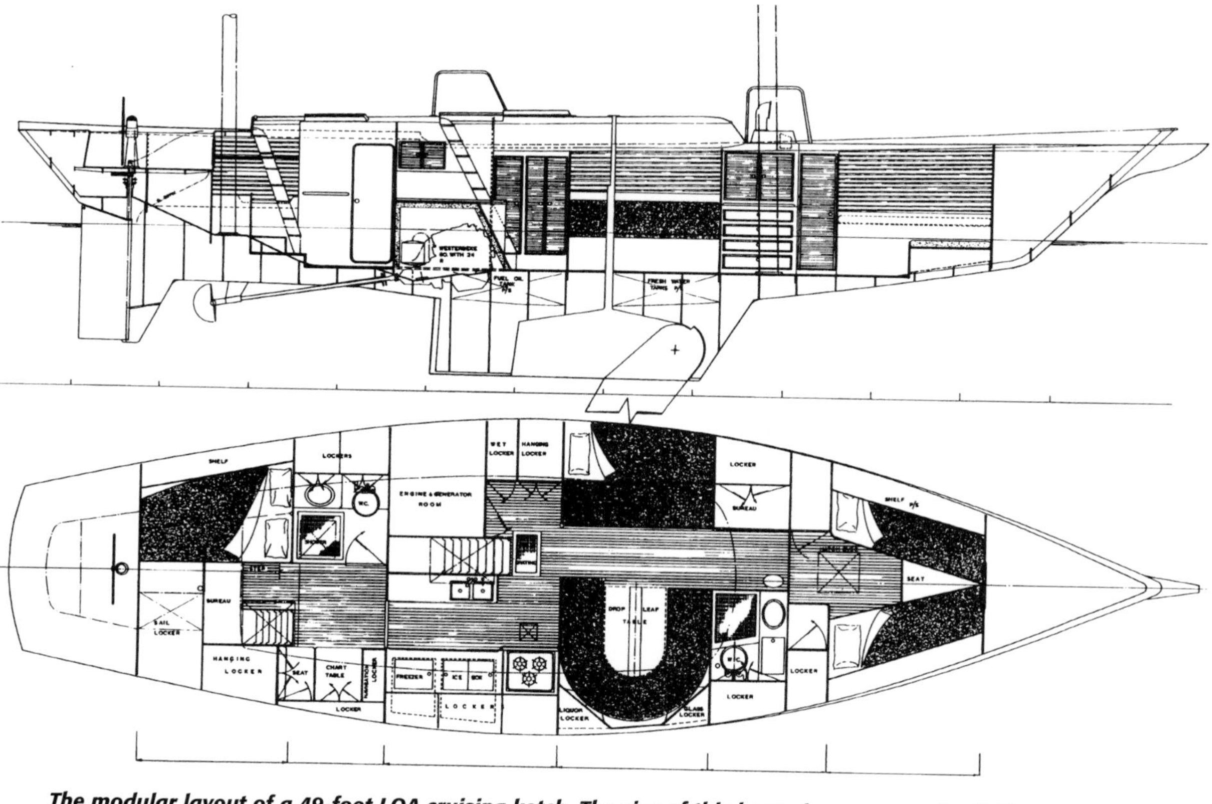

The modular layout of a 49-foot LOA cruising ketch. The size of this boat gives us more flexibility. The forward head fits between the dining area module and the V-berths. Because the boat is so beamy, we can fit a U-shaped dining area. The galley module has been lengthened slightly to fit a large icebox/freezer with sinks on the centerline. An owner's head and the navigation area are in the aft cabin, along with the owner's double berth. An offset companionway leads directly to the aft cockpit. This boat was built in steel and has a centerboard to keep the draft under 6 feet.

Cockpit seats are often built with a straight seat and back. This uncomfortable shape can be modified by adding shaped cockpit cushions to give some lumbar support. A seatback cushion against the coaming can be improved by mounting it on a plywood panel to give a raised seatback.

to support our back. We need the contoured support that seat cushions and seatbacks can provide. If we furnish cushions that are acceptable to different-sized people, we can enjoy more comfort in the cockpit, not less.

Helm seat

The most difficult seat on the boat to design is the helmsman's. It must be close enough to the wheel for a person to sit, yet far enough away to allow him or her to stand. (Seventeen inches from the wheel to the forward edge of the seat is about right.) It must be functional when the boat is upright or heeled. It must accommodate helmsmen who sit to windward and those who sit to leeward. All these requirements pose design problems. Solving them involves trade-offs and

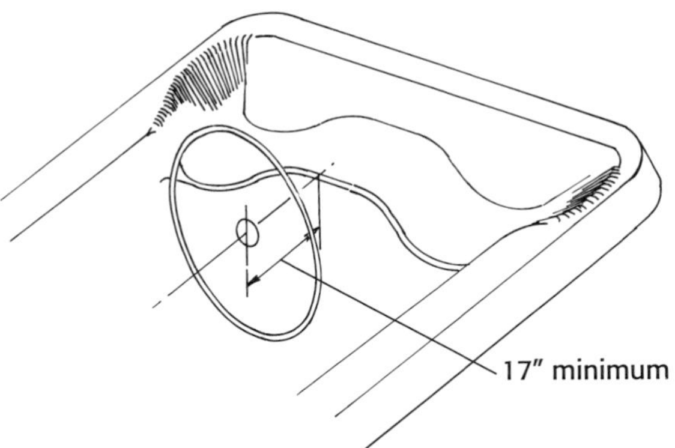

Making a helm seat comfortable requires careful thought. This seat is raised in the middle to boost the helmsman's eye level when sitting down. When the boat is heeled, the helmsman may slide off to one side and steer leaning to leeward or windward. If we ease the coamings and round off all corners, the seat is more comfortable when the boat is heeled.

cushions to adapt the seat. It can also involve modifying the coaming to make the seat more comfortable. Typically, coamings dig into the side of the helmsman as he/she is leaning to leeward to see the sail. By rounding coamings and providing helm cushions, a good compromise seat can be developed.

Dodger

Comfort in the cockpit also means protection from the elements. A dodger shelters the crew and prevents water and spray from going down the companionway. A hardtop or hard dodger (one made from fiberglass rather than canvas) can also be used as a mini-pilothouse.

Bimini top

If you sail in warm, sunny climates, too much sun can be a problem. In this case, a Bimini top might be the answer. Most Biminis are stretched between the end of the boom and the backstay. They work better if the boat has a split backstay and a metal or wooden rod at the boom end. If you want to sail with the Bimini in place, you will need a metal-framed unit. The frame, usually made of aluminum, is bolted to the deck near the stern. Note that a large Bimini will affect the boat's performance when you are sailing upwind in a fresh breeze. You will be better off taking the Bimini down when under sail.

Moving Out of the Cockpit

Making the deck comfortable is not a high priority unless you want to spend time sunbathing there. Still, certain features can make it more pleasant to go forward or easier to handle the sails. These features range from placing chainplates or sheet leads farther outboard or inboard to get them out of walkways, to putting winches on the cabintop under the dodger for easy operation, to putting a seat in the pulpit so you can watch the dolphins playing. It might mean fitting roller-furling gear to avoid headsail changes, or using a self-tacking headsail rather than winding winches on every tack (see chapter 6). Comfort can mean moving an item a few inches or adding another item to make the boat more enjoyable. After all, comfort is really making the boat easier to use.

Chainplates

When moving down the side deck of a boat, look at the chainplate positions. On some boats, the chainplates are located right in the middle of the side decks, making it difficult to go forward. A little compromise (which would affect performance only marginally) could easily position them farther inboard or outboard and make the side deck more functional.

Sheet tracks

How often have you cursed a mainsheet track across the middle of the cockpit, where it is difficult to step over? Moving it out of the cockpit often puts it in a position where it is inefficient. For example, putting the mainsheet on the cabintop puts it in the middle of the boom. Because the highest loads are along the leech of the sail (at the end of the boom), sheeting it from the middle can make the boom bend or break. The ultimate solution in positioning the mainsheet track is to put it on an arch, as I did in the boat for an older client mentioned in chapter 3, and as Hunter Marine has done for a few years. This gets it totally out of the cockpit, transforming it from an essential but annoying feature to a piece of gear that functions almost unnoticed.

A similar problem often exists with headsail tracks. Quite often they are put in the middle of the side deck, where toes get stubbed on them or their cars (fairleads in the U.K.). There is no need for this on a cruising boat. The difference of two or three degrees of track angle is not going to be noticed by the typical cruising sailor. However, the repositioning might be noticed by a racing sailor, who would probably rig a barberhaul to move the sheet lead to the desired angle. In my opinion, headsail tracks on cruising boats should be located either close to the cabinhouse, in grooves to get them lower, or close to the rail where they are not in the walkway.

Our Designs

Having looked at various features that make a boat comfortable, it is time to apply those features to our five designs. The Weekender is a small boat and as such may be the most uncomfortable of all our designs; this means we will have to work hard to raise its comfort level. Both the Cruiser and the Voyager will have relatively high comfort levels, especially the Voyager, which is fitting since its crew will be aboard for the longest time. The Single-Hander will have a high comfort level as well, although in a different sense: because it is designed for arduous solo sailing, "comfort" will amount to painstaking design of the navigation and helming positions. The Cruiser/Racer, on the other hand, will be used mainly for racing and only occasionally for cruising. As performance is a major factor in the design of this boat, comfort levels will be minimal.

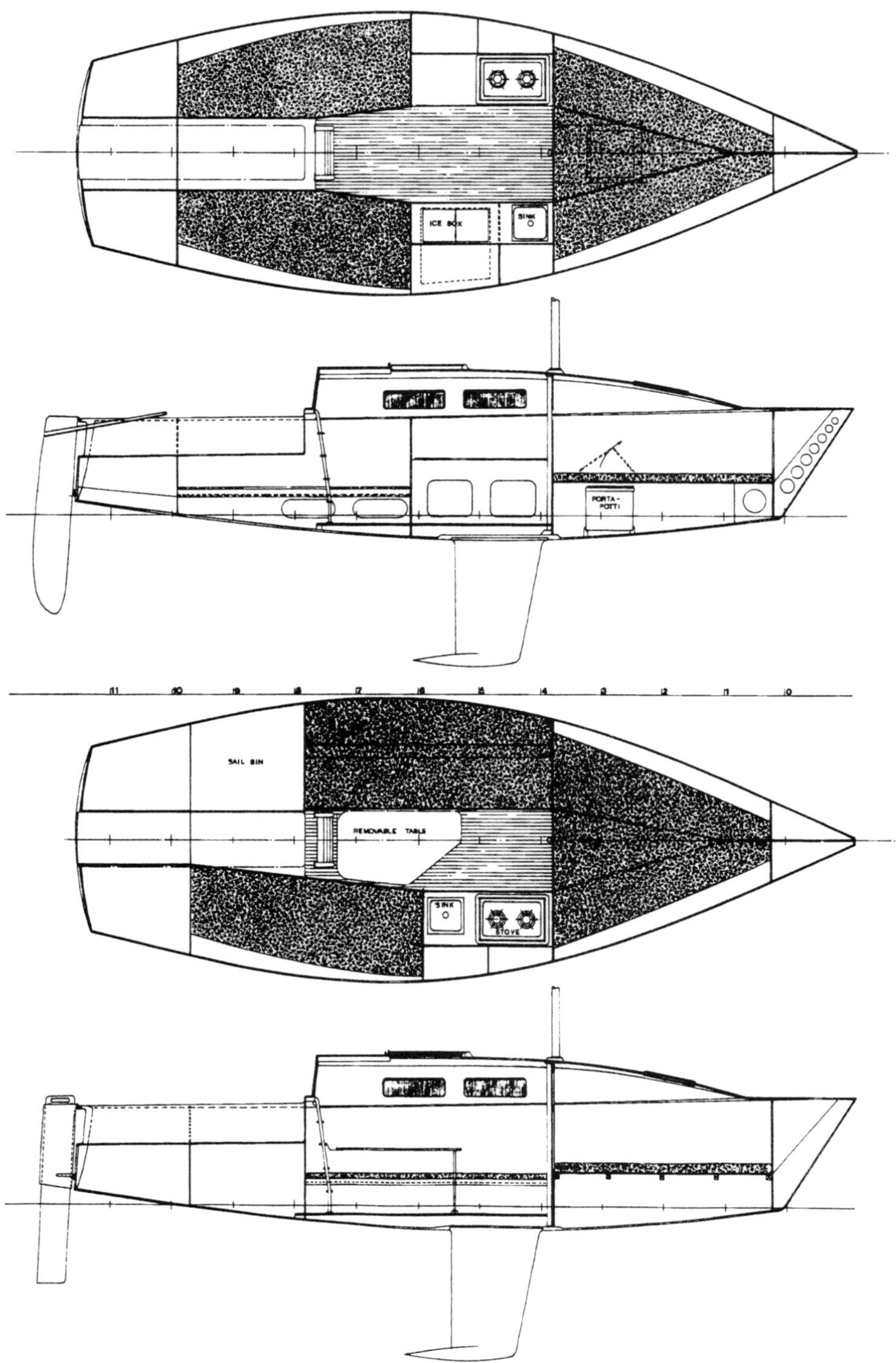

The layout of the Weekender. The original layout is very simple, with two quarter berths and a V-berth forward. The Porta-Potti head is under the V-berth and directly below the hatch. An icebox and sink have been built in amidships, although these might be changed to keep the boat light. In the finished boat a Coleman icebox was used as a companionway step and a square bucket used as the sink. Consequently, there were no through-hulls.

The Weekender

Partly because the Weekender is a small boat, and partly because it is oriented toward higher performance, comfort on this boat is low. Bunks are large enough, but just barely, and the headroom in the cabin is only 5 feet, 1 inch. The galley is basic, and storage space is limited. The Comfort Factor is a meager 3.40 (any factor below 10 is akin to camping out).

Add to this the fact that the boat's motion in any kind of seaway is bumpier than a larger boat's, resulting in crew fatigue and possibly undue stress. Because of these factors, less time is likely to be spent on the Weekender than aboard a larger boat.

Galley

Food preparation on this boat is difficult. The icebox is used as the companionway step to save weight. With headroom restricted, the cook will probably make sandwiches at home rather than cook onboard. For more leisurely cooking, it is assumed that the cook will work at the stove while sitting on the opposite seat. As the crew are onboard for only a short period of time, sandwiches and soft drinks are adequate fare, especially if the owner promises to take them out to dinner when they win a race!

Head

On this boat the head is a simple Porta-Potti located under the forward bunks and the forehatch. This saves making a through-hull and conforms to no-discharge requirements. For privacy, a curtain can be drawn across the forward part of the boat where the main bulkhead is located, but the user will have to sit with his or her head sticking out of the forehatch.

Cockpit

There are no coamings on this cockpit, so the lifelines become seatbacks. Winches are placed for maximum efficiency, and crew comfort is subordinate to gear position. This puts the crew in the open if the weather is inclement. When moored in poor weather, a tent can be stretched between the boom and the backstay to keep rain out of the cabin.

Places to stow gear

When locker space is limited, there are many inventive ways to stow gear. Net hammocks can be fitted above berths for clothes and light gear. Canvas hold-alls can be used for clothes and as

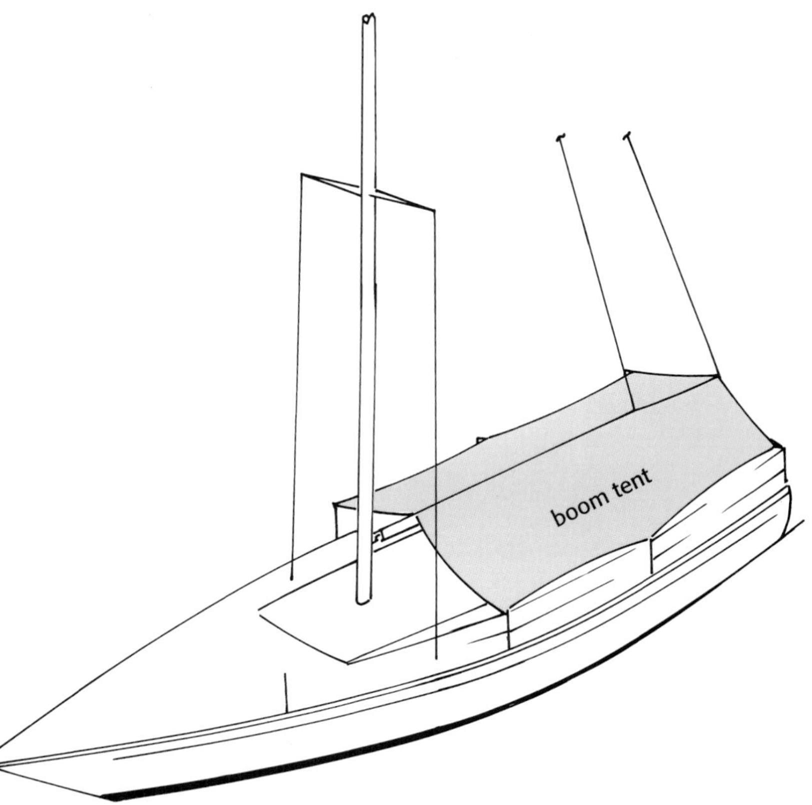

A boom tent can be used to expand the living space in rainy or hot weather.

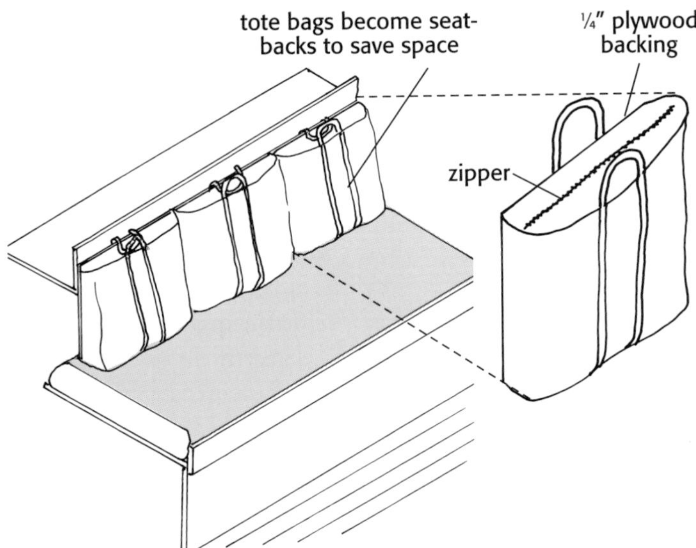

A canvas seabag with a plywood back will double as a seatback.

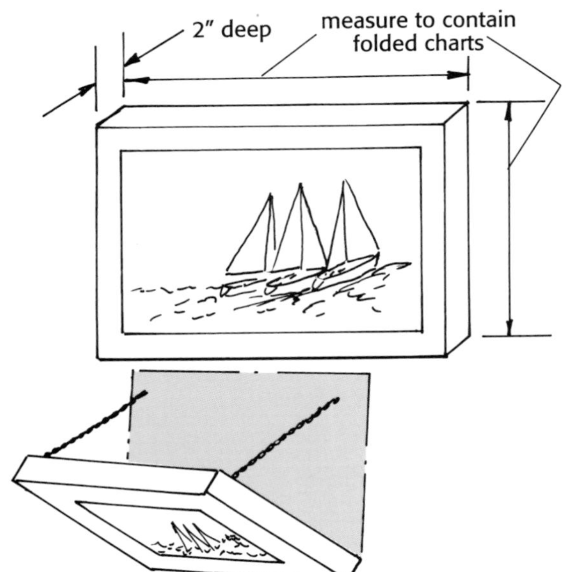

A picture frame with a deep recess will stow charts when they are not in use.

seatbacks. Canvas can also be used for specially made seabags that fit under or behind berths. A picture frame on the main bulkhead can be made to hold charts and flat materials. In the forepeak a 6- or 8-inch-wide shelf can be used as a book rack or for small items, while under the shelf a space-saver stereo or CD player can be fastened.

The Cruiser

With a larger boat comes more comfort. Our 34-foot Cruiser has a higher level of comfort throughout than our Weekender does. The interior has more space for stowing gear, a better galley, a larger dining area, and more comfortable berths. (See the cabin plan in chapter 3.) It is a boat where comfort can be enjoyed to a level comparable to that of home, although the space is still somewhat restricted. In this restricted space, many of the interior features should be made to do double or even triple duty, so the crew can get the maximum enjoyment out of the boat.

The Comfort Factor for the Cruiser is 16.6 with four people aboard, but as the boat is intended for a couple, the Comfort Factor goes to 33.2, which suggests that the boat is fairly comfortable for a boat of this size. A similar style of boat, the Island Packet 37 from Island Packet Yachts, has a Comfort Factor of 34.7 for two. As Island Packet is known for building a comfortable, well-equipped cruiser, the Cruiser is close to its design goals for two crew.

On this boat the galley will be fully equipped, with a three-burner stove with oven, twin sinks, an icebox, and a reasonable amount of locker space. The dining area will be quite spacious for two people. There will be a navigation area, a fully enclosed head, and a quarter berth and a comfortable berth to starboard outboard of the dining area, as well as a V-berth forward.

The hull has a moderate displacement with a displacement/length ratio of 267, which puts it in the moderately heavy range. (Note that the waterline is a little short due to the style of the ends of the boat, which will tend to push up the displacement/length ratio.) This relative heaviness suggests that the boat will sail well in choppy conditions, where it has the heft to keep going. It should also have a good motion through the water that will help to reduce crew fatigue.

Dining area

The dining table should be large enough for at least four adults. The arrangement shown satisfies that requirement with two settee berths with transoms, and a dropleaf dining table. The settees readily convert to bunks simply by pulling out the transom. When used at sea, leecloths should be attached to the berths (see chapter 3, page 60) and stowed under the seat cushion. The upper berth to starboard can be used to store pillows, sleeping bags, or sheets and blankets during the daytime when guests are aboard. The main cabin berth configuration could easily be altered, of course. As discussed earlier in this chapter, another option is a table that drops to fill in a double berth.

Each part complements the others. The table length nicely fits two people on each side. The bunks convert easily to transom berths. People can get past the table when its leaves are dropped. This simple layout is most common because it works efficiently under all conditions. By maximizing the uses of the dining area, we free up other areas of the boat for other features.

Location of bunks

The bunks are more toward the middle of the boat than in the previous design, but in a seaway the V-berth forward will be virtually uninhabitable. A person trying to sleep forward would be bounced up and down as the boat pitched. The quarter berth, which tends to hold the occupant in more securely, lies alongside the hull inboard of a row of lockers. This means that the person in the leeward bunk would be lying level as the boat heels. The most comfortable bunks on this boat would be the settee berths (sofas that can easily be converted to bunks) because they are nearest the center of pitching, and the starboard upper bunk.

Head

With a little juggling we can fit a head unit in this boat. The head will have a Wilcox-Crittenden toilet leading directly into a sump or holding tank. Next to the WC will be a small hand basin, with the remainder of the space taken up by a hamper and locker space. If an owner should want a shower unit, the inboard bulkhead of the head should be moved to the other side of the mast, making the entire head area available for a shower.

Galley

Sink basins must be a minimum of 9 inches wide (the diameter of most large plates), so twin sinks usually measure 10 inches (including trim) by 20 inches, although in some cases the second sink may be only 6 inches wide by 10 inches deep. Thus, the minimum space required of the sink unit is 10 by 16 inches.

It is difficult to fit an icebox under the stove or the sink, so additional space is required for the icebox. As iceboxes have a wall thickness of 3⅝ inches (3 inches of foam, plus ½ inch of

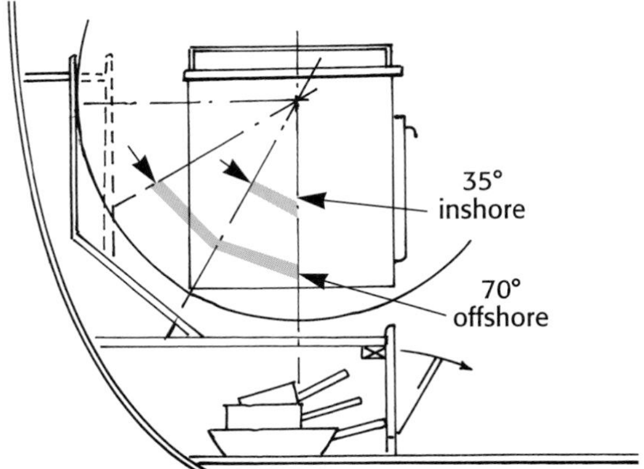

A gimbaled stove must have room to swing as the boat heels. Typically, a minimum of 35 degrees of swing should be allowed for a stove on an inshore boat, and 70 degrees on an offshore boat.

plywood and 1/8 inch of interior fiberglass liner) on all sides, substantially more space is needed to fit them than their interior volume suggests. This icebox is a little small, so it can be pushed back into the sail locker to gain some additional interior space.

When sizing an icebox you must also consider the dimensions of the ice to be put inside to cool it. For example, if you want to store a 12-by-8-by-8-inch block of ice, the bottom of the icebox must be at least 12 by 8 inches and the lid large enough to admit a block of that size. Whatever space is left over is what you have for food storage, and it never seems to be enough, especially on a long trip. A portable cooler is worth considering for additional storage space.

The gimbaled stove also consumes a large chunk of galley space. Typically the space for it is about 20 inches deep by 22 inches wide by 18 inches high, but its swing must be taken into account as well. Inshore boats usually have a more limited range of motion than a boat that is to sail offshore. Inshore boats generally have a swing of 35 to 40 degrees, while an offshore boat might have a swing of up to 70 degrees or more.

All surfaces on either side of the stove mounting should be insulated and covered with stainless steel for easy cleaning. The top of the stove should have fiddle rails and clamps to hold pots in place. Ideally, all your pots should have bases wider than their tops to keep them on the stove in a seaway. According to one study on safety, there should be 7 to 9 inches on either side of the stove to allow locker doors and drawers to open. Another study says that stoves on boats should be placed where items falling off them cannot land on the cook, but there is usually not enough room to allow that distance unless the galley runs along one side of the hull.

Bunks

To the settee berths in the main cabin we'll add a quarter berth and a V-berth forward for children or adults. Each of the bunks should be at least 6 feet, 4 inches long, but we may modify them later if space is tight. By locating lockers outboard of the quarter berth, we reduce the tendency to slide head-down as the boat heels.

Navigation area

The navigator needs an area to lay out charts, check and tune instruments, measure distances, and make calculations—all while heeled over and bouncing around. Even with electronic charts and GPS units in widespread use today, a paper chart is still required onboard. Charts come in many sizes, and chart tables should be laid out to suit most of them. A small chart

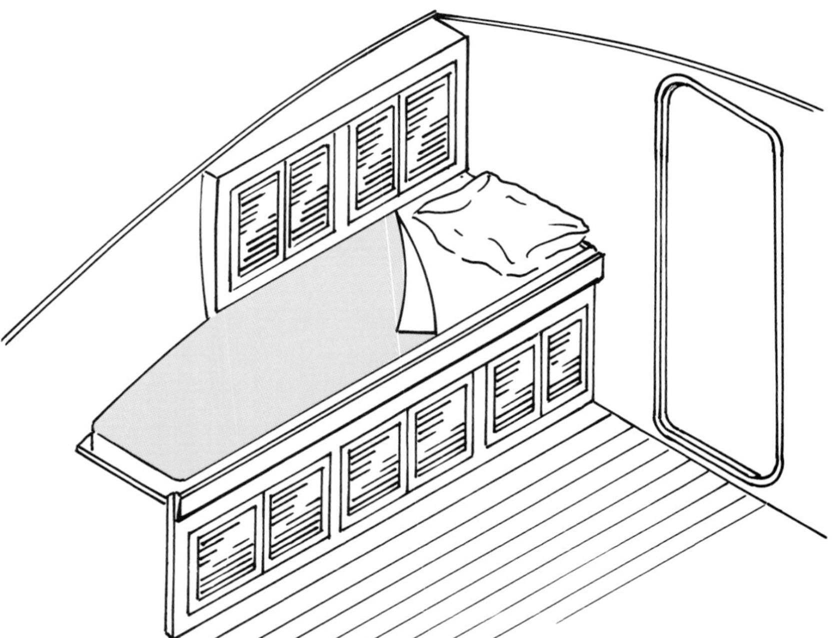

Lockers outboard of a quarter berth prevent sleeping crew from tipping head-downward as the boat heels.

table might measure 18 by 18 inches, while a large table might measure 30 by 36 inches (tables larger than that tend to waste space). Ideally, the table should have a hinged top for chart stowage. The storage tray should not be more than 3 inches deep, or it will make positioning the seat at the right height difficult.

Because space is cramped on this boat, we'll hinge the chart table over the settee berth seats. Chart tables don't get a lot of use on a coastal cruiser, where pilotage is more the norm, so this arrangement should work just fine. The navigator's seat will be on the end of his berth. While this arrangement may seem cramped, instruments can be mounted in the face of the outboard locker and charts stowed in the table. The ideal location for the navigation area is near the companionway, where the navigator has easy access to the person at the helm, and this arrangement accomplishes that.

On deck

On deck the most exposed position is the helmsman's, which is all the way aft behind the wheel. We should make the helm seat as comfortable and functional as possible, perhaps by incorporating the contoured seat design described earlier in this chapter (see page 94).

It may seem a strange topic for a chapter on comfort, but too few and poorly located hatches can make life below deck uncomfortable in a warm climate. There should be a hatch over the galley, one over the dining area, one in each cabin, and a smaller hatch over each head compartment. If the hatch is the only one in the cabin, it should be large enough to allow people to climb through in the event of a fire or capsize. This means that it should be a minimum of 20 by 20 inches, although 24 by 24 inches is better. Ideally, a hatch should not be located over a bunk where it may let water below. Hatches should be provided with screens and also with drains, if they are not horizontal. On the Cruiser there are two large hatches on centerline with Nicro Solarvents over the galley and the head. Both Solarvents will have stainless steel covers in case they are stepped on.

Boats that are going to sail in the tropics should consider opening ports along the sides of the cabin. In an offshore boat, opening ports should be in the aft part of the boat rather than forward where green water could enter a port left open by accident. The Cruiser has opening ports along the entire cabin side.

The Voyager

The Voyager can be very comfortable with the right amount of forethought, but without good design long periods of time spent heeled can mean acute discomfort. On my last Atlantic crossing I spent eight days beating to windward. In the head compartment a clear plastic laminated door to the shower was directly across from the head. It made it almost impossible to use the head on starboard tack; by bracing or leaning against the door, one of the crew fell through the door and shattered it. Thus seemingly minor design oversights can become major problems at sea. Another example is an engine compartment without enough insulation to reduce noise while the engine is running. High levels of noise make talking difficult below, driving the crew up on deck.

The Comfort Factor for this boat is a bit low (32.7) when all six bunks are occupied, but if the boat were to be sailed by four crew it rises to a healthy 49.1. (See the cabin plan in chapter 3.) Four crew is a realistic number for a voyage, as the V-berths forward would probably be unusable in a seaway. The hull shape is intended to give the boat a comfortable motion through the water, although the need to restrict draft has made the bottom of the hull slightly flatter than ideal. This may make the boat slam a little in a good seaway, such as one might find when the wind is blowing hard against a strong tide. But with a displacement/length ratio of 259, the boat should be heavy enough to stow lots of

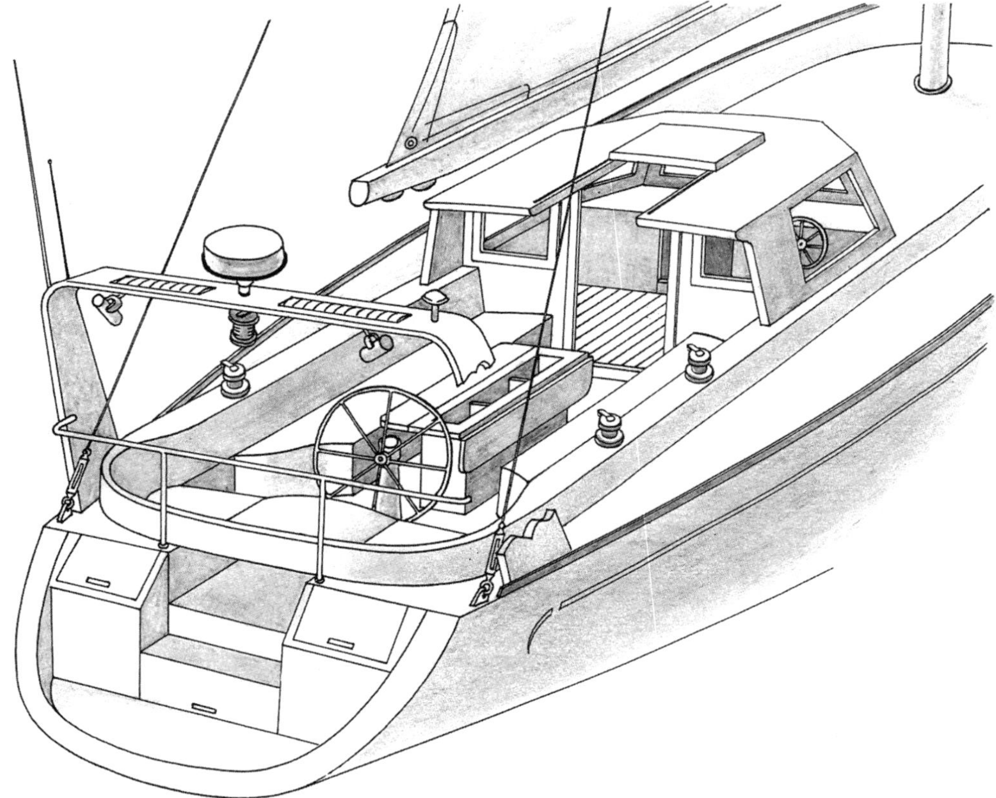

Contoured seatbacks, high cushions, and a pedestal-mounted table contribute to this cockpit's comfort.

stores and to carry its way through big seas without troubling the crew.

Cockpit

To enhance the boat's comfort, both heeled and upright, we'll start in the cockpit. We'll include contoured seats with thick cushions and high seatbacks. In good weather the crew will eat many of their meals in the cockpit, so we'll look to see if a table hinged off the pedestal will fit with the other requirements in the cockpit. Such a table will have deep fiddle rails and holes for drinks, a pair of holes for vacuum flasks to keep food warm, as well as handholds. It will also be strongly fastened to allow the crew to lean against it when the boat is heeled. To illuminate the cockpit dining table for dining at night in harbor, we'll fit a pair of dimmable lights on the underside of the end of the main boom or on the radar arch.

The cockpit will have a small icebox incorporated into the layout, so that the on-watch crew can help themselves to drinks and cold food without having to go below. The icebox will be heavily insulated to keep ice cool.

At the forward end of the cockpit, is the back of the pilothouse. By extending the pilothouse sides back slightly, we can create a comfortable nook for reading while on passage. In harbor, a Bimini can be extended from the radar arch to the pilothouse top; this will provide good shelter in rain or strong sunshine.

We will attempt to set the sole of the cockpit high enough so that water cannot backfill through the scuppers when the boat is heeled. We will also slope the edges of the cockpit sole

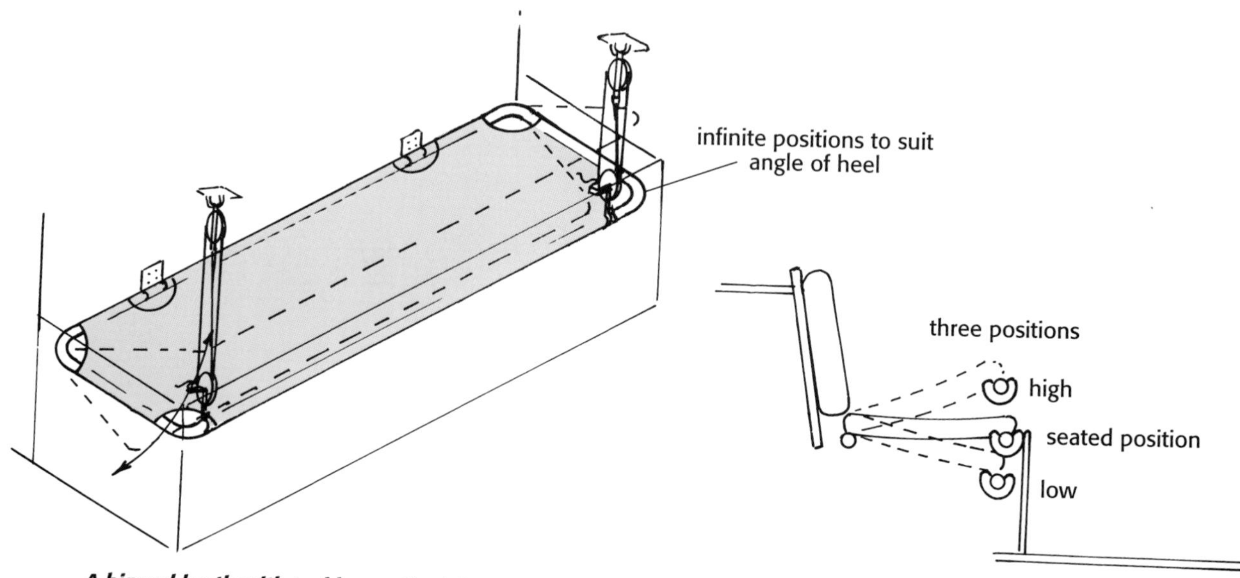

A hinged berth with tackles on the inboard side will adjust easily for heel angle (left). An alternative method is to make the inboard pipe long enough to drop into clamps mounted on bulkheads, as shown in (right).

so that it can be walked on easily when the boat is heeled.

To save work, we could mount electric winches on the coamings, with controls within reach of the helmsman, who could then handle most sail adjustments alone. The anchor windlass could also be a push-button model with controls at the helm station. But while these features save labor, they may add unneeded complexity, so we'll reexamine them when we work up the deck layout.

The reefing gear will be led to the forward end of the cockpit. At the forward end of the cockpit, around the side of the pilothouse, we'll also position the cruising spinnaker lines.

Bunks

On this boat we'll make the non-settee bunks adjustable for heel angle by using leecloths. Another option is a hinged pipe-cot berth, as in the accompanying drawing. A feature to keep in mind is making the settee berths with a seat-back section that hinges up to form a Pullman-

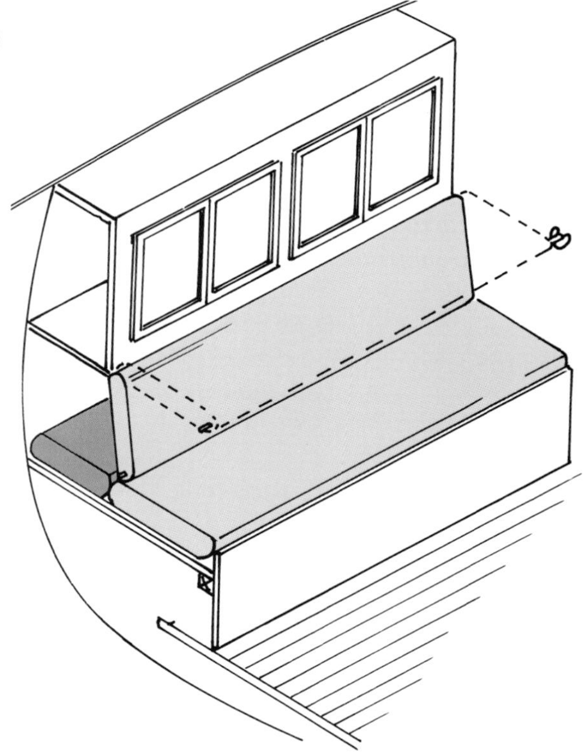

The seatback of a settee can be made to fold up into a Pullman-style berth where space is tight.

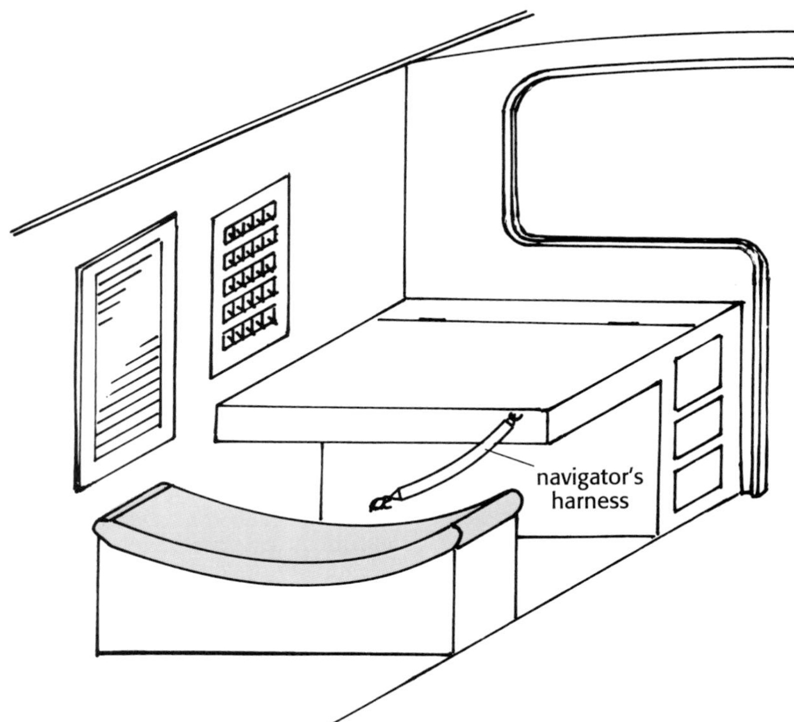

Curving the navigator's seat makes it easier to use when the boat is heeled. A harness strap also helps.

style berth; this can provide an extra adjustable berth in the main saloon. As we get closer to the final design, we'll decide whether to incorporate this feature.

The navigator's seat on this boat will have to be operated at angles of heel. In order to make it comfortable, and to give some storage space under it, we'll make the top curved; this will allow the navigator to sit comfortably at most angles of heel. We will also make sure that no electronic instruments or electrical switches are located outboard of the nav seat. If this area is flat or is a locker door, the navigator can sit comfortably leaning against the door, without being afraid of knocking off a breaker or damaging an electronic dial. When the boat is heeled in the other direction, the navigator can wear a harness to stop sliding to leeward.

On this boat we will make recesses in the countertops near the galley sinks for a pair of vacuum flasks that can be filled and left for the on-watch crew at night; this will save having them turn on galley lights and disturbing those off watch. In bad weather or in a seaway, the flasks can be filled with soup to feed the crew when it might be difficult or impossible to cook.

Cabin lights will have both red and white bulbs to preserve the night vision of the watch on deck while allowing the off-watch to function below. There will be red lights fitted on the companionway steps and in toe recesses to give more red lighting below deck.

The Single-Hander

Discomfort is expected on the Single-Hander, but it can be minimized with innovative features. For example, because of the demands of sailing, navigating, and myriad other chores, the solo sailor is unlikely to spend a lot of time in his bunk. Rather, he or she is likely to spend a lot of time in the main living area of the vessel—in this case, the nav area. Provided with a large swiveling and reclining navigation seat (see chapter 3, page 73), the solo sailor is able to catch a nap in the seat, yet be instantly ready should something unexpected occur. For the single-hander, a comfortable bunk in the middle of the boat is a luxury that is only likely to be used while the boat is in port or while another sailor is aboard. But for those moments when the skipper can retire to a comfortable berth, we'll make it a deep pipe cot that is adjustable for heel angle.

As there is only one person aboard this boat and one bunk, the Comfort Factor soars to a meaningless 116. In other words, one person has all the boat to enjoy.

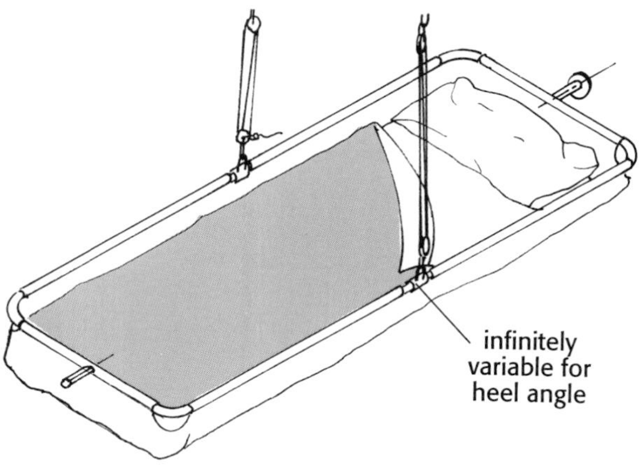

A deep pipe cot, adjustable for heel angle, is installed for those rare moments when the solo sailor can get a good sleep.

The motion, on the other hand, may be rather violent as the boat hits large waves and big seas. With a displacement/length ratio of only 55 the boat has the ability to get up and plane in a lightly loaded condition. While this can be exhilarating, it can also lead to massive broaches and speeds that push the envelope of control. With water ballast and a lot of beam carried well aft, the boat is powerful enough to reach speeds that will maximize the entire waterline length. However, heave, pitch, yaw, and tremendous accelerations will tire the crew quickly. This poses a philosophical dilemma between backing off on the extremes of the design, and making it easier to cruise, or going for speed and hoping that the crew can rest up long enough to stay in control. Only the skipper can answer such a question, and most skippers will look for extra speed and exhilaration.

Comfort aboard the Single-Hander means enough heat in cold conditions and having an area where clothes can be dried, food can be cooked, and a hot drink can be made after the panic of changing sails.

To give the single-handed skipper a comfort zone, there will be a number of alarms tied to

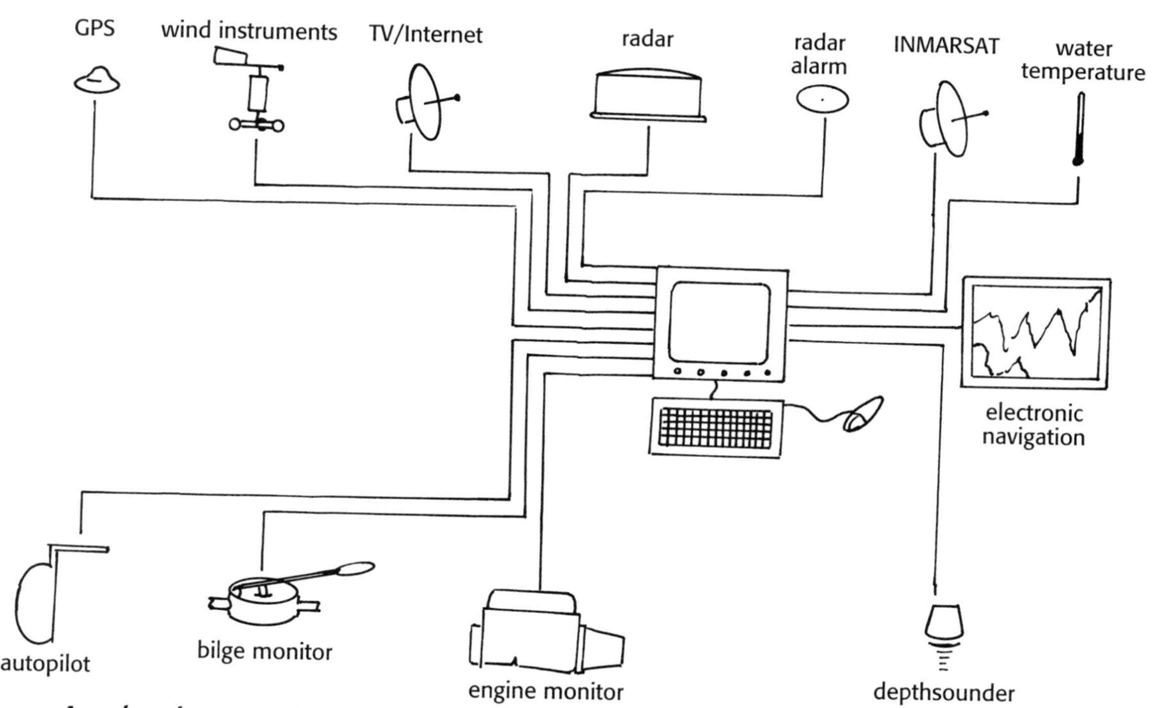

An onboard computer (with backup) monitors all the functions of the boat, from depthsounder to satellite navigation, and sounds an alarm if anything is amiss.

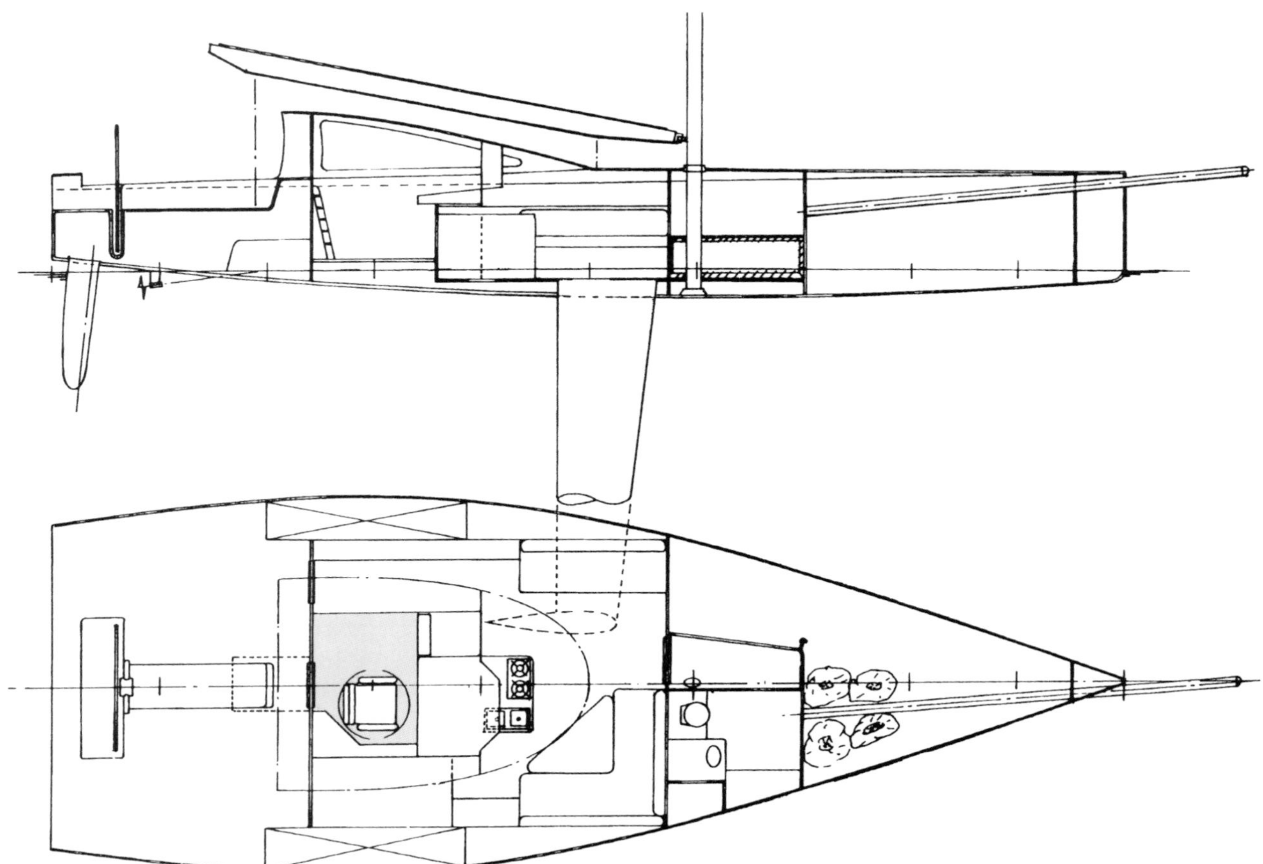

The arrangement plan of the Single-Hander shows a spartan interior with plenty of room to store gear. Sails and the head are forward of the watertight bulkhead abaft the mast. The main living area is in the central section of the hull, with the machinery aft of another watertight bulkhead.

ship systems to wake him should something unusual occur. To make this work well, we will link all the systems into a well-protected computer, which will have at least two backup modes. This system will monitor sail trim, wind angles, boat speed, GPS position, and the autopilot, and display all the information on an electronic chart. It will have a radar-detecting device that can sound an alarm and give bearing and distance to the target. Using a system similar to the Detroit Diesel DDEC engine-monitoring system, it will monitor the engine usage, speed, and condition, as well as fuel, water, and oil levels. In addition, the computer system will accept e-mail, download Internet information, and transmit the boat's position automatically to a remote computer. This entire system is available today, although the various parts are from different vendors and software conflicts may have to be ironed out.

In order to preserve energy for those desperate moments when a shredded sail has to be removed, the boat is designed around having everything to hand. The entire working area is concentrated in a small part of the vessel. The cabin, with its raised house and view of all the sails, the deck, and the area immediately around the boat, contains the nav area, the skipper's chair/berth, and a food storage area (more like a snack storage area). Step out of the cabin through the watertight door, and winches, steering, and other gear are immediately to hand. To the single-handed sailor, comfort is in having everything near and ready to use.

The Cruiser/Racer

On this boat, too, discomfort is expected but can be minimized. At the very top levels of racing, the deck is laid out for efficiency with small regard to comfort. The crewmembers sit on the rail for hours at a time, only moving when the boat turns a mark. If it rains while they are sitting on the rail, they wear foulweather gear. Unlike cruising sailors, they do not go below out of the rain. At lower levels of racing, however, deck efficiency is conditioned by comfort.

At the top levels of racing, the interior is lightweight with pipe cots, a minimal galley and cooler, an open head with curtain, and a large navigation area. At slightly lower racing levels, gear is kept light, but again comfort is of more concern. For example, a cruising couple will probably have a fully enclosed head as shown here, rather than a curtain. The boat might also have a shower and a pressurized hot and cold water system.

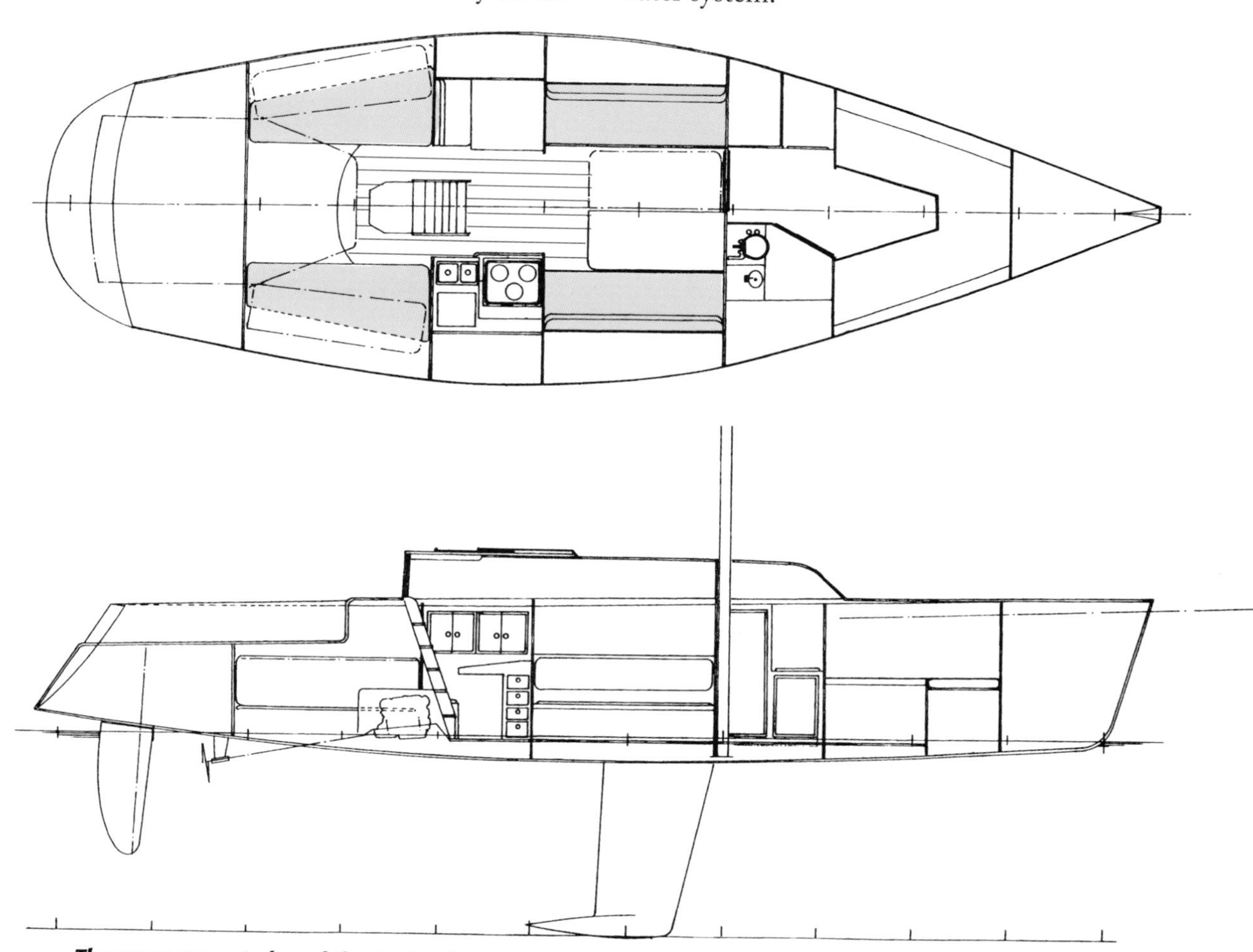

The arrangement plan of the Cruiser/Racer shows a comfortable layout oriented toward a racing crew. Twin quarter berths aft are used as Pullman-style bunks when the boat is not racing. The galley is small, intended for light meals rather than cooking a full dinner for the entire crew.

On this boat the Comfort Factor is a low 14 with a large racing crew aboard. Typically a boat of this size is raced with a crew of eight or nine, which reduces the Comfort Factor to below "camping-out" levels. Experienced racers know that hot bunks (off-watch crew climbing into a bunk recently vacated by a crew going on watch), sails and gear stowed everywhere, and hours spent on the rail are more like camping out on a wet freight train than a comfortable cruise. If the boat is cruised by a crew of three the Comfort Factor rises to 28, but it is still not in the category of a comfortable cruising boat.

The flat-bottomed hull shape with its almost plumb ends also does little for comfort. With almost no reserve buoyancy in the bow, the boat is likely to be wet in a seaway. The flat panels in the bow sides are likely to pound and the flat bottom will make sailing off a large wave a teeth-shaking experience. At 141 the displacement/length ratio is relatively low for this style of boat, which implies that the boat will not have enough weight to slam through waves, and it is likely to be thrown around in a seaway. But again, it is built for its purpose, and a racing crew is unlikely to want to back off and take a more leisurely approach. The cruising crew, on the other hand, will experience even more motion, as they will be sailing with fewer people and less weight. For cruising, this is not likely to be a comfortable boat.

Berths

Comfort on this boat is to be able to go to sleep in a berth. On most races the crew will spend virtually all of their time on the rail. The quarter berths are pipe cots located directly under the people on the rail. In this manner a crew can sleep, but the crew weight remains to windward and on the rail. There may be more berths than crew simply to allow the off-watch to sleep to windward.

The galley will also be minimal: a two-burner stove, no oven, twin lightweight sinks, and an icebox large enough to hold sandwiches and drinks for a two- or three-day race. As an option for the more cruising-oriented racer, a larger stove (three burners plus an oven), an inverter, and a larger icebox can be fitted.

Dining area

The dining area on this boat will also serve as a place to put sails when racing. In order to open up the space below deck, we'll use a fold-down bulkhead table with one leg dropping into a slot in the cabin sole. This type of table also saves weight.

On deck

On deck the layout is clearly oriented toward racing, although some small concessions have been made for comfort. There are no toerails in the mid-deck area, to allow the crew to sit outboard without having the rail cut off circulation in their legs. The helm seat is designed to be very comfortable at any angle of heel. The life raft stows under the seat.

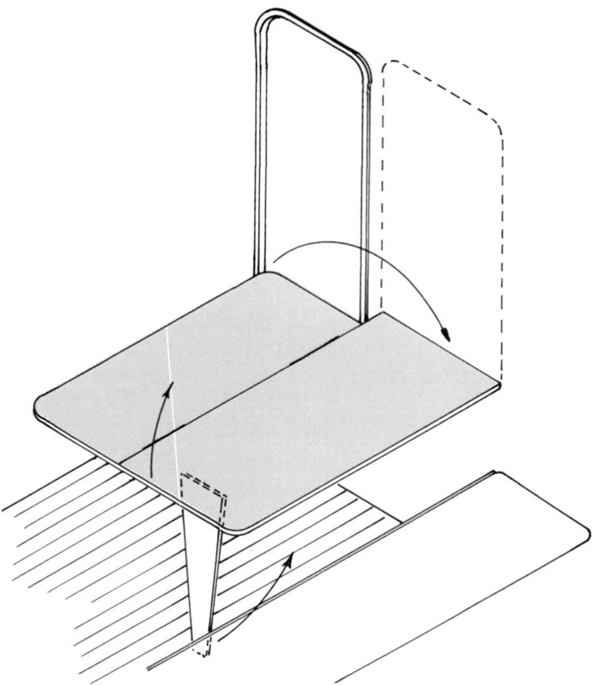

A bulkhead-mounted table drops down for use.

Five

Performance and Efficiency

Although a cruiser should perform well, getting the last ounce of speed from one is not the primary goal of the cruising lifestyle. Many cruising sailors want an easier motion through the water or easier sail handling than is practical for a racing boat. Speed is not so important for a voyager either, although it is helpful in the event of bad weather. Easy motion and minimal crew fatigue are primary factors in the design of a long-distance cruiser.

But for the racing Single-Hander and the Cruiser/Racer, speed and hull efficiency become very important for long-distance or round-the-buoys racing. On these boats almost everything is sacrificed for speed. The crew might sit, eat, sleep, and drink on the rail to generate 1 percent more stability rather than go below. As the crew will get little sleep anyway, crew fatigue and boat motion are not considered in the design equation. Of course, to be fast on the water, a boat must be designed for the prevailing wind and sea conditions. For example, designing a boat with a fairly high prismatic coefficient, which gives it an advantage in heavier winds, is of little value if the boat will be sailing in light air.

So, how do we estimate speed during the design process? Today most designers use a velocity prediction program (VPP) to get an indication of the speed potential of a particular boat. However, even the most computer-literate designer will tell you that these programs are still in their infancy.

Predicting a boat's speed in flat water is relatively easy, but predicting its speed in waves is not. To forecast a boat's speed in waves, a VPP uses a number of "fudge" factors to produce a result that corresponds reasonably well with the actual boat speed. As wind speeds and wave sizes increase, the difficulty of predicting boat speed increases dramatically. In other words, the more you move the rudder to steer the boat, the harder it is to predict boat speed accurately.

As a simpler, more accessible alternative to VPPs, this chapter introduces a few simple ratios that were used before the advent of computers to help give an idea of a boat's speed and performance potential. All of these ratios are nondimensional to allow different-sized boats to be compared, although they work best if the range of waterline lengths is no more than about 10 to 15 feet. Performance assessments should not be based on these ratios alone, of course. But each ratio indicates a trend, and if all the ratios show the same trend, the boat should live up to its design better than a boat whose various ratios pull it in different directions.

For example, the Weekender aims to deliver sprightly sailing in sheltered waters, and may be used in club races. Its displacement/length ratio should therefore tend toward the lower end, and at 138 it *is* fairly low. If this were to be a pure racing boat, this ratio should be under 100 to enable the boat to plane in strong winds. The Hunter 240, a water-ballasted boat, has a displacement/length ratio of 95.

On the Weekender, the sail area/displacement ratio is 25.6, while the Hunter 240 has a ratio of 22. This indicates that the Weekender should sail slightly better in lighter winds than the Hunter 240. On both of these boats, however, the capsize factor is over 2, indicating a vulnerability in that area. This means that both boats should be sailed in sheltered waters and not taken offshore, away from rescue services. We'll look at the ratios for other boats as we discuss each boat.

Performance-Indicating Ratios

Throughout this book we have looked at many factors that go into a good design, but we have not used any hard numbers to determine our ideal boat. For example, in chapter 2 we found that overhangs were important to seaworthiness and the ability to handle anchor gear and the sails, but we never put a quantitative value on the length of the overhangs.

I have developed a simple overhang formula to get an idea of the length of overhangs relative to the boat:

$$(LOA - LWL)/LOA$$

This formula shows that in most cases the overhang is around 16 to 20 percent of the overall length. Some boats have very short overhangs, on the order of 8 percent, but they are recent designs, done to suit the IMS Rule for a cruiser/racer. For a pure cruising boat, overhangs can and probably should be around 15 to 20 percent of the overall length. This means that if we are looking for a 40-foot boat, the overhangs will be between 6 and 8 feet, making the waterline length between 32 and 34 feet.

We can apply similar numbers to other facets of boats, such as their speed potential. If we take a number of boats of various sizes, we can assume that in light winds each boat sails quite slowly, with its speed dependent on sail area and frictional drag. Frictional drag depends upon the boat's wetted surface area (which, to a large extent, depends upon displacement). Hence, we use the sail area/displacement ratio to get an intimation of performance. In heavy winds each boat will sail at a speed dictated by its waterline length. At lesser but increasing wind speeds, boats accelerate; in general, lighter boats both accelerate and decelerate faster than heavier boats as gusts come and go.

Performance-indicating formulae that incorporate these factors (waterline length, wetted surface, sail area, and displacement) will give an idea of the speed potential of a boat. Of course, other factors, not incorporated into these

(continued on page 124)

Production Sailboat Comparisons

The numbers included in the first several columns for each boat in this 13-page table are found in most cruising boat brochures. Using such numbers in the appropriate formulas, you can calculate performance ratios as we have done here. Remember that these numbers indicate trends only: you should confirm them when you trial-sail the boat before buying it.

In this table, we have included the sail area as reported by manufacturers to show how the sail area numbers can be manipulated to give higher ratios of sail area to displacement. By using one definition of sail area—in this case 100 percent of the foretriangle and the triangular mainsail area—we get a more accurate figure for sail area than that given by the manufacturer. You will notice that there are some blanks where prices should be. Many manufacturers decline to give prices, because the boats are often much more expensive than buyers may believe or may include many extras not included in the base price. Remember, too, when looking at pricing, that rates increase about 10 percent or more per year (prices here are current as of 1999).

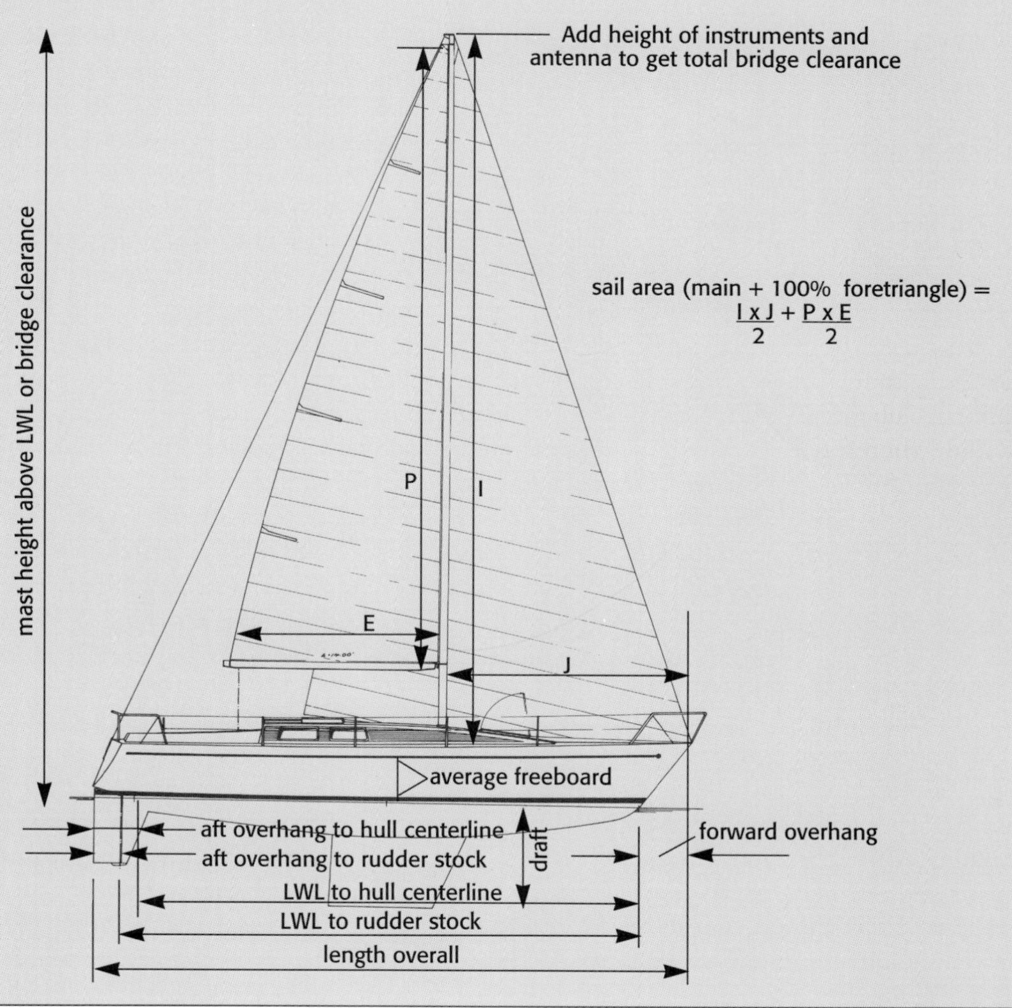

Boat	LOA or LOD, ft.	LWL, ft.	Beam, ft.	Deep Keel Draft	Draft, ft. (wing or shallow) C/B up/down	Displace-ment, lb.	Ballast, lb.	Sail Area, ft.² (given by manufacturer)
Alerion Express 28	28.25	22.84	8.16	4.50		4,400	2,000	352
Alerion Express 38	37.75	29.58	10.85	5.85		12,400		712
Baltic 35	34.90	28.70	11.48	6.07	4.90	9,877	4,145	
Baltic 40	39.37	32.73	12.73	7.25	5.7 5.25	14,990	6,173	
Baltic 43	43.34	35.76	13.78	8.00	6.10	19,750	8,487	
Baltic 47	47.74	39.50	14.40	8.70	6.8 5.9 / 9.9	24,692	10,141	
Baltic 50	50.00	43.60	14.20	9.80		20,503	9,002	
Baltic 52	52.50	43.14	15.40	9.20		31,967	13,228	
Baltic 58	58.50	47.57	16.60	10.50		41,888	18,078	
Baltic 60	60.50	52.00	16.40	9.80		41,888	16,314	
Baltic 64	64.00	51.50	17.30	11.00		56,218	24,652	
Baltic 67	67.00	59.00	17.70	11.90		40,786	15,653	
Baltic 70	70.50	59.10	16.00	12.50		39,249	21,936	
Beneteau 25	24.58	22.20	8.50	5.20		2,755	1,124	349
Beneteau First 33.7	32.80	28.50	11.10	6.10	5.20	10,582	4,800	692
Beneteau First 40.7	39.25	35.10	12.25	7.84	6.16	15,200	5,950	892
Beneteau Oceanis 36cc	36.42	31.20	12.50	5.20		13,382	4,155	
Beneteau Oceanis 40cc	41.00	36.75	12.75	5.58	5.58	18,740	5,300	825
Beneteau Oceanis 411	41.66	36.08	13.00	5.58	4.75	17,196	5,500	883
Beneteau Oceanis 44cc	44.58	36.75	14.00		5.75	20,944	6,835	1,017
Beneteau First 42s7	42.50	35.75	13.50	7.58	5.50	18,220		951
Cabo Rico 36	34.00	26.66	11.00	4.84	4.16	15,500	5,800	588
Cabo Rico 38	38.00	29.25	11.50	5.00		21,000	7,800	969
Cabo Rico 40	40.25	32.00	12.66	5.25		26,800	10,400	1,156
Cabo Rico 45	45.50	35.00	13.16	6.50	5.50	35,600	13,500	1,334
Caliber 35LRC	33.84	29.84	11.33	4.50		13,100	6,100	563
Caliber 40LRC	39.10	32.50	12.66	5.10		21,600	9,500	739
Caliber 47LRC	48.58	39.50	13.16	5.16		33,000	13,000	1,014
Cambria 40	41.50	32.50	12.25	7.25	4.92	22,200	7,500	801
Cambria 44/46	45.86	36.25	13.48		5.00	28,600	11,500	943
Catalina 22 MkII	21.50	19.33	8.33	3.50	2.50	2,290	700	205
Catalina 250	25.00	21.25	8.50	3.50	1.66 / 5.75	3,455	1,050	265
Catalina 270	27.00	23.75	9.84	5.00	3.50	6,240	1,840	316
Catalina C28 MkII	28.33	23.84	10.33	5.25	3.66	13,500	3,200	364
Catalina C30 MkII	29.92	25.00	10.84	5.25	3.84	10,200	4,200	446
Catalina 320	32.50	28.00	11.75	6.00	4.25	11,300	4,000	521
Catalina 34 MkII	34.50	29.84	11.75	7.00	5.33	11,950	5,000	528
Catalina 36 MkII	36.33	30.25	11.92	5.84	4.42	13,500	6,000	555
Catalina C380	38.42	32.42	12.33	7.00	5.33	19,000	6,800	719
Catalina 400	40.50	36.50	13.50	6.75	5.50	19,700	7,250	808
Catalina 42 MkII	41.84	36.00	13.84	6.00	4.84	20,500	8,300	797
Catalina 470	46.50	42.00	14.00	7.84	5.50	27,000	8,800	1,080
Compac 23/3	23.92	20.20	7.84	2.25		3,000	1,340	250
Compac 25	25.00	21.00	8.00	2.50		4,800	1,900	308
Compac 27/2	26.92	24.25	9.50	3.50		6,000	2,500	380
Compac 35	36.75	29.00	11.92	4.00		12,500	5,700	579

Displ. = Displacement; **E** = foot length of mainsail; **FO** = fuel oil tank capacity; **Frac.** = fractional; **ft.** = feet; **FW** = freshwater tank capacity; **gal.** = gallons; **hp** = horsepower; **I** = mast height; **J** = distance from forward side of mast to tack fitting of headsail; **lb.** = pounds; **LOA** = length overall; **LOD** = length on deck; **LWL** = length at waterline; **M/H** = masthead; **Overhangs** = (LOA – LWL) /LOA; **P** = luff length of mainsail; **SA** = Sail area

Sail Area, ft.^{2} Main & 100% Foretriangle	Engine, hp	I, ft.	P, ft.	E, ft.	J, ft.	Mast Height above LWL, ft.
352.50	9	30.00	33.00	12.50	9.75	
653.22	27	43.00	44.50	15.83	14.00	54.25
567.70	18	40.84	41.50	14.93	12.63	
780.87	43	53.81	47.90	15.63	15.11	
901.39	43	57.97	51.67	15.75	17.06	
1,174.08	62	65.29	57.41	20.01	18.37	
1,317.10	78	67.00	60.00	22.24	19.40	
1,310.41	88	70.14	61.81	19.32	20.34	
1,624.96	100	76.60	68.40	23.10	21.80	
1,792.05	100	80.38	72.34	24.10	22.90	
1,971.13	120	86.19	78.10	23.66	24.30	
2,179.94	140	87.60	79.30	26.70	25.60	
2,120.88	140	78.10	81.80	29.80	23.10	
312.08		29.86	30.84	11.98	8.53	38.00
522.97	27	41.67	38.39	14.60	11.65	
806.14	30	51.60	48.85	17.72	14.47	58.80
551.25	27	42.32	35.76	14.44	13.85	41.33
687.17	48	48.23	41.96	15.65	14.88	52.80
695.04	42	47.67	41.50	14.83	16.25	
835.11	85	46.13	52.40	16.31	17.68	59.00
771.85	48	50.86	47.41	17.22	14.30	58.50
611.29	27	41.50	36.00	15.17	16.30	45.00
930.74	50	52.42	46.25	17.58	20.00	50.00
930.74	62	52.42	46.25	17.58	20.00	50.00
1,136.09	75	57.25	51.00	21.17	20.83	50.00
563.38	27	43.00	39.25	12.00	15.25	
738.66	50	50.50	45.75	13.25	17.25	
1,014.17	75	54.50	47.83	18.00	21.42	
821.00	50	55.75	50.00	15.00	16.00	
1,009.46	62	62.00	56.00	16.50	17.66	63.50
217.43	7	25.83	21.00	9.66	8.00	29.10
284.74	10	29.00	24.50	11.00	9.00	36.30
344.61	18	33.33	28.16	11.50	9.25	42.00
415.38	23	39.50	34.00	10.75	10.82	44.40
508.76	23	43.00	37.00	12.00	13.16	47.50
535.34	27	43.58	38.00	13.25	12.33	47.70
558.56	30	46.00	40.50	12.00	13.50	51.58
653.41	30	46.75	41.00	13.00	14.33	52.16
761.21	42	54.00	47.92	15.66	14.66	60.00
810.25	42	52.66	47.00	17.00	15.50	58.00
842.88	50	53.00	46.75	15.60	16.42	58.80
1,010.13	55	58.25	51.50	20.00	17.00	67.60
217.02	9	26.00	22.25	8.50	9.42	30.00
	12					32.75
327.20	18	31.40	25.75	12.00	11.00	35.66
399.25	27	44.50	25.75	12.00	11.00	35.66

(Specifications for these boats continue next page)

Boat	FW, gal.	FO, gal.	No. of Bunks	Rig Type	Base Price, $	In-Water Price (best estimate)	Ratios and Coefficients SA/ Displ.	Displ./ Length
Alerion Express 28			2	Frac. sloop	$47,500	$70,000	21.01	164.86
Alerion Express 38	30	45	4	Frac. sloop	$159,900	$185,000	19.52	213.88
Baltic 35	32	32	4	M/H sloop			19.74	186.52
Baltic 40	50	33	4	M/H sloop			20.56	190.86
Baltic 43	63	45	6	M/H sloop			19.75	192.81
Baltic 47	106	53	6	M/H sloop			22.16	178.86
Baltic 50			6	M/H sloop				
Baltic 52	132	66	6	M/H sloop			20.82	177.75
Baltic 58	212	106	6	M/H sloop			21.57	173.72
Baltic 60			6	M/H sloop			23.78	132.99
Baltic 64	24	370	6	M/H sloop			21.50	183.74
Baltic 67	24	211	6	M/H sloop			29.45	88.66
Baltic 70		58	6	M/H sloop			29.39	84.88
Beneteau 25			2	Frac. sloop	$31,250	$40,000	25.41	112.41
Beneteau First 33.7	40	12	4	M/H sloop	$154,900	$170,000	17.37	204.07
Beneteau First 40.7	79	35	6	M/H sloop	$154,900	$170,000	1.35	156.92
Beneteau Oceanis 36cc	111	40	4	M/H sloop	$126,500	$135,000	15.65	196.70
Beneteau Oceanis 40cc	132	45	4	M/H sloop	$179,280	$200,000	15.59	168.56
Beneteau Oceanis 411	158	40	4	M/H sloop	$168,700	$180,000	16.70	163.45
Beneteau Oceanis 44cc	160	73	4	M/H sloop	$254,600	$275,000	17.59	188.38
Beneteau First 42s7	160	40	4	Frac. sloop	$185,000	$195,000	17.84	178.02
Cabo Rico 36	165	55	6	M/H cutter	$228,000	$245,000	15.74	365.18
Cabo Rico 38	150	56	7	M/H cutter	$266,000	$285,000	19.57	374.62
Cabo Rico 40	200	72	7	M/H cutter	$370,000	$390,000	16.64	365.12
Cabo Rico 45	250	150	7	M/H cutter	$533,000	$556,000	16.80	370.68
Caliber 35LRC	105	120	4	M/H sloop	$139,950		16.23	220.10
Caliber 40LRC	179	212	4	M/H sloop	$212,950		15.24	280.90
Caliber 47LRC	275	275	4	M/H sloop	$311,950		15.78	239.04
Cambria 40	140	60	7	M/H cutter	$330,000	$351,000	16.64	288.71
Cambria 44/46	185	105	7	M/H cutter	$510,000	$533,000	17.28	268.04
Catalina 22 MkII	3	Portable	2	M/H sloop		$12,438	20.03	141.54
Catalina 250	12	14	4	M/H sloop		$17,179	19.94	160.74
Catalina 270	24	14	4	M/H sloop		$46,687	16.27	207.94
Catalina C28 MkII	49	19	4	M/H sloop		$56,917	11.73	444.80
Catalina C30 MkII	50	18	6	M/H sloop		$66,449	17.31	291.43
Catalina 320	50	20	6	M/H sloop		$79,702	17.02	229.80
Catalina 34 MkII	59	25	6	M/H sloop		$89,052	17.10	200.78
Catalina 36 MkII	80	25	6	M/H sloop		$100,669	18.45	217.73
Catalina C380	96	30	6	M/H sloop		$127,742	17.11	248.92
Catalina 400	116	35	6	M/H sloop		$160,566	17.78	180.86
Catalina 42 MkII	116	60	6	M/H sloop		$160,575	18.01	196.15
Catalina 470	204	84	6	M/H sloop		$235,686	17.97	162.69
Compac 23/3	11	6	2	M/H sloop	$21,195	$29,500	16.70	162.49
Compac 25	20	13	2	M/H sloop	$32,500	$54,000		231.39
Compac 27/2	55	13	2	M/H sloop	$67,200	$72,000	15.86	187.83
Compac 35	55	13	2	M/H sloop	$124,000	$140,000	11.86	228.81

Displ. = Displacement; **E** = foot length of mainsail; **FO** = fuel oil tank capacity; **Frac.** = fractional; **ft.** = feet; **FW** = freshwater tank capacity; **gal.** = gallons; **hp** = horsepower; **I** = mast height; **J** = distance from forward side of mast to tack fitting of headsail; **lb.** = pounds; **LOA** = length overall; **LOD** = length on deck; **LWL** = length at waterline; **M/H** = masthead; **Overhangs** = (LOA – LWL) /LOA; **P** = luff length of mainsail; **SA** = Sail area

Capsize Factor	Cost/lb. ($)	FW Ratio	FO Ratio	Displ./hp Ratio	Comfort Space	Overhangs (LOA–LWL)/ LOA	Beam/Length Ratio
1.99	29.17			488.89	16.473	0.192	3.22
1.88	14.92	1.935	2.722	459.26	24.219	0.216	3.13
2.14		2.592	2.430	548.72	18.551	0.178	2.87
2.07		2.668	1.651	348.60	28.175	0.169	2.96
2.04		2.552	1.709	459.30	24.706	0.175	2.98
1.98		3.434	1.610	398.26	30.944	0.173	3.15
1.94		3.303	1.548	363.26	40.049	0.178	3.22
1.92		4.05	1.898	418.88	52.390	0.187	3.29
1.89				418.88	52.600	0.140	3.64
1.81		4.96	4.936	468.48	70.266	0.195	3.42
2.06		3.88	3.880	291.33	51.243	0.119	3.83
1.89			1.108	280.35	48.494	0.162	4.25
2.43	24.52				10.360	0.097	3.00
2.03		3.024	0.851	391.93	19.811	0.131	2.95
1.98		6.112	1.727	506.67	19.083	0.106	3.29
2.11	14.63	6.636	2.242	495.63	25.395	0.143	2.87
1.92	14.88	5.635	1.801	390.42	35.655	0.104	3.31
2.02	15.39	7.351	1.745	409.43	32.604	0.134	3.19
2.04	19.49	6.112	2.614	246.40	39.686	0.176	3.02
2.06	10.70	7.025	1.647	379.58	35.586	0.159	3.04
1.77	25.26	8.516	2.661	574.07	19.492	0.216	2.79
1.67	21.59	5.714	2.000	420.00	22.642	0.230	2.92
1.70	23.78	5.970	2.015	432.26	28.849	0.205	2.91
1.60	25.16	5.618	3.160	474.67	38.355	0.231	3.06
1.93		6.412	6.870	485.19	24.497	0.118	3.03
1.82		6.630	7.361	432.00	40.491	0.169	2.95
1.64		6.667	6.250	440.00	62.132	0.187	3.45
1.75	23.88	5.045	2.027	444.00	24.011	0.217	3.05
1.77	31.17	5.175	2.753	461.29	30.746	0.210	3.09
2.53	7.82	0.873		327.14	8.695	0.101	2.67
2.25	7.14	2.779	3.039	345.50	6.561	0.150	2.87
2.14	10.61	3.077	1.683	346.67	11.859	0.120	2.77
1.74	5.53	2.904	1.056	586.96	25.796	0.158	2.65
2.00	11.07	3.922	1.324	443.48	12.78	0.164	2.65
2.10	10.92	3.504	1.327	418.52	14.237	0.138	2.74
2.06	12.81	3.950	1.569	398.33	14.965	0.135	2.92
2.01	13.42	4.741	1.389	450.00	16.864	0.167	2.92
1.85	10.47	4.042	1.184	452.38	23.930	0.156	3.02
2.00	12.90	4.711	1.332	469.05	24.788	0.099	3.11
2.03	13.16	4.527	2.195	410.00	25.705	0.140	2.99
1.87	12.95	6.044	2.333	490.91	34.109	0.097	3.45
2.18	17.77	2.933	1.500	333.33	11.240	0.156	2.96
1.90	18.62	3.333	2.031	400.00	18.071	0.160	3.02
2.09	20.57	7.333	1.625	333.33	22.545	0.099	2.93
2.06	20.59	3.520	0.780	462.96	46.792	0.211	2.80

Displ./Length Ratio $= \dfrac{\text{Displ. in lbs.}/2{,}240}{(\text{LWL}/100)^3}$

Comfort space $= \dfrac{(\text{Displ.}/64 - \text{Ballast}/700)}{2}/\text{Number of bunks}$

Capsize Factor $= \dfrac{\text{Beam}}{(\text{Displ.}/64)^{1/3}}$

Boat	LOA or LOD, ft.	LWL, ft.	Beam, ft.	Deep Keel Draft	Draft, ft. (wing or shallow) C/B up/down	Displace-ment, lb.	Ballast, lb.	Sail Area, ft.[2] (given by manufacturer)
Freedom 24	24.42	21.50	8.25	6.00	4.50	3,250	1,350	378
Freedom 35	35.35	29.86	12.00	6.50	4.50	14,611	4,465	740
Freedom 40	40.42	35.10	13.50	6.75	5.25	23,762	9,693	1,155
Freedom 45	44.50	34.50	13.50	6.50	4.92	27,500	9,500	954
Gozzard 31	36.20	26.00	11.00	4.33		10,500	4,600	782
Gozzard 37	42.30	31.60	12.00	5.00		19,000	6,800	891
Gozzard 41 & PH	41.00	35.33	13.00	5.25		21,000	7,500	
Gozzard 44 & CC	44.00	37.25	13.66	5.25		28,000	11,700	1,152
Hunter 240	24.10	22.10	8.25		1.5 / 5.5	2,300	1,300	236
Hunter 260	26.25	23.25	8.96	3.50	1.75 / 6	5,000	2,000	320
Hunter 280	27.75	23.58	9.68	5.00		2,100	650	428
Hunter 31	31.93	28.00	10.92	5.50		8,500	3,000	523
Hunter 34	33.75	28.58	11.66	6.00		11,030		682
Hunter 376	37.25	32.00	12.58	6.50		15,000	4,950	810
Hunter 410	40.66	37.84	13.84	6.42		19,500	6,700	875
Hunter 42	42.50	38.00	14.00	4.92		24,000	7,700	949
Hunter 430	42.50	38.00	14.00	4.92		23,800	7,700	970
Hunter 450	44.25	38.58	14.00	5.50		26,000	9,500	981
Island Packet 320	33.25	27.00	11.75	4.25		13,500	6,000	645
Island Packet 350	36.84	29.33	12.00	4.25		16,000	7,500	725
Island Packet 37	38.50	31.00	12.16	4.50		18,500	8,200	800
Island Packet 40	39.33	39.33	12.92	4.66	3.84	22,800	10,000	907
Island Packet 45	45.25	37.58	13.33	4.84		28,400	12,500	1,100
J/120	40.00	35.00	12.00	7.00		13,900	6,000	780
J/130	42.80	38.20	12.80	8.50		15,000	6,350	956
J/160	52.70	47.50	14.50	8.80		31,000	11,000	1,376
J/32	32.60	28.80	11.00	5.90		10,000	3,840	514
J/42	42.00	35.10	12.20	6.60		19,700	7,000	790
J/46	46.00	40.50	13.80	5.90		24,400	9,400	1,021
Jeanneau 34.2	33.75	29.50	10.79	5.66	4.25	10,253	2,866	599
Jeanneau 36.2	36.10	30.50	12.42	6.25		12,320	3,410	659
Jeanneau 40	40.00	33.33	12.92	6.33	4.92	16,094	5,291	894
Jeanneau 42.2	42.00	33.32	13.46	5.42		18,519	5,754	945
Jeanneau 42cc	42.10	33.32	13.46	5.42		18,920	5,742	939
Jeanneau 45.2	45.25	38.42	14.66	6.58		20,570	7,110	997
Jeanneau 47cc	47.25	38.39	14.58	6.92		27,560	9,768	1,200
Jeanneau 52.2	50.50	41.66	15.10	5.92		33,000	12,320	1,302
Morgan 38	38.50	32.50	12.33	7.00	5.33	19,000	6,800	700
Morgan 45	45.25	37.84	13.90	6.50	5.58	25,225	8,975	816
Pacific Seacraft 34V	34.10	26.24	10.00	4.92	4.10	13,500	4,800	534
Pacific Seacraft 37V	36.92	27.75	10.84	5.50	4.42	16,000	6,200	619
Pacific Seacraft 40V	40.33	31.25	12.42	6.10	5.16	24,500	8,600	834
Pacific Seacraft 44V	44.10	33.65	12.80	6.25	5.30	27,500	9,400	1,325
Sabre 362	36.16	30.50	12.00	5.52		13,800	5,520	634
Sabre 402	40.20	34.00	13.33	7.33		19,000	7,400	822
Sabre 452	45.20	38.33	14.10	6.75		26,500	10,200	1,043

Displ. = Displacement; **E** = foot length of mainsail; **FO** = fuel oil tank capacity; **Frac.** = fractional; **ft.** = feet; **FW** = freshwater tank capacity; **gal.** = gallons; **hp** = horsepower; **I** = mast height; **J** = distance from forward side of mast to tack fitting of headsail; **lb.** = pounds; **LOA** = length overall; **LOD** = length on deck; **LWL** = length at waterline; **M/H** = masthead; **Overhangs** = (LOA – LWL) /LOA; **P** = luff length of mainsail; **SA** = Sail area

Sail Area, ft.² Main & 100% Foretriangle	Engine, hp	I, ft.	P, ft.	E, ft.	J, ft.	Mast Height above LWL, ft.
378.00	9	26.00	32.50	11.67	8.62	39.60
740.10	27	39.90	45.30	16.80	11.50	54.50
791.00	45	47.74	51.28	18.85	12.89	61.00
888.50	75	50.83	58.00	18.50	13.85	63.00
613.56	36	40.80	36.00	13.80	17.90	46.00
	63					53.50
	73					58.00
	82					59.00
241.75	5	25.50	24.25	11.00	8.50	32.50
291.88	8	28.30	30.10	10.50	9.46	40.00
338.33	18	31.50	31.66	12.00	9.42	42.00
460.67	18	37.10	39.10	12.50	11.66	48.50
602.61	27	43.00	44.42	16.00	11.50	56.50
683.71	36	48.00	49.00	15.25	12.92	60.10
822.99	50	47.75	45.42	19.25	16.16	58.42
816.00	62	55.50	48.00	15.50	16.00	60.25
837.50	50	50.00	50.00	17.75	15.75	62.42
907.00	59	55.46	49.33	17.75	16.92	63.00
553.77	27	44.00	37.00	12.50	14.66	48.10
614.72	38	44.84	37.00	14.25	15.66	48.33
928.03	38	54.92	47.50	17.50	18.66	49.50
774.34	50	49.84	42.84	15.50	17.75	53.66
928.03	62	54.92	47.50	17.50	18.66	58.84
779.98	38	50.50	46.50	17.80	14.50	56.80
955.88	47	57.00	52.50	18.50	16.50	62.60
1,375.06	88	66.50	62.00	24.16	18.83	74.00
513.98	28	39.20	38.50	15.50	11.00	48.60
789.68	47	50.50	46.50	18.00	14.70	56.50
1,020.80	75	58.50	53.50	19.90	16.70	65.00
472.64	21	41.66	35.42	13.75	11.00	
512.80	27	42.33	36.25	14.42	11.88	
682.40	60	50.00	43.25	15.66	13.75	
703.05	62	50.88	45.58	15.50	13.75	
734.39	62	50.83	44.75	15.50	15.25	
795.01	62	51.14	46.00	16.50	16.25	
	75					
993.61	88	58.58	51.16	17.66	18.50	
700.28	42	50.50	42.16	15.66	14.66	55.50
816.38	50	52.75	46.00	16.00	17.00	58.66
533.19	38	40.33	34.40	14.00	14.50	44.30
618.46	51	44.00	38.17	14.25	15.75	47.75
853.65	51	49.50	44.25	18.00	18.40	55.00
976.44	51	58.88	50.92	16.00	19.33	60.00
634.87	32	48.50	41.60	14.83	13.46	53.20
822.25	50	54.00	47.50	17.00	15.50	57.50
1,027.01	76	59.50	52.50	19.20	17.58	65.00

(Specifications for these boats continue next page)

Boat	FW, gal.	FO, gal.	No. of Bunks	Rig Type	Base Price, $	In-Water Price (best estimate)	Ratios and Coefficients SA/ Displ.	Displ./ Length
Freedom 24	5		2	Frac. sloop	$34,500		27.57	145.99
Freedom 35	80	31	4	Frac. sloop	$152,500		19.82	245.00
Freedom 40	106	62	4	Frac. sloop	$240,500		15.32	245.31
Freedom 45			4	Frac. sloop	As quoted		15.61	298.97
Gozzard 31	81	38	4	M/H cutter	$213,875	$213,875	20.48	266.70
Gozzard 37	121	55	4	M/H cutter	$281,875	$281,875		268.81
Gozzard 41 & PH	126	105	5	M/H cutter	$379,832	$379,832		
Gozzard 44 & CC	150	112	6	M/H cutter	$469,375	$469,375		241.84
Hunter 240	7		4	Frac. sloop	$16,995	$18,694	22.20	95.13
Hunter 260	20	15	4	Frac. sloop	$23,995	$26,394	15.98	177.60
Hunter 280	40	2	4	Frac. sloop	$54,760	$60,236	33.02	71.51
Hunter 31	50	28	4	Frac. sloop	$74,810	$82,291	17.70	172.86
Hunter 34	75	30	4	Frac. sloop	$96,570	$106,227	19.47	210.93
Hunter 376	75	35	4	Frac. sloop	$136,380	$150,018	17.99	204.36
Hunter 410	145	50	4	Frac. sloop	$170,200	$187,220	18.18	160.67
Hunter 42	150	70	4	Frac. sloop	$196,650	$216,315	15.70	195.26
Hunter 430	165	50	4	Frac. sloop			16.20	193.63
Hunter 450	200	100	4	M/H sloop	$259,615	$285,576	16.54	202.13
Island Packet 320	90	45	4	M/H cutter	$144,950	$150,000	15.63	306.19
Island Packet 350	100	30	4	M/H cutter	$167,950	$175,000	15.50	283.10
Island Packet 37	90	50	4	M/H cutter	$189,950	$194,000	21.24	277.23
Island Packet 40	170	90	4	M/H cutter	$226,950	$235,000	15.41	167.31
Island Packet 45	240	140	4	M/H cutter	$284,950	$295,000	15.96	238.89
J/120	75	27	6	Frac. sloop	$209,325		21.59	144.73
J/130	60	30	6	Frac. sloop	$244,660		25.15	120.13
J/160	157	95	9	Frac. sloop	$552,500		22.30	129.13
J/32	50	27	4	Frac. sloop	$120,900		17.72	186.89
J/42	100	31	6	Frac. sloop	$219,290		17.33	203.37
J/46	117	70	7	Frac. sloop	$397,500			
Jeanneau 34.2	37	28	6	M/H sloop	$91,500	$105,000	16.03	178.29
Jeanneau 36.2	78	26	4	M/H sloop	$107,000	$118,000	15.39	193.85
Jeanneau 40	85	36	8	M/H sloop	$107,000	$118,000	17.13	194.05
Jeanneau 42.2	117	46	4	M/H sloop	$187,000	$200,000	16.08	223.49
Jeanneau 42cc	120	60	4	M/H sloop	$224,800	$240,000	16.56	228.33
Jeanneau 45.2	158	54	6	M/H sloop	$248,000	$260,000	16.95	161.93
Jeanneau 47cc	198	62	4	M/H sloop				217.46
Jeanneau 52.2	265	100	6	M/H sloop	$359,900	$380,000	15.46	203.75
Morgan 38	86	44	6	M/H sloop			15.74	247.09
Morgan 45	177	60	7	M/H sloop			15.19	207.84
Pacific Seacraft 34V	75	37	6	M/H sloop	$189,900	$200,000	15.05	333.58
Pacific Seacraft 37V	85	40	6	M/H sloop	$219,900	$240,000	15.59	334.26
Pacific Seacraft 40V	120	70	7	M/H sloop	$332,900	$340,000	16.20	358.40
Pacific Seacraft 44V	84	79	7	M/H sloop	$449,900	$465,000	17.15	322.20
Sabre 362	78	30	4	M/H sloop	$163,900	$190,000	17.66	217.14
Sabre 402	104	50	4	M/H sloop	$234,900	$260,000	18.48	215.81
Sabre 452	200	100	4	M/H sloop	$400,000	$425,000	18.49	210.08

Displ. = Displacement; **E** = foot length of mainsail; **FO** = fuel oil tank capacity; **Frac.** = fractional; **ft.** = feet; **FW** = freshwater tank capacity; **gal.** = gallons; **hp** = horsepower; **I** = mast height; **J** = distance from forward side of mast to tack fitting of headsail; **lb.** = pounds; **LOA** = length overall; **LOD** = length on deck; **LWL** = length at waterline; **M/H** = masthead; **Overhangs** = (LOA – LWL) /LOA; **P** = luff length of mainsail; **SA** = Sail area

Capsize Factor	Cost/lb. ($)	FW Ratio	FO Ratio	Displ./hp Ratio	Comfort Space	Overhangs (LOA–LWL)/ LOA	Beam/Length Ratio
2.23		1.231		361.11	12.213	0.120	3.00
1.97		4.380	1.591	541.15	27.740	0.155	2.86
1.88		3.569	1.957	528.04	44.679	0.132	2.99
1.79				366.67	52.015	0.225	2.94
2.01	36.25	6.171	0.286	291.67	19.686	0.282	2.72
1.80	23.10	5.095	0.158	301.59	24.967	0.253	3.03
1.80	28.80	4.286	0.161	341.46	35.065	0.153	3.13
2.50	18.69	2.261		460.00	1.953	0.083	3.08
2.10	8.80	3.200	2.250	625.00	5.859	0.114	2.98
3.03	41.54	15.238	0.714	116.67	3.985	0.150	2.80
2.14	14.96	4.706	2.471	472.22	16.066	0.123	2.95
2.10	9.63	5.440	2.040	408.52	21.543	0.153	2.82
2.04	14.93	4.000	1.750	416.67	28.413	0.141	2.92
2.06	14.63	5.949	1.923	390.00	36.890	0.069	3.14
1.95	13.27	5.000	2.188	387.10	45.500	0.106	3.12
1.95		5.546	1.576	476.00	45.109	0.106	3.12
1.89	17.31	6.154	2.885	440.68	49.085	0.128	3.17
1.98	20.00	5.333	2.500	500.00	25.296	0.188	2.64
1.91	20.59	5.000	1.406	421.05	29.911	0.204	2.81
1.84	18.83	3.892	2.027	486.84	34.669	0.195	2.93
1.83	18.36	5.965	2.961	456.00	42.746	0.000	3.50
1.75	18.55	6.761	3.697	458.06	53.237	0.170	3.24
2.00	29.11	4.317	1.457	365.79	17.385	0.125	3.35
2.08	30.64	3.200	1.500	319.15	18.775	0.107	3.43
1.85	28.50	4.052	2.298	352.27	26.037	0.099	3.77
2.05	22.73	4.000	2.025	357.14	18.846	0.117	3.01
1.81	18.50	4.061	1.180	419.15	24.818	0.164	3.31
1.99	14.21	2.887	2.048	488.24	13.009	0.126	3.14
2.15	13.24	5.065	1.583	456.30	23.454	0.155	2.82
2.05	10.92	4.225	1.678	268.23	15.244	0.167	2.97
2.04	15.67	5.033	1.872	298.69	35.142	0.207	2.85
2.02	18.21	5.074	2.378	305.16	35.928	0.209	2.85
2.14	19.32	6.145	1.969	331.77	25.937	0.151	3.01
1.93		5.747	1.687	367.47	52.084	0.188	3.03
1.89	18.38	6.424	2.273	375.00	41.502	0.175	3.17
1.85		3.621	1.737	452.38	23.930	0.156	3.03
1.90		5.613	1.784	504.50	27.237	0.164	3.13
1.68		4.444	2.056	355.26	17.007	0.230	3.02
1.72		4.250	1.875	313.73	20.095	0.248	2.94
1.71		3.918	2.143	480.39	26.466	0.225	2.89
1.70		2.444	2.155	539.22	29.733	0.237	3.02
2.00	22.95	4.522	1.630	431.25	25.967	0.157	2.92
2.00	22.41	4.379	1.974	380.00	35.788	0.154	2.93
1.90	26.07	6.038	2.830	348.68	49.936	0.152	3.12

Displ./Length Ratio = $\frac{\text{Displ. in lbs./2,240}}{(\text{LWL}/100)^3}$

Comfort space = $\frac{(\text{Displ.}/64 - \text{Ballast}/700)}{2}$/Number of bunks

Capsize Factor = $\frac{\text{Beam}}{(\text{Displ.}/64)^{1/3}}$

Boat	LOA or LOD, ft.	LWL, ft.	Beam, ft.	Deep Keel Draft	Draft, ft. (wing or shallow) C/B up/down	Displace- ment, lb.	Ballast, lb.	Sail Area, ft.[2] (given by manufacturer)
Santa Cruz 52	53.00	46.50	14.00	9.00		21,000	9,850	1,327
Shannon 39	38.58	32.84	12.00	5.50		18,700	6,900	749
Sundeer	59.92	59.00	13.42	6.00		35,000	10,000	
Sweden Yachts 340	34.12	27.89	11.48	5.25	5.09	12,563	5,179	
Sweden Yachts 370	36.58	29.53	12.07	6.73	5.58	14,987	6,061	
Sweden Yachts 390	38.98	31.50	12.70	7.38	5.58	16,750	6,943	
Sweden Yachts 41	41.01	32.81	12.96	7.38	5.58	18,734	8,155	
Sweden Yachts 45	46.43	37.73	13.71	7.38	5.91	24,244	8,816	
Sweden Yachts 50	50.04	41.34	14.27	8.53	6.56	31,958	13,224	
Sweden Yachts 52	52.04	41.34	14.27	8.53	6.50	33,831	13,224	
Sweden Yachts 70	69.72	52.50	17.00	10.50	8.53	68,324	24,244	
Tartan 3500	35.21	30.00	11.75	6.50	4.84	11,400	4,200	
Tartan 3800	38.00	31.00	12.42	6.84	5.33	16,000	6,500	
Tartan 4100	41.25	35.75	13.50	7.00	5.33	19,000	6,400	
Tartan 4600	46.20	39.58	14.33	8.92	5.5 4.84/9	24,000	8,500	
Trintella 42	42.00	35.75	13.78	5.90		29,750	12,122	1,024
Trintella 47	47.25	37.84	14.76	6.45		35,264		1,030
Valiant 39	37.00	32.00	11.50	5.92	5.25	18,500	7,000	735
Valiant 42	39.90	34.50	12.33	6.00	5.50	24,500	9,500	849
Valiant 50	50.00	40.25	13.84	6.25		35,500	11,000	1,036
Westerly Ocean 33	33.33	28.25	11.16	6.00		9,918	4,453	584
Westerly Oceanquest 35	34.58	27.00	12.25	4.50	3.92 twin keel	14,080	5,698	725
Westerly Oceanranger 38	38.00	30.75	12.66	5.00		15,900	6,600	836
Westerly Oceanlord 41	40.50	35.25	13.50	5.50		20,878	8,000	970
Westerly Ocean 43	43.50	35.92	13.90	5.75		29,767	12,123	1,024
Westerly Ocean 49	48.58	42.16	15.16	7.16		28,940	11,680	1,171
X-Yachts X-99	32.80	27.89	9.80	6.10	5.00	8,677	2,865	667
X-Yachts IMX38	37.28	31.20	12.10	7.15	6.00	11,800	6,173	959
X-Yachts X-302	30.60	26.40	9.80	5.60	4.60	7,929	3,303	567
X-Yachts X-332	33.80	28.90	10.80	5.90	5.00	9,590	3,968	733
X-Yachts X-362	36.10	30.50	11.40	6.20	5.00	11,440	4,960	783
X-Yachts X-382	37.70	31.80	12.20	6.60	5.50	14,333	6,174	950
X-Yachts X-412	42.30	32.40	12.80	6.50		16,314	7,716	1,080
X-Yachts X-442	44.30	36.70	13.60	7.50		21,300	9,480	1,296
X-Yachts X-482	48.00	41.00	14.10	8.20	7.20	26,455	11,023	1,495
X-Yachts X-612	60.00	52.10	16.70	9.50	6.50	47,400	20,060	2,340
OUR BOATS								
Weekender	22.00	18.00	8.33	4.50		1,800	600	
Cruiser	34.00	24.50	10.50	4.00		8,800	2,950	
Voyager	48.00	35.50	13.33	6.25		26,000	9,400	
Single-Hander	50.00	50.00	18.00	16.00		15,500	7,000	
Cruiser/Racer	37.00	33.00	12.00	6.00		10,400	4,400	
Single-Hander fully loaded	50.00	50.00	18.00	16.40		18,000	9,400	

Displ. = Displacement; **E** = foot length of mainsail; **FO** = fuel oil tank capacity; **Frac.** = fractional; **ft.** = feet; **FW** = freshwater tank capacity; **gal.** = gallons; **hp** = horsepower; **I** = mast height; **J** = distance from forward side of mast to tack fitting of headsail; **lb.** = pounds; **LOA** = length overall; **LOD** = length on deck; **LWL** = length at waterline; **M/H** = masthead; **Overhangs** = (LOA – LWL) /LOA; **P** = luff length of mainsail; **SA** = Sail area

Sail Area, ft.² Main & 100% Foretriangle	Engine, hp	I, ft.	P, ft.	E, ft.	J, ft.	Mast Height above LWL, ft.
1,216.98	62	64.55	57.50	21.00	19.00	
748.38	50	52.00	47.00	15.25	15.00	
1,047.24		54.10	54.58	19.70	18.84	64.00
	30					50.86
671.73	30	49.87	46.26	13.12	14.76	56.60
759.39	40	53.15	48.89	13.94	15.75	60.04
	57					59.71
1,072.89	78	59.71	57.75	19.69	16.90	68.24
1,185.44	100	65.62	58.73	18.37	19.69	70.21
1,285.71	100	68.24	61.35	20.01	19.69	72.84
2,074.95	120	82.03	81.20	26.25	24.61	94.49
615.31	27	46.75	41.25	14.25	13.75	53.00
664.93	38	49.75	43.33	14.33	14.25	55.00
810.88	47	54.00	47.75	17.00	15.00	58.50
1,014.00	62	59.50	53.50	19.00	17.00	64.00
982.73	50	60.10	56.76	18.30	15.42	65.00
1,085.08	62	62.00	58.33	18.37	17.72	
	35					54.42
808.38	42	50.33	45.00	13.00	20.50	57.92
	63	53.50	53.00	16.00	20.00	63.20
583.73	20	45.60	41.20	13.45	13.45	
550.54	30	43.77	36.81	12.79	14.40	48.50
654.71	30	48.00	40.65	14.50	15.00	52.00
764.25	40	51.51	45.50	15.48	16.00	55.75
950.11	50	58.00	53.50	18.27	15.91	64.00
1,009.71	78	60.37	52.98	17.72	17.90	65.33
511.27	10.00	36.90	41.00	14.77	11.30	50.4
719.90	28.00	50.97	43.80	16.08	14.43	54.3
435.18	9.00	37.10	37.10	13.12	10.34	46.3
573.43	18.00	43.15	43.15	14.93	11.65	53.0
589.03	20.00	46.75	40.68	14.10	12.93	50.4
703.02	28.00	50.40	43.97	14.44	15.30	54.2
797.18	38.00	54.13	47.58	15.42	15.90	57.7
956.06	59.00	59.39	52.17	16.73	17.50	63.4
1,148.46	75.00	65.13	57.70	18.70	18.70	69.4
1,735.65	110.00	79.00	71.00	23.30	23.00	
237.00	8	28.00	25.00	10.00	8.00	32.50
557.25	23	45.00	38.50	12.00	14.50	49.50
1,005.50	56	60.00	53.00	17.00	18.50	65.00
1,130.00	42	64.00	58.00	18.00	19.00	70.00
665.75	34	46.00	49.00	14.50	13.50	50.50
1,005.50	56	60.00	53.00	17.00	18.50	65.00

(Specifications for these boats continue next page)

Boat	FW, gal.	FO, gal.	No. of Bunks	Rig Type	Base Price, $	In-Water Price (best estimate)	Ratios and Coefficients SA/ Displ.	Displ./ Length
Santa Cruz 52	133	86	6	M/H sloop	$349,000	$375,000	25.59	93.24
Shannon 39	100	60	2	M/H cutter			17.00	235.71
Sundeer	varies	varies	varies	M/H cutter	Semi-custom		15.67	76.08
Sweden Yachts 340	50	41		M/H sloop	Prices direct from factory			258.56
Sweden Yachts 370	55	41		M/H sloop	Prices direct from factory		17.69	259.85
Sweden Yachts 390	105	41		M/H sloop	Prices direct from factory		18.57	239.30
Sweden Yachts 41	88	41		M/H sloop	Prices direct from factory			236.79
Sweden Yachts 45	138	69		M/H sloop	Prices direct from factory		20.50	201.49
Sweden Yachts 50	193	69		M/H sloop	Prices direct from factory		18.84	201.93
Sweden Yachts 52	193	193		M/H sloop	Prices direct from factory		19.67	213.77
Sweden Yachts 70	413	331		M/H sloop	Prices direct from factory		19.87	210.84
Tartan 3500	72	25	4	M/H sloop			19.44	188.49
Tartan 3800	80	38	4	M/H sloop			16.76	239.77
Tartan 4100	100	50	4	M/H sloop			18.23	185.64
Tartan 4600	150	70	4	M/H sloop			19.51	172.80
Trintella 42	200	160	6	M/H sloop		$495,000	16.38	290.68
Trintella 47	225	270	6	M/H sloop		$795,000	16.15	290.56
Valiant 39	128	47	4	M/H sloop	$213,950	$230,000		252.04
Valiant 42	88	77	4	M/H sloop	$253,650	$277,398	15.34	266.35
Valiant 50	207	156	4	M/H sloop	$386,350	$410,000		243.04
Westerly Ocean 33	33	22	5	M/H sloop	$145,738	$150,000	20.24	196.39
Westerly Oceanquest 35	60	35	6	M/H sloop	$179,063	$185,000	15.11	319.35
Westerly Oceanranger 38	70	35	7	M/H sloop	$234,522	$240,000	16.57	244.13
Westerly Oceanlord 41	110	45	7	M/H sloop	$292,403	$300,000	16.13	212.80
Westerly Ocean 43	132	88	7	M/H sloop	$374,171	$380,000	15.83	286.73
Westerly Ocean 49	200	95	7	M/H sloop	$555,425	$560,000	17.15	172.40
X-Yachts X-99	10	14	6	Frac. sloop	$107,000	$112,000	19.38	178.56
X-Yachts IMX38	22	50	6	Frac. sloop	$185,000	$200,000	22.23	173.45
X-Yachts X-302	15	33	6	Frac. sloop	$100,000	$120,000	17.52	192.38
X-Yachts X-332	15	33	6	Frac. sloop	$130,000	$150,000	20.33	177.37
X-Yachts X-362	24	55	6	M/H sloop	$179,000	$210,000	18.57	180.00
X-Yachts X-382	28	55	6	M/H sloop	$213,000	$230,000	19.07	198.98
X-Yachts X-412	29	75	6	M/H sloop	$275,000	$300,000	19.84	214.13
X-Yachts X-442	46	83	6	M/H sloop	$396,000	$415,000	19.92	192.37
X-Yachts X-482	60	120	6	M/H sloop	$563,000	$580,000	20.70	171.36
X-Yachts X-612	192	217	6	M/H sloop	$1,203,000	$1,250,000	21.21	149.63
Our Boats								
Weekender	20		4	Frac. sloop	$15,000	$18,000	25.63	137.79
Cruiser	65	28	4	M/H sloop	$90,000	$125,000	20.92	267.14
Voyager	180	240	6	M/H sloop	$400,000	$480,000	18.34	259.44
Single-Hander	100	40	1	M/H sloop	$400,000	$530,000	29.09	55.36
Cruiser/Racer	75	38	6	Frac Sloop	$187,000	$200,000	22.36	129.19
Single-Hander fully loaded	180	240	1	M/H sloop	Not applicable		23.43	64.29

Displ. = Displacement; **E** = foot length of mainsail; **FO** = fuel oil tank capacity; **Frac.** = fractional; **ft.** = feet; **FW** = freshwater tank capacity; **gal.** = gallons; **hp** = horsepower; **I** = mast height; **J** = distance from forward side of mast to tack fitting of headsail; **lb.** = pounds; **LOA** = length overall; **LOD** = length on deck; **LWL** = length at waterline; **M/H** = masthead; **Overhangs** = (LOA – LWL) /LOA; **P** = luff length of mainsail; **SA** = Sail area

Capsize Factor	Cost/lb. ($)	FW Ratio	FO Ratio	Displ./hp Ratio	Comfort Space	Overhangs (LOA–LWL)/ LOA	Beam/Length Ratio
2.03		5.067	3.071	338.71	26.171	0.123	3.82
1.81		4.278	2.406	374.00	70.583	0.149	3.15
1.64						0.015	5.05
1.98		3.158	2.467	418.76		0.183	2.79
1.96		2.941	2.068	499.57		0.193	2.81
1.99		5.000	1.850	418.76		0.192	2.85
1.96		3.765	1.654	328.67		0.200	2.91
1.90		4.545	2.131	310.82		0.187	3.16
1.80		4.828	1.616	319.58		0.174	3.33
1.77		4.560	4.275	338.31		0.206	3.33
1.67		4.839	3.629	569.37		0.247	3.55
2.09		5.053	1.645	422.22	21.516	0.148	2.93
1.98		4.000	1.781	421.05	30.089	0.184	2.87
2.03		4.211	1.974	404.26	35.967	0.133	3.04
1.99		5.000	2.188	387.10	45.357	0.143	3.17
1.78	28.08	5.378	4.034	595.00	37.294	0.149	2.98
1.80	22.54	5.104	5.742	568.77	45.917	0.199	2.95
1.74	20.00	5.535	1.905	528.57	34.883	0.135	3.20
1.70	18.49	2.873	2.357	583.33	46.155	0.135	3.22
1.69	16.73	4.665	3.296	563.49	67.372	0.195	3.34
2.08	15.12	2.662	1.664	495.90	15.497	0.152	2.91
2.03	22.07	3.409	1.864	469.33	17.655	0.219	2.53
2.02	25.81	3.522	1.651	530.00	17.072	0.191	2.79
1.96	23.30	4.215	1.617	521.95	22.485	0.130	3.00
1.80	21.54	3.548	2.217	595.34	31.985	0.174	2.97
1.98	32.44	5.529	2.462	371.03	31.107	0.132	3.20
1.91	19.27	0.922	1.210	867.70	10.957	0.150	3.27
2.13	35.54	1.492	3.178	421.43	14.630	0.163	2.96
1.97	25.94	1.513	3.121	881.00	9.931	0.137	3.10
2.04	26.68	1.251	2.581	532.78	12.015	0.145	3.08
2.03	32.41	1.678	3.606	572.00	14.305	0.155	3.08
2.01	28.19	1.535	2.878	511.89	17.928	0.156	3.00
2.02	34.89	1.422	3.448	429.32	20.324	0.234	2.91
1.97	35.11	1.728	2.905	361.02	26.606	0.172	3.10
1.90	37.58	1.814	3.402	352.73	33.134	0.146	3.34
1.85	45.72	3.241	3.434	430.91	59.331	0.132	3.59
2.74	15.00	8.889		225.00	3.408	0.182	2.48
2.04	21.37	5.909	2.386	391.11	16.661	0.279	2.68
1.80	28.92	5.538	6.923	464.29	32.735	0.260	3.06
2.89	6.24	5.161	1.935	369.05	116.094	0.000	3.19
2.20	33.33	5.769	2.740	305.88	13.018	0.108	3.16
2.75		8.000	10.000	321.43	133.911	0.000	3.19

Displ./Length Ratio $= \dfrac{\text{Displ. in lbs./2,240}}{(\text{LWL}/100)^3}$

Comfort space $= \dfrac{\text{Displ.}/64 - \text{Ballast}/700}{2}$/Number of bunks

Capsize Factor $= \dfrac{\text{Beam}}{(\text{Displ.}/64)^{1/3}}$

(continued from page 110)
formulae, can also influence speed. That is why a VPP is to date the best method of estimating boat speed. For our purposes, however, traditional formulae are a good place to start.

Displacement/Length Ratio

It is commonly believed that heavy boats withstand heavy weather better, but a boat's weight or displacement (the terms are interchangeable) has little to do with its ability to withstand heavy conditions. The engineering of the boat is what determines its ability to hold together in bad weather. The weight of a boat does, however, affect its motion in a seaway. A light boat will usually stay afloat easily, but its motion is quick and bouncy and can cause crew fatigue fairly quickly. A heavy boat, on the other hand, is a stable platform in heavier winds, but in light airs it is slow and cumbersome.

To get an idea of the best weight for a cruiser, we use the displacement/length ratio. Because it is nondimensional, it's applicable to any size boat. The ratio is found from the formula:

$$\frac{\text{Displacement in lbs}/2{,}240}{(\text{LWL}/100)^3}$$

This number might range from 60 to 400, with lightweight boats at the lower end of the scale and real heavyweights at the upper end. The majority of production cruising boats fall between 150 and 250. For the sake of this discussion we will assume that the ideal cruiser is between 175 and 225, although a smaller boat, such as a weekender, would tend toward the lighter end of the scale. A single-hander might also be light, with a ratio around 100 to 120, and a cruiser/racer would be in the 100-to-150 range. A voyager, on the other hand, can reasonably be expected to be a little heavier because it needs to sail well whether it is laden with stores at the beginning of a trip or empty at the end. The Voyager might be around 250, at the heavier end of the spectrum.

Beam/Length Ratio

Once again, in order to compare boats of different dimensions, we generally express beam as a function of the length of the boat. Because it is very easy to change the length of a boat (by adding a bowsprit or sloping the transom differently) without changing the displacement or the beam, designers usually use the waterline beam and the waterline length. In the accompanying chart, I have used the waterline length and, because waterline beams are not published numbers, a factor of 0.9 times beam to approximate the waterline beam. This makes the ratio (0.9 × beam)/LWL.

In general, a boat with a high beam to length ratio has plenty of volume for accommodation, but depending on the ends of the boat it may not sail to windward as well. Boats with a lower beam/length ratio, such as a 12-Meter, sail to windward better. Offwind, boats with a larger beam/length ratio tend to be more powerful.

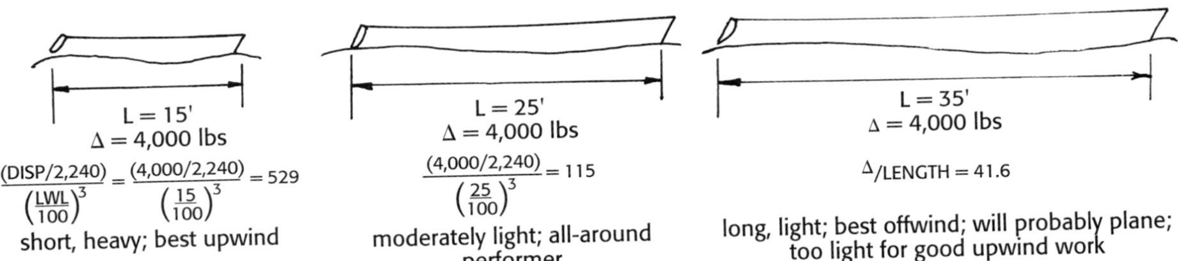

The displacement/length ratio shown graphically. If hull length increases while displacement holds constant, the displacement/length ratio drops dramatically. A ratio of 300 indicates a heavy boat, while 50 is exceptionally light. Boats with a displacement/length ratio under 60 will plane (theoretically, at least).

Sail Area/Displacement Ratio

This ratio is the sail area in square feet, divided by the displacement in pounds divided by 64 (64 pounds of seawater in 1 cubic foot gives the volume of displacement), raised to the ⅔ power:

$$SA/(Disp/64)^{2/3}$$

(Because sail area is in square feet and the volume of displacement is in cubic feet, raising the volume of displacement by the ⅔ power gives a square foot value, making the entire formula nondimensional.)

The sail area/displacement ratio gives an idea of the amount of sail area available on a boat to push each pound of weight. The higher the number, the better the boat will accelerate. A boat with a high sail area/displacement value will gain more distance in light winds or when the fleet is accelerating than a heavier boat will. (When the wind is blowing hard and all boats are sailing at their maximum speeds, waterline length is a better speed indicator than the sail area/displacement ratio.) A boat with a sail area/displacement ratio of 27 has more sail area and more get-up-and-go than a boat with a number of 18 pushing the same displacement. Displacement is also directly proportional to wetted surface, so the sail area/displacement ratio bears some relationship to the sail area/wetted surface ratio (see below), which is a better indicator of light-air speed potential.

Capsize formula

As a result of the Fastnet Race disaster of 1979, in which 15 sailors died in the Irish Sea when 24 boats sank or were abandoned in a Force 10 storm, experts developed a formula aimed at determining a boat's *tendency* to capsize. In this formula, values less than 2 indicate a lower risk of capsizing, while boats with values above 2 should not be sailed in deep ocean storms. The formula is:

$$\frac{\text{Beam}}{(\text{disp}^{1/3}/64)}$$

It assumes that beamy boats are harder to capsize but also harder to reright, and that heavier boats are harder to capsize. Note that the cap-

Typical SA/Δ values are 15 to 35
Smaller boats have higher values

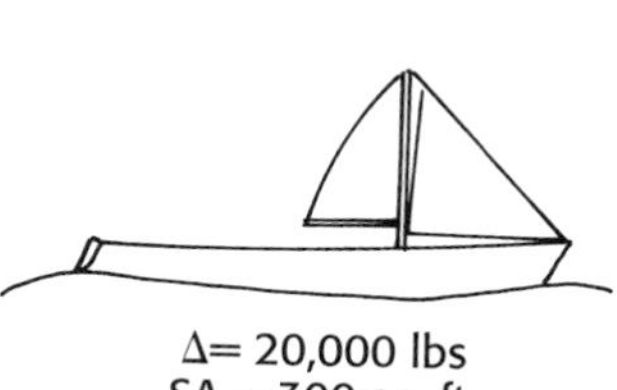

Δ= 20,000 lbs
SA = 300 sq. ft.

$$SA/\left(\frac{DISP}{64}\right)^{2/3} = \frac{300}{\left(\frac{20{,}000}{64}\right)^{66}} = 6.52$$

ridiculously undercanvased

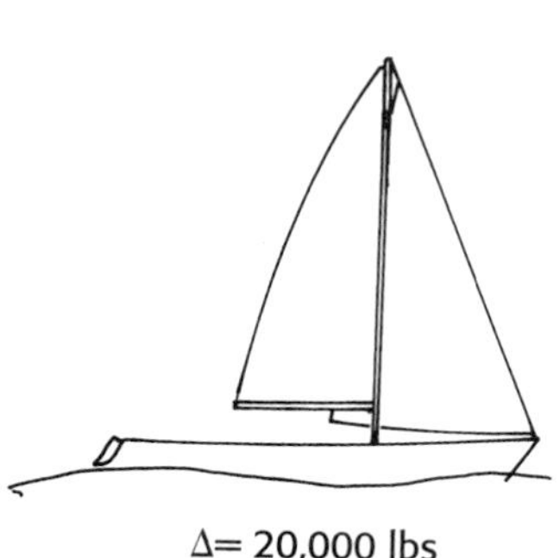

Δ= 20,000 lbs
SA = 1,000 sq. ft.

$$SA/\Delta = \frac{1{,}000}{\left(\frac{20{,}000}{64}\right)^{66}} = 21.74$$

faster in heavy air

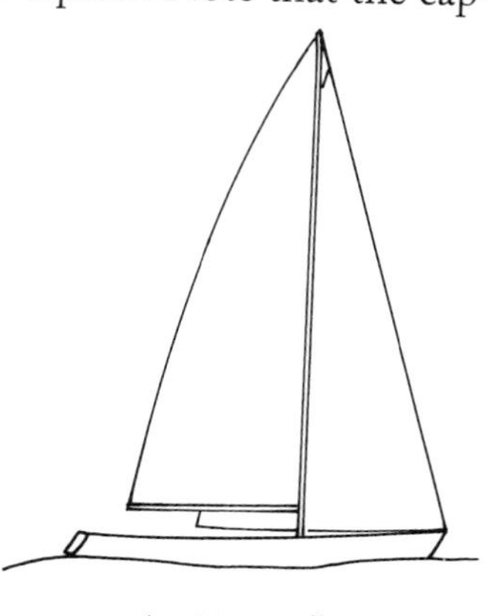

Δ= 20,000 lbs
SA = 1,500 sq. ft.

$$SA/\Delta = \frac{1{,}500}{\left(\frac{20{,}000}{64}\right)^{66}} = 32.61$$

fast in light air

The sail area/displacement ratio shown graphically. Typical ratios are in the 14-to-35 range, with higher numbers belonging to boats that are faster in light winds.

size factor is only an indication of capsizability, not a hard-and-fast rule. The angle at which the righting moment curve turns negative is a lot more accurate in a static condition. The accompanying drawing shows a righting moment curve for a hypothetical boat. The solid line indicates that at 90 degrees of heel the curve turns negative. If the curve is inverted (turn the page upside down), the righting moment is the same upside down as it is rightside up. This means that the boat is as stable upside down as it is rightside up! A wave that tips the boat beyond 90 degrees will probably roll it over until another wave rerights it, and it is rare that two large waves follow each other.

Fortunately, most boats have a righting moment curve that turns negative at around 140 to 160 degrees, which means that the boat has to heel a long way before it wants to stay inverted and it will come back upright more easily. The dashed line shows a righting moment curve for a typical production cruiser.

Sail Area/Wetted Surface Ratio

Another useful ratio is the sail area divided by the wetted surface area. If this ratio is high, the indications are that the boat will perform better in lighter winds. Typical values for the ratio are between 2 and 6. When used in conjunction with the previous ratios, a clear trend starts to emerge regarding the potential performance of the boat. Unfortunately, the wetted surface areas of production cruising sailboats are rarely if ever published. You can approximate the number using the displacement/length ratio and waterline beam/waterline length ratio, but since waterline beam is itself an approximation, what you get is an informed guess at best.

The drawing opposite shows the evolution of a long-keeled sailboat into a modern bulbed-keel form. The long keel has a lot of wetted surface and will be slow in light winds. However, it will track well in a straight line (known as having good directional stability). To increase the boat's speed in lighter winds the keel is cut away and a skeg-hung rudder is fitted. This reduces wetted surface by 40 to 50 percent, making the boat faster in lighter conditions. Note that

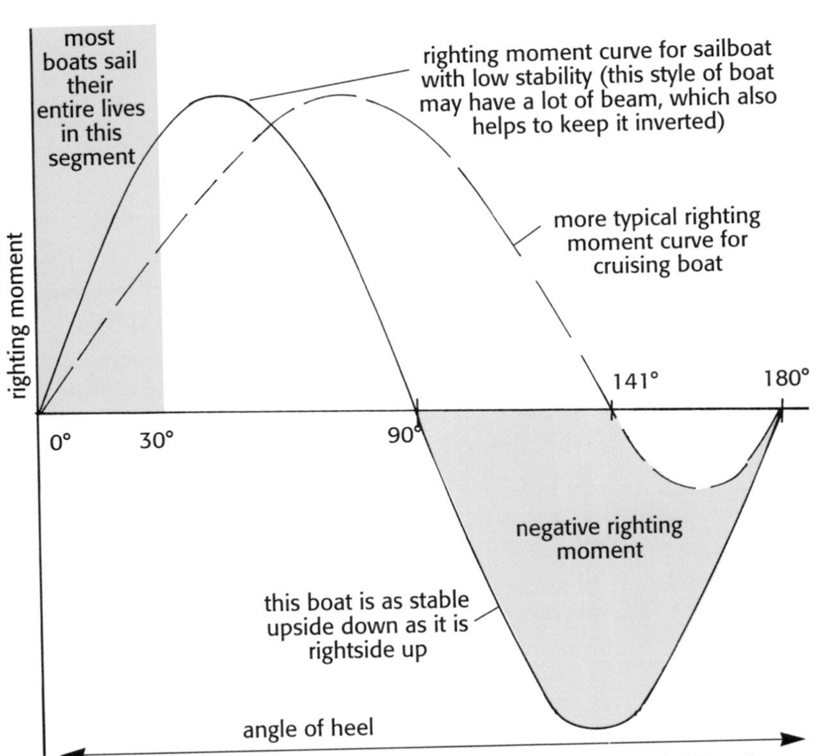

Righting moment curves for two hypothetical boats. The solid line shows a righting moment that turns negative at 90 degrees of heel. But don't worry; very few monohulls turn negative at this angle of heel. Most turn negative at around 140 to 160 degrees, as shown in the dashed curve. The amount of area under the curve shows the boat's tendency to stay inverted. (If you turn the book upside down, you will see that the lower part of the solid curve has the same area as the upper part; this boat is as likely to stay upside down as it is to stay upright.)

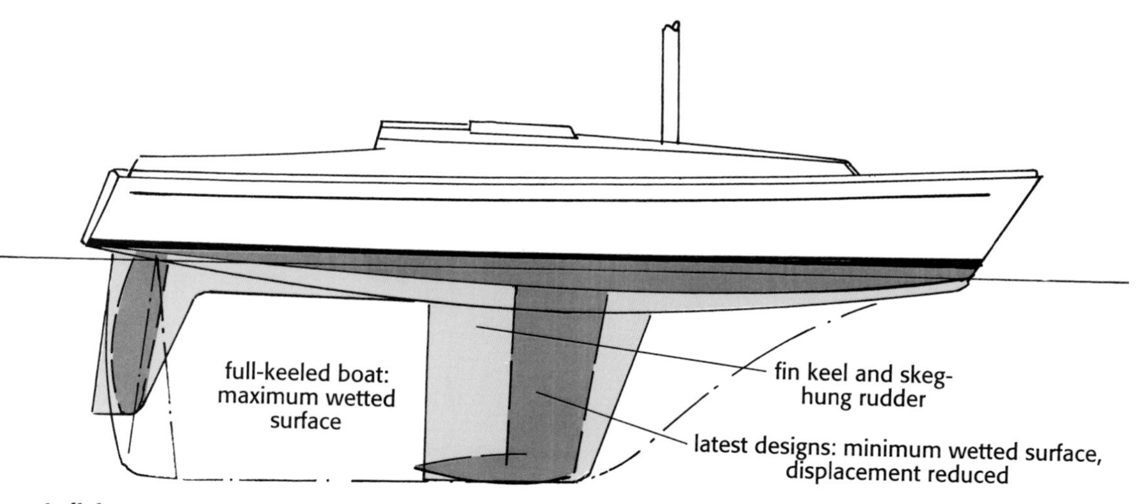

In light winds, frictional drag accounts for most of the resistance of a boat under sail. Frictional drag is comprised of two major parts, the roughness of the hull's surface and the surface area of boat in contact with the water (wetted surface). A long-keeled boat presents a large amount of wetted surface, which can be reduced by whittling away the underbody until the boat has a fin keel, skeg, and rudder. To get rid of still more wetted surface, you have to reduce the displacement and fit a balanced rudder and bulbed keel.

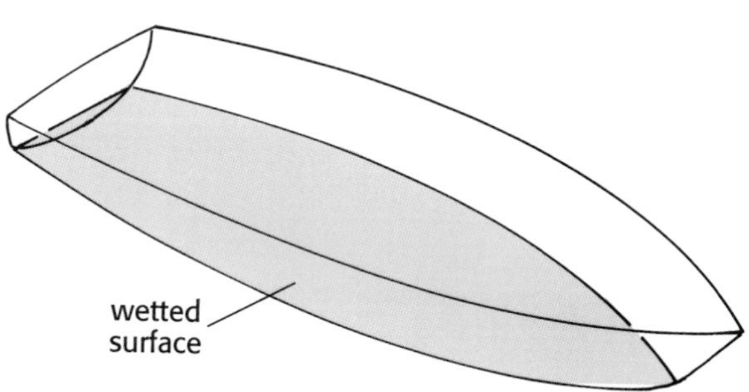

The wetted surface of a boat is any part of the hull in contact with the water, including keel and rudder.

stability has not changed, only wetted surface. The latest step in this trend is to cut away wetted surface even further by putting a bulbed keel (to increase stability) and a balanced rudder on the hull, and reducing the displacement using more up-to-date materials. Now the boat has become considerably faster under all conditions because stability (and the power to carry sail) has increased, wetted surface has decreased, and displacement has decreased.

The trade-off in making each of these steps is a reduction in the boat's ability to heave-to and resist capsize. (Before you decide that only a long-keeled boat will suit you, consider that most sailors spend less than 1 percent of their sailing time in serious heavy-weather conditions where they could be capsized.) The original hull with a long keel is hard to capsize because of the inertia of the hull and the volume of water that has to be moved as the boat is tipped over. (Imagine the lateral area of the keel acting as a huge scoop and, as the boat is capsized, moving all the water between the keel in the vertical condition and the keel in the horizontal position.) Compare that with the amount of water to be moved by the smallest keel.

Another trade-off is that in heavy wind conditions a boat with a small keel can only be hove-to with difficulty. The long-keeled boat can be hove-to under most conditions. This means that more modern boats must be sailed aggressively away from heavy weather, rather than taking a more passive approach. Because of the faster motion and continual sailing, crew fatigue and helming skill are likely to play a big role in keeping the boat safe in heavy conditions.

Prismatic Coefficient

Even if all the above ratios indicate that the boat will be a light-air flyer or a heavier cruiser, the wrong prismatic coefficient can spell disaster. The prismatic coefficient is the ratio of the volume of displacement to the largest sectional area multiplied by the waterline length:

$$\text{Prismatic coefficient} = \frac{\text{Displacement (ft}^3\text{)}}{\text{Midship area (ft}^2\text{) x LWL (ft)}}$$

Typically, a designer would use the immersed section at station 5 to find the coefficient, but the most accurate method is to calculate the volume of displacement under the curve of areas—that is, the area of each section is graphed along a baseline representing the waterline of the boat—and divide that into the largest area times the waterline length. This is the method used by most computer programs.

It makes sense to calculate the prismatic coefficient with the keel and rudder on the boat, because they go through the water too. But since the keel section can unduly influence the size of the midship section and skew the results, most designers use the hull without the keel or rudder.

When asking about the prismatic coefficient, make sure to find out how it was taken. Typical values of the prismatic coefficient are between .51 (best for light-air performance) and about .59 (best for heavier-air performance). The prismatic coefficient should also be modified depending on the load-carrying ability of the boat. For example, a barge has a prismatic coefficient of over .9, so a boat that is designed to carry a lot of stores may have a slightly

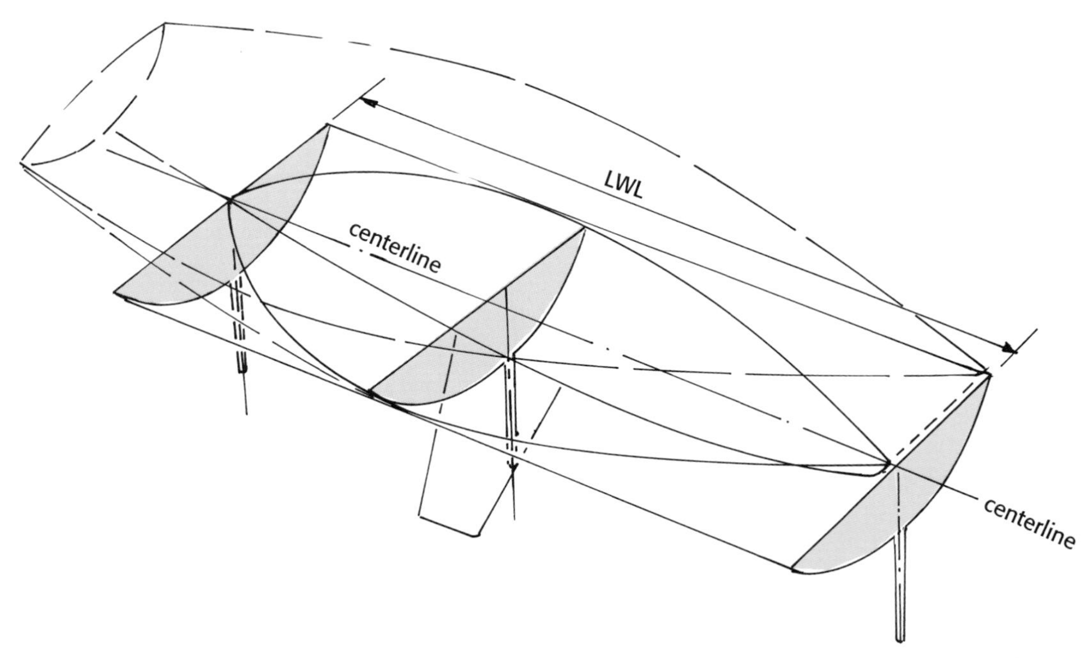

The prismatic coefficient is the volume of displacement divided by the largest midship sectional area multiplied by the waterline length. It is usually between .51 for a boat that sails best in a zephyr and .59 for a boat that sails best in half a gale. It should include the keel and rudder area although some designers prefer not to include them.

higher prismatic than a stripped-out racer. Also note that the prismatic coefficient will vary according to the length of the boat. In general, smaller boats sail at higher relative speeds for longer periods than larger boats and their prismatic coefficients will be slightly higher than those of a larger sailboat. By picking the right prismatic coefficient, a boat's performance can be enhanced considerably.

Speed-Increasing Factors

Usually a trade-off between speed-enhancing and speed-detracting factors is required to make the all-around best-performing boat. For example, a speed-enhancing factor is to have the minimum amount of keel lateral profile and wetted surface. This may be combined with a bulbed keel and minimal section thickness to get the very best performance. But if the lateral profile is made too small, the boat will make a lot of leeway, and the speed gain from reducing keel profile will be lost to slippage when the boat goes to weather in stronger winds. If you reduce the keel section thickness too much (usually less than 6 percent thickness ratio), you open yourself to early stalling and increased leeway angle. To strike the right balance in lateral profile takes skill and experience on the part of the designer.

Another factor in making a boat sail well to windward is the profile area above the water. If you can feel the wind on a boat, you are offering some resistance to the boat's forward motion. By minimizing the profile of the boat (lowering the freeboard, tucking halyards behind the mast, getting the crew to stay below deck or keeping them low), you can increase boat speed by a small amount.

The roughness of a boat's bottom is another factor in boat speed. For a boat to sail well in light winds, the hull bottom must be smooth. In light-air conditions, the drag or resistance of the hull comes from two major sources: frictional drag, and form or wave-making resistance. In light winds frictional drag contributes by far the largest percentage (up to 90 percent) of the overall drag. As the wind increases, frictional resistance shrinks to a few percent of the overall drag, and wave-making drag becomes the largest contributing factor.

As the wind increases, the amount of sail area a boat can carry becomes an important factor. Provided it can be carried efficiently, more sail area equals faster boat speed. If the boat carries maximum sail area but heels to 30 degrees, that sail area is not doing it any good. Most modern hull shapes are designed to sail at less than 25 degrees of heel, and the flatter

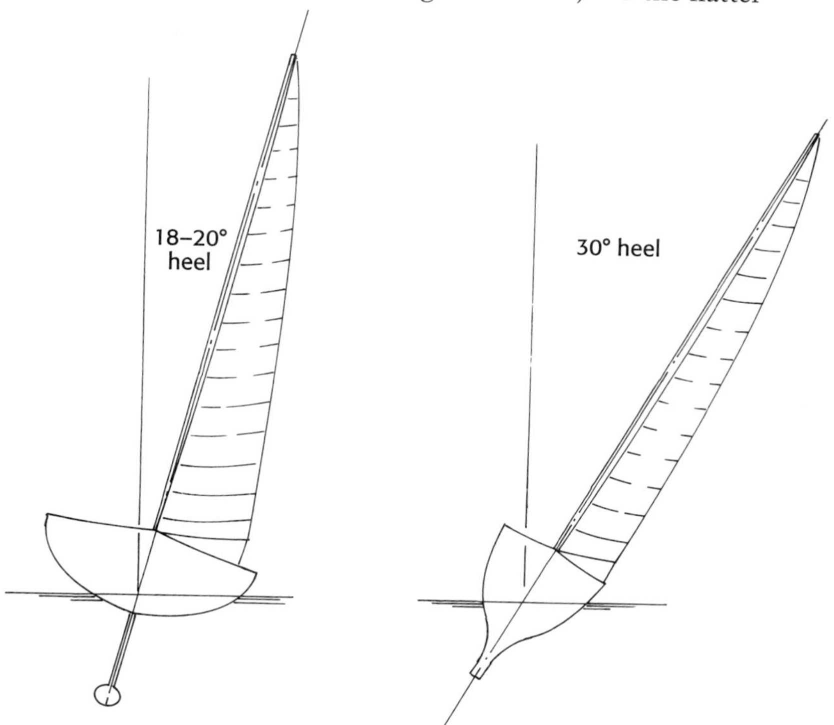

In general, a lightly ballasted, flat-bottomed boat should be sailed more upright than a heavily ballasted, narrow boat.

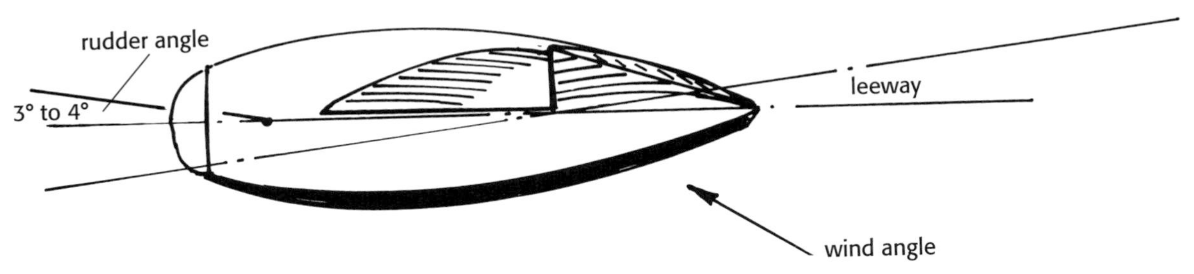

A rudder is most efficient when the rudder angle is around 3 to 4 degrees. If the rudder angle is excessive, it's time to reduce sail.

the hull bottom, the flatter the boat should be sailed. In other words, a very flat-bottomed boat should not be sailed at more than 15 to 18 degrees of heel.

Most sailors make the mistake of keeping full sail on the boat too long as the wind increases, and the boat slows appreciably. The slowing is due to heel angle and the movement aft of the center of pressure of the sail area, which requires more rudder angle to correct. If the rudder angle increases to more than about 6 or 7 degrees, the rudder is creating extra drag and slowing the boat. At that point, the mainsail should be reefed to lower the pressure on the rudder and restore the rudder angle to 3 or 4 degrees, which is when the rudder is creating maximum lift and minimal drag.

Boat Stability

What keeps a boat upright is its stability. Stability is a function of the height of the center of gravity of the boat and the vessel's waterline beam. The wider the beam, the more likely a boat is to stay upright. The best example of this is the nonballasted catamaran, where the hulls are placed far apart. At the other end of the scale is a narrow-hulled boat, such as a 12-Meter, where nearly 70 percent of the total displacement is ballast.

The cruising boat stability curve on page 131 tells you several things about a monohull's stability compared to that of a multihull. First, it indicates how stiff the boat is when the wind blows. (Designers use the righting moment at 1 degree or 30 degrees to compare boats when the complete curve is not available.) The curve also shows when a boat is likely to capsize. For example, the cruising boat curve on page 131 shows that if the boat is heeled to 145 degrees it will continue to turn over. The righting moment has turned negative at 145 degrees. Once the boat is inverted, the area under the curve shows how likely it is that the boat will turn back upright again. Based on their righting moment curves, most cruising monohulls have to heel to at least 140 degrees before they turn over; the negative side of a typical curve is small enough that the boat will right itself fairly quickly. Multihulls, on the other hand, show curves that are much steeper initially, but turn negative faster and tend to stay negative. When a multihull is upside down, it tends to stay that way because the drag of the sails and rig make it hard to reright.

Minimum Pitching

If a boat pitches a lot, it cannot sail fast—too much energy is expended slamming into waves. To reduce pitching, the weights of the boat need to be concentrated amidships and the hull shape needs to be thought out carefully. Perhaps the best way to understand this factor is to look at a curve of displacement, which shows the volume of the hull from forward to aft. If we

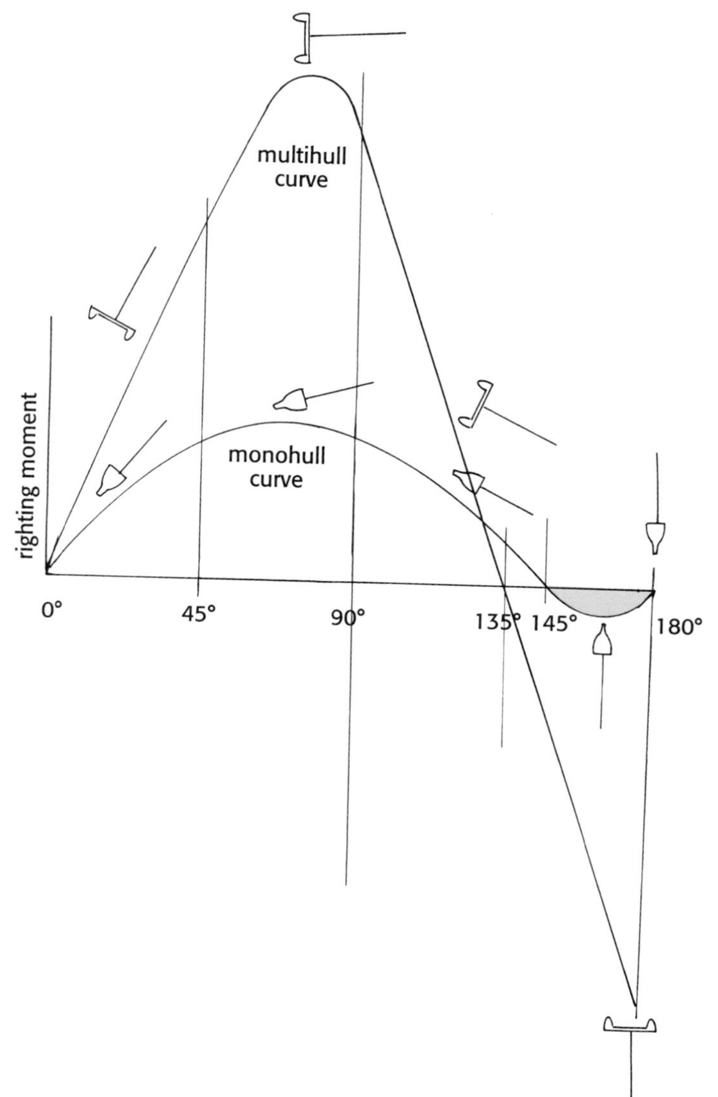

A righting moment curve for a multihull and a monohull. The monohull curve turns negative about 145 degrees, but the heavy keel wants to reright the boat as soon as possible. The multihull curve has far greater initial stability (it is harder to turn over), but as the multihull approaches 85 degrees it wants to turn over. Once over it will stay upside down because of the additional weight of the rig below the water's surface.

superimpose a table of weight distribution on top of this curve, we can immediately see whether there is enough volume of displacement to support the weight. If the weight distribution table stays inside the displacement curve, the boat is less likely to pitch.

Another factor that dampens pitching is the shape of the hull above the waterline. A boat with a fine bow and stern and wide midbody will pitch more than a boat with a fine bow and fat stern. A fat stern tends to dampen pitching.

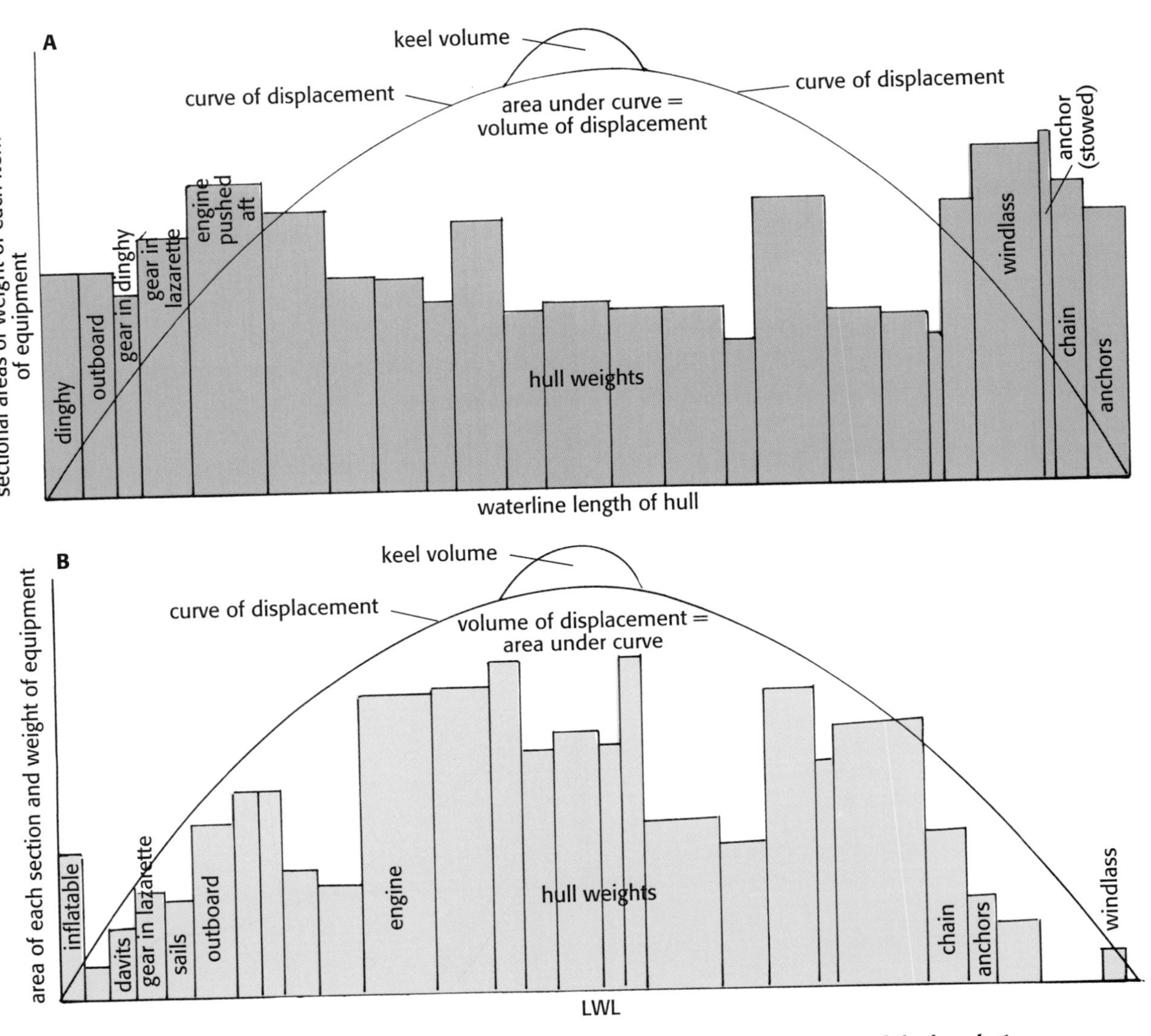

A weight distribution curve can indicate a boat's tendency to pitch. In A many of the heaviest weights are in the ends of the boat and outside the displacement distribution (area) curve. Just like a seesaw, weights on each end will tend to make the boat pitch. In B the major weights are inside the curve, indicating that the boat is less likely to pitch.

Crew Stability

Crew location can make a difference in a boat's performance. Positioning the crew as far outboard as possible can add stability, depending on the number of crew carried. For example, four crew on the rail of a 24-footer, each weighing 160 pounds, add 2,560 foot-pounds to the righting moment. If the 24-footer's righting moment is around 1,000 foot-pounds at 1 degree of heel, adding four crew on the rail increases the righting moment and the power to carry sail considerably. The same rule holds true on a maxi (the largest racing class). If there are 20 crew on the rail, each weighing 160 pounds,

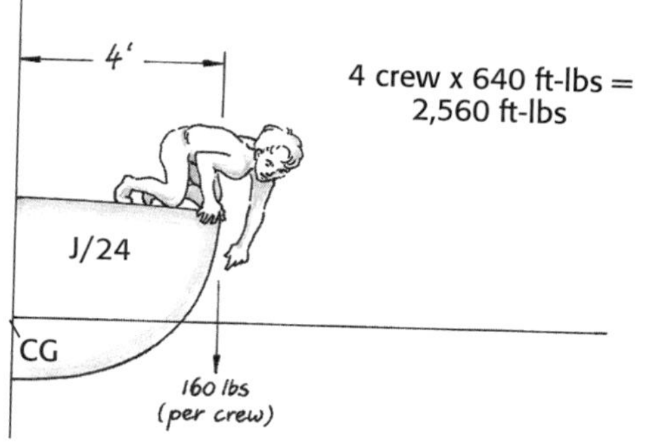

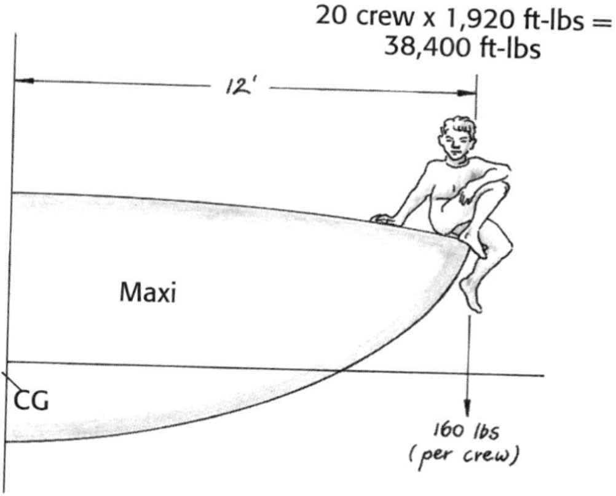

Crew weight can make a difference. Crew on a boat about 24 feet long sit out about 4 feet from the centerline. On a maxi the crew may be 12 feet from the centerline.

the righting moment increases by 38,400 foot-pounds. If the maxi's righting moment at 1 degree of heel is about 3,000 foot-pounds, the power to carry sail has increased considerably. These, of course, are merely typical values; actual figures may vary substantially.

Racing Performance Features

Speed-enhancing factors
Low wetted surface
Low to moderate displacement
High sail area
A prismatic coefficient suited to the sailing conditions
Minimal above-water profile (when sailing to windward)
Smooth hull bottom
Low center of gravity (which gives high stability)
Low pitching moment
Small mast section
Properly tuned mast
Properly set sails
Proper distribution of crew weight

Speed-reducing factors
High wetted surface
High displacement
End shapes poorly suited to sailing conditions
High pitching
Low stability
Rough underbody
Poorly shaped or poorly set sails
Poorly tuned rigging
Weight in the ends

Crewing factors that make a boat slow under sail
A lot of movement onboard
Excessive use of rudder
Poor sail setting
Poor positioning of heavy gear

Optimizing the Hull Design

Optimizing a design means tailoring it for the expected wind and sea conditions. For example, a boat that is to sail on the Great Lakes or Long Island Sound, where winds are usually light, is optimized by including factors that increase speed in light winds. These might be a relatively low prismatic coefficient, minimal wetted surface, high sail area, sails designed for light winds, and light weight. If the boat is going to race, and the courses are predominantly to windward, it might also have a fine bow, minimum waterline beam, and a deep, high-lift rudder and keel. For a boat that is to sail offwind, the bow may be fuller, the stern wider, and the keel and rudder of minimal size. In fact, the most efficient offwind hull shape is a semicircular cross section with no keel!

As the average expected wind strength increases, so should the prismatic coefficient. Displacement should also increase somewhat if the boat is to encounter larger waves. This can be done by adding lead ballast. For upwind sailing, the bow should be made slightly finer and the lateral profile of the keel should be increased slightly, which is easy to do if a centerboard is used.

If the expected winds are still higher, the prismatic coefficient should be increased even more, the position of maximum beam carried slightly farther aft, the hull made narrower, the bow made even finer, and the hull weight increased. Wetted surface area contributes less to drag in higher winds, so it can be increased if desired. Of course, apart from increasing weight, all these modifications are impossible in a boat that is already built and sailing. Substantial reconstruction would be required.

Making a Design Work over a Wide Range of Conditions

If we must design a boat to suit all conditions—upwind and downwind sailing, heeled and upright conditions, heavy and light winds, at an angle of leeway and in a seaway—the design process becomes difficult. Specific features incorporated into a hull design to solve one set of problems may affect other factors in a different way. For example, a hull may be made flat-bottomed to help reduce the vessel's overall draft. The flat bottom makes the boat easier to build, but it also allows any bilge water to wash up over the interior of the boat. Consequently, special measure must be taken to keep bilge water to a minimum at all times.

Obviously, a hull cannot be made to change shape to suit the sailing conditions, so the designer must either compromise to get the best all-round performance, or optimize the hull shape for the most frequent conditions in the area where the boat is likely to sail. For this reason, it is very important to define exactly what is required of a new design before the design work begins, or in the case of a production boat, to find out what conditions the boat is designed for before you purchase it.

But even that is not the entire picture. For a boat to perform well consistently it must have a good crew, good sails, reasonably good tactics, and a spot of good luck. While good design can go a long way toward producing a high-performance boat, in the absence of these other factors, a boat may be a great cruiser but never win a race.

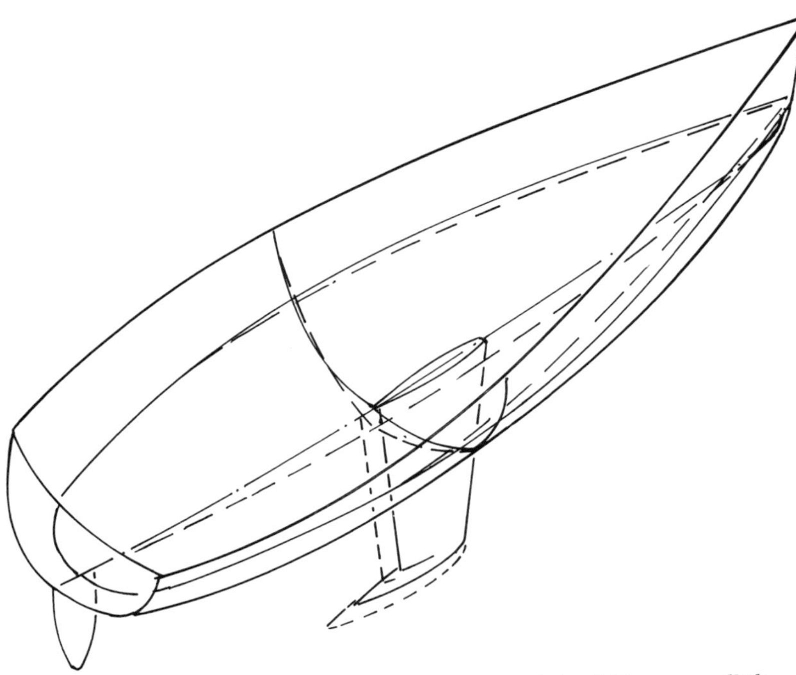

As wind speeds increase, a boat going upwind should become a little finer in the bow, deeper in canoe-body draft, and deeper in keel draft to optimize its performance (dashed lines). That is impossible, of course, so a designer has to pick the best compromise to suit anticipated weather conditions.

Considering the Rating Rules

A boat intended for flat-out racing is optimized in every area that will increase speed or produce a lower rating. Obtaining a lower rating is like making the boat faster *all* the time it is racing. However, factors that can be adjusted to lower a rating often relate to speed, and the virtual speed gained by a rating change can be more than offset by the actual speed lost. For example, if long overhangs are taxed by a rating rule because they add extra waterline length when the boat is heeled, shortening them will reduce the boat's rating, but it may also reduce real speed potential.

Not many boats are optimized for speed. Most make compromises in one or two areas. Cruiser/racers make a lot of compromises. For example, the IMS Rule requires that boats have an interior so that the boat can be cruised. On the fastest IMS boats the interior fittings are sophisticated lightweight structures aimed at reducing weight and concentrating it in the center of the boat to reduce pitching. Bulkheads and tables may be made of a core material with two layers of wood veneer on each side. On a more cruising-oriented boat, the interior furniture is made of solid plywood and weighs more. The compromise Cruiser/Racer is slower than a flat-out cruiser/racer simply because of the weight difference.

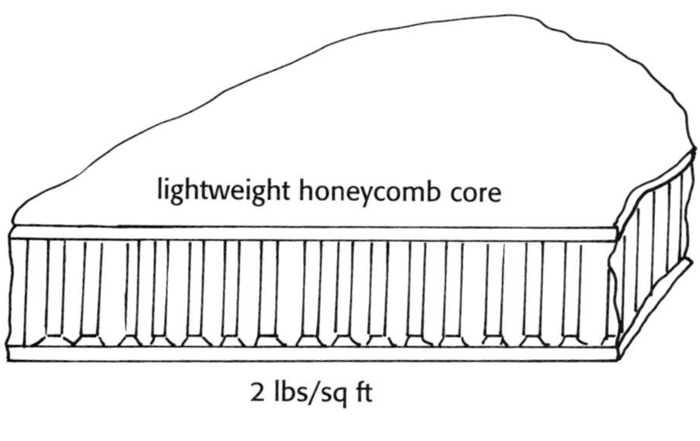

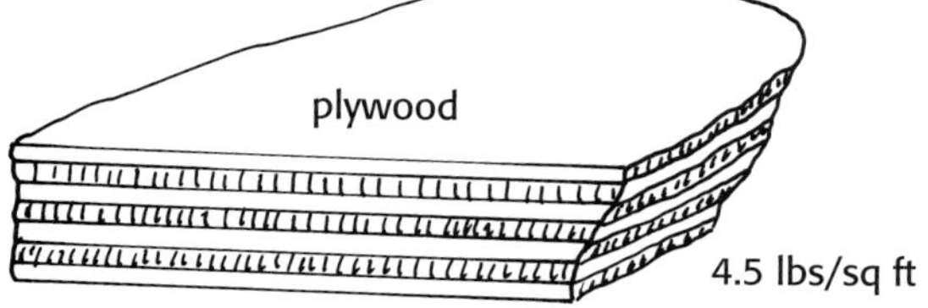

A Hexel core is mostly paper and air and weighs around 1 to 2 pounds per square foot. A plywood bulkhead weighs around 4 to 5 pounds per square foot. Both look the same on the outside, but a boat with cored bulkheads will be much lighter and will perform better.

Tracking

Tracking is controlled by the lateral plane of the hull. In general, a boat with a long keel and a rudder hung on the aft end of the keel will want to sail in a straight line all the time, making it track well. It will also be slow in light winds, slow to respond to the helm, and will take longer on a trip. However, against that you must balance the fact that there will be much less work for the autopilot, and your batteries will last longer (they will need to).

A boat with a short keel and a balanced rudder will be more sensitive to sail, and much more responsive to the helm. Because of its sensitivity, the autopilot will work harder but helm movements will be smaller, making it somewhat easier for the pilot to keep the boat on course in lighter winds. As the weather worsens the pilot will have to work a lot harder.

Turning Radius

A boat with a long keel will also have a large turning radius. In general, the less lateral profile a boat has, the easier and faster it will turn. This also means that such a hull will be more sensitive to steer. Boats with skeg-hung rudders also have a relatively large turning radius, because the skeg helps to keep the boat going in a straight line. The smallest turning radius is on a boat with a short keel chord and a balanced rudder, and that is one reason you see these features on performance-oriented cruisers.

Boat-Handling Techniques and Maneuvers

Heaving-to

Heaving-to is a way to tame the savage beast when the gales blow, the crew tire, and fear lurks. To accomplish it, you back the jib (sheet it to windward) and let the mainsail drive the boat. In theory, the main will turn the boat into the wind and the backed jib will force it off again, and these two opposing tendencies will achieve a stasis in which the boat is comfortably "parked." In practice, the two sails should be close to the same size, and you may need to adjust the rudder to get the boat to balance properly. Once the boat is in balance, the helm can be lashed. I believe that heaving-to is a relatively safe maneuver in non-breaking seas and in winds up to Force 7. If you try it in breaking seas or winds much stronger than Force 7, you stand a good chance of being rolled.

Under the right conditions, the boat sits comfortably on the water. It may fore-reach slightly, or it may slide backward slightly. It *will* make a lot of leeway, which your DR plot should recognize.

Heaving-to is not a good maneuver for a highly responsive, short-keeled Cruiser/Racer. It best suits old-style long-keeled cruisers with plenty of directional stability. A short-keeled racing boat should be actively sailed out of trouble, but that's a story for another book.

Broaching

If a cruising boat is properly balanced, it will rarely broach. Broaching is caused by allowing sail forces to get out of alignment and by overpowering the hull forces (see the accompanying drawings). When a boat is sailing along to windward the aerodynamic forces balance the hydrodynamic forces. Note how the forces are shown to be acting through the center of effort (CE)of the sails and the center of lateral resistance (CLR). As the wind increases the aerodynamic forces increase, creating a little more heeling force and more driving force. The increased aerodynamic forces are balanced by a slight increase in lift from the hull and keel and an increase in the drag force, but this happens more slowly than the aerodynamic increase and temporarily the helmsman will have to use some rudder to counter the increased aerodynamic forces. As soon as the forces are back in balance the helmsman centers the wheel, removing the temporary balancing force created by the rudder.

Now suppose a powerful gust hits, as in the figure (C) on page 137. The boat heels much further. Helm is applied to correct the increase in aerodynamic forces, but the wind force is too strong and the boat heels further. Because the boat is heeled, the counteracting hydrodynamic forces are acting nearer the water's surface and are less effective, plus the heel angle has shortened the longitudinal distance between the two forces (known as the lead and shown as α). Shortening the lead and increasing the aerodynamic forces requires even more rudder angle to correct it. But the rudder is also acting nearer to the water's surface where it may be ventilating (drawing surface air over the rudder blade). It may also be turned to its maximum and stalled (the water flow is no longer attached to the rudder blade so there is no lift from the blade). If the rudder blade is not stalled or ventilated it is operating in turbulent water where its efficiency is lowered. The result is that the boat slides into a windward broach.

Offwind the aerodynamic and hydrodynamic forces function in a similar manner. As long as the aerodynamic forces stay above the hydrodynamic forces the boat stays in balance. But as rolling increases the forces become increasingly unbalanced. At first, the unbalanced forces can easily be countered with the rudder. But further rolling requires that a counteracting force be in place *before* the aerodynamic forces become

(continued on page 138)

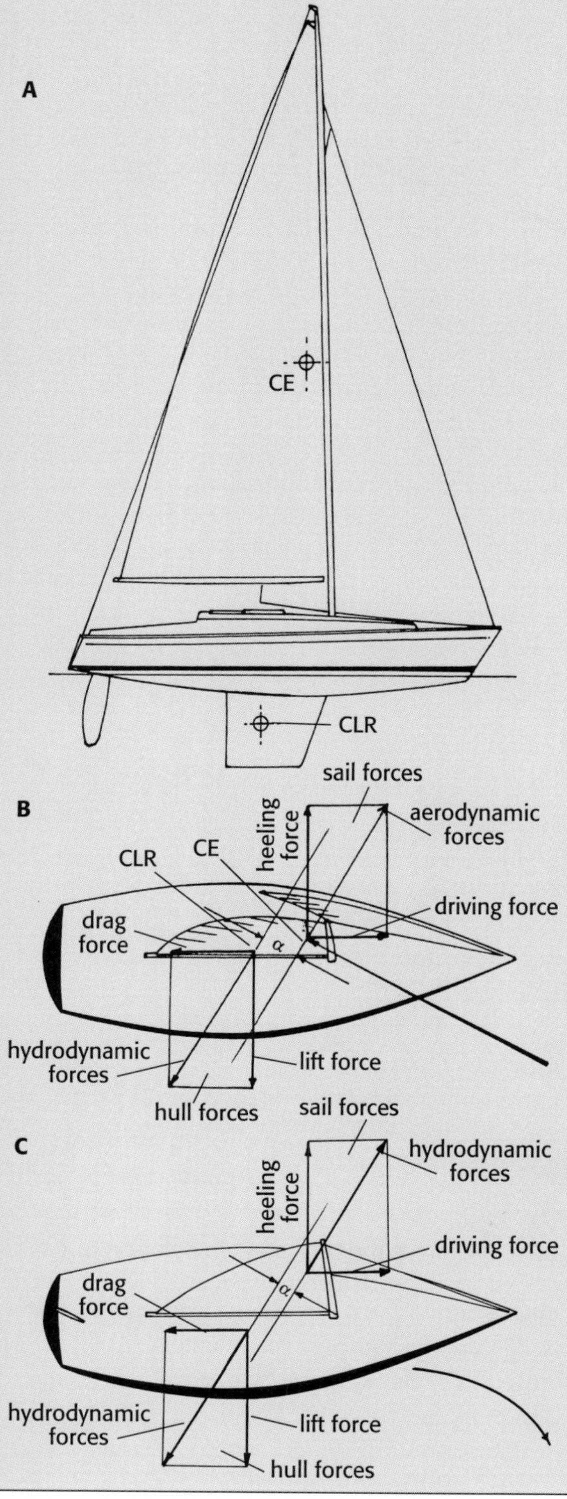

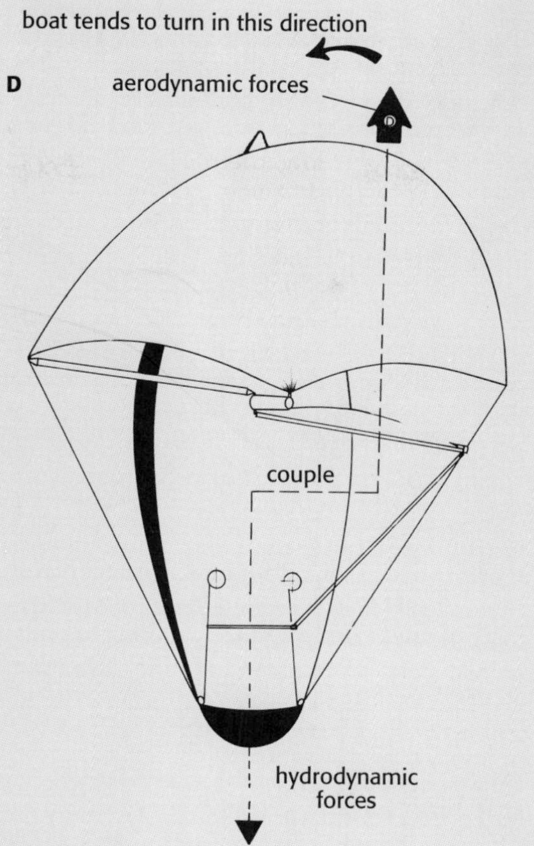

When a boat is sailing along normally, the sail forces can be said to be acting through the center of effort (CE) and the hull forces can be said to be acting through the center of lateral resistance (CLR). Under normal conditions, these forces form a couple acting as shown in B. As the wind overpowers the sails, the sail forces tend to move aft, making the distance shorter. We can counteract this with the rudder (complaining of "weather helm" as we do so), but if the movement is far enough the sail forces overpower the rudder's ability to control the boat and a broach results, as shown in C. When a boat is running downwind, the sail (aerodynamic) forces are normally directly above the hull (hydrodynamic) drag forces. As long as these forces are in line, the boat sails in a straight line. When these forces get slightly out of line, turning the rudder will usually serve to pull them back. If they get far out of line, as shown in D, they overpower the rudder's ability to counter them, and a broach results.

Boat-Handling Techniques and Maneuvers, *continued*

too large, because the rudder force cannot counter the aerodynamic forces *after* the boat is at the extreme end of a roll. If the helmsman gets in sync with the rolling and applies rudder force before the boat rolls to an extreme, quite often the rolling can be controlled. If not, bye, bye. The boat rolls into a broach with white-knuckled crew draped everywhere. Going downwind the broach can be to leeward or windward, depending on what side the helmsman lost control. Neither is particularly enjoyable and both can cause damage to sails and rigging, not to mention the helmsman's ego.

Backing under Power

If your boat has a right-handed propeller, and most do, the stern will kick to port when you back the boat down. (In fact, when you power ahead, the prop wants to turn the boat to starboard, but the effect is almost unnoticeable because of the propeller's effect at the aft end of the hull and the size of the rudder blade just astern of it.) The effect is lessened on boats with long keels and propellers in the deadwood.

To avoid problems, the trick is to start backing down some distance from the point you want to arrive at and build some speed in reverse. As soon as the boat has some way on, you will be able to steer it with the rudder. Note, however, that the rudder is acting like a bow rudder rather than the conventional stern rudder, and its effect will be much more severe. When you have some way on astern, do not let go the helm. The rudder is unbalanced and will want to turn to one side or the other, all the way to hard over, and you may have difficulty getting it back to the centerline.

Other Performance Features for Cruisers

Performance should not be limited to how a boat does on the race course. In fact, cruising boats designed without the restrictions imposed by rating rules may actually sail faster than racing boats. But cruising boats have different criteria of performance, and these vary according to the type of sailing that is being planned. A successful design is one that fulfills its intended purpose. For example, a boat designed to explore remote areas may not have scintillating speed, but it will have features that make it self-sufficient, such as strongly built hatches incorporated into a well-built hull.

Other cruising performance features can range from having a shallow draft to maximizing the usable locker space. A totally self-contained energy generation system, such as solar cells, an inverter, and a wind generator, can also be considered performance features on a cruising boat. These items will allow the boat to generate enough electricity to run onboard systems without resorting to a diesel-powered genset. In an area where diesel fuel is scarce, being able to generate power from an alternate source is a very high-performance feature.

Dinghy Storage

Dinghy storage is of major import to many cruisers. Poor stowage can affect visibility, control, and use of the boat. Dinghies can be stored on davits, either aft or on one side of the boat, on chocks on deck, or, in the case of inflatables, in a locker. In the Cruiser we have installed dinghy chocks on the cabintop. In another design I built davits into the radar arch. When required, the davits were locked in place and the dinghy was lifted out of the water, as we show for the Voyager; when not in use, they folded away into the arch. In another case, I recom-

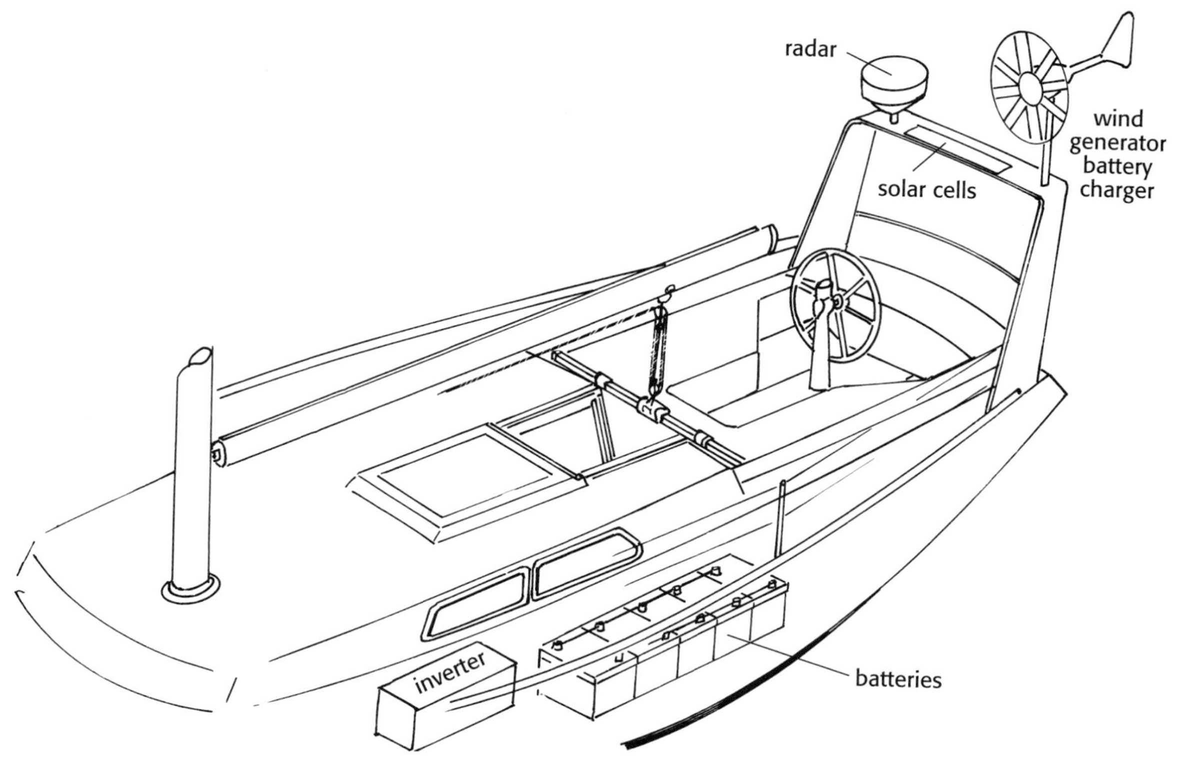

A wind generator and solar cells can be used to charge the battery bank. Having a fully charged battery bank will allow the crew to use an inverter or run an autopilot.

mended the use of Edson davits, through-bolted to the transom. These davits keep the dinghy above sea level and in a secure position out of the way of the on-deck crew.

J. J. Marie, president of Zodiac America, believes that you can get more fun out of an inflatable than you can any other kind of boat. For example, the Zodiac Fastroller, with its pressurized floor, can be stowed in a locker aboard most medium-sized cruisers and used virtually anywhere for going ashore, fishing, scuba diving, and many other things. On a boat with davits, a hard-bottomed inflatable, such as Zodiac's 11-footer, can be stowed with its tubes deflated. This kind of boat gives a wider range and much faster speeds than a soft-bottomed inflatable. Having one of these aboard can make your cruising more fun.

The Workshop

While a workshop is not in itself a performance item, it can be an area that enhances the efficiency of the entire boat. For example, bringing a pump or a piece of gear to a workbench, where the correct tools are available, makes it easier to repair. Workbenches should be laid out so that tools are safely stowed in clips or holders and cannot become dislodged.

Ideally, a workshop should be next to the engine compartment to keep the tools in a relatively dry environment. The workbench utilizes the maximum space available, with lockers positioned above it. This allows lights to be fitted in the overhead locker valance for greater illumination. If desired, storage containers can be screwed to the underside of the lockers. Note that heavy gear (the vise, the genset, heavy

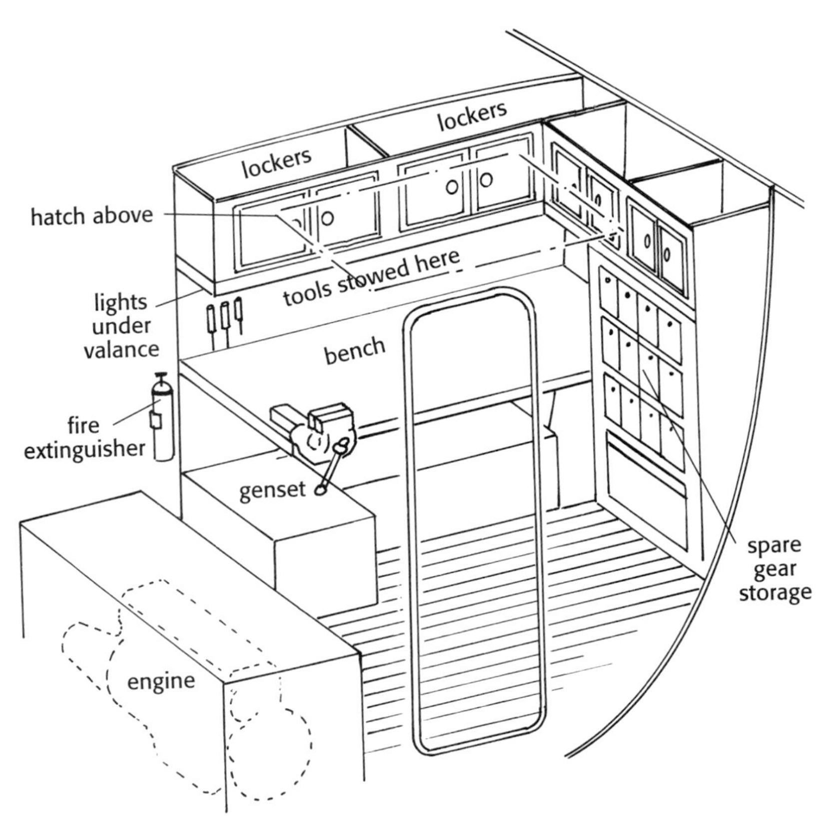

A well-organized workshop might be laid out as shown, with heavy weights concentrated low and toward the middle of the boat. Overhead lockers are used to store spares and to hide lights under the valance. The bench has a heavy-duty vise, with tools stored along the bulkhead (not on magnetic holders). In the overhead is a large hatch through which heavy objects can be lowered.

tools) are located low and toward the center of the boat if possible. Lighter gear is positioned in the overhead lockers. Directly above the workshop is a large hatch. This serves several purposes: a vent, an escape hatch, and an opening for lowering large pieces of gear, such as the capstan, into the workshop.

Sail-Handling Efficiency

Another performance feature on cruising boats is an efficient method of handling the sails. For a cruising boat that is to sail in winds under 20 knots, efficiency might be a roller-furling headsail and staysail. As the wind speed increases, a roller-furled sail tends to get fuller and the boat's performance loses efficiency. To keep efficiency high in these conditions, a flatter sail is necessary.

Sail-handling efficiency for single-handed sailing may include a self-tacking system. By sizing the jib to fill the foretriangle area and run on its own transverse track, a boat can be made to self-tack easily. There is some loss of boat speed compared to a boat with a full genoa, but tacking efficiency is increased. A single-handed boat that tacks frequently should include this feature.

An Efficient Rudder

When a sailor refers to a high-performance rudder, most people think of a carbon-fiber pre-preg laminate on a high-tech raceboat. The rudder on a cruising boat can be just as high-tech, but the performance criteria are different. For example, on one 48-foot cruising design, the rudder had to retract because the owner's mooring was in 4 feet of water. This rudder was designed on the job site (Howdy Bailey's Boatyard in Virginia) with a lifting section that enabled it to slide up inside the outer section without restricting the turning arc of the rudder. This innovative rudder has performed well.

Keel

Efficiency for a keel may mean many things: getting the highest lift to windward, being able

Non-Racing Performance Features

Efficient cruising rudder
Self-contained power-generating system
Protected crew environment with a steering position
Cockpit entertainment area
Method of getting on or off the boat efficiently
Efficient deck layout for the intended use of the boat
Good dinghy storage area
Efficient and nonintrusive sail stowage
A workbench or work area
Efficient navigation area
Efficient galley
Comfortable bunks
Good cockpit layout
Easy sail handling

to moor in shallow water, being able to settle on an even keel when the tide goes out, or keeping the boat as upright as possible (in the case of a boat designed for the handicapped). To fulfill these diverse goals a designer may resort to a centerboard or a daggerboard; the latter is less efficient for upwind sailing but can be retracted when the boat ventures into shallow water. In the case of a boat intended to settle upright in a mud berth, a centerboard might get clogged with mud. In this case, a twin-keeled boat with a skeg-hung rudder, although terribly slow in light winds, would serve the purpose. See pages 38 to 40 for more on keels.

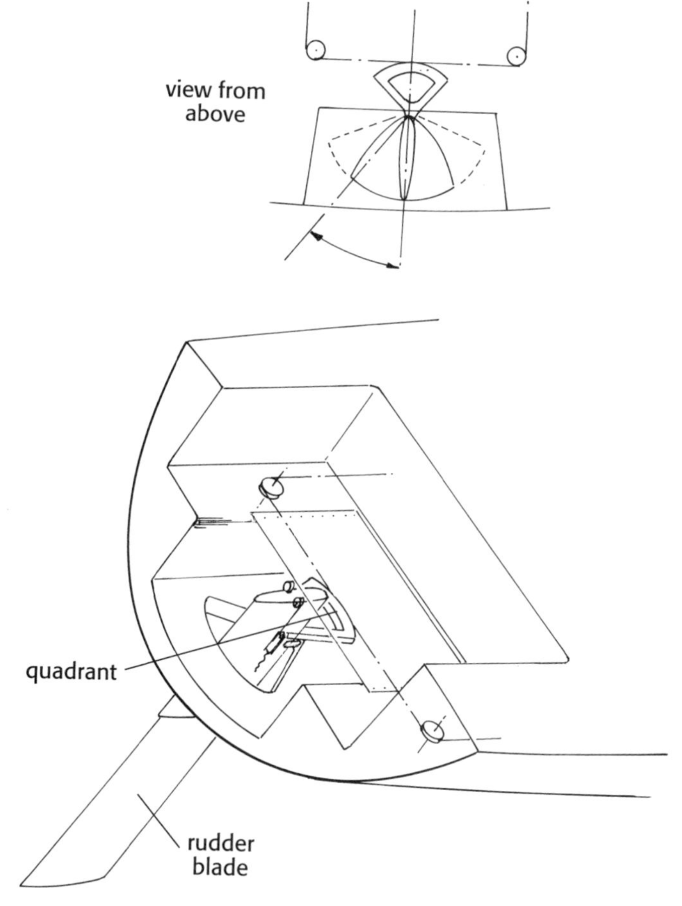

This rudder was designed to retract when the boat enters shallow water. Because it is completely exposed, the crew can tell immediately if a problem has occurred. The top section is welded to a quadrant and the pintles, and houses the blade, which is raised and lowered by taglines. A plate against the hull stops the hull aperture from creating additional drag when the boat is under sail.

Our Designs

In chapter 4 we looked at comfort aboard each of our designs. In this chapter performance and efficiency come under scrutiny. In most cases higher-performance boats will sail faster and make port sooner than a lower-performance boat, but they may also have a more violent motion. Does that matter? How do you rate your comfort/performance ratio?

Each of the designs that follow has its own performance requirements; the trade-off between performance and comfort differs for each one. The Weekender, for example, is primarily an inshore boat with an emphasis on cruising and evening races. Comfort and performance rate about 50/50 on this boat.

Although the Cruiser may sail offshore, the primary focus of its crew is on living aboard for two- or three-day cruises without the rigors of long ocean passages. In this case, comfort rates higher than performance, a ratio of about 65/35.

The Single-Hander's goals are different: to cruise or race relatively long distances. This skipper of this boat may cross oceans and be out of contact for weeks at a time. Under these conditions, reliability ranks higher than speed, and speed ranks higher than comfort. Such a boat would probably get a comfort/performance ratio of about 30/70.

The Voyager will also cruise long distances, making reliability a major factor for it too. Performance and comfort are also important, probably equally so. This gives the Voyager a comfort/performance ratio of about 50/50.

The Cruiser/Racer is an inshore boat with a hull and deck layout for racing, while the interior retains a lot of cruising appeal. The emphasis is on performance, so the comfort/performance ratio should be about 20/80, as is shown by the comfort ratio in the comparison of 100 new production boats on page 112.

The Weekender

The Weekender's focus is on fun sailing, whether it is cruising or racing. To that end, the boat is simple and has few performance features. One such feature is the 600-pound bulbed keel, which enhances stability. Rather than being totally round, the bulb is elliptical to lower the bulb center of gravity (CG) by another 2 inches. While this change may not seem much, it increases the righting moment by 100 foot-pounds, equivalent to half a person's weight on the rail. The bulb also reduces wetted surface by providing an end-plate effect (see chapter 3, page 71) and making the blade of the keel more efficient. While this gain is hard to quantify, there is definitely an improvement in upwind ability.

The retractable sprit also increases the effi-

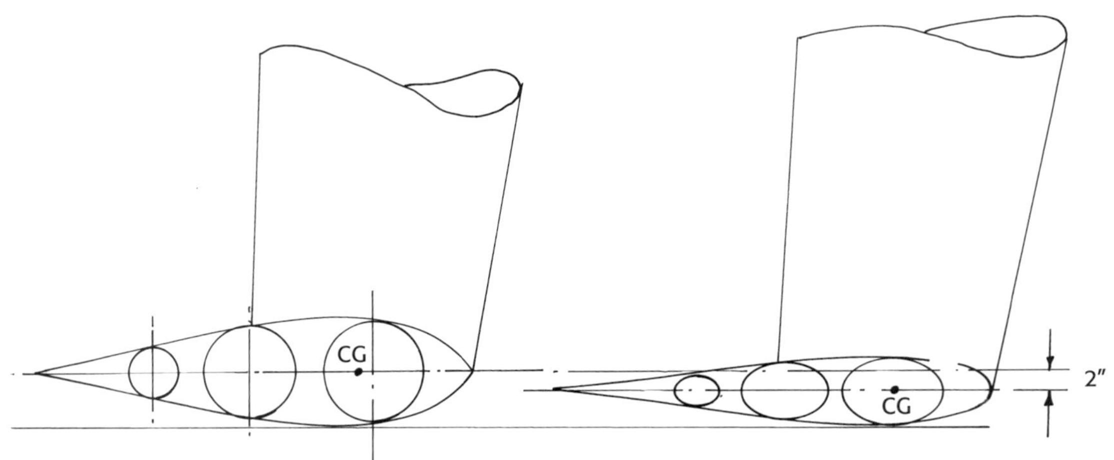

Making the keel ballast bulb oval rather than round lowers its center of gravity by 2 inches, which increases the righting moment by an additional 100 pounds.

ciency of the sail plan (see page 151), but at the expense of having a tube passing through the forepeak. Because a spinnaker can be set without a crewmember going forward, the boat will not slow approaching a turning mark, and overall speed around the course is improved. The same gain is made when it is time to take the spinnaker down.

On the Weekender the performance ratios are intended to produce a powerful small cruiser with the ability to race at club level and to cruise for a weekend. As we saw earlier, the displacement/length ratio is relatively low (138), but not so low that the boat could plane and possibly be overpowered. To get it lower one could decrease the displacement or increase the waterline length, of course, but there is a simpler if counterintuitive solution: to *increase* displacement slightly, which, because the aft end of the boat is very flat, will increase the waterline by nearly 20 inches. This same effect will be obtained when the crew step aboard and the stern is pushed further into the water, so we don't really have to worry about lowering the displacement/length ratio. With two crew onboard, displacement might increase by 2 × 160 pounds = 320 pounds, and the waterline length might increase by 19 inches, changing the displacement/length ratio to 117. This is much closer to a fast sport-boat and promises much better performance.

This also should indicate how these ratios can easily be manipulated by a competent designer and why they must be viewed with caution. Ideally, to get realistic values for comparison, performance-indicating ratios should be recalculated for a boat in sailing condition with a full crew, half the stores, half of the water and fuel, and a full load of sails. To do that we have to make a number of assumptions about the weight of the crew and the weight of stores, fuel, water, and sail, which can vary tremendously. Consequently, in order to simplify things, we accept these numbers warily.

If we check the sail area/displacement ratio (25.6), we find that this could be increased for better performance (up to about 28, or even 30). This would have the effect of increasing speed in light winds, but at a cost of less stability and earlier reefing.

Note that the capsize figure is 2.74. This seems high, but to lower it we would have to decrease beam or increase displacement. However, if we look through the new-boat data chart we find that many smaller boats have a high ratio, and the capsize report is aimed at boats that are likely to sail offshore. As long as we recognize that the ratio is high and sail accordingly in areas where rescue services are at hand, the high value should not be a problem.

The prismatic coefficient for this boat is .57, which is quite high. But with the large sail plan, such a small boat is likely to be sailing at a relatively high hull speed most of the time, and consequently a high prismatic coefficient is desirable.

The Cruiser

The Cruiser has different efficiency requirements, one of which is the ability for the helmsman to see over the cabintop when sitting down at the helm. This might require raising the helm step or lowering the cabintop if a potential obstruction is discovered on the drawing board. Because drawings are two-dimensional and a boat is not, requirements such as visibility over the cabin often seem satisfied on paper, but leave something to be desired in reality. The high-cut jib is another design feature to increase the overall efficiency of the Cruiser. This will enable the helmsman to see to leeward without having to peer around the jib. While a high-cut jib sacrifices some sail efficiency, the level of safety increases dramatically.

The numbers indicate that this boat should have moderate performance under most conditions. For example, the displacement/length ratio is a moderate to heavy 267. Because the buttock lines are fairly shallow at both ends of the boat, the waterline length is likely to increase considerably as stores are added in an upright condition, so the displacement/length ratio can be expected to drop slightly when the boat is loaded for a cruise.

The sail area/displacement ratio is good at 20.9, which will compensate for the increased wetted surface of the long keel. Still, the sail area/wetted surface ratio is undoubtedly fairly low and indicates that some cutting away would increase performance. Against that we must weigh the fact that a long keel makes the boat track better and many people don't really care how fast the boat is going, only that they are comfortable making the trip.

Other numbers that are important on this boat are the freshwater (FW)/displacement ratio and the fuel oil (FO)/displacement ratio. Both are about right for a cruising boat, with 5.9 for FW/displacement and 2.4 for FO/displacement. (An ideal FW ratio would be about 5, and a good FO ratio would be about 3.) This indicates that the boat has plenty of fresh water and fuel for a weekend jaunt or a longer cruise, but that a weeklong trip should be planned with fuel and water stops in mind.

The Voyager

The Voyager has different requirements from the Weekender or the Cruiser. This boat will cross oceans, so seaworthiness is likely to be of more importance than speed. Efficiency in this case amounts to self-sufficiency, an easier motion through the water, and a less tiring hull shape, rather than speed or a high-powered sail plan. The displacement/length ratio is fairly high at 259. This number reflects the increased weight of construction, the need for greater stores, and the desire to have backup systems and reliability. Note that the Valiant 42, a boat that has made over a hundred round-the-world cruises, also has a high displacement/length ratio of 266. The sail area/displacement ratio also reflects the weight of this cruiser: the relatively low number of 18.3 is dragged down a bit by the higher displacement. The Voyager has the lowest capsize factor of all our boats, as it should. This is a boat that should not be prone to capsizing, because it may be exploring a remote location far from rescue.

The prismatic coefficient for this boat is a moderate .56, which puts it in the middle of the range. The idea is to have a boat that will perform over a wide range of wind speeds and weather conditions. The FO/displacement ratio seems high at around 6.9, but the boat has a generator and a main engine to power. On the other hand, the FW/displacement ratio seems low, but the boat has a watermaker, and the value of 5.5 is appropriate or even may be a little high. This is a good example of how equipment influences the ratios, and why that influence should be carefully considered when designing boats for different functions.

Notice how the Comfort Factor on this boat is almost as high as that of the Cruiser when the boat is cruised with six people. Typically, six people might be required for a long, arduous trip. If the boat were to be cruised with four, more space would be available and relative comfort for the crew would go up to 49. It would appear that comfort should be in the 25-to-60 range for a comfortable cruiser, with readings over 65 bordering on luxurious.

Efficiency on the Voyager may also come through features such as additional displacement to accommodate plenty of stores and provisions, ease of handling the sail plan (see page 173), ease of self-steering, ease of riding to a sea anchor or drogue, and other factors that may not be recognized in racier designs.

Windage on deck may not seem like a terribly important factor, but its importance becomes apparent when the wind is howling at about 50 knots. Because of windage considerations, the Voyager's life raft has its own stowage area in the transom step, and the pilothouse has

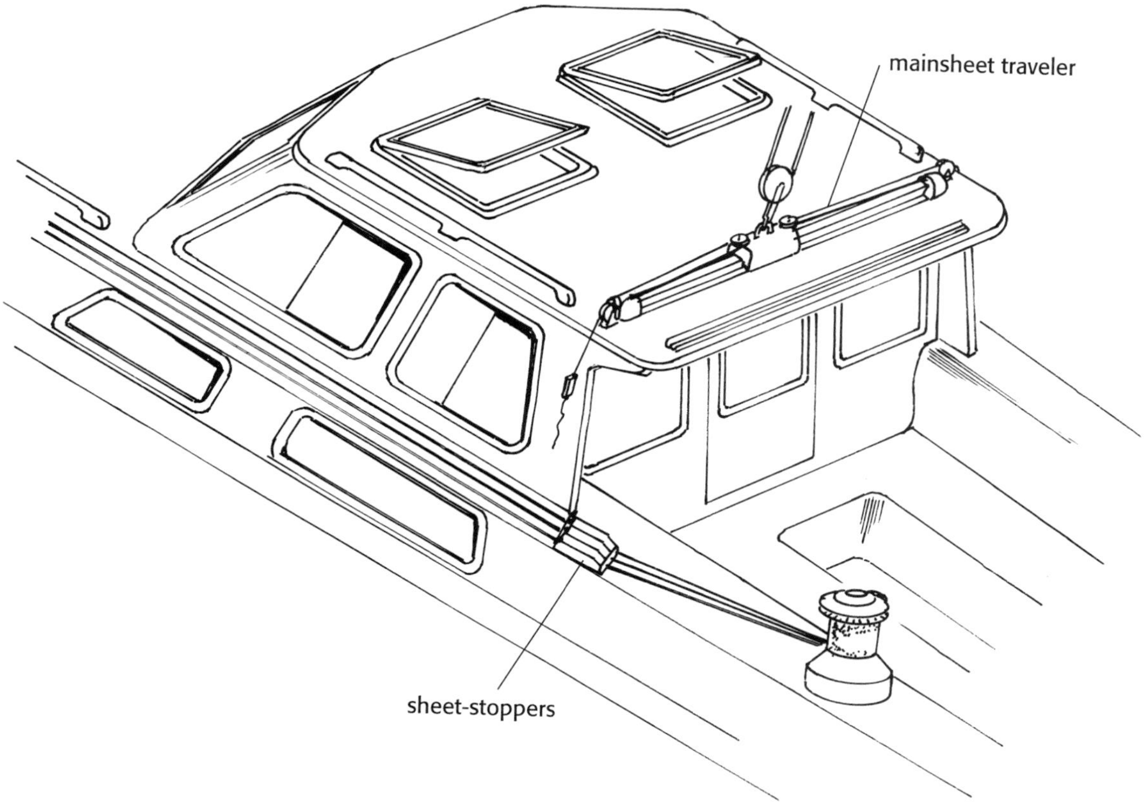

mainsheet traveler

sheet-stoppers

The Voyager's pilothouse shows hatches for the crew to view the sails. Sheetleads lead along the side of the cabin to sheet-stoppers and then to the winch. The mainsheet track is on top of the cabin to get it out of the cockpit, with taglines led down the side of the house.

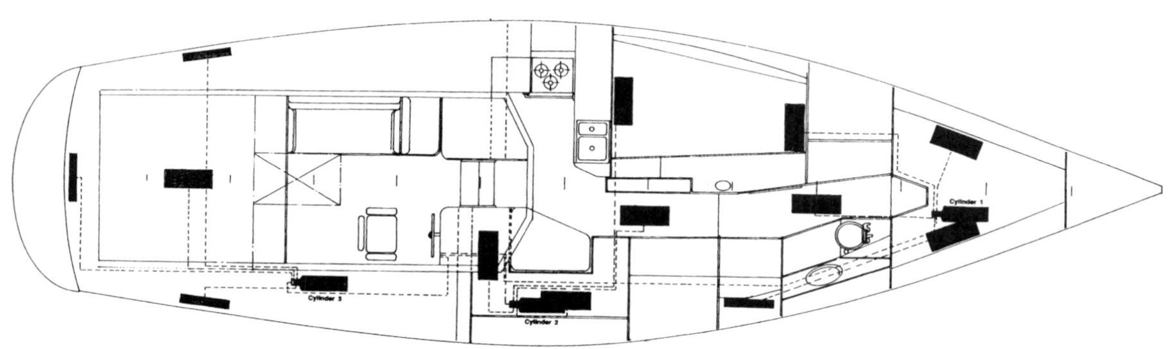

The layout of Yachtsaver airbags on a cruising design for one of our clients. According to Yachtsaver, these airbags can be built into furniture and will inflate when a line led to the helm position is pulled.

windshield wipers for better visibility. The dinghy is an inflatable that can be carried on davits for short distances or collapsed and stowed in a locker for transoceanic sailing.

Efficiency in this boat may be as simple as being able to work at the chart table while the autopilot steers. This is why the navigation area on this boat is located in the pilothouse where the skipper can see all around the boat, navigate, and adjust the autopilot while still in comfortable surroundings. There are also hatches in the pilothouse roof to enable the skipper to see the sails without leaving the pilothouse.

A relatively new feature we are going to install in the Voyager is the Yachtsaver bag, made by Yachtsaver in Round Pond, Maine. These bags are built into the lockers and joinerwork of the boat, and should it be holed and in danger of sinking, the skipper can tug on an emergency line which sets off CO_2 cylinders to inflate the bags and keep the boat afloat. With the boat afloat but a thousand miles from shore, the crew has time to repair the hole and pump out the boat. After repairs are made, the Yachtsaver bags can be deflated and the boat can continue to shore.

The Single-Hander

Speed is a factor for the racing single-handed sailer, but not so much for the cruising single-hander. A quick check of the ratios shows that speed rates vary highly. The sail area/displacement ratio is a whopping 29.09, while the displacement/length ratio is a minimal 55 (well within the planing regime). The capsize factor is high at 2.89, but in order to get it down, displacement will have to be increased as beam is already extreme. A look at the numbers when the boat is in sailing condition shows us that these numbers are not so extreme after all. For example, the displacement/length ratio rises to 64.3, the sail area/displacement ratio drops to 23.4, and the capsize factor goes to 2.75 without water ballast. While it is still not below 2, the curve of transverse stability gives a more reassuring picture, showing that the boat fulfills the criterion developed by the BOC—now Around Alone—race committee that the curve not go negative until the heel angle is at least 145 degrees.

Another feature that will be built into the Single-Hander is self-righting ability. One of the problems with large-beamed single-handed boats is that they stay inverted when capsized. While naval architecture calculations show that a wide-beamed boat can theoretically reright itself, the suction caused by the relatively flat hull in contact with the water plays a large part in restricting its ability to do so. In this boat we will install small airbags (similar to the Yachtsaver bags, described above for the Voyager) that can be inflated to lift the hull above the water and enable it to reright itself.

Along with speed goes the need to make the boat comfortable for the crew. A boat that can win races only at the expense of totally exhausting the crew may not win many races at all. A boat that can sail fast *and* be handled comfortably will do a lot more winning. Note that the Comfort Factor is a whopping 116, but this is an extreme boat with one crew that renders the Comfort Factor meaningless. If four crew were sailing the boat, the Comfort Factor would be a more reasonable 29, at the low end of the comfort range.

Sail handling is also a problem for a single-hander, and sails are the engine of the boat. With the wrong sail, the boat may perform badly. Sails are heavy and need to be kept below deck, but in an area where they can be easily accessed. The headsails will be stowed with their luffs tied tightly and in turtles where they can be easily pulled through the forehatch (with a halyard if necessary) and hoisted. Likewise, spinnakers are stopped (tied loosely with yarn or elastic bands to prevent the sail opening when it is being hoisted) and then stowed ready

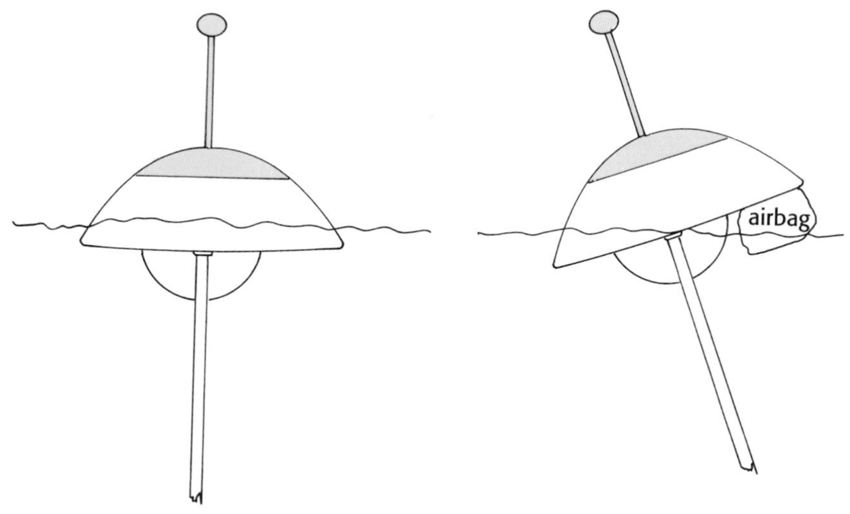

One of the problems with beamy boats is that when they capsize, water suction helps to prevent them from returning to the upright position. On this boat we'll install an airbag to break the water suction and help the boat return to the upright.

for use in turtles. We'll place a stopping bucket (a bucket with the bottom cut off, through which a sail is passed and elastic bands threaded on to the sail) in a nonwatertight bulkhead to allow the spinnaker to be pulled through and stopped with elastic bands; this will make it easier to hoist.

With a small cockpit, and a small overhang on the main cabin, the solo sailor doesn't have a lot of comfort space on deck. On-deck boat and sail handling are critical, but the deck should not be cluttered with fittings. Elegant simplicity is the rule. All the headsails in use are roller furled, while the fully battened mainsail can be reefed with a jiffy-reefing system. When the mainsail is dropped, it falls into lazyjacks, which can be removed and stowed at the mast for long trips.

This is a beamy boat with a water ballast system. The wide deck gives plenty of room for a wide shroud base, which allows the skipper to sheet inside the shrouds if required. But if the wind comes ahead on a long-distance race or cruise, the skipper will not usually pound to windward unless the end is in sight, but will instead sail as fast as possible and hope that the wind will free up later. To help the boat close-reach faster, the shroud base is likely to be wider than normal, although not extraordinarily wide. Its width is governed by the amount the sail can be sheeted. If the spreaders are too long, they will poke through the sail when it is pulled in; if they are too short, the rig will not have a stable staying base.

Because the anchor handling system needs to be relatively light, there will not be a large windlass on deck. The anchor rode will be rope, with anchors stowed below and hauled on deck when required. The major concern here is that the chocks, cleats, and cars (fairleads) do not chafe the anchor rode.

The Cruiser/Racer

At the top of the racing pyramid, speed is not so great a factor as getting the right rating. Of course, optimizing the rating can lead to bad naval architecture, as it did in the early part of this century. In America between 1890 to 1920, the rating rule produced boats with large beam, low freeboard, and light displacement. In Britain, it produced boats with a very narrow beam, deep draft, and poor sailing qualities. The rules rated both styles of boat very low, but both styles were prone to sinking, and it is tough to finish a race when your boat has sunk!

The ratios show that the Cruiser/Racer has performance consistent with other boats of this ilk. The displacement/length ratio is 129, which is moderately light, right where it should be. The sail area/displacement ratio is 22.4, which is on the low side. A reduction in displacement using

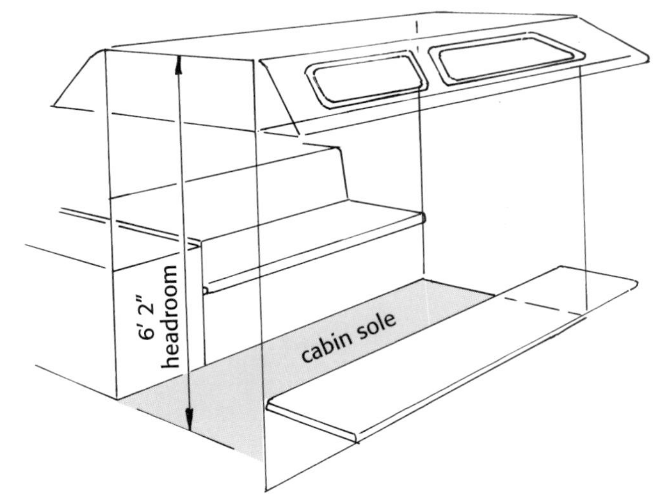

We can get full headroom (6 feet, 2 inches) inside the Cruiser/Racer with a narrow cabin trunk, still leaving wide side decks for a racing crew.

a more high-tech laminate may be appropriate to get this boat going even faster, although the cost might be prohibitive. The capsize factor is over 2, but as this boat is likely to be raced in the company of other boats, that number is tolerable. The FW ratio is high; if the boat is to be raced, smaller freshwater tanks should be fitted. The cruising version can have the present tanks. Notice how the numbers influence the racing and cruising aspects of the design. In this case a pure racing design might have a carbon fiber hull, smaller freshwater and fuel tanks, cored bulkheads and furniture, and possibly a lightweight rig to save weight. The cruising version might look identical, but it would have a regular fiberglass hull laminate, plywood bulkheads, larger fuel tanks, and a double-spreader rather than a triple-spreader rig. This why it is so hard for a designer to design a true cruiser/racer. The demands of performance skew the design in one direction, while the cruiser seeks the other tack.

The dominant characteristic of the Cruiser/Racer is the large cockpit intended to improve crew efficiency and to make sail handling easier. Today racing hulls are very similar, and it is in the area of crew efficiency that many extra yards can be gained. The large-diameter steering wheel (see page 168) makes it easy for the helmsman to get well out to windward, while the winch positioning makes it easier for the crew to operate the winches without getting in each other's way.

In our Cruiser/Racer the cabin trunk is relatively small to reduce windage yet still give enough headroom below deck directly above the area where people are likely to stand.

The mainsheet is at the end of the boom, with a five-part tackle and wire strop to reduce windage. The main traveler has three-part taglines for maximum control of the mainsail.

To minimize the number and weight of winches, the halyards and spinnaker lines are all led through line organizers and sheet-stoppers to self-tailing winches. The primary winches are non-self-tailing for faster cast-offs, plus there are no foot blocks to hang up the line. The genoa sheet tracks (two per side) are oriented to allow the boat to sail to windward at as high an angle as possible. Each track has a tagline to allow a crewmember to adjust the position of the car at any time.

While racing this boat is likely to be fun, it does not offer the comfort of a true cruising boat. There is little room for stores, other than those for winches and deck gear. The sail inventory is often taken to the rule maximum, and during a race sails are stowed on the cabin sole. This is the best place for them in terms of weight, but it leaves something to be desired in comfort. When cruising, the sails are stowed forward where they tend to give the boat a bow-down attitude, which is not the best for seakeeping.

Six

Sails and Deck

Elegant simplicity was how one person described the deck of a new ocean racer. The boat was designed to race efficiently and sail fast, and the deck layout reflected that thinking. Cruising boats, on the other hand, do not have quite as sharp a focus on the deck layout. The requirements of comfort and ease of use play a much larger role.

Comfort and ease of use also apply to the sails. The latest technology in sail design and material is not much use if the boat is to be sitting at anchor with roller-furled headsails for long periods of time. In that case, a UV-stabilized sailcloth that can be rolled up easily is of more importance.

Making the deck and rig easy to handle also affects seamanship. A boat that is hard to reef might not get reefed as soon as it should. A boat on which it is difficult to trim the sails properly may not go to windward very well and may get into trouble when trying to sail off a lee shore. Ease of handling, then, affects more than just the way the crew operates the boat. It affects seamanship, stability, comfort, and many other facets of the vessel.

Some Sail Plans

Most of today's sail plans have evolved from the days of wooden masts and iron men. With the advent of high-strength carbon fibers, different rig shapes are appearing. In the future, we will no doubt see many more variations as designers use the advances in technology to develop new rig ideas and sail plans.

Cat Rig

Probably the simplest rig of all is the cat rig. This can take the form of the traditional catboat rig, or it can be a more modern version as seen in the line of Nonsuch cruisers designed by Mark Ellis. Both rigs are reasonably efficient and versatile. Note that cat rigs do not sail to windward well, which permits the designer to make the bow sections of the hull very full. This has the benefit of providing a large hull volume well forward to support the weight of the mast.

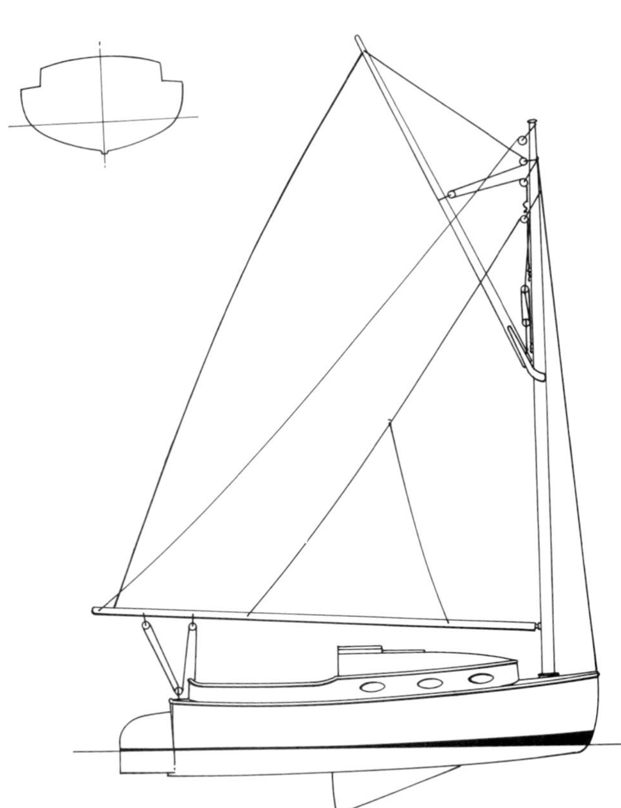

The old-style catboat with its barn-door rudder can be fun to sail. But as the wind increases, the helm becomes very heavy because of the single sail with its large area aft of the center of lateral resistance.

Sloop

For ease of operation, the single-masted sloop rig is one of the most versatile rigs of all. It is best when sailing upwind, but with the addition of a spinnaker it becomes powerful downwind also. Because of the rig's simplicity and spinnaker, this is the favorite sail plan of the racing fraternity.

The sloop sail plan can either be fractional or masthead, as shown in the accompanying sail plan. On a fractional rig the headstay is attached to the mast at a point lower than the

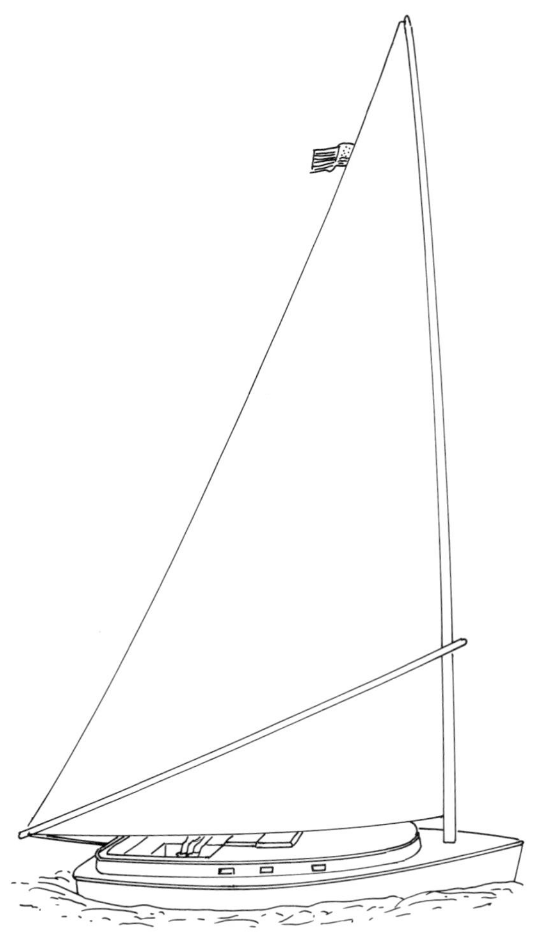

The Nonsuch-style catboat uses a wishbone rig to accomplish the same goals as the traditional catboat. Sail depth is controlled by pulling the wishbone slightly forward at the mast end. Mast bend is often considerable, but the boat is easy to control.

masthead. This point may be anywhere between 65 and 90 percent of the mast height. The fractional rig (B) is harder to control because mast bend affects the shape of the mainsail and it takes some skill to bend the mast just the right amount. But the fractional rig requires fewer sail changes, because the headsail is relatively small and the mainsail can be eased to relieve pressure on the helm. A masthead rig (A), in which the headsail reaches all the way to the top of the mast, is more forgiving, in that it can be set up and virtually forgotten underway. It is easier for a less-experienced sailor to get the best from a masthead rig, especially if the boat is to be cruised over long distances.

Generally, the sloop rig is set with one mainsail and one headsail. The headsail may be either a jib (less than 100 percent of J, where J is the distance from the front of the mast to the headstay fitting on deck) or a genoa (more than 100 percent of J, and up to 160 or even 175 percent of J). A sail that is 150 percent of J is one that overlaps the mast by 50 percent, parallel to the headstay.

Working jibs and mainsails usually have battens. Fitting battens on an overlapping headsail is not a good idea because the battens are likely to be broken by slamming against the mast as the boat tacks. The mainsail may have short battens, full-length battens, or a combination of the two. Short battens are holdovers from the days of the IOR Rule and are not seen much on newer sails. Full-length battens give better performance and make the sail last

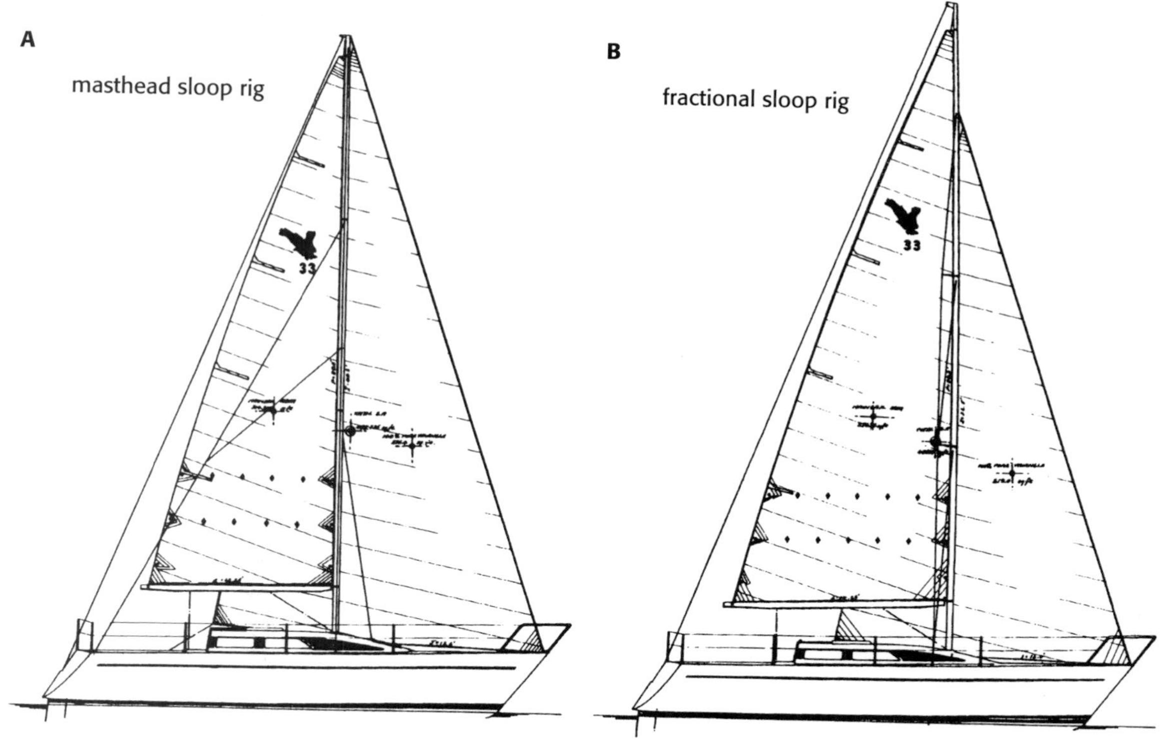

The sloop rig can be masthead (A) or fractional (B). In general, masthead rigs are easier to control. For the cruising sailor, the masthead rig is less work and needs less attention. On a fractional rig the headsail is smaller and the mainsail needs more trim. Most racers bend the mast to get the best from the mainsail, but cruisers rarely bother.

Some sloop rigs use battened headsails to make them more efficient. Battens stiffen the leech (eliminating cupped leeches) and make the departing airflow smoother. If battens are used in the headsails, the sail should not overlap the mast. If it does, the battens are likely to get broken when the boat tacks. The dashed line shows the extent of a battened headsail.

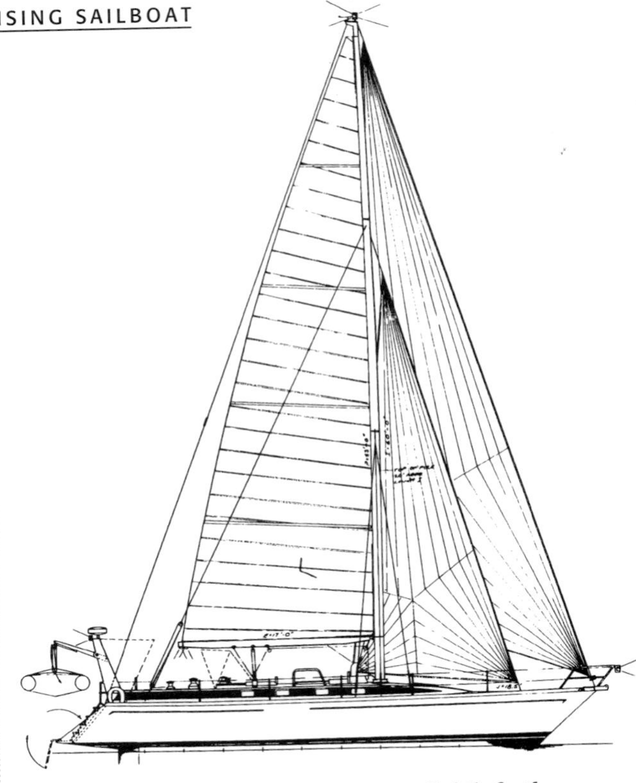

Cutter rigs generally have the mast set slightly farther aft than a sloop and set twin headsails in the foretriangle. The staysail and topsail (yankee in Britain) break the sail plan into smaller pieces, increase visibility, and make the sail plan more efficient when the sheets are eased. This is not the most efficient rig for sailing to windward, however, because of the double slot and the difficulty of sheeting both headsails in tightly.

longer, plus they can be used to increase the amount of roach in the sail.

Cutter

The cutter rig is almost as versatile as the sloop, but it has two headsails. For reaching this makes it much more powerful, but if the boat is to sail to windward for any length of time, the sloop rig is better. The bow sections of the hull can be slightly fuller for a cutter rig because the sail plan is not intended to go to windward like a sloop. Such a cutter might be well suited for long-distance cruising, where windward performance is not as essential as powerful reaching and a slightly wider bow platform is required for anchor handling.

Ketch

For offshore cruising under a wide range of conditions, the ketch rig is one of the finest rigs of all. The sail plan is broken down into manageable areas, and it has a lot of power under a wide range of conditions. Additional sails such as a mizzen staysail (shown dashed in the figure on page 153) can be set to go downwind

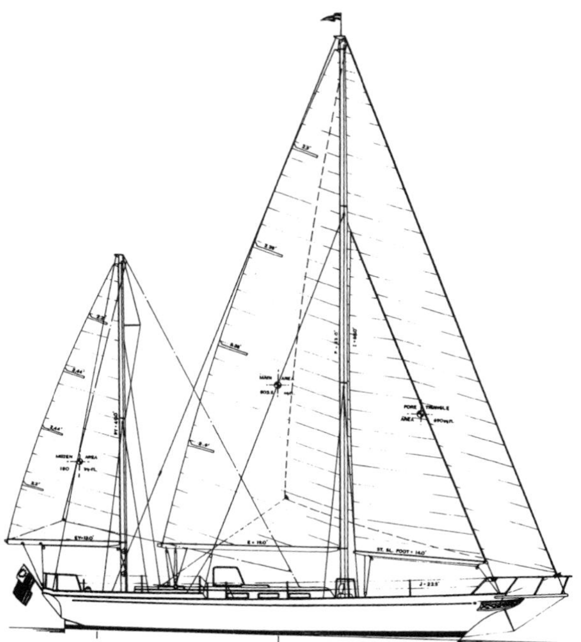

The ketch rig splits the sail area into easily handled parts for a small crew. On a reach a mizzen staysail can be set to increase sail area. On this steel design, I made the staysail self-tacking for convenience. Note that the masts are independently stayed.

without using an unstable spinnaker. If a cruising sailor wishes, a spinnaker or a multipurpose spinnaker (MPS or genniker) can be used to deliver fast reaching under a variety of conditions. For the sailor who wants to travel long distances with limited crew, the ketch rig provides a variety of options. One common practice I recommend against, however, is that of sailing with no mainsail and a full headsail and mizzen. Granted, this is an easy way to "reef," but with no mainsail load on its back edge, the mast will tend to bend forward and can easily get out of column and collapse in a seaway. In my opinion, you should never sail without some mainsail, especially with today's lighter spars.

Yawl

The difference between the ketch and the yawl is the position of the mizzenmast relative to the rudderstock. If the mizzen is forward of the rudderstock, the boat is a ketch; aft of the rudderstock, and the boat becomes a yawl. While the yawl has many of the advantages of the ketch, the mizzenmast is usually so small that these advantages are minimal. The theory behind a mizzen is that its size overcomes its windage and it can be used to help the boat reach better, but the benefit is small on a yawl. You are usually better off furling the mizzen when sailing to windward in either a ketch or a yawl, as the mizzen on both rigs is operating in the turbulent air off the mainsail. Setting the mizzen when the boat is at anchor keeps the boat head-to-wind at a cost of increased wear on the sail.

Schooner

The schooner rig is probably the most romantic rig seen today. We all have visions of reaching across a deep blue sea in a well-found schooner. But while the schooner will reach like the wind, it is not a windward rig. The efficiency of the

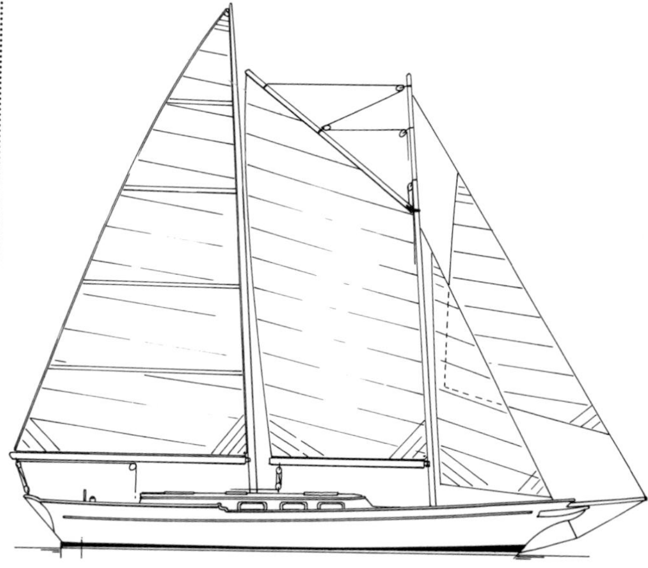

Schooners can set many combinations of sails. This schooner rig shows a typical staysail, topsail, foresail, and mainsail. For light-wind sailing a main topsail and a gollywobbler can be added. The schooner sail plan is best for offwind sailing, but is not very efficient for sailing upwind.

large mainsail is very much reduced by the foresail and the headsails in front of it. The hull shape also requires a lot of lateral profile well aft to balance the large mainsail, which can make the boat difficult to haul and may make it deep-drafted. Nevertheless, with its wide array of sails, the schooner rig can be very versatile. You can set a huge amount of sail area in light winds and easily reduce that area as the wind increases.

These are by no means all of the sail plans that can be fitted on a boat. Other rigs, such as a junk rig, can be used if desired. But remember that the hull shape should be carefully matched to the desired sail plan to get the best out of the boat.

How Many Sails?

How many sails should you have aboard your boat? The number will depend on the size of your boat, the area in which you sail, and the type of sailing you do. For example, if you cruise in a sheltered bay, you may feel that a mainsail and a working jib are all the sails you require. But if you decide to race your boat in the same sheltered bay, you might add a spinnaker and a genoa to the sail inventory. The accompanying table suggests sail inventories for various-size sloops under a range of conditions.

Heavy-Weather Sails

Boats going offshore should carry heavy-weather sails—not just for storms, but for a range of conditions, from fresh breeze to gale to storm. For example, as the wind increases, you might change from a full-size jib to a smaller one, a number three or four, before going to a storm jib. Many sailors assume that a partially roller-furled headsail will suffice for heavy weather, but it won't. As a headsail is roller-furled, the middle of the sail, due to fabric distortion, rolls more slowly than the top and bottom; consequently, more fabric is left in the middle of the sail, making it fuller, which is exactly the opposite of what should happen when you go to a heavier sail. The heavier sail should be flatter. A fuller sail causes the boat to heel more, sail slower, and run the risk of broaching.

For this reason, boats that travel offshore change sails to suit the weather. They may use old-fashioned hank-on sails, or they may have an extra headstay strictly for heavy-weather sails. Some carry headsails that can be tied over the roller-furled sail. Whatever system you use should be based on the amount of time you intend sailing offshore and the amount of sail handling you are prepared to undertake. I prefer a separate stay for heavy-weather sails on a boat that will be at sea for a long time. For a cruising boat that might get caught out occasionally, a heavy-weather headsail that is fitted over the roller-furled sail can be used. Practice your headsail changes in reasonably heavy winds *before* you get caught out in a whole gale. You'll be glad you did.

Roller-Furled Sails

Roller-furled sails have revolutionized the job of sailing a boat. No longer do you have to carry enough crew to change a headsail as the wind increases in strength, you can simply roll the sail around the headstay. But roller-furled sails do have some drawbacks, and the lousy shape of a partially rolled headsail in heavy weather is only one of them. They can also degrade on the headfoil unless an ultraviolet cover is fitted; and when the boat is anchored or moored in heavy weather, a roller-furled headsail can unroll, cause all sorts of mischief, and be destroyed in the process. (To reduce the risk of this, remove the roller-furled sail when a storm is forecast.) But these drawbacks are minor compared to the benefits: easy handling, fewer crew, a smaller sail inventory, and the ability to fine-tune sail area to the conditions. One headsail can often be made to do it all on an inshore cruiser.

Sail Inventories for a Sloop Rig

Possible sail inventory for a small boat up to 27 feet

	Basic sails inventory	Medium inventory (Basic inventory plus the following)	Racing inventory (Medium inventory plus the following)
Sheltered bay	Main, working jib	110% or 130% roller-furled genoa	Spinnaker
Close to shoreline Up to 20 miles offshore	Main, working jib	110% or 130% roller-furled genoa Medium spinnaker	Light spinnaker
Offshore	Main, working jib Storm jib	Medium spinnaker	

Possible sail inventory for a cruising boat between 28 and 39 feet

	Basic sails inventory	Medium inventory (Basic inventory plus the following)	Racing inventory (Medium inventory plus the following)
Sheltered bay	Main, working jib 110% genoa	130% genoa 150% genoa	¾-oz spinnaker Spinnaker staysail
Close to shoreline	Main, working jib 110% genoa Spinnaker staysail	130% genoa 150% genoa	½-oz light spinnaker ¾-oz medium spinnaker
Offshore	Main, working jib 110% genoa 130% genoa	150% medium/heavy genoa Storm jib	1½-oz medium spinnaker Spinnaker staysail

Possible sail inventory for a boat between 40 and 55 feet

(Headsails would be high cut for cutter-rigged boat and a staysail used under the headsail)

	Basic sails inventory	Medium inventory (Basic inventory plus the following)	Racing inventory (Medium inventory plus the following)
Sheltered bay	Main, working jib	150% light genoa	¾-oz spinnaker
Close to shoreline Up to 20 miles offshore	staysail 130% headsail Spinnaker staysail	150% medium headsail 1½-oz reaching spinnaker	¾-oz spinnaker
Offshore	110% #3 genoa 130% #2 genoa Storm jib	150% medium/heavy genoa Spinnaker staysail	¾-oz medium spinnaker 1½-oz spinnaker
Transoceanic in addition to offshore sails	Main, working jib	150% light genoa	½-oz light spinnaker

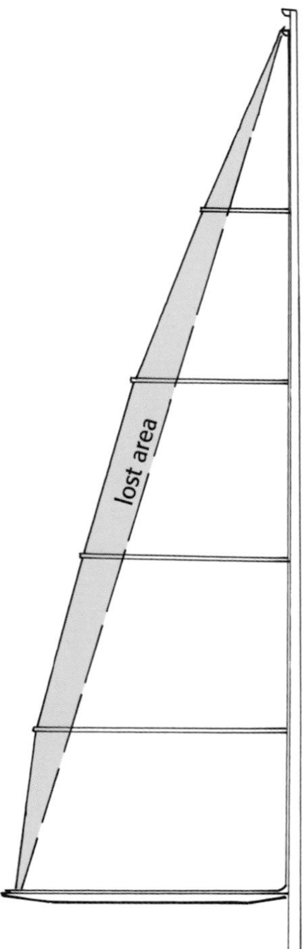

A battenless, roller-furling mainsail carries less area on given lengths of foot and luff due to the loss of the roach—the area outside the dashed line in this drawing.

Frankly, I'm not a fan of mainsails that furl inside the mast. Because the sail has to be tightly rolled, it cannot have battens, although some sailmakers have tried vertical battens and others have tried hydraulic ones. This means that an appreciable amount of sail area (in the roach) is lost. If a roller-furled mast is requested at the design stage, the lack of sail area can be compensated for and the mast height increased, but only rarely does this happen. Typically, a new mast with roller furling is put in the boat and sail area is decreased, even though the sail dimensions are exactly the same as before.

The other problem with roller-furling masts is the additional weight aloft. A roller-furling spar will typically increase the weight of the mast tube by 25 to 40 percent. This additional weight reduces stability, makes it more difficult for the boat to drive into a seaway, and, together with the reduced sail area, makes the boat perform worse in light winds. However, in a situation where the owner would not sail the boat without a roller-furling main—for example, an older single-handed sailor—the roller-furled mainsail can and should be used, as long as its drawbacks are recognized.

Rig Considerations

If the sails are the engine of a boat, the rig is the foundation; consequently, a well-thought-out rig is essential to getting the most from your sails. Several calculations go into the right-sized rig. Simply put, the righting moment and the distances between the spreaders and other attachments to the mast are used to establish the mast fore-and-aft inertias. These inertias let the designer determine the thickness of the mast wall and the fore-and-aft dimensions of the spar, which in turn determines its weight.

The designer has a number of options to adjust the size and weight of the mast. For example, by adding spreaders and reducing the mast wall thickness, the mast may be made lighter, but at the expense of increased difficulty tuning the rig. To reduce the diameter, a designer might use a thicker mast wall with intermediate shrouds and more spreaders. Depending upon the number of spreaders used and their spacing, identical boats could have very different spars.

The USYRU/SNAME capsize study referred to in previous chapters determined that rigs have become about 30 percent lighter on the latest boats than they were 20 years ago. Since heavier rigs have more resistance (or *greater inertia*) to capsize than almost any other

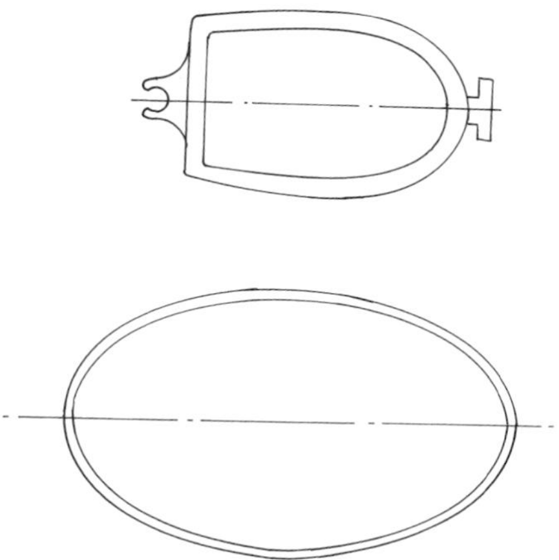

A conventional thin-walled mast with one or two spreaders results in a large-diameter spar. With a slightly thicker wall and multiple sets of spreaders, the mast diameter can be made much smaller. The result is a lighter, bendier, harder-to-tune spar, but one that allows better airflow over the mainsail. Cruisers may have more peace of mind with the larger, less bendy mast.

factor in the design of the boat—in other words, they slow the speed at which a boat rolls into a capsize, making the capsize less likely to occur—the study recommends that masts used today be made slightly heavier for greater resistance to capsizing. Another recommendation is for the development of sealed masts to help reright a boat if it should capsize. (A sealed mast provides additional righting moment.) The only way I see to do this is to use external halyards or to install plastic halyard tubes in a carbon fiber mast and seal the remainder. But a carbon fiber spar is much more expensive than an alloy spar, even without the additional expense of halyard tubes.

Tuning a Rig

A single-spreader rig is the easiest to tune, has the largest mast diameter, and usually has the heaviest weight. To reduce weight and windage aloft, a double-spreader rig might be used. The tuning of a double-spreader rig is only marginally more difficult than a single-spreader. It is when you get into three and four sets of spreaders that tuning becomes difficult: the mast diameter and weight are usually considerably smaller and the mast is more likely to get out of column. To benefit from the smaller diameter and reduced windage, a three- or four-spreader mast should be tuned by an expert.

In general, cruising boats should have relatively simple rigs. A crew enjoying a cruise should not have to worry about multiple spreaders, keeping the mast in column, and getting just the right amount of mast bend to make the boat sail superbly well. In other words, when

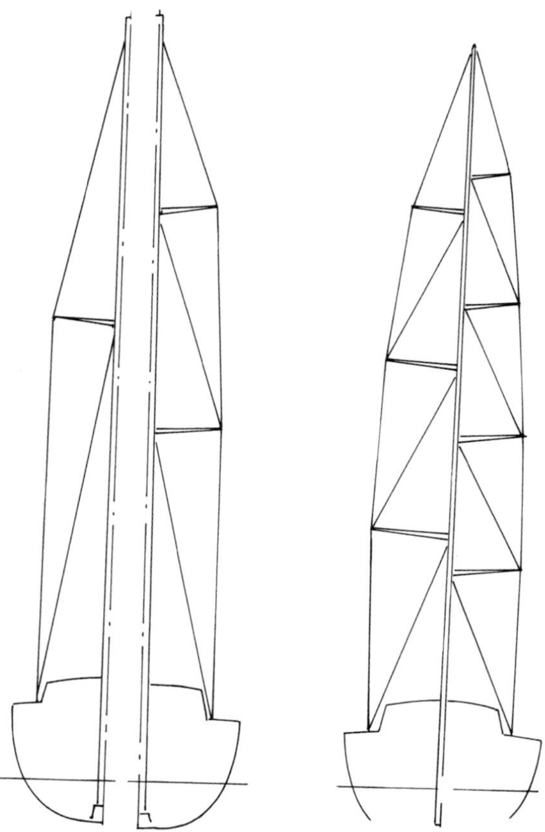

Single-spreader masts have the largest diameter and are the stiffest spars. Double-spreader masts are about as far as a hard-core cruiser should go. Cruiser/Racers can benefit from a triple-spreader mast, and extreme racers will make their sails marginally more efficient with a four- or five-spreader rig.

selecting a rig for a cruising boat, ease of use and tuning become major factors.

Standing Rigging

How do you keep your mast upright? Unless it is a freestanding spar, you use standing rigging.

The trend today is to use solid rod for all standing rigging, but in my opinion that is not the best option for an offshore cruising boat. I like to have a little "give" to the rig. The reason for this goes back to a tropical storm I encountered on a trip to Bermuda. The boat had solid rod rigging, and as the storm's fury increased we cranked up the backstay to keep the boat heading up toward Bermuda. Even so, by the time we were down to the storm jib, the headstay had an appreciable sag to leeward. When the storm had passed by, we took stock of our situation. The rig was still standing and the boat was secure, but on close inspection we found a compression dimple about the size of a fist in the mast tube. Had we not had a thick mast wall, we could have lost the spar. Apparently, the tight rig had transmitted the shroud loads directly to the mast tube, which led to the dimple. If the hydraulic backstay had been slacked slightly, the rig would have had more give and we would probably not have seen a compression dimple. For this reason, I like to use 1 × 19 stainless steel wire for the backstay and lower shrouds on a cruising boat. This allows the rig a little freedom to move and absorbs some of the shock loads that travel through the hull when the boat sails off a wave.

Of course, on a racing boat the story is different. The rig needs to be as tight as possible to go to windward, and the mast is often set up with some pre-bend. Because it stretches so little, rod rigging is the only option to get the performance required. Note that discontinuous rod rigging should be used to reduce stretching and to cut down on the possibility of failure. (Continuous rod rigging is when the vertical shroud is merely bent over the end of the spreaders and runs from masthead to chainplate. Discontinuous rod rigging is installed in sections, with one section running from chainplate to lower spreader, another section from lower spreader to upper spreader, and a third section from upper spreader to masthead. Discontinuous rod rigging is less likely to lead to a catastrophic mast failure if a single shroud breaks.)

Running Rigging

While standing rigging supports the mast, running rigging controls the sails. It needs to have low stretch characteristics and flexibility, even when immersed in salt water for long periods of time. Most running rigging is low-stretch braided line. (Only anchor lines still use three-strand.) Running rigging should be sized to suit the anticipated load; tracks and other deck gear should suit the diameter and load of the line.

The least expensive choice for running rigging is low-stretch braided Dacron. As the loads get higher, the diameter of the line can be increased to suit the increased load. But at some point, Dacron lines become too large to handle easily yet still have low-stretch characteristics; this typically happens on boats around 45 to 50 feet LOA.

Rather than resort to large-diameter lines (which would in turn require larger winch drums, larger blocks, and larger cleats), rope manufacturers have added Kevlar or Spectra fibers to their lines. Early Kevlar and Spectra lines had problems; Kevlar abraded itself, and Spectra suffered from creep—that is, it stretched and didn't return to its original length. But gradually, rope manufacturers developed a blend of Kevlar, Dacron, and Spectra that works satisfactorily. These lines are easy to use, durable, and, if properly sized, will carry the load without problems.

What should you buy? If your boat is small, you do not need high-strength lines; Dacron will do the job. High-strength lines tend to be of smaller diameter, and the smallest line that you can hold comfortably is about 1/4 inch diameter. As boat size increases, lines get larger. Kevlar should be used first on spinnaker sheets and guys, which tend to carry the highest loads. If you don't set a spinnaker, chances are you can get away without any high-strength lines. If your boat is over 50 feet, however, you will need higher-strength lines to keep the rope diameter to a manageable size.

On Deck

How do you lay out a deck that is easy to operate and conducive to good sail trim? First, you need to arrange the deck so that each part can do its job properly without chafe and without interfering with other gear. You do this by considering each component of the deck layout separately and then integrating them into the layout.

Experienced designers know that there are certain areas that can cause problems when translating a two-dimensional drawing onto a three-dimensional deck. For example, problems occur around the coaming when a line is led from the track car or turning block to the winch. It is difficult to spot on a drawing, but the line will often chafe on the coaming. To prevent such snags, the deck layout drawing should serve as a basic plan of where gear will go. Those responsible for installation should always be free to adjust gear as required to eliminate chafe. This means that a line should be run to make sure that all leads are fair before drilling any holes or gluing anything down.

Mainsheet

Mainsheet tracks are most efficient when they are located directly under the boom and about a foot in from the end; this is where the highest leech loading occurs on the mainsail. However, on most boats this location is directly abaft the companionway hatch. Most sailors, with visions of being decapitated by the mainsheet during a jibe, dislike having the track in the cockpit. Consequently, many production boat manufacturers have moved the sheet to a location on the cabintop, just forward of the companionway hatch. This positions the track near the middle of the main boom, so a system of two or three blocks is used to spread the load somewhat. Without spreading the loads, the mainsheet could bend or break the boom.

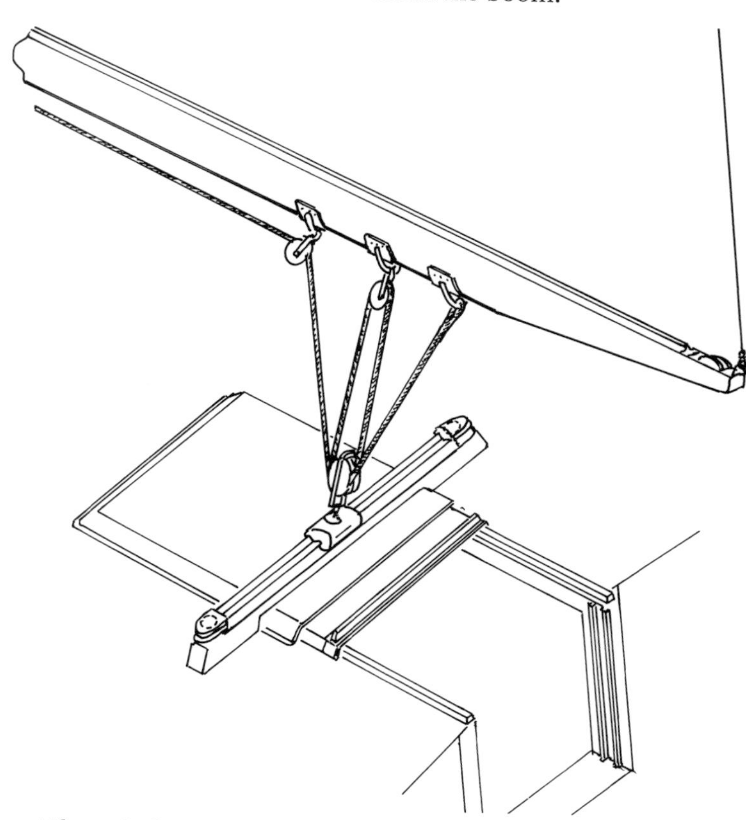

To get the mainsheet track out of the cockpit, many builders are locating it over the companionway hatch. A single-point attachment to the boom can bend the boom and may eventually cause it to fail. A better arrangement is the three-point attachment shown here.

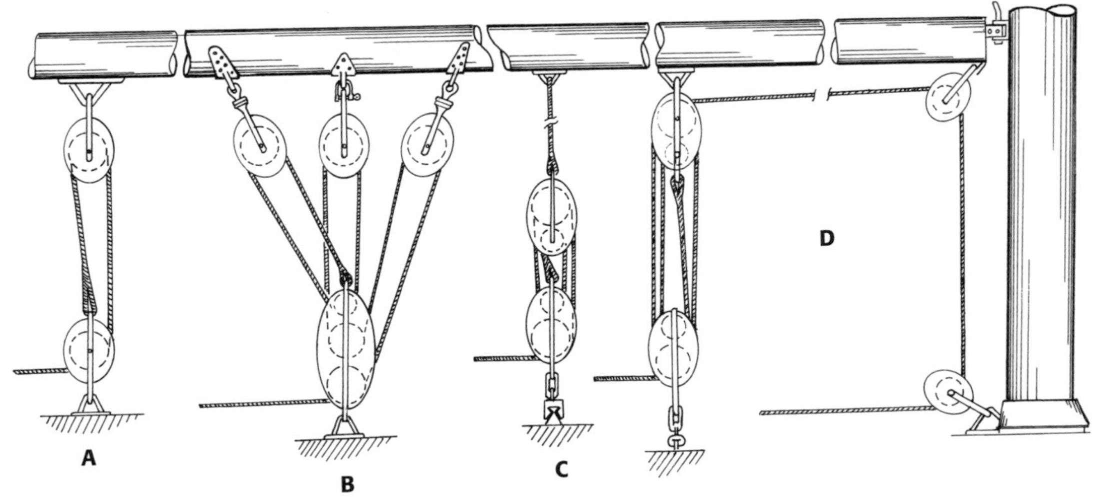

Various mainsheet arrangements. A shows a two-part mainsheet tackle, as may be found on a smaller boat. B is a six-part tackle that might be used on a 40-to-50 footer. C is a four-part tackle led to a winch, as is found on many cruisers. D is a four-part tackle led forward to the mast and back to a cleat or a winch in the cockpit.

Regardless of the mainsheet track location, a two-or-more-part tackle is used to gain enough downward tension on the main boom. The layout of the mainsheet may use any one of several configurations, as shown in the accompanying drawing. A is a two-part sheet operated from the lower block. Typically, this system is used on a smaller boat. B shows a six-part tackle for a larger boat. C shows a four-part tackle from a single point on the boom, often the boom end. D shows a four-part tackle for a larger boat. In this system the line is led along the boom and back to a winch on the cabintop. The more complex systems generate a lot of friction, making them harder to use. It usually does not pay to use more than a four-part tackle. In a five- or six-part tackle, a lot of line is required to ease the sheet out fully, which will fill the cockpit when the mainsheet is pulled in tightly.

Today, the mainsheet traveler plays an essential part in setting the mainsail. If the mainsail controls (halyard, outhaul, leech line, and foot line) are used to set the mainsail up properly, the traveler should be thought of as the item that adjusts the angle of the sail to the wind. For example, the traveler may often be above the centerline when sailing to windward to put the boom on the centerline. As the boat comes onto a close reach, the sail shape may not change, but the sail's angle to the wind should be changed by easing the traveler down using the taglines. In a gusty wind the traveler should be eased before the mainsheet; this will maintain sail shape and feather the sail as a gust hits.

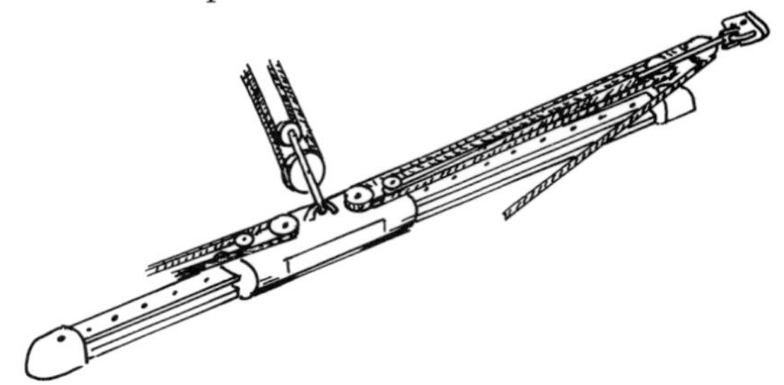

Taglines on the main traveler should be used to control the angle of attack of the sail. Set the sail up to suit the wind strength and use taglines (instead of the mainsheet) to move the boom up and down on the track. If you ease the tagline in a puff, the sail shape does not change. If you ease the mainsheet, the sail shape changes and must be reset when the puff subsides.

Headsail Sheet Tracks

Headsail sheet tracks should be positioned fore-and-aft to enable a 150-percent headsail to be sheeted near the aft end of the track and a 110-percent headsail or a working jib to be sheeted at the front end of the track. Usually this means a long length of track. Manufacturers often use a shorter track for the 150-to-110-percent headsail and a padeye for the working jib, with another padeye for the storm jib.

When a boat sails to windward, the headsails are sheeted fully in. We have already seen how the fullness of the bow and the type of rig affect the boat's ability to go to windward. Another factor that affects windward ability is the sheeting angle. The farthest-outboard track for a windward headsail produces an angle around 10 degrees, while the most inboard track should not be below 7½ degrees, unless the sail is a staysail. Staysails are sheeted on a 6-to-8-degree track. The angle is measured from the tack fitting at the bow. Ideally, tracks are located so that the sheeting angle opens up slightly as a smaller sail is used in higher wind strengths. In the accompanying drawing a boat's port side shows tracks at 7½-degree and 10-degree angles. The starboard side shows a compromise track where the angle varies; it also shows a 6-degree staysail track.

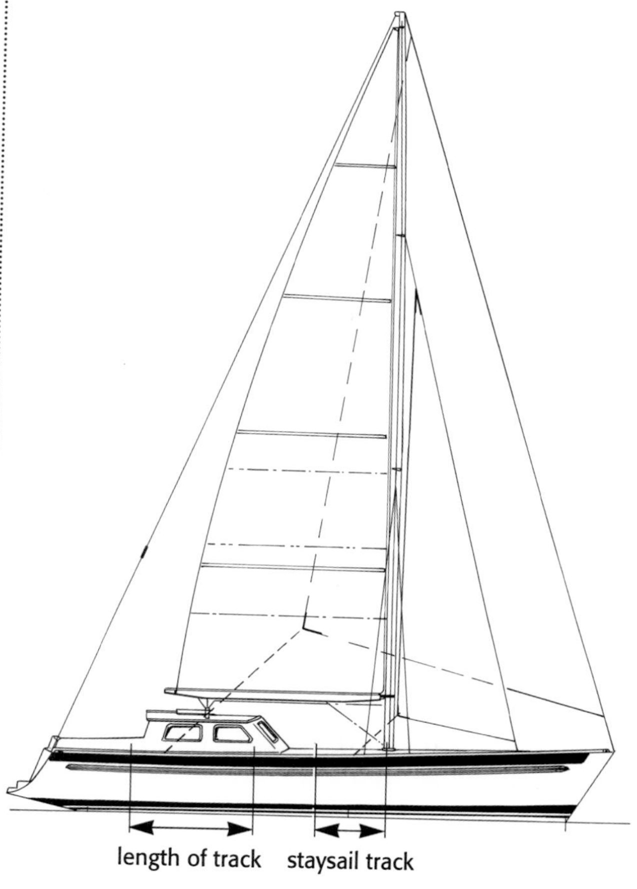

By projecting sheet leads to the deck, a designer can determine the fore-and-aft positions of the headsail tracks.

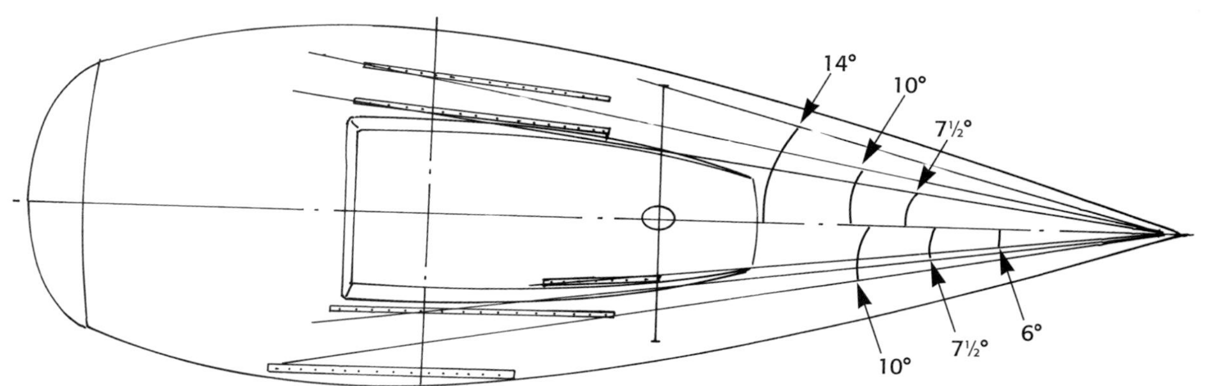

When the fore-and-aft track locations have been set, the distance outboard must be found. In general, staysail tracks are located on a 6-to-8-degree line projected back from the sail tack. Headsail tracks are located at 7 to 10 degrees from the centerline, depending on the width of the house.

Winches

As soon as the loads on lines become higher than a person can pull, the load must be reduced to a point where it can be handled. One method of doing this is to use a block and tackle; another is to use a winch. Smaller winches may have one or two gears, while large powerful winches can have up to four gears and a backwind capacity. Geared winches tend to be heavy and expensive. As a consequence, boatbuilders use line organizers and sheet-stoppers (described in the next section) to cut down on the number of winches on deck.

Winches used for trimming the sheets (and often the spinnaker guys) are primary winches. These tend to be the largest and most powerful winches on the boat, but in most cases little thought is given to their placement. They are stuck on the coaming, and the crew is expected to adapt to their location.

Secondary winches tend to be smaller than primaries and are used to trim staysail and spinnaker sheets. Secondary winches may be independent from the halyard winches, but with sheet-stoppers halyard winches can double as secondaries, cutting the minimum number of winches onboard to four. If the halyard winches are not used as secondaries, at least six winches must be carried.

The power of winches is a function of the gear ratio and the power ratio. The gear ratio is quite simple:

$$\text{Gear ratio} = \frac{\text{Number of handle revolutions}}{\text{Number of drum revolutions}}$$

Lewmar sizes its winches according to the gear ratio. For example, using Lewmar 40 in low gear takes 40 turns of the handle to turn the drum once.

The power ratio of a winch is the manufacturer's term for mechanical advantage. This depends on three factors: the gear ratio, the winch handle length, and the diameter of the drum.

$$\text{Power ratio} = \frac{\text{Gear ratio x (2 x handle length)}}{\text{Diameter of drum}}$$

This means that the power ratio of a winch with a 1-to-1 gear ratio, a 10-inch handle, and a drum diameter of 4.5 inches is:

$$\frac{1 \text{ x } (2 \text{ x } 10)}{4.5} = 4.44$$

Thus, a person who can exert 60 pounds on the handle can pull in a sheet load of

$$4.44 \text{ x } 60 = 266.7 \text{ pounds}$$

When the operator uses another winch speed with a gear ratio of 40 to 1, that same person could pull in a load of 10,667 pounds!

Line Organizers

In the mid-1970s and early 1980s we used to lead lines through fairleads and then to a winch. The only problem was that each lead took up a lot of space on deck. Today we use line organizers to align halyards or sheets before leading them to a winch.

Sheet-stoppers

Sheet-stoppers (also called rope clutches) are used extensively on today's boats to reduce the cost and weight of winches. They can be ob-

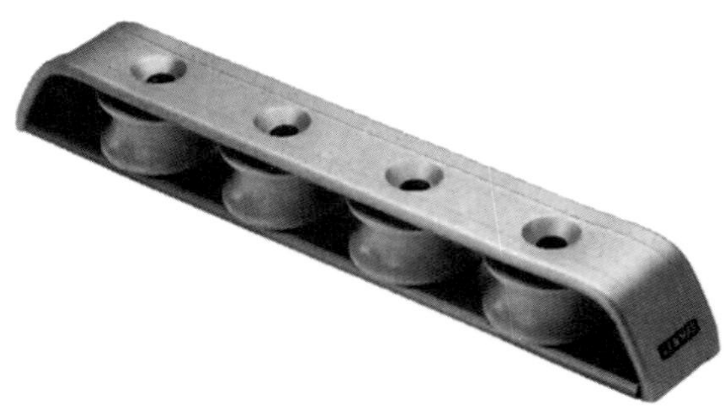

Line organizers are used to align halyards and small lines properly with winches. *(Photo courtesy of Lewmar)*

Sheet-stoppers, also called rope clutches, are used to reduce the number of winches onboard. By using a clutch, one winch can be used for three to five lines. This is Lewmar's single Superlock rope clutch. *(Photo courtesy of Lewmar)*

tained either singly or in banks of up to four. When selecting and placing sheet-stoppers, you should make sure that no lines going to a winch will conflict during each of the evolutions made onboard. For example, if you want to fly a staysail and a spinnaker at the same time, you cannot lead the staysail and spinnaker halyards or sheets to the same winch. It is not a good idea to lead more than four lines to a single winch, because, despite the best-laid plans, you can be sure that at some point you'll want to get two lines on the same winch simultaneously.

Cleats

Conventional cleats are essential for tying off and locking lines. Cleats on the foredeck will be used for mooring and may well be used for towing, so they should be slightly larger than the mid-deck or aft cleats. The accompanying illustration, from an earlier book of mine, *Designed to Win*, shows cleat sizes for conventional boats.

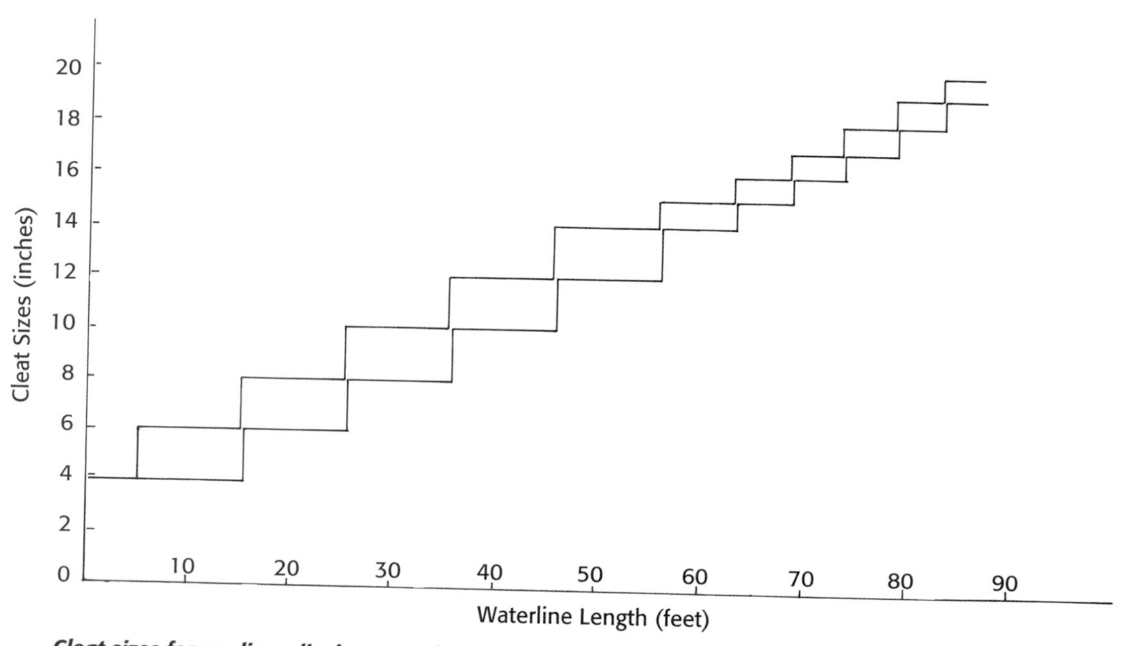

Cleat sizes for medium-displacement boats. Bow cleats should be one size larger to allow the boat to be towed.

You can go one or two sizes down for lightweight boats.

Conventional cleat sizes should be sized by multiplying the diameter of the line by 16. For example, ½-inch line requires an 8-inch cleat. Other types of cleats, such as jam and cam cleats, should also be sized according to the line size. When selecting a cam or jam cleat, make sure the line load is low enough so that the line cannot be pulled through the cleat; if that happens, it will burn the plastic "teeth" and ruin the cleat.

Anchor Handling

Handling the anchor can be of critical importance on a cruising boat. Having adequate anchors and chain aboard can be a lifesaver, but a weak link anywhere along the system—in the bow roller, the capstan or windlass, the chain or anchor line, or the strongpoint to which the rode is fastened—can result in the loss of the boat.

Bow Roller

Bow rollers should hold the anchor captive, allow the chain to pay out easily, and allow the anchor line to be retrieved without chafing or snagging. This means that a bow roller needs a reasonably large-diameter roller and flared jaws to allow the rode to move easily. A well-made bow roller should also be strong enough to carry the load of the boat as it snubs against the anchor rode in a seaway, and should provide a way of securing the anchor tightly.

Windlass or Capstan

Whether you choose a windlass or a capstan (a windlass has a horizontal axis and a capstan has a vertical axis) depends on the location of the unit. For example, on a boat with two bow rollers, the chain or line approaches the unit from different horizontal angles. In this case a capstan would work best. When the unit is located in a locker or has only one line leading to it, a horizontal-axis windlass will be better. Whether you choose a windlass or a capstan, it should have a chain gypsy and a rope drum on it.

Some of the latest windlasses are low profile, reversible, and draw relatively low power. They do have some drawbacks next to conventional windlasses, primarily that the motors are small and may cut out after several minutes of hard hauling. But where virtually automatic handling is required, they are hard to beat. With one of these windlasses an anchor can be raised and lowered from the cockpit.

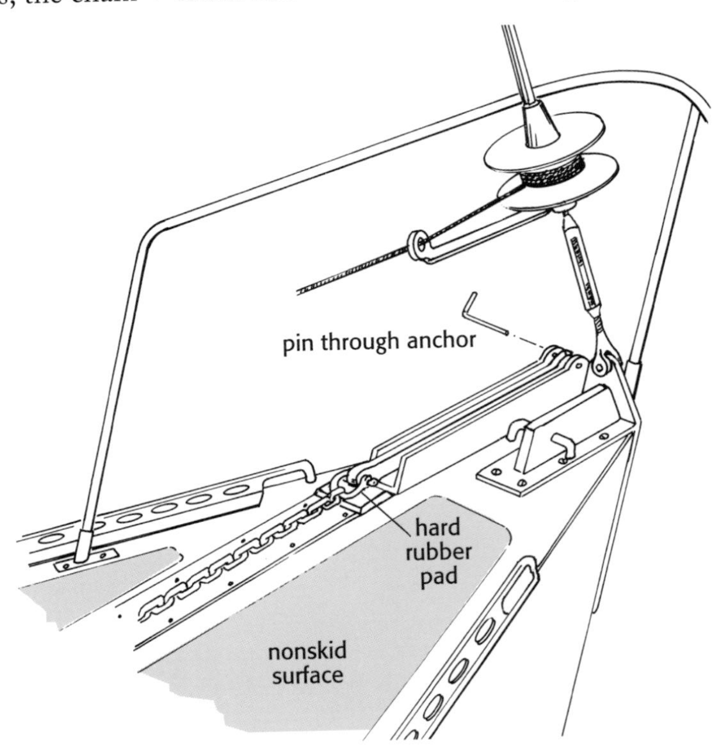

If a bow roller is fitted, it should be possible to pin the anchor tightly in position. Here a pin is inserted through the anchor and a hard rubber pad is positioned at the inboard end to stop the anchor banging on the deck. In heavy weather the anchor should be removed or lashed securely to the rail.

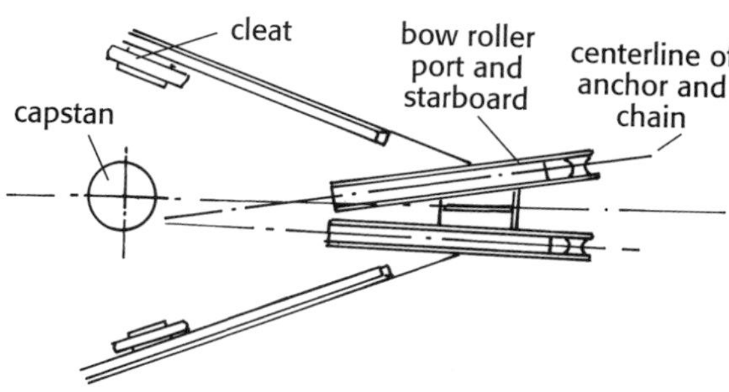

A capstan is best if you have two anchors on bow rollers. Both rollers can be oriented toward the chain gypsy.

A larger anchor capstan should have a chain gypsy, as shown on this Lewmar 3000. *(Photo courtesy of Lewmar)*

The Lewmar Concept low-profile windlass with the chain spliced to the anchor line is hard to beat on a small boat. When selecting such a windlass, make sure it has enough power to haul the entire anchor rode in before it overheats or cuts out. *(Photo courtesy of Lewmar)*

Anchor Rode

Unless you are going to anchor in coral or on rocks, you do not need an all-chain anchor rode. A nylon line works better and has some stretch to it. But you should have a length of chain (about 2 fathoms, or 10 to 15 feet) between the anchor and the line. This will help to keep the anchor pulling parallel to the seabed, plus it helps hold the rope catenary down to give more shock absorption to the line.

If the rope is spliced into the anchor chain it runs around the chain gypsy much more easily, as shown in the accompanying photo on this page. On the other hand, an eyesplice will let you shackle the chain to the line, which is best if you change anchors or line often. If you use a shackle, make sure it is moused properly so that it cannot come undone underwater.

Anchors

What type of bottom do you expect to anchor on? Mud, sand, rock, coral, shale, shingle, stone? There's an anchor for each place. Fortunately, anchors can be divided into two major categories—those for anchoring in mud or sandy bottoms, and those for anchoring in harder bottoms such as shingle or stone. Responsible sailors do not anchor on rock or in areas where they are likely to damage coral.

Anchors have parts that make them easy to distinguish. For example, a plow anchor does not have a stock, while a fisherman and a Danforth do. It helps to remember the parts when describing an anchor.

Anchors for soft bottoms are of the Danforth, plow (CQR), or Bruce types. All of these anchors dig into the bottom and stay dug in as the boat swings around it. If they were to be used in an area of rock or weed, these anchors might not hold properly.

Because of the space required for stowage, plow or Bruce anchors, (A) in the accompanying sketch, are usually stowed on a bow roller. A lightweight Danforth (B), which is comparatively flat, can be kept in a deck locker ready for use. Many production boats have a built-in locker on the foredeck. The problem with such a locker is that it may fill with water in bad weather, plus it puts the anchor high on the bow where the weight is detrimental to performance.

Anchors for harder bottoms are grapnel or fisherman types (C), with their smaller flukes that can dig into cracks or between rocks. In general, the style of the fluke gives the anchor its name. This type of anchor should not be used on soft bottoms, as they will pull out easily. Stowage is a major problem with fisherman-style anchors. A fisherman-style anchor made by Paul Luke will collapse into three parts for easier storage, but it must be reassembled before it can be used.

The designer or boatbuilder should know what type of anchor a boat is to carry to enable the correct stowage to be incorporated into the design. For example, a boat designed to carry a Danforth lightweight anchor may have a special anchor locker on the foredeck. If a Bruce or plow (CQR) anchor is to be carried, stowage may be in a hawsepipe or on a roller. A fisherman anchor may be stowed below.

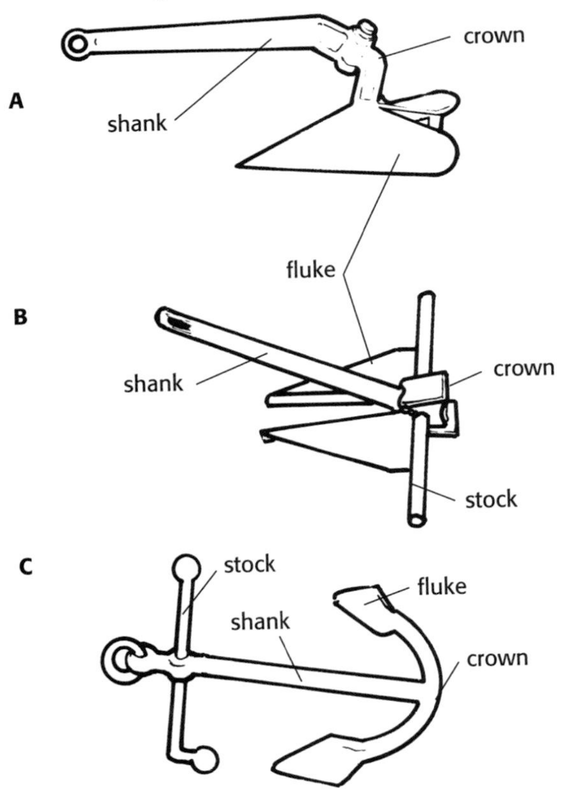

Different types of anchors. A is a CQR or plow-style anchor, B is a Danforth lightweight anchor, and C is a fisherman-style anchor.

Chain Locker

A chain locker should have a grating at the bottom to allow water to drain into the bilge. We have already (in chapter 3) looked at the hawsepipe and how it should be slightly sloped to prevent the chain from rattling. It should also have access through the top to allow the anchor line to be organized so that it won't block the hawse.

When the anchor is stowed, the chain usually rattles around on deck. If the anchor is not stowed properly and slips off the roller, it can run out until it hits bottom. For this reason, a chain claw, or stopper, is often used to secure the chain when the boat puts to sea.

The chain locker requires a strongpoint to which the chain should be secured, to ensure that the anchor and chain do not disappear over the side.

Ports and Hatches

On a cruising boat, having enough hatches and opening ports can be critical, especially for a boat that will sail in the tropics. It is also of major importance that hatches not leak (you would be surprised how many do).

Hatch frames today are usually made of aluminum alloy, which means that they can be distorted if they are not installed properly. If they get distorted, hatches will leak. Hatches should have screens to keep insects out. If it rains a lot in your area, you might want to have a dodger over the hatch, although a dodger cuts down on airflow.

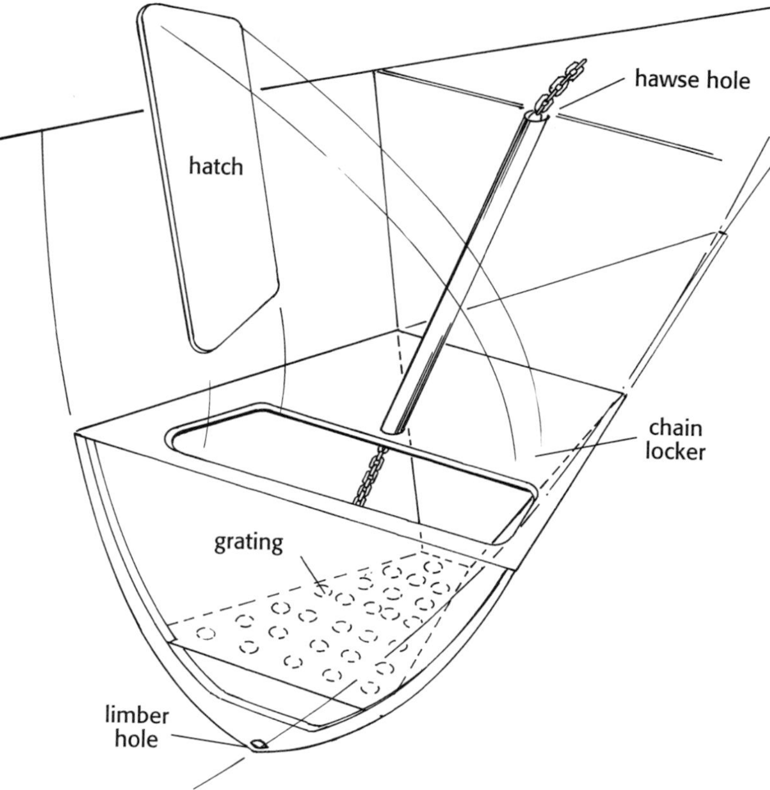

The chain locker. Chain enters through the hawse and lands on the grating at the bottom of the locker. The grating has holes in it to allow water to drain to the bilge or to a sump. The locker has a removable lid to enable a crew to spread the chain evenly around the locker.

If there is only one hatch to a compartment, it should be large enough for a person to climb through. The minimum size is around 18 by 18 inches. (In the head compartment there is rarely enough space for an escape hatch, so the head door should be designed to open inward.)

In the days of sailing ships, ports were cut in the sides of ships for guns or for cargo loading. When open they provided cross-ventilation. Whenever possible I like to specify opening ports in the sides of the cabin to obtain some cross-ventilation. Like hatches, opening ports should be fitted with screens to keep insects out.

Steering

The steering system is one of the most critical parts of the boat. It comprises many parts, and each should be installed and operated properly for the system to be most efficient. The chain and wire steering system includes the pedestal, which houses a chain sprocket attached to the wheel shaft. A chain attached at either end to cables runs around the sprocket. The cables are led via turning blocks to the quadrant, which is bolted to the rudderstock.

Some systems on smaller boats use a single wire housed in a sheath. Steering gear manufacturer Edson calls this a push/pull or a push/push system. Other manufacturers, such as Whitlock, make a linked system where the steering column turns a bevel gear, which, in turn, drives another shaft, connected to an arm on the rudderstock. On very large boats the

A chain stopper should be placed between the windlass and the bow roller to take the strain off the windlass. *(Photo courtesy of Lewmar)*

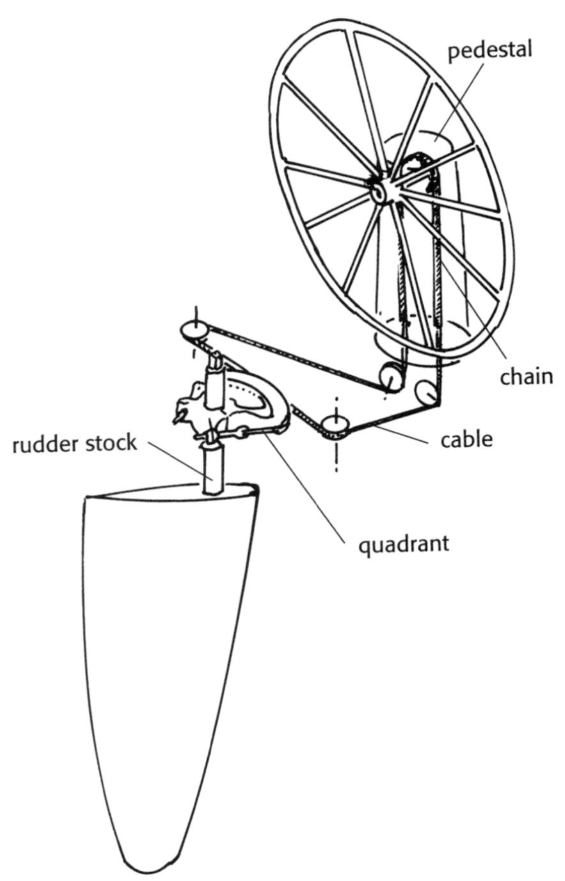

Cable steering is most commonly used on sailboats. Cables are led from the quadrant via blocks to a chain that runs over a sprocket in the steering pedestal.

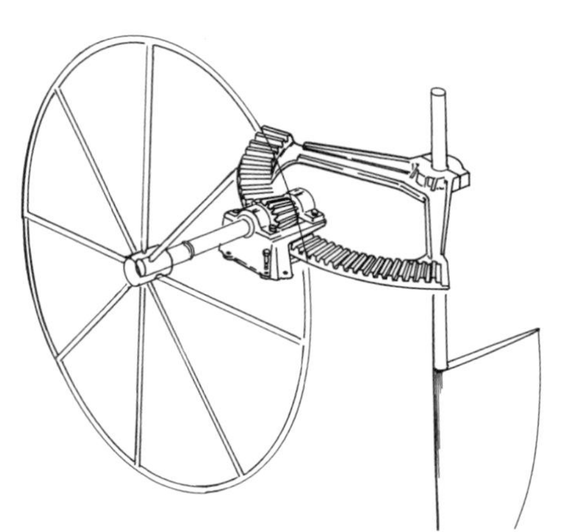

Geared steering is used on boats, such as large catboats, where the feedback from the helm may become overwhelming.

steering loads are so high that a hydraulic system is be used. The drawback of a hydraulic system is the lack of feedback to the helmsman.

On boats with transom-hung rudders, the simplest steering system of all is the tiller. It allows for great sensitivity, immediate control and feedback, and easy maintenance and repair. The only problem with a tiller is that on large boats it needs to be quite long to get enough leverage, and as the boat tacks the tiller sweeps the cockpit. Thus, tiller steering is usually restricted to smaller boats.

On some boats (catboats, for example) weather helm increases dramatically as the wind and heel angle increases. In such cases geared steering is sometimes used. Geared steering reduces the feedback from the helm and can be used to increase the mechanical advantage of the steering gear.

Wheel

The steering wheel should be as large as possible within the confines of the cockpit space. A larger wheel makes it easier to steer, and in the case of a racing boat enables the crew to get farther outboard. The only restriction on the size of the wheel on a cruising boat is that the crew should be able to move past the wheel without leaving the cockpit. Usually this limits the wheel diameter to around 42 inches.

Quadrant or Steering Arm

Quadrants should have large diameters to cut down on the steering effort. They should also be perfectly aligned with the sheaves on either side of the hull. The best quadrants are keyed and clamped to the rudderstock. They should never be simply clamped, because the bolts can loosen, allowing the quadrant to slip.

Emergency Steering

On every wheel-steered boat the top of the rudderstock should be taken to deck level and squared off to provide an emergency steering system. This will enable you to get home if the cable breaks or the pedestal jams. One of the first things you should try out on a new boat is the emergency steering to make sure it works flawlessly. You may depend on it someday.

Ventilation

Proper ventilation keeps odors, bacteria, and mold spores under control. There are several methods of circulating air through a boat: using opening hatches, Dorade-style vents, or low-profile power vents and solar vents, such as those made by Nicro. The Dorade vent (so named because it was first used on Olin and Rod Stephens's *Dorade*) conducts air below yet prevents water from entering. Alternatively, you could use a power vent to continuously circulate air. The unit shown in the photo has a built-in solar cell and ni-cad battery that powers a fan. The fan runs for up to 48 hours and continually refreshes the air inside the hull.

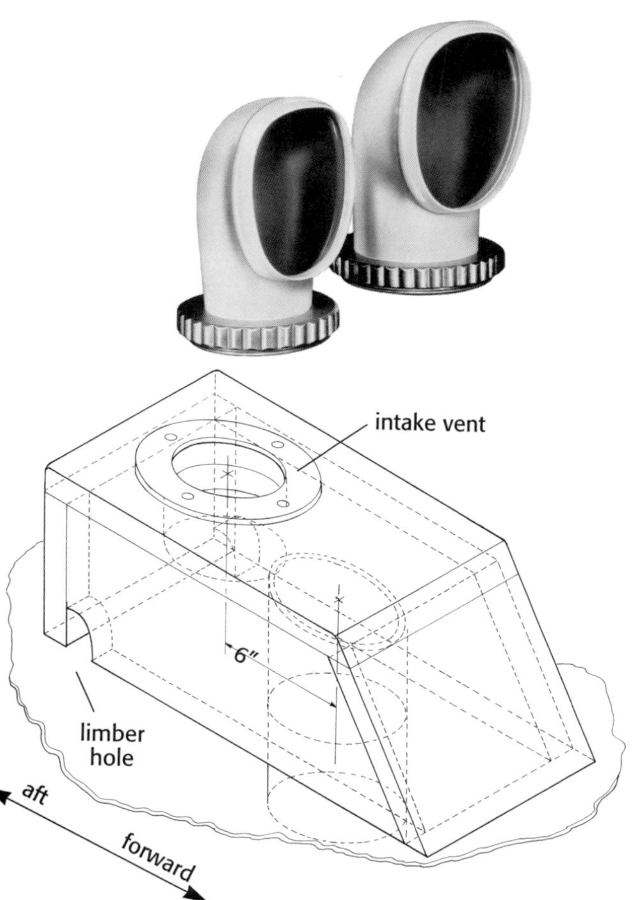

As shown in the drawing, a Dorade vent is a box through which air flows into the boat. The vent into the boat is forward of the intake vent to allow water to drain out. Cowls such as these from Vetus Den Ouden can be purchased in most chandleries. *(Photo courtesy of Vetus Den Ouden)*

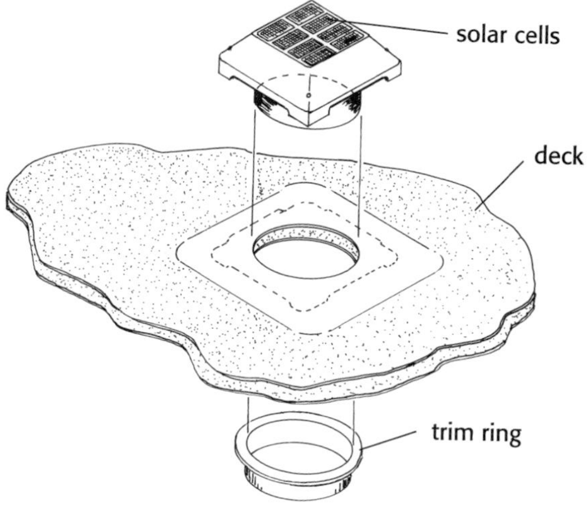

The Nicro power vent can be used where low-profile continuous ventilation is required. It is driven by solar cells and a ni-cad battery which gives it enough power to run for 48 hours continuously without recharging. It is installed by drilling a hole through the deck, caulking the area, and dropping the vent in place (see drawing). A trim ring fits on the underside. I tested this vent and found that when it is closed, no water can get through it. *(Photo courtesy of Marinco)*

Our Designs

The deck layouts of our five boats differ significantly according to the different purposes of each boat. For example, in keeping with its light weight, the Weekender requires a minimum number of winches. The Voyager, on the other hand, should have some redundancy so that if a winch breaks in a remote area, another can be used.

The Weekender

The deck layout of the Weekender is simple, consistent with a light, easily handled boat. There are four winches on deck—two on either side of the cockpit and two on the aft end of the cabintop. All lines lead from the mast aft, through sheet-stoppers, to the winches. Leads to the sheet winches are direct from the track cars to minimize frictional losses; this puts the car at a slight angle but stays within its tolerances. The companionway hatch has no dodger or covering board. It is as simple as possible, with just a cover and a single washboard. One steps through the hatch onto the winch-handling platform, which is really the top of a

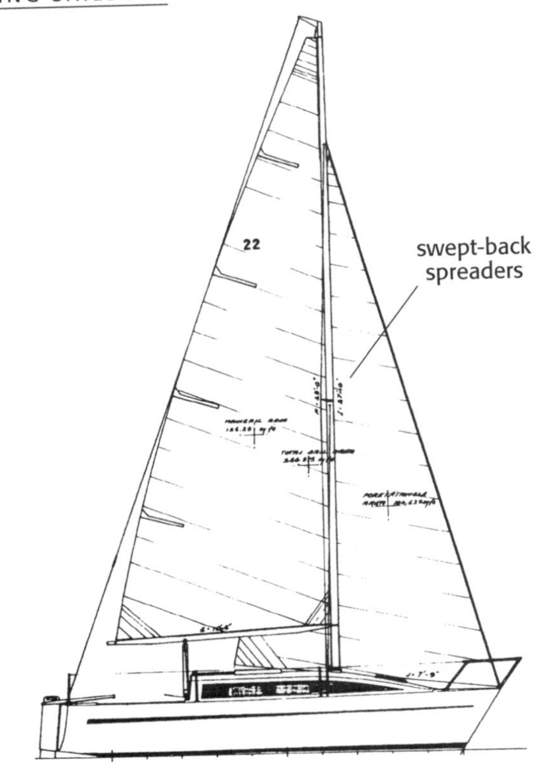

The sail plan of the Weekender. The deck-stepped mast and fractional rig give this boat good light-air performance. Note the swept-back spreaders and absence of running backstays for easy rig control.

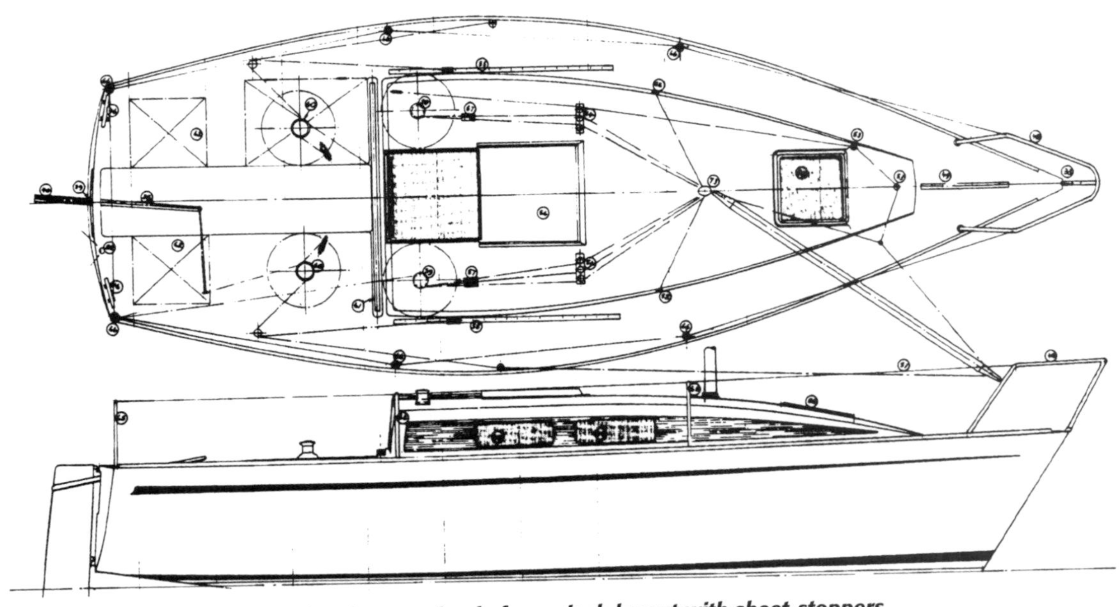

The deck of the Weekender shows a simple four-winch layout with sheet-stoppers.

portable ice chest. This boat has no Dorade vents, but it does have one solar vent in the cabintop over the galley. Additional ventilation is achieved by opening the hatches.

Because the cabintop is fairly wide (to give headroom below), sheet tracks are located alongside the cabinhouse to minimize sheeting angles. In this case they are slightly outside the 10-degree line. This still allows the leads to go directly to the winches, but we will have to watch for chafe on the edges of the cabin. The mainsheet traveler runs across the cockpit to make it easy for the helmsman to operate, dividing the crew area from the helm position.

The rig on the Weekender is also simple. It is a deck-stepped fractional rig with swept-back spreaders to eliminate running backstays and to keep the headstay taut. The chainplates are bolted directly to the master bulkhead, which is cut away below deck to save weight. Standing rigging is 1/8-inch and 3/16-inch 1 × 19 stainless steel wire. The mast is intended to be easy for one or two people to raise and lower. All halyards are low-stretch polyester.

The Cruiser

On the Cruiser deck there are two large hatches, with solar vents over the galley and heads. At the forward end of the main saloon there are a pair of Dorade-style vents which can be kept open in all but the worst weather. To make sure air can circulate throughout the entire boat, there are louvered vents in all doors.

On a cruising boat the location of the tracks, chainplates, and sail leads is less aggressive than on a racing boat. In other words, rather than minimize the genoa track angle to get the very best windward performance, the location of the track is more of a compromise among performance, structural rigidity, and its effect on the interior layout. Instead of a 7½-degree angle for the entire track and another track outboard of the first, a cruising boat will typically have a genoa track parallel to the centerline and close

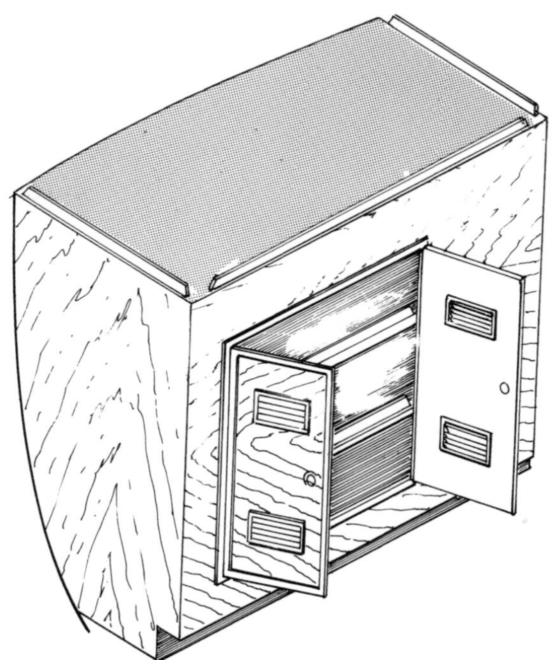

Lockers should have vented doors for good air circulation.

to the cabintop, as on this boat. This may put the aft end of the track at a 7½-degree angle and the forward end at a 10-degree angle, which has the effect of making the boat sail farther off the wind as the wind strength increases and smaller sails are used. (In turn, the slightly lower windward performance is another reason not to give the boat a fine bow.)

On a racing boat the shroud base may be very narrow to enable the crew to sheet the sail in as tightly as possible. This positions the chainplates well inboard. On a Cruiser, however, the shroud base and chainplates can be somewhat wider, at an angle of around 14 degrees rather than 11 or 12. In order to minimize the intrusion of the chainplate brackets into the interior, the chainplates are located next to the cabin side, which allows the brackets to be mounted on bulkheads and clears the deck walkway.

Compared with the Weekender, the sail-handling systems on the Cruiser are slightly more complex, with a cruising spinnaker and

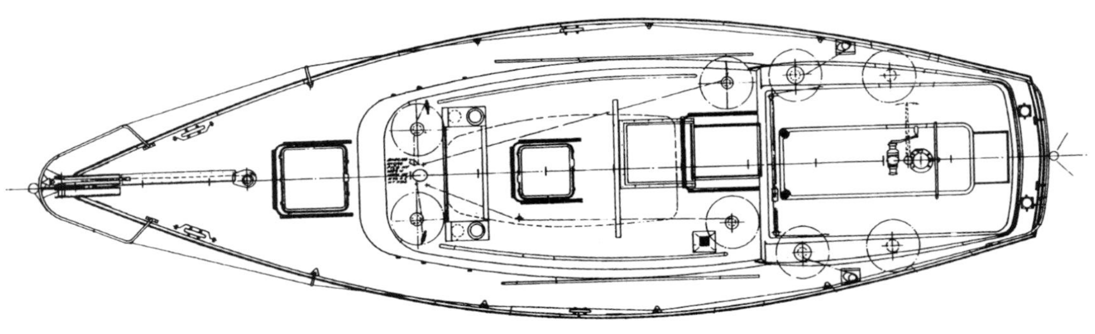

The Cruiser shows a conventional layout with winches centered around the cockpit. This layout shows the ketch version, although the sloop version would be similar apart from the mizzen in the cockpit and the additional rigging.

several headsails on a mast stepped through the deck. The mainmast is a double-spreader aluminum spar with a tapered top section to reduce windage. The mizzen is a single-spreader, independently stayed mast. Rod rigging is used for the V1s, V2s, and D3s shrouds, but with a 1 × 19 stainless steel backstay and D1 lowers so the rig has a little "give." All halyards are prestretched polyester with an eye spliced into both ends to prolong the life of the halyard. (By end-for-ending it as it gets worn, a halyard can be used twice as long.)

All the sheet winches on this boat are located on the cockpit coamings. Halyard

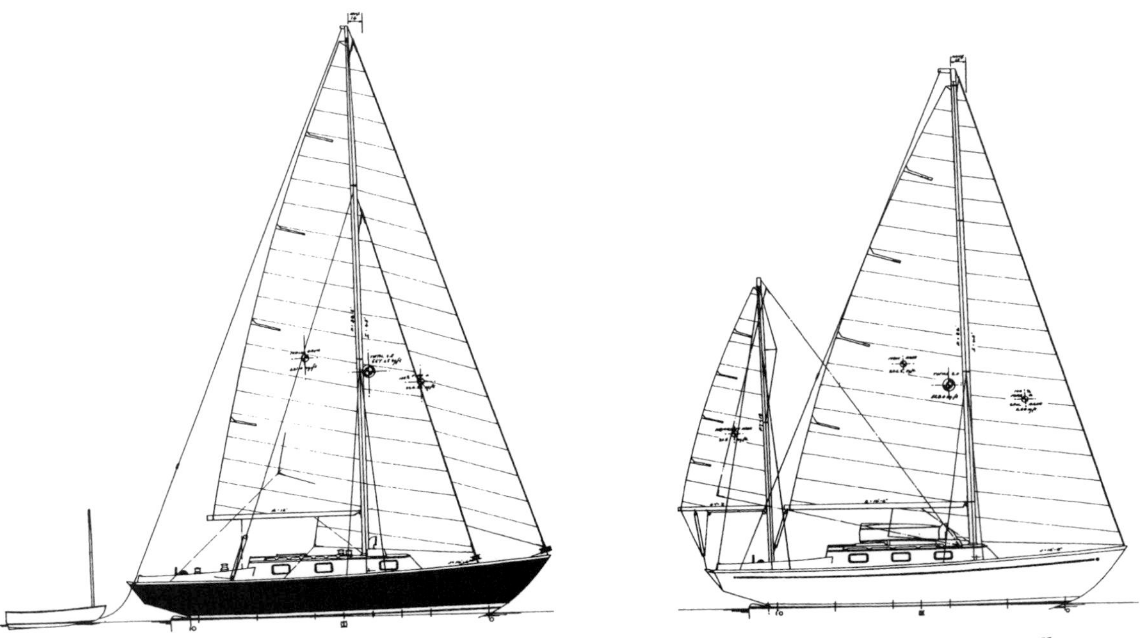

Two sail plans of the Cruiser. The sloop rig is taller, with running backstays to carry the staysail loads. Both headsails are roller furled for easy handling.

winches on the cabintop enable halyards to be led aft via line organizers and sheet-stoppers. Behind the primary winches are the secondary winches, with sheets coming directly from turning blocks. The mizzenmast winches are located on the mast, where they can be operated by any of the cockpit crew. For single-handing, the secondary winches (which can be trimmed from the helm) can be used as primaries.

To accommodate a hard dinghy on the cabintop, the mainsheet track on the Cruiser has been located at the forward end of the cockpit. The mizzen sheet is taken to a short length of track on the taffrail, with the lead coming forward along the boom to a winch on the mast.

The sail plan shows both a double-headsail sloop and a ketch rig. Both rigs will fit on this boat, although headroom under the mizzen boom is critical for the helmsman. The double-headsail sloop version has running backstays, which can be a pain to use but are required to balance the staysail load on the mast. Note also that both rigs are conservative in sail area. If the boat were to be sailed in light wind areas such as the Great Lakes or the Chesapeake, the rig height could be increased by a few feet.

The Voyager

On deck the Voyager is set up for a cruising spinnaker or for double-headsail wing-and-wing sailing. The cruising spinnaker will be tacked to the headstay, so no pole is required. A pair of whisker poles will be located forward for wing-and-wing sailing. In this configuration the mainsail will be dropped; this should give the boat an easy motion downwind with minimal crew labor.

To make sail handling easier on this boat, we could look at splitting the sail plan into either a yawl or ketch. Upwind the ketch would sail with no mizzen, while on a reach the boat would be able to set a mizzen staysail for more sail area. In heavy weather the skipper might set

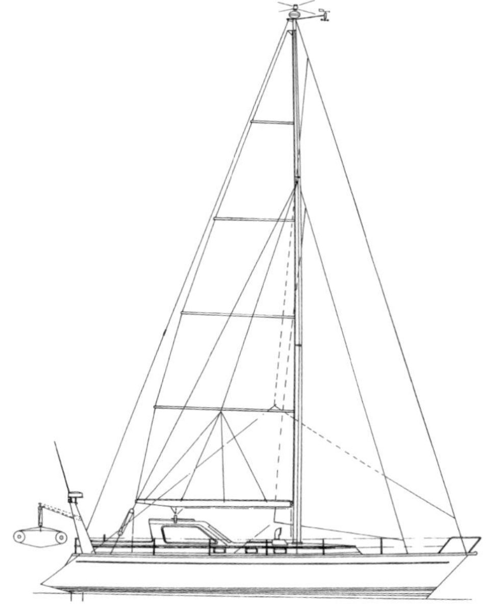

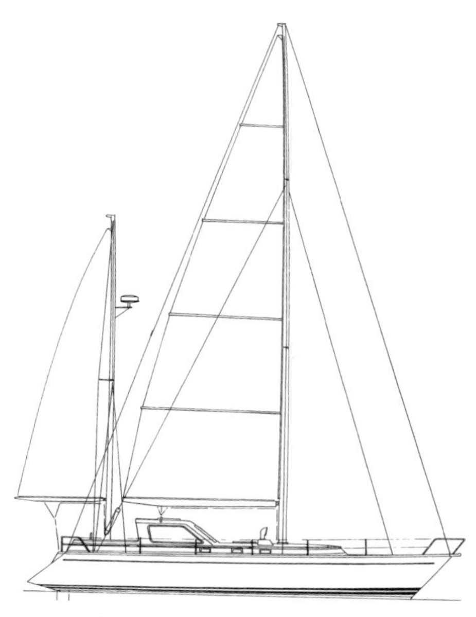

Sail plan options for the Voyager: double-headsail sloop versus ketch. On the ketch rig the mizzenmast increases the amount of standing rigging around the cockpit; this may make it difficult to get in and out of the cockpit when the boat is heeled. On the sloop rig dinghy stowage has been sacrificed for extra sail area. On this version the dinghy might be stowed against the transom or on the cabintop in front of the pilothouse. The ketch's additional rigging and other complications with the mizzen make the sloop rig with the radar arch a better choice.

Two views of an aluminum flush-decked version of the Voyager under construction in Howdy Bailey's Virginia boatyard. *(Photos courtesy of Dr. Joe Dealteris)*

a mizzen and headsail and a very small mainsail. I am partial to the concept of a ketch rig on a long-distance cruising boat. If the masts are stayed independently and one mast is lost, the other can be used to hoist a jury rig or it can be used alone to get the boat home. This is not an academic point when the boat is likely to be far from help. Another consideration is the division of the sail plan to make it easy for a short-handed crew to get the best from the boat under different wind conditions. However, if we fit a mizzenmast we will have to eliminate the radar arch and put that gear on the mizzen. Plus we will need davits for the dinghy. These are the trade-offs. In this case we'll go with the radar arch, rather than the added complexity of the mizzenmast and its extra rigging.

On this boat the rig will use wire lower shrouds and backstays, with discontinuous rod upper shrouds and a roller headfoil from Furlex, as I consider the Furlex system to be one of the best available. Running rigging will be low-stretch Technora from New England Ropes. The boat will also carry at least two spare halyards and sheets.

As with most voyagers, the sail inventory will be large and cockpit locker space will have to be found for sail storage. The mainsail will be fully battened and will use removable lazyjacks to contain it when it is lowered. (Lazyjacks

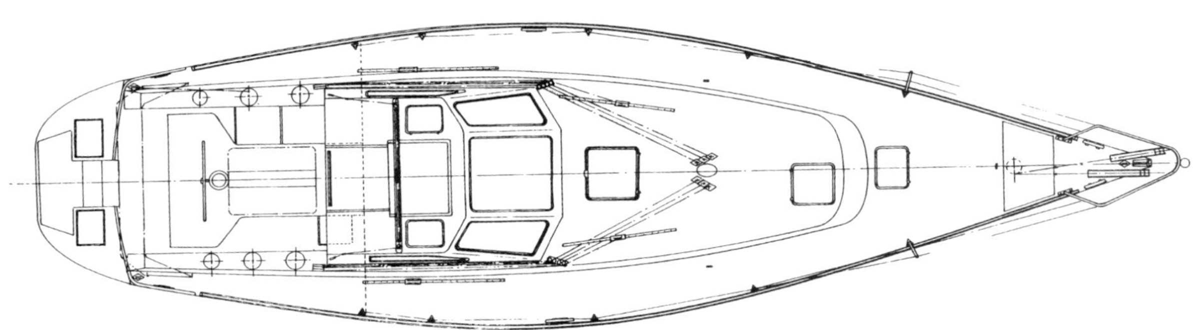

The deck layout of the Voyager. All halyards lead aft to the cockpit via line organizers and sheet-stoppers. The mainsheet is clearly visible on the pilothouse top. Notice also the dropleaf table in the cockpit, the transom steps, and propane stowage in the transom locker.

cause chafe and should be removed on long trips.) The mainsail will be furled on the boom. The headsails (topsail and staysail) will be roller furled, with a removable stay for the staysail. In a storm, a second staysail stay will be brought forward and the storm jib hanked to it. With removable stays great care must be taken to tension them tightly enough to stop them slapping the mast when not in use. We'll use a specially curved plate and a tackle for this job. If we add a mizzen, we'll use a fully battened mizzen and a mizzen staysail to improve reaching efficiency. For power reaching we'll use a multipurpose spinnaker (MPS), although the boat will also carry medium and heavy running spinnakers. Spinnakers, MPS, and mizzen staysail will all be stowed in the aft sail locker.

The mainsheet track will often be in the way as it bisects the cockpit, so we'll move it to a less efficient position on the pilothouse top and, as described earlier, spread the load on the boom.

The Single-Hander

On the Single-Hander gear is concentrated for maximum efficiency and minimum movement. The mainsail is fully battened for efficiency and easy handling. It will also have a large roach to maximize the sail power on a boat with a very large beam aft. Gear is located around the small cockpit, and lines are led aft. The vang is located on its own track rather than the more conventional single-point fitting; this will keep the boom down when the boat is sailing at large wind angles.

The rig on this boat will be an efficient four-

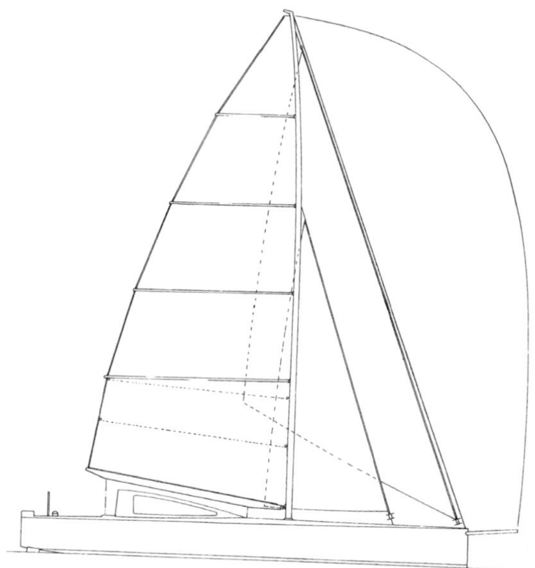

The sail plan of the Single-Hander shows a large roach on the mainsail for maximum power. With its blunt ends, the boat looks ungainly but shows a lot of sail power.

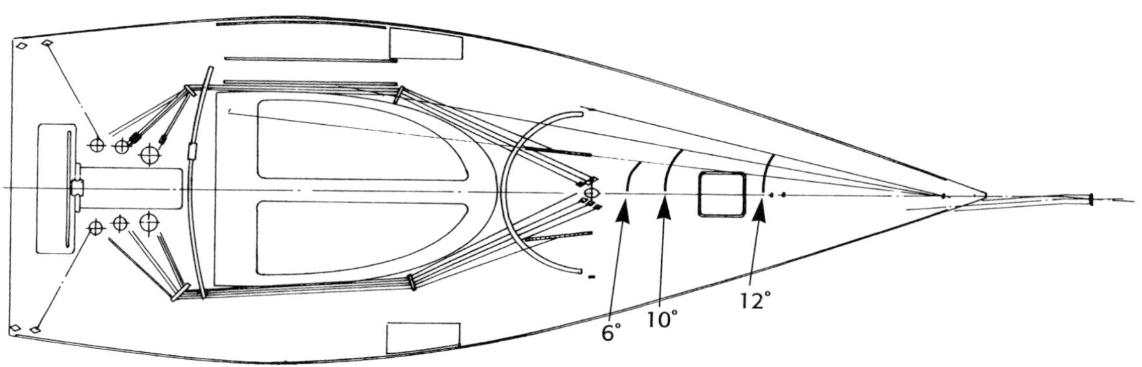

The deck plan of the Single-Hander. The angles of the various tracks have been shown (to port) on this layout. By pushing the inner track against the cabinhouse, we've attained a sheeting angle of around 10 degrees. For power reaching, tracks have been placed farther outboard. All lines are led to the cockpit via organizers and sheet-stoppers, where they can be led to any one of three winches on each side of the boat.

spreader carbon fiber mast with running backstays and a staysail stay. This will reduce weight aloft and help stability. Both the staysail stay and the headstay will be roller furled for easy sail handling. A second headstay will be set ahead of the roller-furling stay for heavy-weather sails. All rigging will be discontinuous rod rigging to minimize stretch on this highly tuned rig. We will also consider titanium fittings to reduce weight aloft at the spreader ends and the masthead. All running rigging will be Technora for minimal stretch.

The Cruiser/Racer

The sail inventory of the Cruiser/Racer includes the widest range of sails allowed by the rating rules to maximize speed. The boat is set up for a racing spinnaker, with one pole and three spinnakers: a ¾-ounce flat-cut reaching spinnaker, a ½-ounce lightweight runner, and a ¾-ounce running spinnaker. Deck gear is laid out specifically to handle these sails, as well as the headsails, within the restraints imposed by a cruising interior.

With this extensive sail inventory, a triple-spreader rig with running backstays and single lower shrouds, Technora running rigging, and hydraulic rig tensioning, this boat will go to the limit allowed by the rating rules to reduce weight aloft and maximize speed. All sails will be designed for racing, although a set of cruising sails—typically worn-out racing sails—will be kept at hand for cruising.

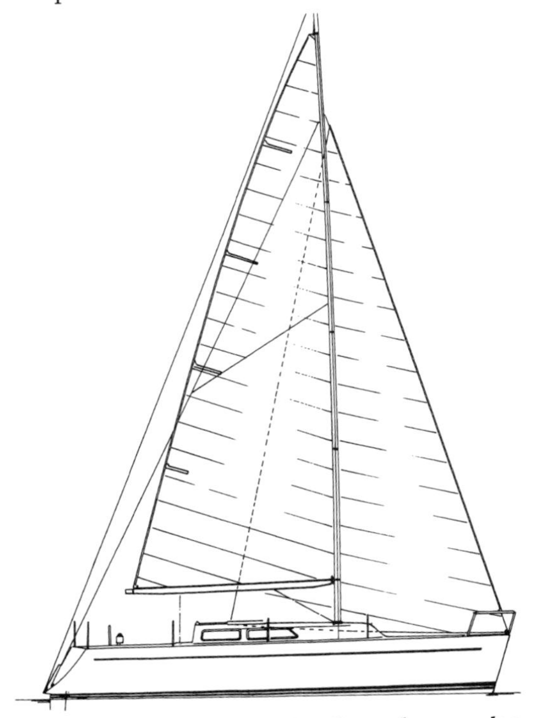

The fractional rig of the Cruiser/Racer has running backstays and checkstays to keep the rig under control at all times. The simple sail plan is efficient but not overly seaworthy, with its deck-level headsail and poor visibility to leeward.

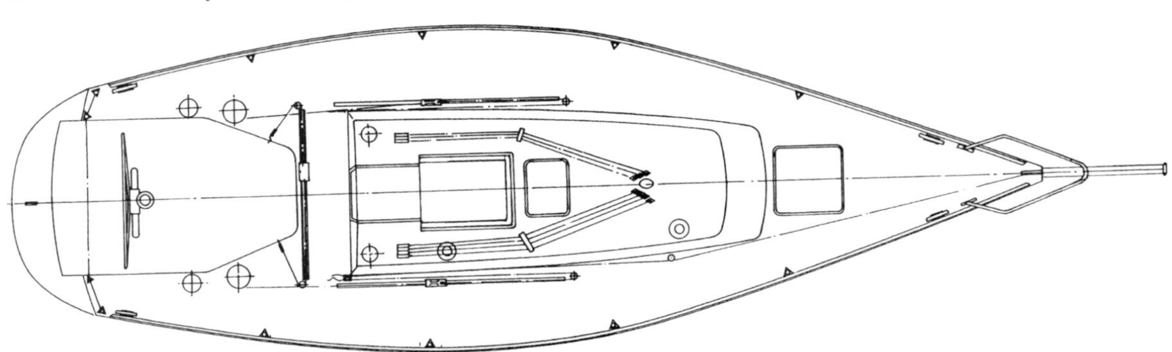

The deck plan of the Cruiser/Racer shows a very simple layout designed to allow fast, efficient maneuvers to be carried out quickly and easily. The cabintop is a concession to the cruising side of this boat, as it extends well forward to give headroom below deck to the fore cabin. Even though the halyards are led aft, a crew will be working at the mast during all sail hoists, so the halyards will emerge from the mast at around 8 feet above deck.

Seven

How Much Does It Really Cost?

When a neighbor of mine, Victor Calebreta, wanted a new boat, he decided to buy a Pearson 30. He and his wife had been out with friends on their Pearson 30, and it had everything they wanted for their style of sailing. Vic did a lot of research before he went looking at used Pearson 30s, and he learned that the boat suffered from two major problems. The first concerned the mast, which was deck-stepped on a balsa-cored deck with a support pillar below. On boats that had been raced, or when the shrouds had been cranked up tight, the deck compressed slightly and caused stress cracks to appear in the deckhead near the support pillar. The second problem was that the rudder bearing would sometimes bind to the rudderstock and the entire bearing would turn in the support tube, making the rudder assembly rattle. According to Vic, either condition, if it existed, could be found within minutes of boarding the boat. "We got it down to where we could spend five minutes on a boat and determine if it had a problem," he said. This meant that he would often drive for hours to look at a boat, discover a problem in the first few minutes, and then have to get in the car and drive hours to get back home.

He looked at a lot of boats before he found the one he wanted. "Then," he said, "emotion took over. We were so happy to have found a satisfactory boat that we wanted to take possession of it immediately. We paid to move two other boats so we could get the boat out of a Maine boatyard and down here to Rhode Island where we could work on it. At that point price didn't matter. We got the boat we wanted, and we got it here fast."

This story illustrates the role that emotion plays in buying any boat, new or used. Once you have decided which boat to buy, you'll often pay more than you should to get it home where you can show it off or start to work on it. It becomes your baby, your toy, and is deemed worthy of all your attention. Although it is hard to eliminate emotion from boat buying, emotion should not dominate your choices. You need to step back and make a hard-eyed critical analysis of the costs so that you don't end up with too much boat or one that is overpriced. Research the style of boat you want. Make sure you know the problems of a particular make, as well as its strong points. If you look for information in magazines, remember that most magazine boat reviews deal only with the high points, and are almost useless for finding out about problems. Most of all, take your time to find the boat that best suits your family and your budget. Then estimate the ongoing costs of boat ownership. If you do your homework, you don't have to wonder whether you can afford it, and you will enjoy your sailing more without having to worry about paying next month's boat bills.

Evaluating the Cost of a New Boat

Typically, the cost of a new boat can be evaluated by figuring its cost per pound, but you must make sure you are comparing boats with

The Valiant 42 under sail. Valiant Yachts can document that more of their boats have sailed around the world than those of any other builder. Many have set out straight from the building plant without any modifications. *(Photo courtesy of Valiant Yachts)*

similar features. For example, each boat in the Hunter line comes equipped with a CruisePac. This extra equipment will allow you to get sailing almost immediately. Suppose another builder does not provide the equivalent of a CruisePac, but the cost of its boat in your range is about the same. If you compare the two boats by dividing the displacement into the purchase price, you will get a misleading number, because you still have to buy the equivalent of Hunter's CruisePac for the second boat.

To make accurate comparisons among boats, then, you need to determine what comes with each boat and what gear you will need to purchase later. See the table in chapter 5 on page 112 for the base price of many cruisers. I recommend that you get an inventory from the manufacturer or yacht broker and list the gear that comes with the boat (see pages 179 and 181.) Then make a list of additional gear you will need and, using a retail catalog, such as one from Boat/US or West Marine, price out that gear.

The Valiant 42, for example, is a popular boat among sailors who want to cruise long distances or even circumnavigate. The base price (as of January 1, 1999) for the Valiant 42 is $253,650. Rich Worstell, president of Valiant, says that "to go sailing you need to install instruments, buy sails, and add fuel." Even Valiant can forget the last of these items. I took a brand-new 42 for a sail out on Lake Texoma and ran out of fuel leaving the harbor. We found out afterward that the mechanic simply forgot to put fuel in the boat!

I asked Henry Little at North Sails in Newport, Rhode Island, for a typical package of sails for the Valiant. We decided on a 135 percent roller-furling genoa, a fully battened mainsail, and a heavy staysail. These sails would be long-lasting Dacron rather than a more exotic material. The North Sails quote (see the sidebar) covers everything, even a UV cover over the mainsail. This package came to $9,588.

Electronic instruments need to be added. Here I decided that a complete package from one manufacturer was the best route to go. The list included wind instruments, a depthsounder, an autopilot, a plotter with a built-in GPS, and a handheld GPS as a backup. Handheld GPS units come in many styles and sizes from Magellan, Garmin, and others at prices ranging from $99 for the smallest Magellan to around $600 for the Magellan 6000 handheld GPS plotter. We chose a Magellan 2000 as a backup for the main unit at a cost of $299. For the rest of the instruments, I called Roger Brudenell at Cetrek USA. He suggested that we go with the

How Expensive Are the Sails? A North Sails Quote

Mainsail

NorDac Fullbatten Main (8.8-oz. PremDac, 387 sq. ft.): $2,770.
Price includes four full-length battens
Foot shelf: $136
Insignia: $97
Cunningham: N/C
Two reefs: $479
Sailcover: $285

Headsails

135% #2 NorDac genoa (up to 28 knots, 6.6-oz.
PremDac, 704 sq. ft.): $3,388
UV leech and foot: $477
Furling patch: N/C
Foam luff: $423

Dacron Staysail (for up to 35 knots): $1,533

This gives a total sail package of $9,588 for two headsails and a mainsail. You can go sailing with this package in most areas and make offshore voyages, but if you want to sail around the world, you should definitely add storm sails, and probably a multipurpose spinnaker (MPS).

Evaluating the Brochure

If you pick up a typical brochure at a boat show and go through it carefully, you'll find that many items are not included. For example, some builders do not include bottom paint or commissioning; others don't include any electronics or sails. One or two builders do not include an engine or the head unit; you must pay extra for them.

When fitting out a new boat, it often seems that you should have parked it next to a marine store or marina chandlery. You will make countless trips to the store. You can, however, cut down on the trips to the chandlery and the rude awakenings if you start by making a list of what comes with your boat, and what you think you need to purchase. Quite often you can cut a deal with a chandlery or the boatbuilder to purchase everything from them in one trip and get a volume discount rather than buying gear piecemeal at top price.

Boat Price per Pound—An Example

Weight of base boat = 20,000 lbs.
Weight of ballast = 7,800 lbs.
Hull less ballast = 12,200 lbs.

Cost of base boat = $284,000

$$\text{Dollars per pound with ballast} = \frac{\$284{,}000}{20{,}000\text{ lbs.}} = \$14.20$$

$$\text{Dollars per pound less ballast} = \frac{\$284{,}000}{12{,}200\text{ lbs.}} = \$23.28$$

Of the two values, with or without ballast, the latter, $23.28 per pound, is a more accurate indicator. If, for example, the keel were redesigned and the weight of ballast dropped to 6,000 pounds, the calculation would be:

$$20{,}000 - 6{,}000 = 14{,}000\text{ lbs.}$$

$$\frac{\$284{,}000}{14{,}000\text{ lbs.}} = \$20.29$$

The weight and cost of the remainder of the boat have not changed. Since the cost of ballast ranges from about $1.30 to $1.70 per pound in a finished keel, subtracting ballast weight gives a more accurate number.

C-Net 200 instrument package, a multiunit full-function electronics package that includes depth, speed, temperature, navigation, wind, and battery monitoring functions. It can accept three NMEA data inputs (in case you want to use it with your computer and GPS), and it will output one NMEA data string (to send info to your computer). Roger also suggested that the boat use a single multifunction system incorporating input from a masthead unit for wind direction and speed, a transducer for depth, speed, and temperature, and position data from a GPS unit. If desired, the boatowner can add extra dedicated individual displays. (For example, you might want to have the multifunction unit in the navigation area and additional displays near the steering wheel.)

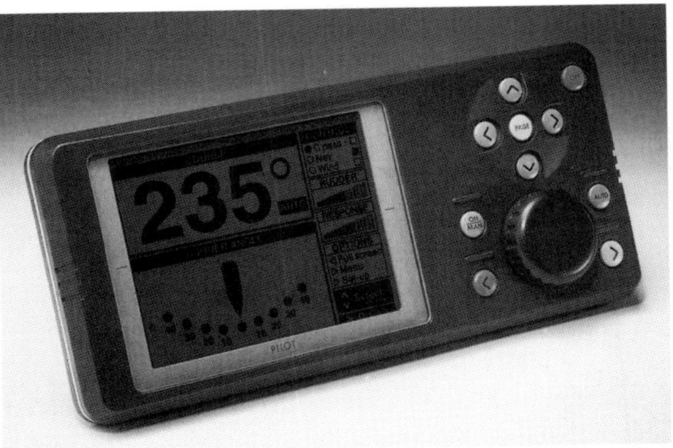

The Cetrek C-Net 780 instrument panel. *(Photo courtesy of Cetrek)*

The cost of all this equipment is $995 for the multifunction display, $795 for the masthead unit, $400 for the transducer pack, and $895 for the wind display. Add three displays at the helm (wind, tacking angles, and depth/speed/temperature), and the price goes up another $1,980. Throw in a Propilot 700 autopilot at a cost of $2,495 and about $600 for installation, and we get a total of $8,459 for electronics.

This brings the total cost of the Valiant 42—with sails and electronics—to $271,697. We should probably factor in another $3,000 to cover bedding, crockery, cutlery, provisions, and other small items. As the boat is not yet in the water, a dealer will charge about $3,000 (see commissioning prices later in this chapter) to launch and check out the boat before you actually step aboard. So the final figure comes to about $277,697.

The total cost of your boat plus additional gear divided by the displacement will give a dollars-per-pound value for the boat. If you want to be even more accurate, you can subtract the weight of ballast from the displacement, as figured in the example (see the sidebar "Boat Price per Pound—An Example," on this page).

In the case of the Valiant 42, the total price comes to $277,697 to get the boat in the water. If we divide that figure by the displacement (24,600 pounds), we get a price of $11.29 per

What Gear Do You Need?

If we take a boat, say a 1980 Bristol 35.5, and look at its inventory, we can sort out what gear is included and what extras we would have to buy. The information here, from a yacht broker, is typical of an inventory you might get with a used boat. In addition to the basic boat, with a 22-horsepower Yanmar diesel, you will get

Mainsail and working jib
Loran
Compass
Wind speed indicator (Brooks & Gatehouse)
Combination speed and distance logs
Icom VHF radio
Combination depthsounder
Two CQR anchors with 300 feet of ¾-inch anchor line
Bimini top
Dodger with cockpit awning
Seven adult life jackets (plus two child-sized)
Fenders and docklines
A Dyer Dink dinghy with oars and sails
Six harnesses
Six-man life raft
Cockpit cushions
Coast Guard–recommended safety package with flares and other items

This represents a nice package for the basic boat. Still, you will need to buy personal gear, such as kitchen utensils, dishes, flatware, and sleeping bags or blankets. If you decide that you want an inflatable and outboard instead of the Dyer dinghy, you will have to add its cost to your budget. You should also have a GPS unit onboard. They are not expensive anymore. (The Pioneer from Magellan retails for $99; at that price, if it breaks you can almost afford to buy another.)

The sails on this boat are tired. According to the broker, the sails were replaced in 1989, so you will have to purchase new sails. You might want to expand the sail inventory with a multipurpose spinnaker (MPS) plus a spinnaker pole, sheets and guys, and a 130- or 150-percent genoa.

The life raft should be serviced, at a cost of a few hundred dollars. If the flares have passed their expiration date—an unfortunately common occurrence on a used boat—you will have to buy a new set. In addition you will probably need

An additional bilge pump to be operated from the cockpit
A horseshoe life ring and holder
A windex
A fishing pole and trolling lures

Thus, for a used boat the list of extras can be fairly short. The price you pay will depend upon what is offered, how well the boat surveys, and how much the seller is willing to negotiate.

pound. By subtracting the ballast weight from the boat (because ballast costs about $1 per pound for any boat and its weight can easily be changed, subtracting it from the overall weight gives a more accurate figure for the cost of construction), we get a dollars-per-pound value of $277,697/(24,600 – 9,500), or $18.39 per pound. When you compare that number with other boats listed in chapter 5's new-boat data chart, on page 112, you will see that the Valiant is a good value, in spite of being slightly heavier than other boats.

Having done your analyses, compare the numbers. If one boat is, say, $15 per pound and another is $25 per pound, you need to find out whether the more expensive boat is really worth it. The more expensive boat may have additional features, such as carbon fiber in the hull, to justify the extra cost. If the only discernible difference is in price, you should inquire into less obvious features, such as the hull construction, joinerwork, core materials, or the mast and rig materials. A more expensive boat should have better gear and better joinerwork.

Evaluating the Cost of a Used Boat

You will usually get more for your dollar if you buy a used boat, because it will often include gear installed by the previous owner; gear that is not suitable for the seller's next boat is often left

Commissioning as Listed in the Brochure

Usually this means that the yard will paint the bottom, install the rig, launch the boat, check that the engine runs and that the engine instruments work, find the fenders, and tie the boat alongside. If you need instruction you might have a yard person help you, but you might be better off hiring a competent instructor to take you out sailing for several days.

What you need to sail the boat

Life jackets (enough for every person on board, including children)
Life rings, horseshoes, or throwable flotation cushions
A whistle, foghorn, or similar signaling device (and a bell in boats of 12 meters [39.4 feet] or more)
Flares (day and night use)
Fire extinguisher of correct grade
Correct navigation lights (if sailing after dark is a possibility)
Charts of the area in which you sail (electronic charts are not acceptable)

Additional safety gear

Bilge pump
First-aid kit
VHF radio capable of receiving weather forecasts
GPS unit (not essential but prudent)
Leadline
Offshore harnesses for every person onboard
Searchlight
Spare navigation lights and batteries
Bungs ready to hammer into a failed through-hull
A life raft large enough to hold everyone onboard if you go offshore
A mirror or other signaling device

In the engine compartment

Spare lube oil
Filters
Spare belts
Adequate fuel in the fuel tank
Spare impeller (if engine-mounted bilge pump is installed)
Pump spares kits

Ship systems

Plumbing
Freshwater filters (if the freshwater tanks are new, you might need to scrub them and install filters)

Electrical

Spare fuses or breakers
Spare bulbs including red ones

In the navigation area

Charts
Dividers
Triangles or parallel rules
Pencils
VHF radio
GPS or sextant
Flags
Flashlights
Batteries/spare bulbs
Foghorn

Optional extras that will need to be wired in (probably a yard job)

Radar
Wind instruments
Autopilot

aboard. If you work with a broker, you will get an inventory of everything that comes with the boat. Some inventories are extensive, including everything except the owner's personal belongings; others are minimal, and you will have to buy gear. Either way, you should make an additional list of the gear you need to purchase.

How do you know if the boat you are about to buy is priced competitively? The simple answer is that you don't, unless you do a fair amount of research. To get a feel for how fairly boats are priced, I went through the pages of

Loran
Radio (VHF and possibly SSB)
Water temperature indicator (for crossing the Gulf Stream, for example)
Red light bulbs for nighttime use

Bunks and bedding
Sleeping bags or sheets and blankets
Sleeping bag liners
Leecloths and strongpoints to tie the leecloths to
Pillows and pillow cases

In the galley
Cutlery—knives, forks, spoons, galley knives, bottle and can openers
Crockery—plates, bowls, mugs, serving plates
Pots and pans, kettle, vacuum flasks, bowls, trays
Possibly an additional filled propane tank
Disposables—soap, sponges, scrubbers
Trash-can liners
Cook's harness or safety strap
Cutting board

You will also need food and drinks as well as napkins, condiments, herbs and seasonings, aluminum foil, plastic wrap, and all the other small items that fill kitchen shelves at home. It is hard to go to the supermarket when you are 50 miles at sea.

If you go offshore, you should have onboard emergency foods (freeze-dried foods or canned goods) and emergency water supplies (a gallon jug of fresh water for each crewmember).

In the head
Towels
Soap
Toilet roll
Mug
Spare toothbrushes
First-aid kit
Sunscreen
Toilet brush and plunger
Spare-parts kit with hoses and lube oil

On deck
Docklines
Sheets/guys/spare halyards
Fenders
Tape (for taping over cotter pins)
Spare shackles
Shackle key and sharp knife
Sail ties
Varnish or teak oil for all brightwork (typically the builder or yard put only two or three coats of varnish on wood; you need at least eight to ten coats for good winter protection)
Nonskid tape for covering hatches or slippery areas
Extra winch handles (if you go sailing with one handle, you can be sure that someone will drop it over the side)
Winch handle pockets
Light line for foredeck lifelines (and to make a net to keep sails onboard, to tie the sail feeders to the tack fitting, and to put a Turk's Head knot in the center of the steering wheel)
Sails (see page 155 for sample inventories)

Soundings Boats for Sale and checked a number of other magazines before going to Scott Heckard at Annapolis Sailyard—one of the most helpful yacht brokers I have ever had the pleasure of meeting. He helped me get information on a number of boats, and then I graphed the results. The accompanying graph includes every Catalina 30 I was able to find. The dealer quoted me $72,500 as the price of a new (1998) Catalina 30. As you can see, the projected average price line on my chart came remarkably close to the actual new-boat price. This gave me confidence that the average price line was close to right on. If a boat were priced above the line, it should have extra gear or be superbly maintained. The price for a Catalina 30 in rough shape should fall below the line. There may be local variations in price; for example, boats on the West Coast may have a higher asking price than those on the East Coast.

Getting the Best Value

Suppose you bought a 1984 Catalina 30 in poor condition for $26,000. If, over the next four years, you put your own time and a few dollars into bringing the boat up to a high standard, you would increase the boat's market value to or near the well-maintained or well-equipped line. On the graph of Catalina 30 values, try moving to the left from a starting value of $26,000 for a 1984 model until your line strikes the

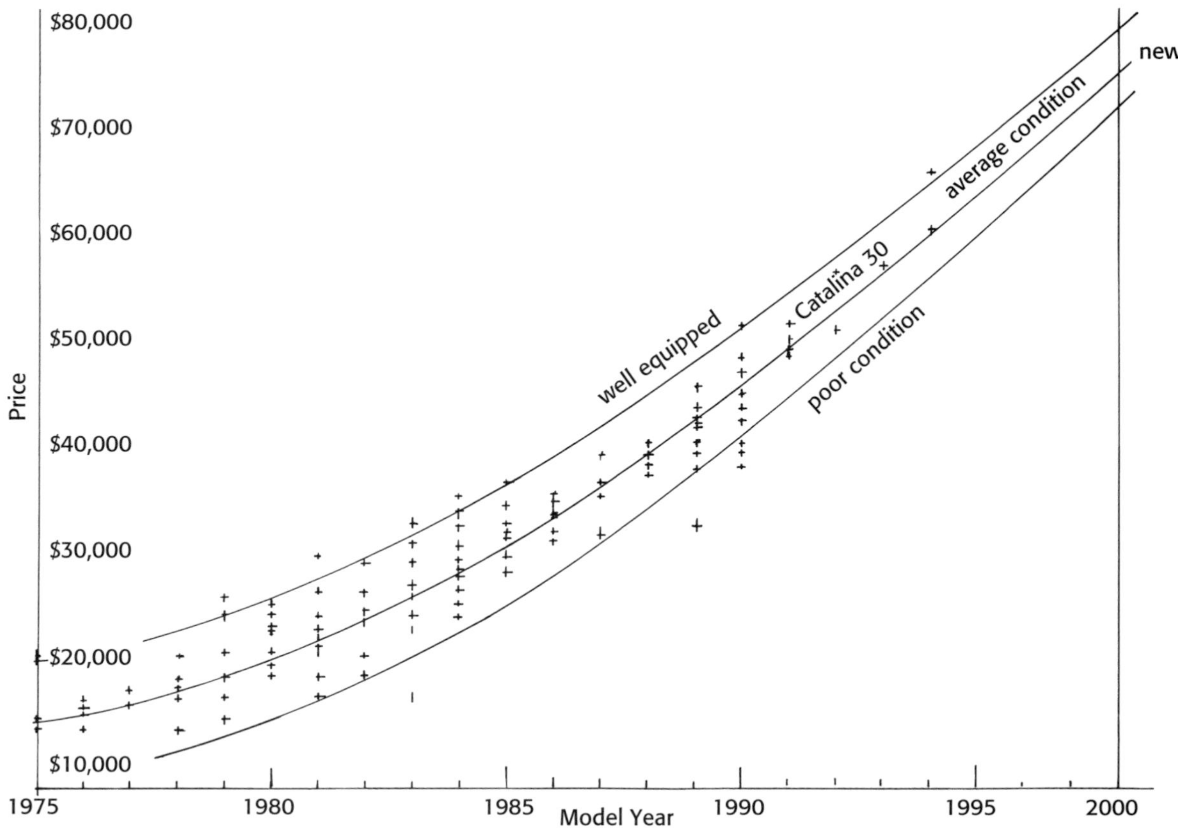

A graph of the price of Catalina 30 sailboats against the year manufactured. The middle line represents average prices. On the lower line one expects to find boats with minimal inventory or boats that are not in very good condition. Boats with prices on the highest line should be in top-notch condition and/or very well equipped.

curve of top value, which happens at model year 1980. It may be stretching the data a bit, but we may reasonably conclude that your upgraded Catalina 30 will sell four years later for about what you paid for it. In other words, by buying cheap and improving the boat over the time you own it, you are able to recoup the money you spent after four years. If you sell the boat sooner, you could actually make a profit: provided you have upgraded the boat sufficiently, you should be able to ask about $27,800 for the boat in three years. Of course, there are no guarantees that Catalina 30s will depreciate at the same rate in the future.

While it seems that sailing is free, in fact you have spent both time and money over your period of ownership. Plus you have not taken inflation into account. But by working over the numbers carefully, you can go sailing for little more than the cost of operation and maintenance.

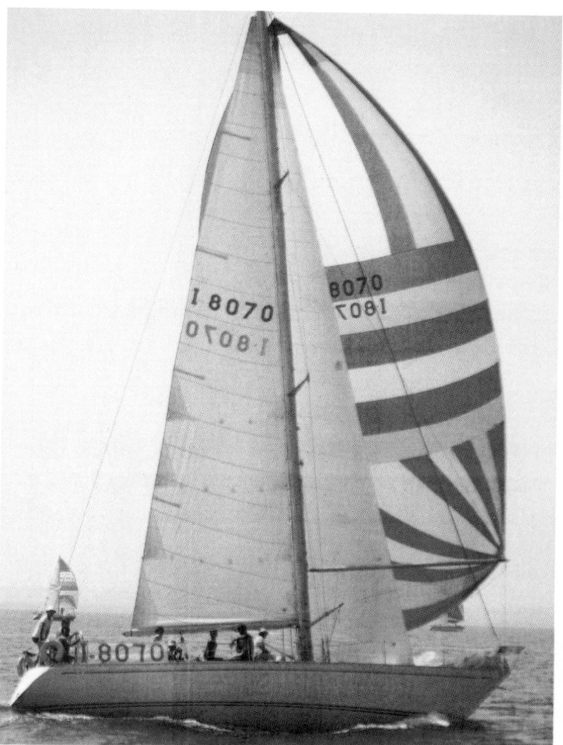

This older model Swan 48 is an ideal used boat for long-distance cruising.

The Survey

If your boat is new and comes from a well-established line, it probably doesn't need to be surveyed, although many banks make it a condition of financing. However, if the boat is used or is one of the first five or six off the production line, it should be surveyed by a competent surveyor. I recommend that my clients use a surveyor who has been accredited by NAMS (National Association of Marine Surveyors) or certified by SAMS (Society of Accredited Marine Surveyors). A NAMS surveyor has to take an eight-hour test to become qualified. There probably is a NAMS surveyor in your area; you can get a list in *Marshall's Marine*

Boat Buyers' Websites

The number of websites changes daily, so you should use links or search engines to find new sites. Here is a sampling of websites for new and used boats (all addresses are preceded by http://).

www.clipperbay.com
www.info@crusaderyachts.com
www.theyachtgroup.com
www.hellieryachts.com
www.thehinckleyco.com
www.by-the-sea.com/cannellpayne&page
www.by-the-sea.com/edey&duff
www.sail@rcryachts.com
www.bbyacht.com
www.sailingspecialities.com
www.easternyacht.com
www.yachtworld.com/hillowden
www.ecys.com
www.northrup&johnson.com
www.boatshow.com
www.allaboutboats.com

Other useful resources are magazines such as *Soundings*, *SAILING*, *SAIL*, *Cruising World*, and *Northeast Sailing Life*, which provide access to boat sellers worldwide.

Source Book, one of my earlier books.

You can expect that a survey will cost around 2 to 8 percent of the cost of the boat, depending on the distance the surveyor has to travel and how long it takes to do the job. NAMS surveyor Bob Wallstrom, of Delta Marine in Blue Hill, Maine, points out that a survey can lower the price paid for a boat by revealing overlooked defects that you can bring to the negotiating table. Ultimately, you may save more than the cost of the survey.

Ongoing Costs

Now that you have bought a boat, you are about to find out about the many costs of boat own-

Ongoing Costs for Decommissioning and Recommissioning

(By permission of the Jamestown Boatyard)

Storage

Prices for labor only unless specified

( ) Haul, store outside, and launch (mast out) ____ LOA x $25/ft. =
( ) Haul, store outside, and launch (mast in) ____ LOA x $30/ft. =
( ) Haul, store inside, and launch length x beam x $7.25 =
( ) Power-wash bottom when hauling ____ LOA x $2.50 =
( ) Boat stand rental (number of stands by yard) ____ stands x $21.50 =
( ) Frame and cover (custom-fit canvas with metal frame)
    Cover with mast out _____ LOA x $75 =
    Cover with mast in _____ LOA x $85 =
( ) Tarp rental @ $0.15 per square foot =
( ) Shrink wrap (call for pricing)
( ) Install/remove/store frame and cover _____ LOA x $12 =
( ) Storage lockers
    ( ) Half container (8′ x 10′) $70/month x 6 months minimum =
    ( ) Full container (8′ x 20′) $130/month x 6 months minimum =
( ) Winterize outboard (remove, winterize, gear lube oil changed, stored for winter and commissioned in the spring; repairs and materials extra) = $150

Rigging

Includes unstepping and storing mast(s), stepping in the spring. Test and disconnect electrics. Disconnect roller-furling unit and store on inside rack. Remove spreaders and masthead antennas.

In the spring, the lights are tested, the rig is visually inspected. The rig is installed, taped, and tuned. Booms are installed, and running rigging is re-led.

Any repairs or modifications are extra.

( ) Outside-stored mast(s) (includes unstepping, storage, and stepping)
    ( ) Boats 29 ft. LOA and under ____ Mast length x $13.00/ft. =
    ( ) Boats 30 to 45 ft. LOA ____ Mast length x $18.50/ft. =
    ( ) Boats 46+ ft. LOA ____ Mast length x $20.50/ft. =

Plus:

    ( ) Furling unit storage $100

ership—the cost of insurance, launching every spring, hauling every fall, bottom painting, and ongoing maintenance. Insurance costs, which can be estimated by calling your local agent, vary depending on the area of the country in which you sail; for example, premiums will be lower if you sail a 40-footer on a small lake than if you take that same boat on a transoceanic voyage. Premiums will also vary depending on the type of insurance and the equipment you want to cover.

Maintenance costs can be predicted by calling your local boatyard and asking what they charge for a given boat size for launching, bottom painting and commissioning in the spring, hauling, removing the mast, washing the bot-

- or -

( ) Inside-stored mast(s) (includes unstepping mast and furling unit, storage and stepping)

    ( ) Boats 29 ft. LOA and under ____ Mast length x $18.00/ft. =
    ( ) Boats 30 to 45 ft. LOA ____ Mast length x $23.50/ft. =
    ( ) Boats 46+ ft. LOA ____ Mast length x $25.50/ft. =

( ) Remove and bend on sails

    ( ) Boats under 40 ft. LOA $48.00 per sail =
    ( ) Boats 40 to 50 ft. LOA $72.00 per sail =
    ( ) Boats 50+ ft. LOA $96.00 per sail =

Subcontracted work

( ) Clean, inspect, and store sails (invoiced by yard in the spring)
( ) Service life raft

Work Authorization for Standard Winter and Spring Expenses

Prices are for labor only unless otherwise specified

( ) Spray-paint bottom: Labor only; one coat, includes sanding = _____ feet LOA x $20.00/ft. This requires about 50% to 75% more paint than rolling. We suggest this for boats with multi-year paints.
( ) Additional fairing and sanding for racing =

- or -

( ) Roll-paint bottom: Labor only; one coat, includes sanding = _____ feet LOA x $14.00/ft.

- or -

( ) Sand bottom only: _____ feet LOA x $8.00 =
(Note: Environmental and health concerns dictate the use of vacuum equipment for sanding all bottom paint.)

- or -

( ) Our equipment for rental for those who wish to do their own painting.
$100/day (minimum 1 day)

Note: The above prices do not include painting the centerboard, which will be done at time-and-materials rate.

tom, and storage over the winter. They should be able to give you a good idea of these expenses. For instance, I called my local boatyard, The Jamestown Boatyard, and got their price breakdown for the above work, as detailed in the accompanying sidebar, "Ongoing Costs for Decommissioning and Recommissioning," page 186. Their contract is typical.

As you can see, the cost of decommissioning and commissioning a boat each winter can be significant. Using a Valiant 42 as an example, we figured that the boat would be hauled and stored with its mast out. Masts that remain stepped during the winter can impose significant stress on the hull, as the rig vibrates in winter storms (not to mention the wear and tear on the mast itself). Removing the mast and storing it under cover is better for the boat and for the rig. The boat will be power-washed on hauling, covered with a frame, and the mast stored inside.

According to the schedule, the cost of hauling would be 42 feet × $25 = $1,050. Unstepping and storing the mast for the winter would be 59 feet × $23.50 = $1,386.50. We would remove our own sails and install our own frame and cover, removing them in the spring. Bottom painting would cost 42 feet × $14 = $588 for labor and $320 for paint. This figure might vary depending on the type and amount of paint used. We would first want to apply a barrier coat, such as Interlux's Interprotect, for protection against blistering, even though Valiant used vinyl ester resin during construction (a barrier coat should last indefinitely). On top of this we would use Interlux Micron CRS antifouling paint to give us multi-season use. The total amounts to $3,344 before any maintenance work is done. Extras can boost the total very quickly. For example, if the yard installs your frame and cover, the cost can be an additional $3,150. You should carefully figure out what you intend to do and what the yard will do, and keep track of the total. Otherwise, asking the yard to perform extra work can get a winter bill up to $10,000 in a hurry.

Once you have fitted out a new boat for the first year of sailing, your expenses are going to be fuel (for both the boat and the crew) and maintenance, as well as insurance and other costs. As you can see from the Valiant 42 example, the first year you should probably allow about 2 to 5 percent for maintenance. There will be things that you have to do, such as bottom painting and building up the layers of varnish, but there should not be a lot of engine or equipment repairs, and those that do appear should be covered by the builder's warranty. As soon as the warranty expires on any boat, you can be sure that gear will start to fail, and that is when your expenses start to rise. After about three years you can expect to be paying per year about 5 percent of the cost of the boat in maintenance costs. A used boat will have higher ongoing expenses (5 to 10 percent) right from the start, although those expenses can be kept down if the surveyor has done a good job and you get them taken care of before the ownership documents are signed.

In addition to maintenance there is the cost of mooring, both in your home port and in marinas you visit (called transient fees). Transient fees can easily add up to a sizable amount over the course of a busy season. If you visit foreign ports, there may be entry and departure fees as well as fees for visas and other unexpected items (graft, or baksheesh in some ports!). All these hidden costs should be factored in if you are to get at the true cost of operating your boat. Now add another 10 percent; that will give you a cushion for items that you have forgotten and will put you reasonably near the total cost of the boat.

Finally, if you want to be a real masochist, you can divide the total costs by the number of hours you spend on your boat to get the dollars spent per hour. This final value should probably be hidden from your spouse.

Eight

Ease of Maintenance

Good design leads to good maintenance. That's what an old-time builder told me when I was first starting to design boats. In those days, fiberglass boats were built heavily with a single laminate of fiberglass. Many boats were still built of wood. The primary maintenance consideration was to get adequate ventilation throughout the boat. Ventilation is still important, but today there are many other factors that go into designing a low-maintenance boat. These factors can affect the upkeep of a boat over the long term, as well as the boat's resale value.

As we have seen, the ongoing cost of maintenance is a large factor in the yearly operating cost of the boat. But how do you tell what might become a maintenance nightmare down the road and what will be easy to maintain? Often it is difficult to tell exactly, but you can certainly get some indication of future problems with a careful inspection of the boat prior to purchase.

The subject of boat maintenance could fill several books. Here we will limit our focus to the ways in which design influences maintenance. I'll also cover the things you might check when buying a boat, and discuss how to set up an ongoing maintenance manual (using manufacturer's manuals) and schedule specifically for your boat. If you cannot get maintenance manuals from the manufacturer of the gear on your boat, I would recommend that you get Nigel Calder's *Boatowner's Mechanical and Electrical Manual*, available from International Marine. This is one of the best books on maintaining your mechanical systems that I have seen in a long time.

Eliminating Maintenance during Building

The place to start your inspection is in the boatshop when the boat is being constructed. Look first at the way the boat is being put together. As we have seen in chapter 3, production boats typically have a molded deck backed with a molded headliner. Once the headliner is in place, the inside of the molded deck is completely hidden. On the production line, wiring, winches, and other deck fittings are often bolted in place *before* the liner and the deck mold are mated. This is not good practice, because it may hide wiring and the backing plates for deck fittings. If deck gear is installed *after* the deck mold and liner are mated, the underside of the equipment is usually accessible.

Wiring can be a problem, however. Builders don't want wiring showing, so it is usually hidden inside the liner. You should check if wiring is being run in conduits (see page 200) or if it is simply clipped to the underside of the deck and covered with the headliner; if this is the case, you will have to remove the headliner to get at the wiring. This may be difficult if the headliner is a one-piece molding. If you have to drill through the deck to mount a new piece of gear, you may inadvertently go through wiring behind a one-piece headliner. If wiring is in a conduit, you can at least pull the wire out and replace it with a new one.

You should have additional wires run at the building stage if you intend to fit extra lights, a stereo, a TV, or other electronic systems later. A few minutes of work now might save you hours later. The same forethought should be put into the navigation area. Have additional wires run for wind instruments, radar, or other gear you might want to fit later.

When checking the deckhead, make sure you can reach the backing plates for all the deck gear. Deck gear breaks, warps, and needs replacement. You should be able to do this yourself, or have a yard do it, without ripping the boat apart to undo a few nuts and bolts.

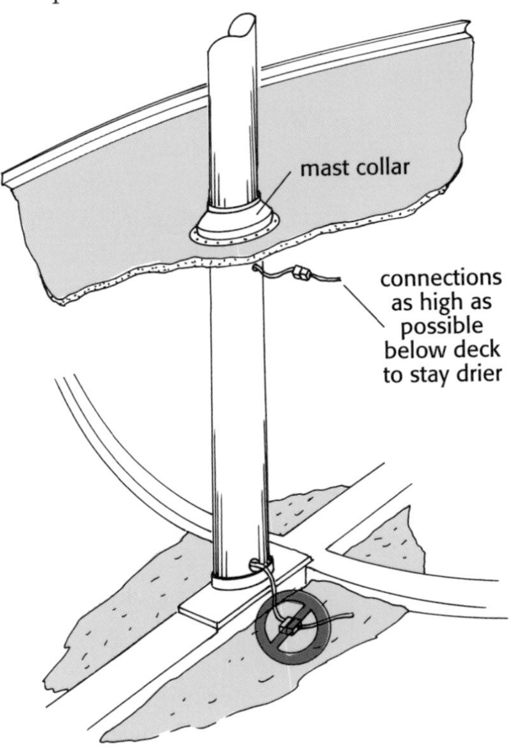

Mast wiring should never go through the bilge, where it can be soaked with bilgewater. It should always exit the mast as high as possible.

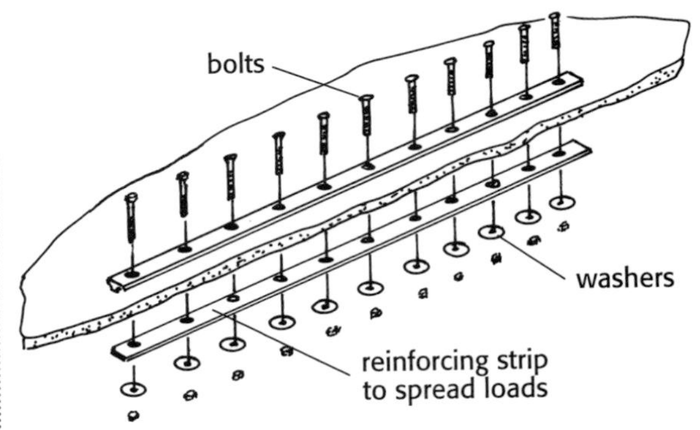

All deck tracks should have backing plates and large washers to help spread the upward loads of sheets and guys.

Check that the mast wiring and electronics emerge from the mast just under the deck, not at the bottom of the mast in the bilge. For obvious reasons, mast wiring that runs through the bilge often has problems with dampness in the connections.

When checking deck gear, make sure it is through-bolted if it is to take any strain. If the strain is likely to be upward, as in tracks or padeyes, there should be backing plates under the deck.

What to Check When Looking over a Boat

When going to look at a boat, do what Bob Wallstrom, a NAMS-certified marine surveyor based in Blue Hill, Maine, recommends: Take along a tape measure, a flashlight, and a magnet. The tape measure is to make sure furniture is properly sized, that you can get into spaces to work on gear (hatches, for example, should be 18 inches square to allow you to climb through them), and to measure dimensions should you decide that you want to change something. The flashlight enables you to see into the dark corners of lockers, or into the engine sump where normal lighting cannot reach. The magnet is to check whether metal is ferrous or nonferrous. Magnetic materials on a boat can play hell with the compass, and some types of so-called stainless steel are often found to be magnetic (true stainless steel is nonmagnetic).

Whether you are about to buy the boat or already own it, first check the steering gear and other mechanical items. Then go through the interior, look under the hull, and finally look over the deck and the rig. A good mini-survey might take a few hours, but it is time well spent if you are trying to decide whether to proceed with a professional survey in advance of buying the boat, or if you want to assess your present boat. Make notes and ask a professional surveyor or boatyard expert about anything you don't understand. Later you can use your notes to work up a maintenance schedule for the boat. This will allow you to spread out chores rather than trying to get them all done before you go on a cruise. Remember that maintenance can always be done during the winter to avoid the spring rush.

Steering Gear

According to the USYRU/SNAME report that followed the Fastnet disaster, one of the most important features on a sailboat is the steering gear. They found that steering failures led to some boats getting beam-on to the sea and being rolled. For this reason, you should make sure that the boat you buy has a strongly made steering system. Systems such as those from Edson International or other reputable manufacturers are designed to be strong and secure, but sometimes the installation leaves something to be desired. On one boat I sailed, the steering system worked properly except that the turning blocks below deck were screwed to a ½-inch plywood bulkhead and eventually tore loose. All steering blocks should be solidly through-bolted to glassed-in blocks or heavy bulkheads.

When looking at a boat, make sure you go aft and check access to all the parts of the steering system. Now, having found everything within reach, imagine the boat heeled 25 degrees and bouncing around. Can you still reach everything? Then climb on deck to check the emergency steering system. If you do buy the boat, you should take a few minutes to mount the emergency tiller and try steering the boat with it *before* you get into weather where you might require emergency steering. You may find that the emergency tiller slips off the rudderstock, or that you can barely move the tiller because the wheel or binnacle is in the way. If you have to use relieving tackles because the steering gear cannot be moved with the tiller, you should make some up in advance and store them with the emergency tiller. All the maintenance work in the world may be in vain if you cannot fit emergency steering gear.

Check that all turning blocks have guards on them. When a steering cable stretches as the helm is turned, the other side may come loose and drop off the sheave. A guard will keep the cable on the sheave. Check the movement of the tiller or wheel from on deck. Any grating or grinding shows that there may be problems. Steering cables, blocks, and chains should look slightly oily, not rusty.

Check the number of turns on the wheel. Ideally, there should be a maximum of three to four turns from lock to lock. More than four turns, and the helmsman has to work. If this is the case, you should probably change the gear sprocket inside the steering pedestal (check with the manufacturer to see if that is possible), or fit a larger quadrant.

Look carefully at the quadrant. It should be keyed to the rudderstock, not just clamped. Clamped fittings can come loose over time and eventually slip.

If the boat has tiller steering, check the gudgeons and pintles for wear. A sloppy fit may mean that you should replace them. On smaller boats, check that there is some method of stopping the gudgeons from lifting off the pintles. Check also the fit of the tiller into the rudder; it should not slop around.

Engine Compartment

Take a careful look at the engine box. The engine box or panels surrounding the engine box should be easy to remove. If you have to dismantle half the boat to get the engine box off the engine, not a lot of engine maintenance will get done. Access panels should be provided to allow the dipstick, belts, water-intake line, and fuel filters to be checked frequently. The engine, batteries, pumps, and other gear should look clean and well maintained.

The very first thing to do when you lift the engine compartment cover is to look inside the cover. Black oily deposits show where the engine may be leaking oil. Black grime may show if the exhaust line has cracked and is venting fumes and carbon into the engine box. Next look over the engine. Do you see signs of oil trickling from joints anywhere on the engine? If you do, you could be looking at major problems, the least of which is a blown gasket. If you see major areas of rust and corrosion around the engine (most marine engines eventually shown some rust), have a mechanic look at it. Corrosion of electrical wiring could lead to electrical problems.

Next look at the shaft. Is it electrically bonded to the engine? In most cases it should be. Are there signs of wear on the shaft bearings or joints? Misalignment is very common on prop shafts. Go outside the boat and check the strut and Cutless bearing for wear—any misalignment will show up here. Check to see if the prop shaft can be withdrawn without hitting the rudder. Usually, if there is any chance that it will, it is set a few degrees to one side of the rudder.

Check for corrosion on the generator, any pumps, plumbing and wiring connected to pumps, and intake and outlet lines. Signs of

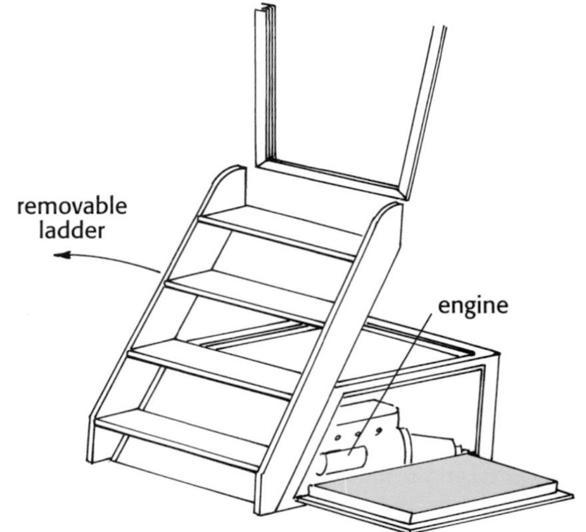

Good engine access is critical to good maintenance. Typically the companionway ladder can be removed along with engine panels to provide easy access all around the engine.

heavy corrosion should be checked by a competent surveyor. Look at the fuel line filters to see if there is air, dirt, or water trapped in them. If any of these is present, you could have dirty fuel tanks and possibly engine problems later on.

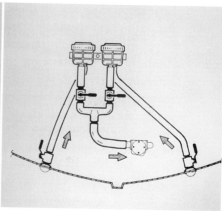

A seawater intake strainer should be fitted on all boats. This strainer from Vetus den Ouden is fitted between the through-hulls and the saltwater pump. (Photo courtesy of Vetus den Ouden)

Checking the oil

Pull the dipstick and take a look at the engine oil. A fairly clean oil tells you that some care has been taken with the engine. A thick, black, tar-like oil suggests that there may be engine problems developing. Ask when the oil and filters were last changed. If it was longer ago than the beginning of the previous season, run, don't walk, away from the boat.

Strainers

When you own your own boat, one of the first steps you should take toward improving your engine maintenance is to install a strainer in the seawater intake if one is not already fitted. A seawater strainer will prevent debris from getting into the saltwater cooling system of your engine.

The next step is to install fuel filters. The first filter should be in your fuel tank fill line to strain out large particles as they come from the filler hose. The next filter, between the tank and the engine, strains out particles down to 20 microns; Racor or CAV/Lucas filters are typically fitted here. Make sure that you have a supply of the proper filter elements onboard in case you get a batch of dirty fuel and have to change the filter. The final filter is usually fitted by the engine manufacturer and strains out particles down to 10 microns. All these filters should be changed at least once per season, more if the engine is used extensively.

Make sure that your fuel system has good filters and that you carry spare elements to suit the filters. (Photo courtesy of Racor, Division of Parker Hannifin Corp.)

Grounding

Another point to check is that the engine, rudder shaft, mast, and prop shaft are all grounded properly. A 1/8-by-1-inch copper strap or 18-gauge wire should be used to bond any large metal item to the keel to help prevent electrolysis. If one is not fitted on your boat, check with the builder or local boatyard to see if one should be. Some manufacturers use other systems.

Exhaust system

If you have the opportunity, check the exhaust system while the boat is under construction. It should be firmly mounted with flexible brackets. The engine vibrates when it is running, and the exhaust system will vibrate along with it. If the exhaust is tightly fastened to frames or bulkheads, it will eventually crack and leak, letting CO_2 fumes get into the boat. On a used boat, gain access to the entire exhaust line and check it for leaks (you may see black or gray marks on the hull adjacent to the leak). Check, too, that the exhaust brackets are heat-resistant and that any furniture or fittings near the exhaust line are protected against heat. Exhaust lines get hot and can set fire to anything flammable they come into contact with.

Make sure that a through-hull is fitted at the outboard end, especially if the through-hull is located forward of the transom. If you get into bad weather you might want to close the through-hull to prevent water from draining back into the engine.

Metering your engine

You should sound-test the area below deck with a decibel meter. I have recorded levels of up to 95 decibels in some sailboat cabins, which can cause ear problems. High levels of noise when the engine is running make it uncomfortable below deck and eventually can cause ear damage.

Another meter you should have on your boat is an hour meter on the engine. You will then be able to tell when the engine requires servicing. If you do not have an hour meter, make sure that the oil, filters, and freshwater cooling system are changed at the *end* of every season. Changing them at the end of the season gets rid of acids that may be in the oil. Engine belts should also be checked at this time and changed as necessary.

Wood in the engine compartment

You should check that all wood used in the construction of the boat is encapsulated with fiberglass. For example, if the engine beds are made of wood, the wood should be totally encapsulated. The styrene in the fiberglass will prevent rot from starting as long as there are no holes in the fiberglass coating. Wood that is not totally encapsulated will absorb moisture and may eventually warp or bend.

Interior

Maintenance of the interior starts with good design, such as eliminating corners in which dirt

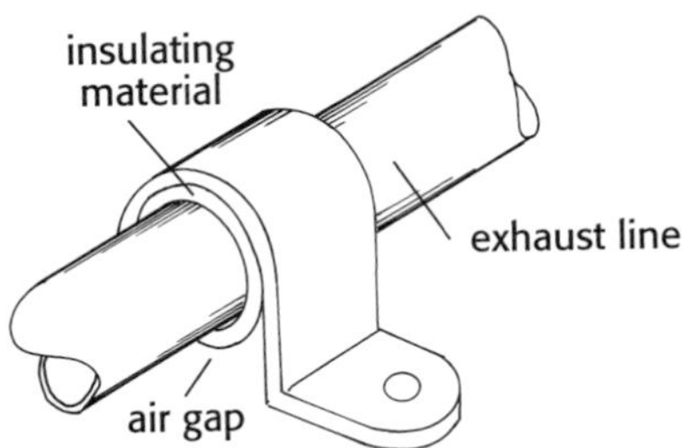

Hot-exhaust lines should be insulated from the hull to prevent burning the hull laminate.

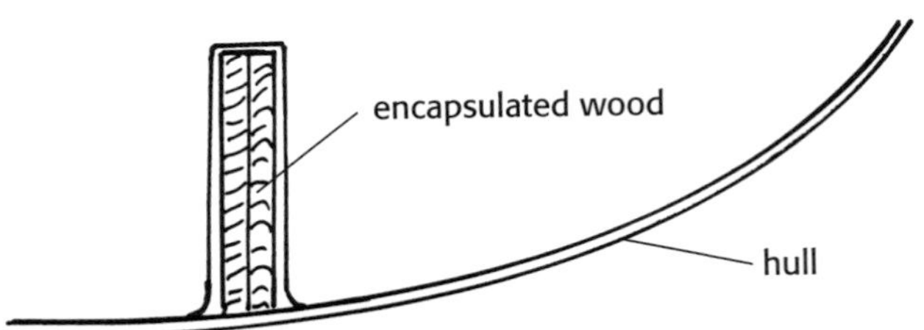

All wood that is built into the hull laminate—for example, engine beds—should be fully encapsulated.

and grime can accumulate. It continues with regular work on the part of the owner and crew. Even when sailing, routine maintenance chores can be done to keep the boat looking pristine and to keep all the systems working well.

Galley

Maintenance in the galley is an ongoing chore that requires a thorough initial inspection and then constant vigilance. You need to start with the galley stove. Make sure that the gas line or fuel system can be turned off at the stove. Check, too, that the gas line cannot get damaged as the stove swings. Look at the stove gimbals: there should be a lock and a damping mechanism in good working order. Stove fiddle rails should be high—at least to half the height of any pans on the stovetop. Check that you can reach all parts of the stove enclosure. If a pot boils over, you want to be able to clean up the mess.

Next look at the galley lighting. All work surfaces should be illuminated properly. Surfaces that are not may require additional lighting. If your plans include night sailing, you might also install red lights here.

Look in the icebox to ensure that it does not smell. If it does, you will have to clean it with a powerful cleaner and keep it well ventilated when not in use. Check the icebox insulation, if you can. The thicker it is, the longer your food will stay cool. Check that the icebox drain works properly and drains into a sump tank, not into the bilge. A drain into the bilge will eventually make the bilge smell.

Look in each locker, especially the lowest ones. Bilgewater may be able to slop up into the lockers, wetting your pots and pans. Check those lockers that you keep food in. The inside of a locked boat on a hot summer day can reach 140 degrees, and food can be ruined. Make sure, as part of your ongoing maintenance schedule, that you remove old food and drinks that might get spoiled by high temperatures.

Lockers

As in the galley, you need to be vigilant about what gear is stored in lockers throughout the boat. A life jacket that got soaked by a few waves will eventually smell if it is not washed in fresh water before being put away. Similarly, harnesses, foulweather gear, and clothes should be put away clean. You might want to stow clean clothes in plastic bags to keep them clean and fresh if you leave them onboard for long periods.

Lockers with tools in them should also be kept clean. Ideally, you will use a tightly sealed toolbox for metal tools. To minimize rust, either lightly grease your ferrous tools before putting them away or put some Bullfrog corrosion-resistant pads in the toolbox before locking it.

Head

The challenge in the head is hygiene and cleanliness. After each trip the head should be thoroughly cleaned with a commercial toilet cleaner. Even so, you will find that the toilet will eventually smell. Most of the time, the smell comes from the intake line of the toilet. When seawater is drawn into the intake line, it sits until it is used; meanwhile the microorganisms in the water rot. Eventually, the odor permeates the rubber of the intake line, causing the entire head compartment to smell. The only sure way to eliminate this odor is to replace the intake line every few years. When doing so, make sure that it has a high loop with an antisiphon valve to prevent water from siphoning back into the head.

To maintain the head itself, pour soapy washing-up water down it and lubricate the seals lightly once or twice a season. When the boat is hauled in the fall, make sure the entire head is drained, flushed with nontoxic antifreeze taken in through the intake line, and lubricated.

Bunks

Bunks and bedding should be aired out as often as possible to keep them fresh. Check that leecloths are correctly positioned and securely fastened in place. Also check to see that there are enough attachment points for leecloth lines. The best material for seats and bunks is smooth and water resistant, without buttons or cording. Water-absorbent material tends to soak up any seawater that gets below and the salt in the seawater absorbs still more water, making the cushions feel damp all the time. Eventually they will smell. Avoid buying cushions with buttons, which are uncomfortable to sleep on. Also try not to buy vinyl-covered cushions, which tend to make people sleeping on them sweat.

Navigator's space

The navigator's space contains a variety of different gear: electronics, charts, plotting tools and pencils, navigation instruments, lighting, and seating. It may also house the electrical panel, a bunk, and even windows or hatches to the cockpit.

Each item requires specific maintenance. Charts, for example, need to be kept dry. This means that they should be stowed in their own dry place, usually in the chart table. Laminated charts should be used if the chart table is near the companionway or likely to get wet.

Electronics should also be protected from getting wet. Electronic connectors are the most common source of problems, and you should spray them with CRC or an equivalent product for protection. If you have an electronics malfunction the first step is to undo the connections, one by one, and clean them. In many cases this will solve your problem. Remove the batteries from battery-powered items at the end of each season, and replace with new batteries in the spring. (Remember to write down your GPS waypoints, though, before removing the batteries.) This will help prevent corrosion and give your electronics gear a longer life. If you can, take all of your electronics gear home and store it in a dry place for the winter.

Additional items that need to be kept dry include flags, sextants, and other navigation instruments. Wet flags will mildew fairly quickly. You might also want to put pouches of silica gel or Bullfrog desiccants in the box with delicate navigation instruments, such as your sextant, to keep them dry.

Electrical maintenance

Like most of your electronics gear, electrical gear will corrode near joints. If you think about it, by putting a steel-based light bulb in a copper socket and soaking it with seawater, you are creating a battery. By definition, one side of the battery will corrode. This is what happens in every light socket that gets wet. For longest life, you need to keep all your electrical connections dry aboard a boat. This may mean a light spray of nonconductive lubricant or a light greasing.

Wiring should be checked where it passes through bulkheads, the mast, and frames to ensure that it is protected against chafe. If a wire chafes through, not only could you lose power to a major piece of gear, such as a navigation light, but you might also create a stray secondary current that could lead to electrolytic corrosion throughout the boat.

Bulkheads

Check to see that all the vessel's main bulkheads are glassed properly to the hull. In some production boats minor bulkheads are not glassed in, but all the main bulkheads should be. An overlap of 3 to 6 inches of fiberglass onto the plywood is normal.

Cabin sole

Ideally, a yacht's cabin sole boards should be a snug fit and locked down, but still removable. They should never be allowed to rest on the floor timbers without being fastened; otherwise, there is a danger that they will shift when the boat heels. If the sole boards swell, they become tight and may not be removable in an emergency. A locking device should be one that is not tripped over but easily used.

Varnished sole boards look wonderful on a boat in the showroom, but as soon as they get wet and the boat heels they can be very slippery. If you really want varnished sole boards, have the finisher sprinkle some sand or other gritty substance on them while the varnish is wet to give them some nonskid properties.

Frankly, I don't like carpets below deck, but some people prefer them. If you have carpets on the cabin sole, make sure they are fastened down and can be lifted easily during an emergency.

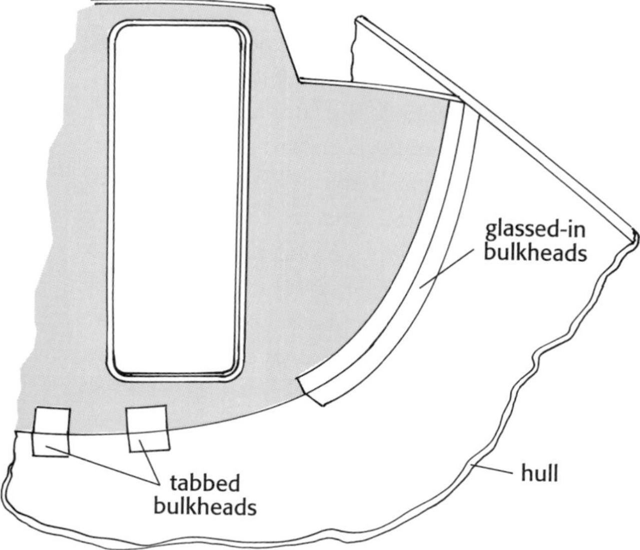

Bulkheads should be properly glassed to the hull as shown on the right, not tabbed lightly as shown on the left. If the bulkhead is lightly tabbed to the hull, it is prone to break free in heavy weather.

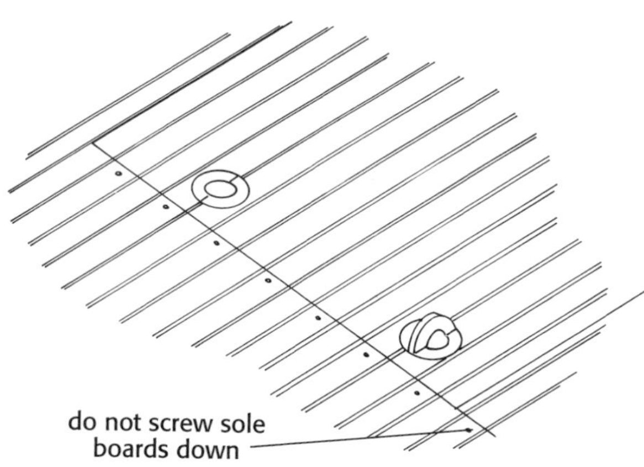

Recessed catches can be used to lift cabin sole boards. Sole boards should never be screwed down, but should be locked in place. If they are screwed down and the hull is holed, you might not be able to get the sole board up fast enough to stop the boat from sinking.

Underbody

Go under the boat and check the keel to make sure it is fair and that bottom paint, if present, is applied properly. Go inside the boat and check that the keelbolts all have oversized washers on them and that there is some form of backing plate under them. The first sign of keel problems is usually a loose keelbolt or two. When the boat stands are removed in preparation for launching, touch up the bottom of the keel and any area that was not painted. If you notice a crack between the keel and the hull, don't worry too much about it as long as the crack is in the paint layer. In winter, when the boat is out of the water, the hull and keel expand and shrink at different rates and a crack develops. If you can get a fingernail into the crack, ask a surveyor about it. If you can get a finger into the crack, the boat has serious problems.

Check the rudder bearings by moving the rudder blade. If the blade moves or wobbles in the bearings, it might be a sign that the bearings are shot and need replacing.

Deck Gear

When first inspecting deck gear, look for signs of heavy strain on it. A prime spot for problems is on alloy genoa tracks. The stainless steel pins holding cars in place are often bent or corroded, indicating that the boat has not been properly maintained. Shackles, blocks, and swivels should not show signs of strain or bending. Tracks should not be bent upward or otherwise distorted. If you find any distortions, go below and check out the underside of the deck; there could be damage here, too. You should oil or lightly grease all shackles, blocks, track cars, and other movable gear at least once a season.

Winches are another source for continual maintenance. At the very least you should strip, clean, oil, and regrease your winches once per season. Ideally, you should work them over two or even three times during the course of a normal sailing season.

Maintenance Log

Every boat should have a maintenance log. This log is quite simple to lay out and update. Take any book and rule it into columns for date, problem, solution, date of solution, date of warranty expiration, and who performed the work. When you are out sailing and something breaks, you simply write up the job that needs to be done. You can either have a yard do it or do the work yourself. As soon as the work is completed, enter what was done, who did it, and when.

You can also lay out a maintenance schedule so that you will know when to service a piece of equipment. For example, you may service the winches once per season. If the service work is written up when the work is done and a note is made to show when the next service is required, you will have an automatic prompt.

A good maintenance log can show if a part is breaking regularly (indicating that it may need to be replaced with a sturdier item). It will also remind you what gear is still under warranty and for how much longer. If you add a column for the cost of repairs, the log can help you keep track of your sailing expenses, too. Finally, when you go to sell the boat you will be able to show that each piece of gear was properly maintained and what was done to it. This should help to raise the resale value of your boat.

Our Designs

Not surprisingly, the maintenance of our boats varies according to the function of the boat. The Weekender has simple systems and will be used lightly; consequently, it is unlikely that a large amount of maintenance will be required. The Cruiser will spend a lot of time during the week sitting on a mooring, which will give a yard or an owner time to do any work required. On weekends the boat should be in tip-top condition for an enjoyable cruise. On this boat a maintenance log will be essential to keep track of any projects that might need work.

On the other hand, the Single-Hander and the Voyager will need constant maintenance, even during a cruise. During extended cruises halyards will chafe and must be closely watched. Sails will be abraded on rigging and may need to be repaired underway. Because both boats will be constantly in use, maintenance will have to be worked in around daily watch-keeping chores.

The Cruiser/Racer is a lot like the Cruiser, in that it will usually be raced on weekends or evenings and maintenance work will be done during the week. On this boat most of the work will be concentrated around the sails, winches, rig and engine systems, with major interior work taking place at the beginning and end of the season.

The Weekender

As there are only a few systems and not a lot of structure, not many things should go wrong on the Weekender. The basic systems, such as the portable head or two-burner stove, can easily be replaced if they break down. Any major problems would concern the hull and deck construction.

One of the design maintenance problems the builder should be aware of occurs where the edges of cabinhouses and cockpits turn to meet the deck. This area can become a "hard spot." Typical areas are at the front corners of a cockpit where the corner meets the deck, or at the outer corner of a cabinhouse where it meets the deck. Hard spots are localized areas of high stress which may produce cracking and let water into the core material. If the deck core material is end-grain balsa wood, it may rot,

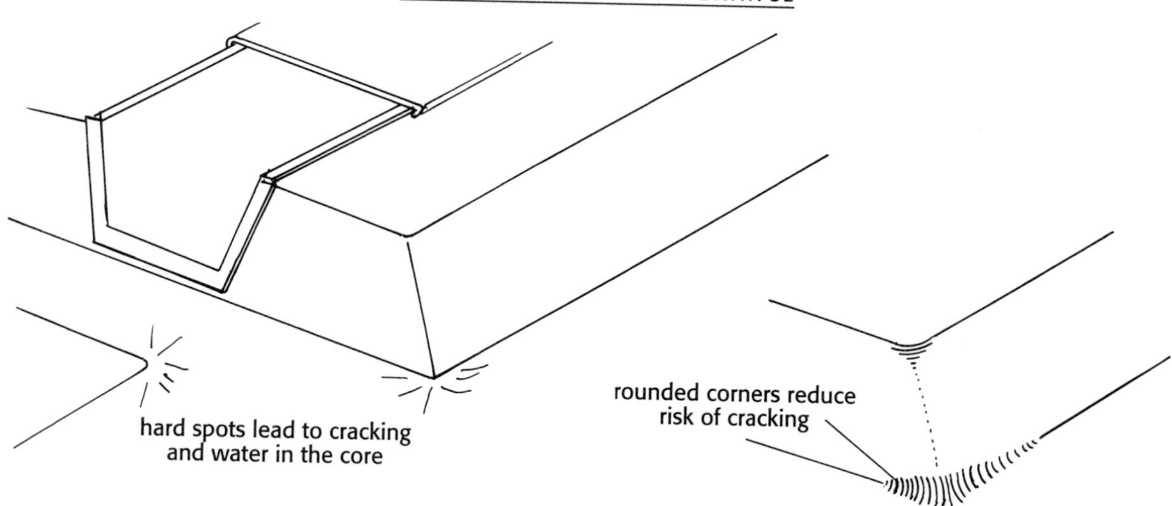

Corners on deck should not have "hard spots," because these tend to crack the laminate and allow water into the deck core. Corners should be rounded slightly as shown on the right.

although balsa totally encapsulated in fiberglass will not rot. Styrene in the laminating adhesive prevents rotting. But as soon as the encapsulating material is fractured and water is allowed in, rot can start. The solution in this case is to make the cabintop or cockpit-to-deck radius slightly larger. This eases the transition from a vertical surface to a horizontal one.

Another area of potential problems is the hull/deck joint. Few builders glass the deck on small boats such as this because of the man-hours involved. The deck is bedded in adhesive and bolted together. A poorly designed hull/deck joint can lead to problems if the boat is used heavily. It behooves the designer to use a strong joint and possibly an alloy toerail to increase the rigidity of the joint. (See illustration on page 56 of hull/deck joint types.)

A third area that may develop problems is the hull/keel joint (also described in chapter 3). With a bulbed keel and a narrow blade, there may be too little "meat" at the top of the keel to make a strong joint. Eventually, this may lead to cracking and possibly failure of the joint. By making the keel wider at the top or installing it with a flange, such problems can be eliminated.

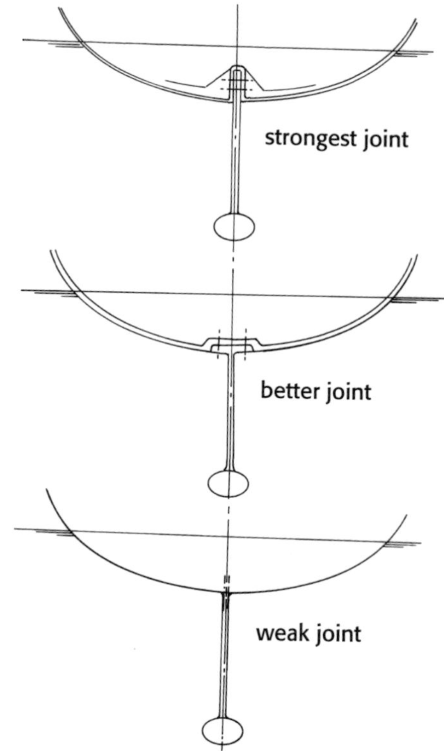

Modern bulbed keels are very narrow at the top and can cause problems when bolted in the conventional manner (bottom). A better method is to weld the keel to a top plate and through-bolt it (middle), or to fit the keel into a recess in the hull and bolt it transversely (top).

The Cruiser

On a cruising boat, systems maintenance is ongoing, so it is essential that you keep a good maintenance log. Cruising boats have a number of systems, and as a rule complexity increases with size. At the design stage there are several things that can be done to facilitate maintenance. For example, all wiring should be done to the American Boat and Yacht Council (ABYC) standard, so that any boat electrician can track and repair cables.

There is a lot of wiring on the Cruiser, so all wiring will be put in plastic conduits glassed into the hull when the boat is under construction. When wiring we will be careful to avoid hard spots where the wire may be chafed. This entails rounding or padding all sharp edges.

With a number of systems requiring spares and replacement parts, it is often a good idea to make a list showing where parts are stored and what is available. This list can be as short or as detailed as you wish. Accompanying the list can be repair manuals, exploded views of the system, and similar supporting materials.

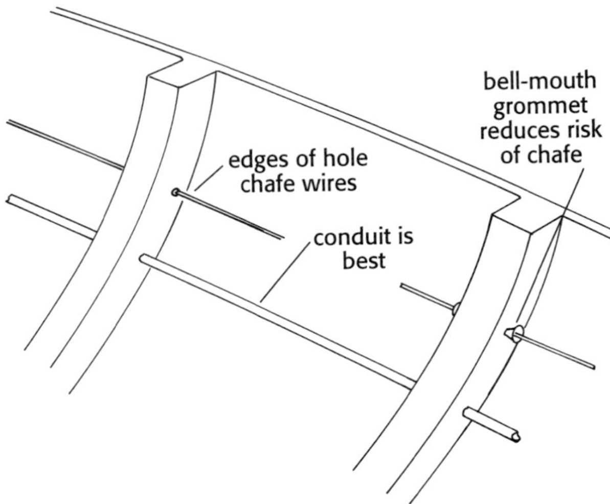

When wiring is run through the hull, the best installation method uses conduits. Failing that, some kind of flared fitting should be used to prevent the wiring from chafing on a hole drilled through fiberglass.

The Voyager

On the Voyager spares should be carried for virtually everything, as this boat may be far from a supplier when something breaks. A spares list might include a spare injector for the main engine, spare filters and belts, as well as more unusual parts such as gaskets and watermaker membranes.

Maintenance will be part of an ongoing process, and a sizable area of the boat may be given over to storing maintenance materials. A comprehensive list of spare parts, maintenance materials, and their location is a must on this boat.

On a boat this large it is not unusual to carry a computer, and a lot of maintenance information is available either on CD-ROM or online. With Internet access, ordering or assembly information may be downloaded, reducing the number of manuals that need to be carried.

Where there are a large number of systems and parts required, it helps to make as many parts identical. For example, gear from the same manufacturer often has interchangeable parts. On a boat that is likely to be wandering away from conventional stores, having interchangeable parts can be a big plus.

The Single-Hander

As on the Voyager, maintenance on the Single-Hander is ongoing. Downtime can be used for routine maintenance (in addition to sleep). As with the Voyager, a large number of spares should be carried.

The water ballast system will demand a lot of attention. The pumps that fill and transfer the ballast water need to be maintained in tiptop condition. As a result, all the pumps on board may be identical, which would cut down on spares and provide a layer of redundancy (if one pump were damaged, another, less-used one could be substituted).

Another area where maintenance can be minimized is through-hulls. If we limit the boat to three through-hulls, the owner will likely know exactly where each one is and have an emergency plan to deal with a failure. If there were 20 or more through-hulls, typically of different sizes and styles, maintenance demands in that area would increase dramatically.

The Cruiser/Racer

Most of the maintenance on this boat will be aimed at racing. The cost of gear failure on the Cruiser/Racer is measured in time—and lost races. The thrust of the maintenance process is to increase the efficiency of the gear. For example, the winches may be oiled regularly rather than being greased, which will make them turn faster and shave a few seconds. Snapshackles might have short tails to make them easy to open quickly. The sheaves and halyards will be checked regularly to ensure that they run smoothly.

Maintenance is in little things as well. Carrying spare batteries and extra light bulbs can make a difference. It is hard to steer a good course during the night if the light bulb in the compass blows and no spare can be found.

Nine

Getting It Together

If you think about it, sailboats are amazingly complex pieces of equipment. The hull is designed to move efficiently through the water, where it is acted upon by wind and waves. Wind and waves can vary in size and strength, making structural strength a major factor in the design of the vessel. Inside the hull are living accommodations for a number of people. The hull also holds a mast, on which sails are set. Sails are tweaked into various shapes to sail the boat well in a range of conditions. This tweaking is performed with gear mounted on the deck, which is also the roof of the accommodations. All these different functions must come together in a way that allows each to work without interfering with the others. Putting all of these functions together often requires trade-offs.

For example, in chapter 6 we considered giving the Voyager a ketch rig. As the design progressed, however, it became apparent that the mizzenmast and its rigging would clutter the cockpit area, and getting forward would become difficult. A trade-off of some kind was needed. Rather than go with the ketch rig, we opted to keep the radar arch and, as a bonus, incorporated davits to carry the dinghy for short distances.

Other, more subtle factors also influence the design. For example, a boat's construction may determine how chainplates are fastened through the deck and to the hull. In an aluminum hull the chainplates are simply welded into the aluminum structure. In a fiberglass hull, stainless steel chainplates need to be designed to be bolted to wooden bulkheads, or bolted and fiberglassed to the hull structure. A large chainplate mounting that ends up going through a bunk may ruin that space.

In this chapter we will take a final look at our five boats to consider how all the various pieces go together, and what trade-offs may be needed to make the design work. (Any of the designs in this book is available from my design office in Jamestown, Rhode Island, see page ii.)

The Weekender

This design did not require a lot of compromise during development, because the starting assumptions for such a small, simple boat already entail great compromises to comfort and seaworthiness. Again, the interior shows four berths, two forward and two quarter berths, separated by the galley to starboard and stowage to

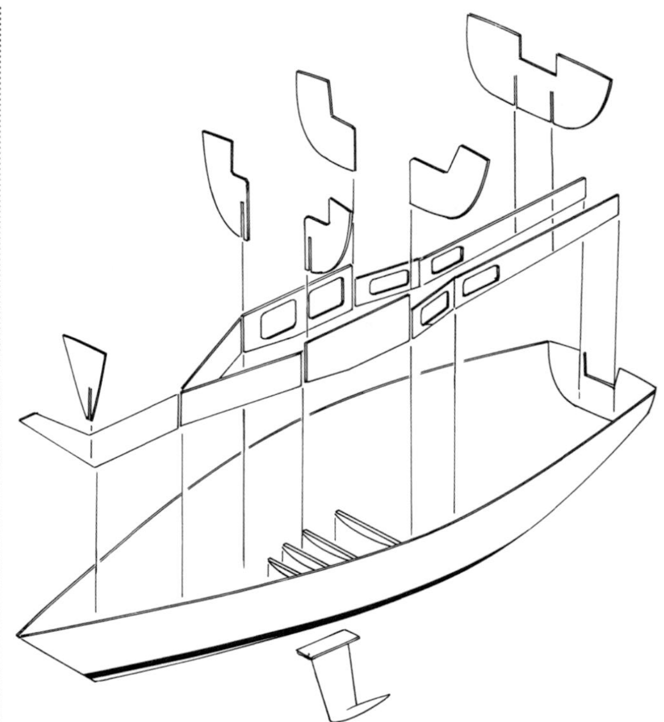

The furniture of the Weekender is all structural and is assembled as shown.

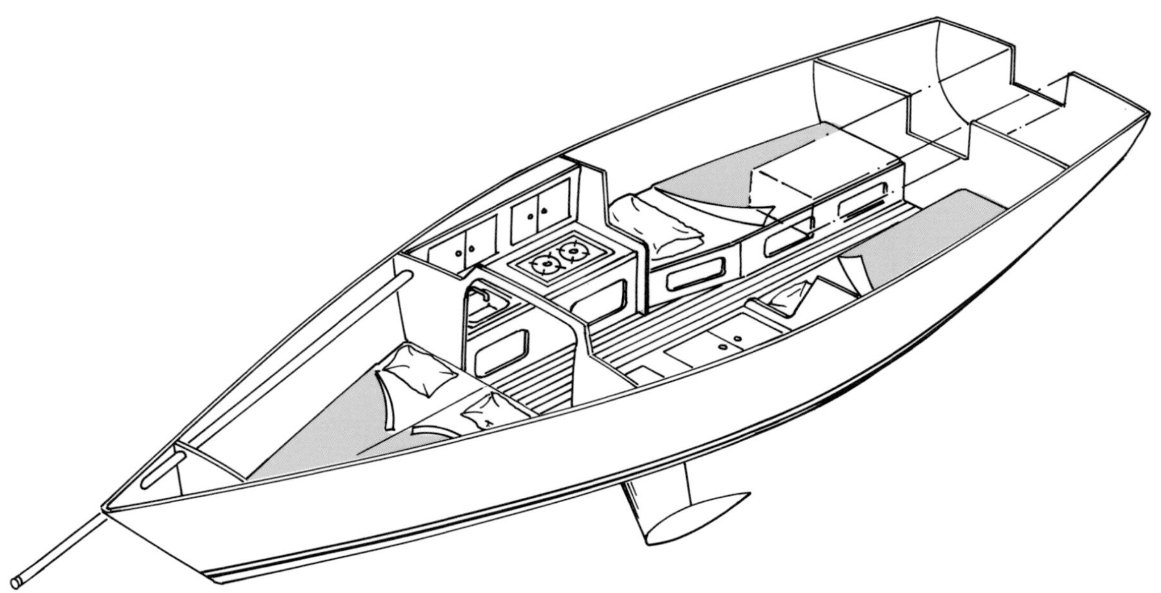

The layout of the Weekender is extremely simple, with a V-berth forward, two quarter berths, and a small galley amidships.

port. The icebox, a 48-quart cooler, serves as a step to get in and out the cabin. The stove is not gimbaled, as it is unlikely to be used when the boat is underway. Typically, food will be cooked when the boat is at anchor; hot drinks will be made up and left in a vacuum flask in the sink.

The interesting feature of this hull is the longitudinal structure, in that the plywood bunk faces and the galley faces become structural bulkheads throughout the boat. This simplifies construction because the transverse bulkheads have slots cut in them and drop into place over the longitudinal bulkheads.

In keeping with the theme of simplicity, the deck layout is minimal, with a few twists. The pulpit is designed to let the spinnaker be launched through it. With a belly-button line, the kite can be pulled down by a crew, either below the forehatch or in the cockpit.

The swept spreaders allow the rig to bend slightly without the use of running backstays. This gives the crew full sail control should they want to race the boat. In cruising mode, they can simply set the rig up and ignore it. The fully battened mainsail is trimmed by the helmsman, leaving the rest of the crew free to work on other jobs or lie in the sun.

The Cruiser

The Cruiser gets a lot of accommodations into a 34-foot hull. We accomplished this by compromising on the nav table and galley to some extent, making them suit the boat's inshore habits rather than equipping them heavily. The boat can sleep five in a pinch, but it is intended to be cruised by two. The cockpit is a little small but adequate for a crew of two.

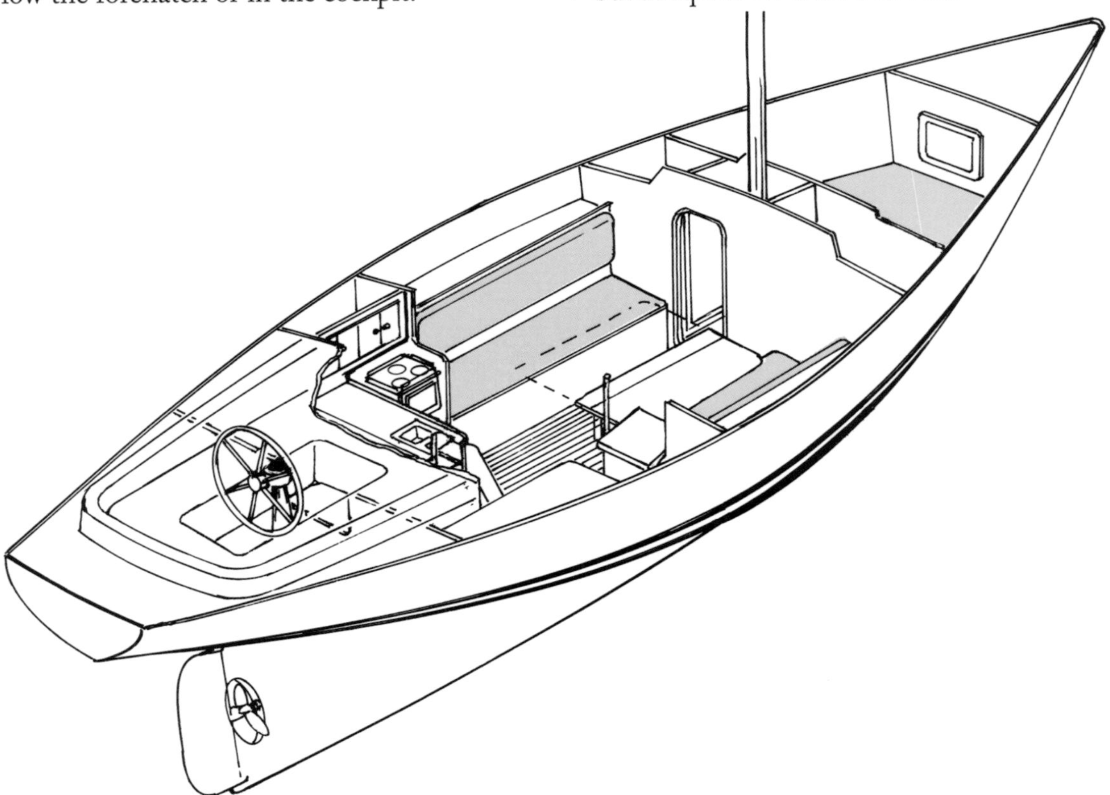

The Cruiser has a traditional interior in keeping with its traditional exterior. Note the three-bladed propeller in an aperture to reduce vibrations.

The deck view (see page 172) shows a simple deck plan with opening ports and a pair of large deck hatches. Sails are stowed on the spars or in the cockpit locker, with only a small difference between the sloop and ketch sail plans.

At the bow the boat has one anchor with its own capstan and a below-deck chain locker. There is only one headsail shown for the sloop rig. The ketch can have a similar arrangement or carry double headsails, in which case both sails are roller furled for ease of use. I would guess that the best way to tack the double-headsail rig would be to partially furl the topsail, tack the boat, and unroll the headsail. A running backstay is shown for the double-headsail rig to keep tension on the staysail stay, but the spreaders could be swept back to eliminate running backstays on a boat this small. In keeping with the user-friendly sail plan, the mainsail drops into lazyjacks, where it can be tied off and stowed.

Below deck the accommodations are aimed at a couple. There is a relatively simple V-berth forward and a dining area in the main saloon. Both settees in the dining area can be made up into berths. The galley is functional, as is the head/shower. A five-step ladder leads into the cockpit, which has a bridge deck.

The underbody is distinguished by a long keel and a keel-hung rudder. There are no surprises with this boat. It is simple and traditional, intended for solid seaworthy performance under all conditions.

The Voyager

The Voyager is a fairly large boat, designed for one or two couples. The interior has a V-berth/suite forward, and a double berth/suite aft with the berth pushed under the pilothouse. This arrangement gives two couples the middle of the boat for socializing yet privacy at night; on a long trip the settee berths can be used for sleeping. The dining table is wrapped around the mast, making the forward area of

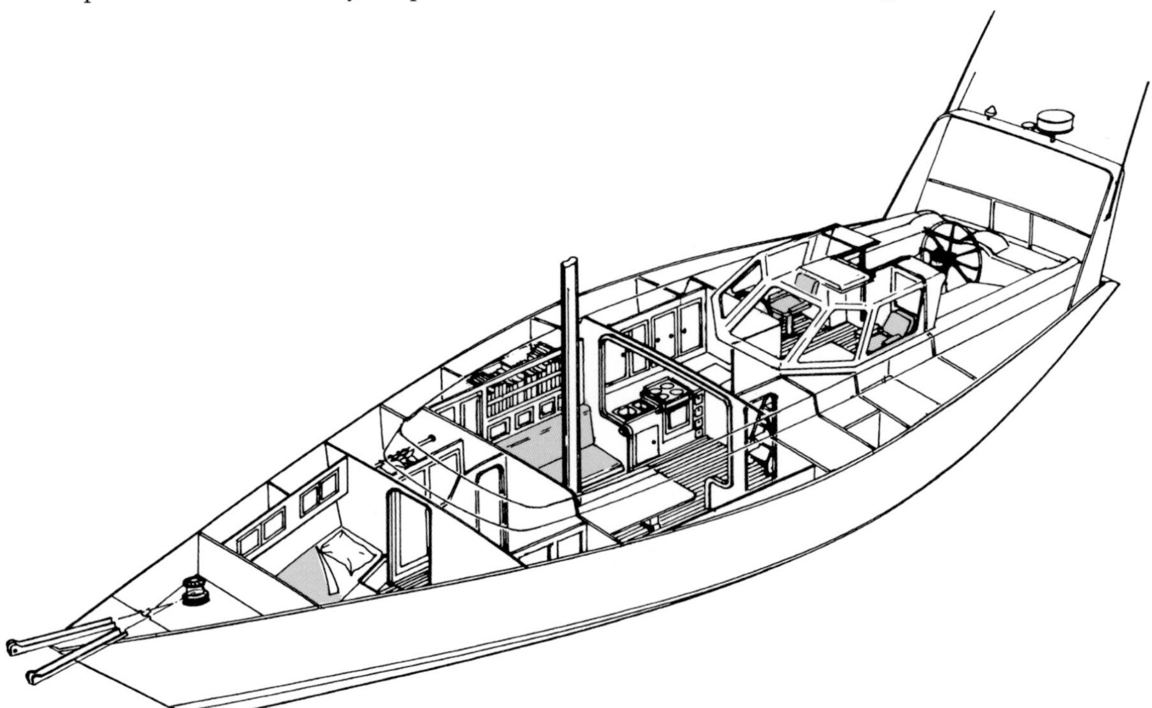

The layout of the Voyager emphasizes comfort for long-distance cruising.

the boat into a comfortable saloon. Outboard of the settee berths are bookshelves and lockers for stowage of glassware and the like. Aft of the dining area is a galley to starboard and the aft cabin. The engine compartment is under the pilothouse sole and houses a generator and a watermaker. The locker in the pilothouse aft of the helm seat serves as an area to hang wet foul-weather gear. The aft cabin has its own head compartment to port and a large double berth for the owners. The pilothouse has an inside steering station and the navigation area, as well as a single berth. The latter would be used on passage by the off-watch when just two people are aboard. The interior is designed to be light and airy, with good air circulation for when the boat is in the tropics.

On deck the boat is relatively simple, with halyards and sheets led aft via organizers and sheet-stoppers to primary winches on the coamings. In warm weather or when the boat is in southern waters, a Bimini top can be extended from the radar arch to the pilothouse to provide plenty of shade. All the windows of the pilothouse will open to allow cool drafts to blow through.

The mast has a double-spreader rig for straightforward tuning, with a double headsail rig for good boat speed under most conditions. Running backstays are required to keep tension on the staysail luff, and additional winches are provided on the cockpit coaming. This boat will have a multipurpose spinnaker (MPS) tacked on a strop fastened to the headstay tack fitting rather than a pole.

There are plenty of hatches on deck to allow good air circulation. At the forward end of the deck is a locker housing a windlass. This keeps the windlass out of the way of most of the heavy seas that come aboard and still allows a pair of heavy-duty anchors to be stowed on the bow. These anchors can be left in place or stowed below deck on a long passage. Any water that makes its way into the bow locker will drain out through a drain hole in the bow.

Aft, the radar arch houses davits for the dinghy, a shower unit, cockpit lights and the stern light, and solar panels, as well as antennas for the radar, GPS, and VHF and SSB radios. It also contains stereo speakers and lifebuoy holders.

The Single-Hander

The Single-Hander contains more innovative and specialized features intended to make the boat manageable by one person. Even so, it is not as groundbreaking as some of the latest Single-Handers, which incorporate gimbaled chart table/galleys, extremely low freeboard, shrouds that project outside the plane of the hull, and extensive electronics.

The emptiness and the ballast tanks are the two main features of this hull. Rather than cram the hull with accommodations, we have aimed to keep the weight down. Below deck, sails are stowed forward behind a watertight door. Note the small collision bulkhead all the way forward. The main accommodation area has minimal headroom, but also houses stores, a workbench, the galley, a small dining area, the head, and a single bunk for the skipper. It is up in the cabin/pilothouse where the real action takes place. Here the skipper has a chart table, helm controls, a computer, and a comfortable chair that can be used for sleeping.

Step out of the pilothouse, and the deck is laid out so that everything can be operated from the cockpit. The skipper does not need to go forward except to hook up the spinnaker. The deck edge is rounded, with the toerail set inboard to reduce drag going upwind.

The rig is high performance, with triple spreaders, running backstays, and roller-furling sails. A fully battened mainsail gives plenty of light-air power (and provides a huge billboard for prospective sponsors). The boom has a low tack fitting to increase sail area and to enable

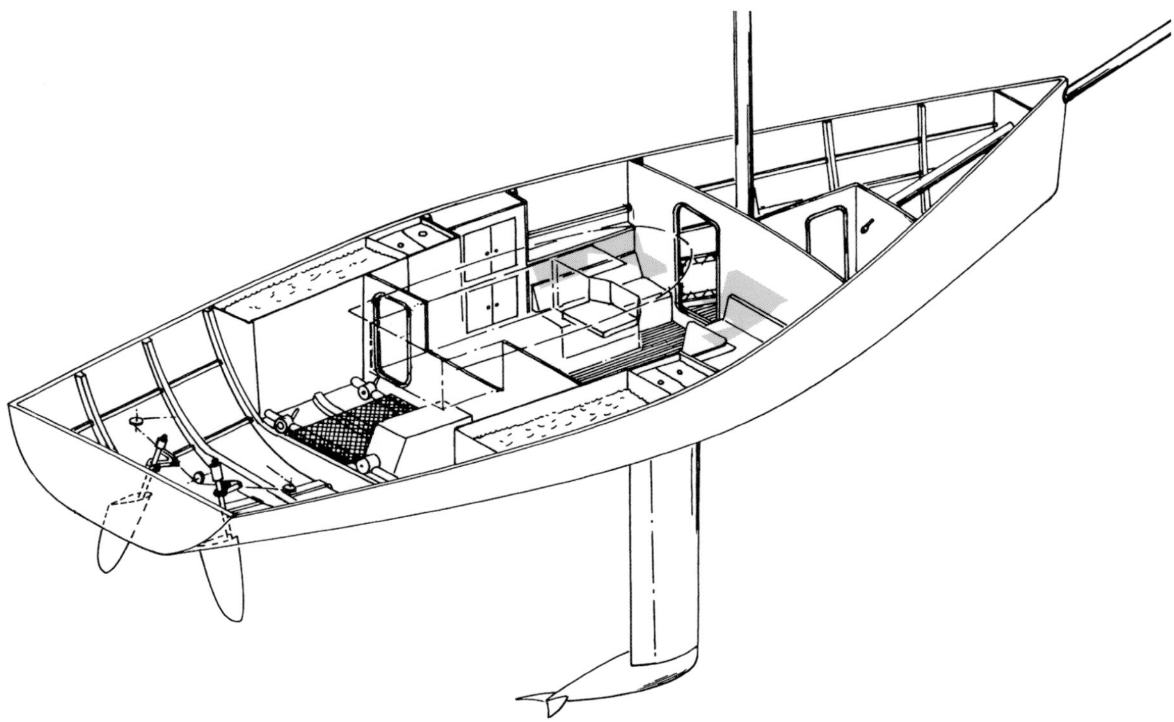

The Single-Hander's interior is stripped out, with lots of hull structure showing. This helps to keep the boat light and fast.

the boom to sit close to the cabintop when the boat is beating to windward. Putting the boom this close to the cabintop promotes the end-plate effect to increase the efficiency of the mainsail. This boat is intended for efficient fast sailing under all conditions.

The Cruiser/Racer

Compromise is inherent to the Cruiser/Racer. The racer wants speed; the cruiser cares more about comfort. For both the designer and the builder, a fast boat is a way of attracting attention and getting more commissions. These factors tend to tip the balance toward racing, and cruising takes a back seat.

Our Cruiser/Racer has a cruising interior and a racing exterior, but even the interior is oriented somewhat toward racing. Inside, the boat has two quarter berths, a small galley to port, and opposite the galley a navigation area. The quarter berths are pushed out to the extreme sides of the hull by the width of the cockpit. As the cockpit is optimized for sail handling, the bunks are secondary, but having the bunks outboard also puts the weight of a sleeping crew where it is most needed. In the middle part of the boat is the dining area, with the head just forward. Typically, this part of the boat will be full of sails during a race; sails are kept forward when not racing. There are pipe cots in the forepeak should the entire crew decide to sleep aboard.

The hull is designed for maximum speed under the prevailing rating rule, with a bulbed keel and an efficient balanced rudder. The sail plan is typical of racing boats: a fractional rig with a large spinnaker and a minimal deck layout. The deck layout is designed to minimize gear (and its weight) yet still be very efficient.

There are no toerails in the middle of the boat so that the crew can sit comfortably with their legs over the side to increase stability.

These five boats are clearly designed to suit the conditions under which they are intended to sail. Boats that engage in even more specialized sailing will be designed even more narrowly. For example, on an *America*'s Cup boat all turns are made leaving the buoy to port, so the spinnaker hatch is to port; there is usually no hatch to starboard.

Boats designed for specific conditions should stick to the kind of sailing they were built for. Taking a boat designed for lake sailing on a voyage around the world would be asking for trouble unless the boat could be substantially rebuilt. A lake boat might have an extra-high mast to pick up the lightest zephyr. Stability may be marginal because the boat is designed to sail with a large crew. Other features inappropriate for bluewater sailing may be less obvious. The rigging may be light or designed without a thought given to chafe prevention, because the boat will be sailed sporadically and maintained constantly. Chafe prevention is a major factor on an offshore boat. On the other hand, it is overkill to buy a boat with the capability to cross oceans, such as a Swan 50, to sail on a small freshwater lake, and you will enjoy much more exciting sailing if you choose a boat specifically designed for lake sailing. Selecting the best boat for your style of sailing requires candid appraisal of your goals and interests (as

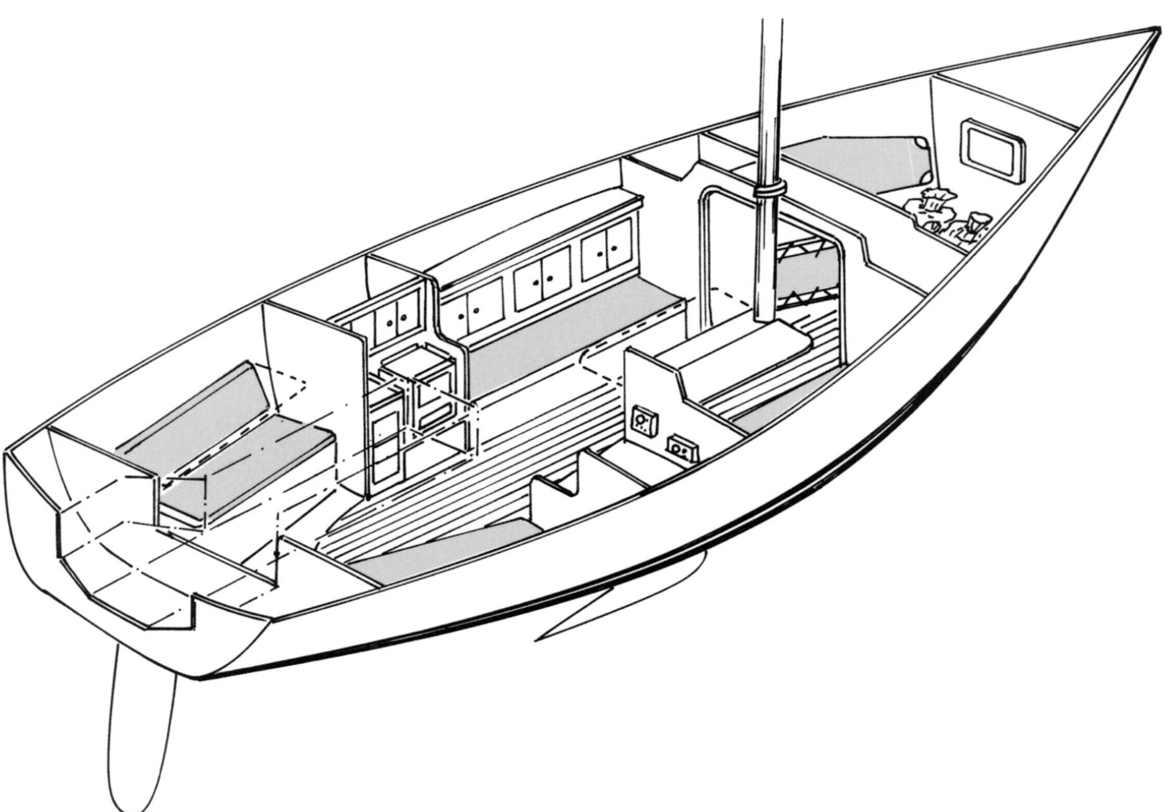

The Cruiser/Racer layout is wide open to give the crew room to move around sails. For a more cruising-oriented layout, a V-berth could be fitted forward, and a double quarter berth aft. Options such as these are typically offered by builders of high-performance cruiser/racers.

in the quiz in chapter 1) and then careful technical analysis. This book guides you along the way; the rest you will learn from experience and lots of sailing.

A Concept Cruiser

In closing, let's look into a crystal ball and see what cruising boat ideas might be in store in the years ahead. My office has developed a 54-foot concept design for an easily handled cruising boat. It is intended to be comfortably fast—that is, it will carry all the stores required for an ocean crossing without losing a lot of performance. It is intended to be virtually unsinkable, with a double bottom containing all the tankage and side-mounted water ballast tanks.

The sail plan is a roller-furled cutter rig with both sails high cut for maximum visibility to leeward. The rig is totally boomless and much more efficient than a conventional mast. It also creates more lift, presents less windage, and eliminates standing rigging, apart from the roller-furling foils and the backstay. The curved spars perfectly match the leech curvature of the sail to become virtually invisible to the wind. The mainsail, if it can be called that, is sheeted to the radar arch, which also doubles as dinghy davits and holds a roller-furled Bimini top. (We'll use a rigid-bottomed 9-foot hard-bottom inflatable as a tender.) The radar arch has several features of its own. Not only does it have davits, but it has a freshwater shower, stereo speakers, radar, a GPS antenna, cockpit lights, and the stern light—plus three gun-mounts for fishing poles.

The windshield is curved acrylic and is fixed in place. More curved acrylic panels are stowed in the back of the cockpit seat and can be raised over the cockpit in bad weather.

For offwind sailing, a recessed MPS pole/sprit is used to help keep the foredeck clear. A Danforth and a CQR anchor are recessed into the bow to minimize interference with the sprit. A Bruce anchor may also be carried on the centerline at the stem.

On deck, visibility is enhanced by raising the helmsman's cockpit and the crew cockpit. This has two benefits: the helmsman can see over the cabintop, and there is additional space inside the boat to allow a large aft cabin under the cockpit. All sheet winches are located entirely below deck where they can be easily accessed. There are no tracks, because the headsail sheets are led directly to a winch located below deck.

The transverse swinging keel enables the boat to sail at the optimum angle of heel in any wind. The hull is designed to sail fastest when heeled 10 to 15 degrees. An onboard computer constantly adjusts hull/keel angles to maximize the boat's speed.

Inside the hull, the accommodations and features will not be so radical. After all, humans still have to enjoy the sail. All the bunks are gimbaled, so that they remain horizontal. As the boat is programmed to heel no more than 10 degrees, gimbaling the bunks is relatively easy. The galley and nav station are mounted so that they can be used easily on either tack without major adjustments.

The nav station is completely electronic, with three levels of backup. Electronic charting, autopilot steering, heel angle (plus ballast-tank water levels), boat speed, engine and generator functions, freshwater levels, search and rescue transponders, visibility (with automatic radar activation), and the proximity of other vessels are all monitored continually. Of course, this requires a fair amount of electrical power, which is generated by a constantly running super-quiet Panda generator located inboard to one side of the keel. A secondary, smaller generator for use at night is located on the other side.

For heavy-weather sailing, we'll install a pair of drogues (a Jordan series drogue and a Gale-rider) in their own lockers in the transom. Also in the transom will be a locker for a sailboard and mast, twin 40-pound propane tanks, boarding steps and ladder, and a man-overboard pole. We have also placed all cleats on the outside of the hull to eliminate chafe (from the chocks) if a sea anchor or drogue is deployed. The toerail is eliminated in favor of a curved deck edge to reduce windage.

This is a lot of equipment to shoehorn into a 54-footer, but it still leaves room for four people to enjoy a remarkable sailing experience on a boat where safety is paramount yet unobtrusive. The ideas and designs laid out in this book are intended to give you an insight into what goes into designing several types of cruising boat. They are a product of my experience as a designer, as a lecturer (where I learn what other people like), and as a sailor. I hope this book has prompted some ideas as to what you would like in your next boat. Good luck, and good sailing.

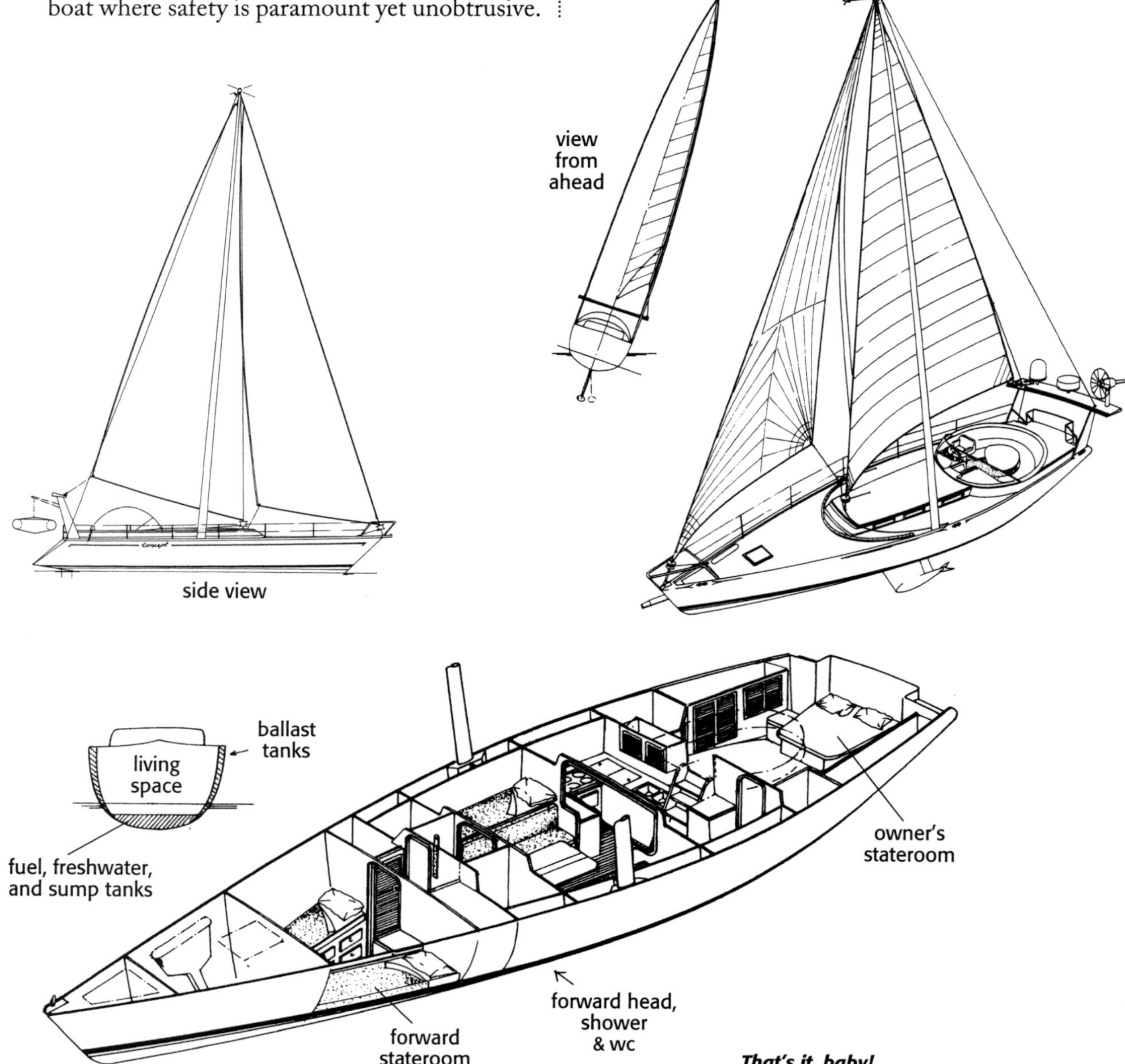

That's it, baby!

Index

Pages in **bold** refer to illustrations

t

u

v

w

x

y

z